Becoming Zimbabwe

Becoming Zimbabwe

A History from the Pre-colonial Period to 2008

Edited by

Brian Raftopoulos and A. S. Mlambo

INSTITUTE FOR
JUSTICE AND RECONCILIATION

First published in 2009 by
Weaver Press, P.O. Box A1922, Avondale, Harare

Published in South Africa in 2009 by
Jacana Media, 10 Orange Street, Sunnyside, Auckland Park, Johannesburg

Weaver Press ISBN: 978 0 77922 083 7
Jacana Media ISBN: 978 1 77009 763 6

Published in collaboration with the Institute for Justice and Reconciliation, Cape Town,
which aids the building of fair, democratic and inclusive societies in Africa
before, during and after political transition.

The publishers would like to express their gratitude to the Ford Foundation
whose financial assistance made this publication possible.

Cover: Danes Design, Harare
Cover photograph: Annie Mpalume
Typesetting and layout: TextPertise, Harare
Printed and bound by CTP Book Printers, Cape Town

Contents

Tables

Maps

Acronyms

AAG   Affirmative Action Group
ACP   African, Caribbean and Pacific countries
AEU   Amalgamated Engineering Union
AIPPA   Access to Information and Protection of Privacy Act
ANC   African National Congress or African National Council
BSAC   British South Africa Company
BSAP   British South Africa Police
CAS   Capricorn Africa Society
CCJPZ   Catholic Commission for Justice and Peace in Zimbabwe
CFU   Commercial Farmers Union
CHRA   Combined Harare Residents' Association
CIO   Central Intelligence Organization
CYL   City Youth League
DSA   District Security Assistant
ESAP   Economic Structural Adjustment Programme
EU   European Union
FBAWU   Federation of Bulawayo African Workers Union
FLS   Frontline States
FRELIMO   Front for the Liberation of Mozambique
FROLIZI   Front for the Liberation of Zimbabwe
IBDC   Indigenous Business Development Centre
IBWO   Indigenous Business Women's Organisation
ICFTU   International Confederation of Free Trade Unions
IMF   International Monetary Fund
IRA   Inter-racial Association
JMO   Joint Marketing Organisation
LDO   Land Development Officer
MDC   Movement for Democratic Change
MK   Umkhonto we Sizwe
NAM   Non-aligned Movement
NCA   National Constitutional Assembly
NDP   National Democratic Party
NEPCO   National Export Promotion Council
NGO   Non-governmental Organization
NIBMAR   No Independence Before Majority Rule

Figures

NLHA   Native Land Husbandry Act
OAU   Organisation of African Unity
PF-ZAPU   Patriotic Front – Zimbabwe African People's Union
POSA   Public Order and Security Act
RAR   Rhodesian African Rifles
RENAMO   Mozambique National Resistance
RF   Rhodesian Front
RICU   Reformed Industrial and Commercial Workers' Union
RRAEA   Rhodesian Railways African Employees Association
SADC   Southern African Development Community
SADCC   Southern African Development Co-ordination Conference
SRATUC   Southern Rhodesian African Trade Union Congress
SRBVA   Southern Rhodesian Bantu Voters' Association
TILCOR   Tribal Trust Lands Development Corporation
TTL   Tribal Trust Lands
TUC   Trade Union Congress
UANC   United African National Council
UDI   Unilateral Declaration of Independence
UFP   United Federal Party
UN   United Nations
UNICEF   United Nations Children's Fund
VIDCO   Village Development Committee
WADCO   Ward Development Committee
WOZA   Woman of Zimbabwe Arise
ZACU   Zimbabwe African Congress of Unions
ZANLA   Zimbabwe National Liberation Army
ZANU   Zimbabwe African National Union
ZANU(PF)   Zimbabwe African National Union (Patriotic Front)
ZAPU   Zimbabwe African People's Union
ZCTU   Zimbabwe Congress of Trade Unions
ZIPA   Zimbabwe People's Army
ZIPRA   Zimbabwe People's Revolutionary Army
ZLC   Zimbabwe Liberation Council
ZNLWVA   Zimbabwe National Liberation War Veterans Association
ZWW   Zimbabwe Women Writers

Chronology

c.600-900   Zhizo people populate and dominate the Limpopo region.

c.900   Leopard's Kopje people replace the Zhizo, who move west into the Kalahari to form the Toutswemogala culture.

1220-1290   Mapungubwe, the first Leopard's Kopje settlement to exhibit the characteristics of a state is established and thrives.

1325-1450   Great Zimbabwe succeeds Mapungubwe and establishes itself as the biggest political and economic centre south of the Zambezi.

1450   Great Zimbabwe succeeded by two contemporaneous states, Khami to the west and Mutapa to the north-east.

1490   Torwa ruler briefly usurps Mutapa throne before he is deposed four years later by Chikuyo Chisamarengu.

1506   Portuguese establish presence in the Mutapa state.

1515-30   Sachiteve Nyamunda establishes an independent state in the south-east which blocks trade between the Portuguese on the coast and the Mutapa state.

1550   Venda language fully established in the Limpopo region, combining some Sotho and Shona elements.

1569/77   Portuguese attempt to invade the Mutapa state.

1600   Goba people move into the area around the confluence of the Zambezi and Sanyati rivers.

1606-09   Mutapa Gatsi Rusere experiences the Matuzianhe revolt.

1629   Mutapa Mavhura Mhande signs the 'capitulations' and begins the reign of puppet Munhumutapas.

1663-1704   Mutapa Kamharapasu Mukombwe's reign reverses losses to the Portuguese incurred during the reign of puppet Munhumutapas, expelling the Portuguese and redistributing land.

1684   Changamire Dombo defeats the Portuguese at the battle of Maungwe.

1690   Rozvi state and Changamire dynasty established in the west.

c.1700   Large-scale migrations out of Mbire and Buhera begin.

1720s   Hlengwe groups begin to form in the south-east, disrupting trade between the interior and Inhambane.

1750   Civil wars reach their peak in the Rozvi state.

c.1750   Sections of the Rozvi migrate out of the central state to form the Nambiya dynasty in the north-west and the Singo dynasty south of the Limpopo.

1768 The Hiya attempt an invasion of the Rozvi state.

1824-32 Several Nguni groups enter the Zimbabwean plateau and each fights the Rozvi state.

1838 Ndebele state established in the west, effectively replacing the Rozvi state.

1857 Ndebele successfully subject most major Shona chieftaincies to their rule.

1870 Lobengula signs the Tati Concession.

1878 Portuguese soldier-capitalist Paiva de Andrada seeks to convert the riverine and costal province of Mozambique into an empire covering the entire Zimbabwean plateau working on behalf of *Companhia de Mozambique*.

1879 Ndebele experience the first serious military defeat by the Shona at Nyaningwe Chivi.

1884-85 German Chancellor Otto von Bismarck hosts the Berlin Conference.

1886 Rich goldfields discovered on the Witwatersrand.

1887 Lobengula signs the Grobler Treaty.

1888 (Feb.) Lobengula signs the Moffat Treaty.

1888 (Mar.) Lobengula signs the Rudd Concession.

1889 (Oct.) Queen of England grants Cecil John Rhodes a Royal Charter.

1890 (Sept.) Pioneer Column occupies Mashonaland and raises the Union Jack in Salisbury (Harare).

1893 Anglo-Ndebele War/Matabele War or *Imfazo* I.

1894 Hut Tax introduced.

1894 (July) Matabeleland Order-in-Council instituted.

1894 Gwayi and Shangani Reserves created.

1895 (May) British South Africa Company officially adopts the name Southern Rhodesia.

1896 (Mar.) Outbreak of Ndebele uprising/*Umzukela Wokuqala* or *Imfazo* II.

1896 (June) Outbreak of Shona uprising or First Chimurenga.

1898 Southern Rhodesia Order-in-Council recognised by the British imperial government as the governing instrument of Rhodesia.

1903 Colonial Legislative Council introduced.

1903 Masters and Servants Act introduced.

1905 Sixty Reserves created.

1910 Southern Rhodesia Native Regulations introduced.

1912 South African Native African Congress (SNANC) formed.

1914 Reserves' Commission established.

1914 P. S. Ngwenya forms the African Home Mission.

1919   Matabele Home Movement petitions the Crown for the return of alien-
        ated Ndebele land.
1923   Responsible Government succeeds Company Rule.
1923   Southern Rhodesia Bantu Voters' Association formed.
1924   Morris Carter Commission appointed.
1927   Native Affairs Act introduced.
1927   South African Industrial and Commercial Workers Union opened
        branches in Rhodesia.
1930   Land Apportionment Bill adopted as the Land Apportionment Act.
1931   Land Apportionment Act put into effect.
1931   Maize Control Act introduced.
1934   Women's League of the Southern Rhodesia Bantu Voters' Association
        organises a successful boycott of beer halls.
1936   Bantu Congress of Southern Rhodesia formed.
1943   Howman Commission Report.
1945   Railway Workers Strike.
1945   African National Council (ANC) revived under Revd Thompson
        Samkange.
1947   Urban Areas Act.
1946   Revival of the Reformed Industrial and Commercial Workers' Union
        (RICU), by Charles Mzingeli.
1947   African Voice Association (the Voice), founded by Benjamin Burombo.
1948   General Strike.
1951   Native Land Husbandry Act (NLHA) passed.
1953   Garfield Todd becomes Prime Minister of Southern Rhodesia.
1953   Establishment of the Federation of Rhodesia and Nyasaland.
1954   Launch of the Southern Rhodesia Trade Union Congress (SRTUC).
1955   Formation of the City Youth League (CYL).
1956   Salisbury Bus Boycott.
1957   Formation of the Southern Rhodesian African National Congress
        (SRANC).
1959   Industrial Conciliation Act.
1960   Formation of the National Democratic Party (NDP).
1960   Monckton Commission Report.
1961   NDP banned and replaced by Zimbabwe African People's Union
        (ZAPU).
        New Southern Rhodesian constitution spearheaded by Edgar Whitehead.
1962   Rhodesian Front formed in March and wins election in December.

ZAPU banned in September.

Formation of the Southern Rhodesian African Trade Union Congress (ATUC).

1963   Dissolution of the Federation of Rhodesia and Nyasaland.

Zimbabwe African National Union (ZANU) formed on 8 August.

ZAPU and ZANU begin to send recruits for military training in socialist bloc countries.

1964   Ian Douglas Smith becomes Prime Minister of Rhodesia.

1965   Unilateral Declaration of Independence (UDI) on 11 November.

Britain imposes sanctions on selected Rhodesian goods.

1966   Britain imposes full embargo on Rhodesian trade.

UN imposes oil embargo on Rhodesia.

Britain adopts the NIBMAR principle.

ZANLA guerrillas engage Rhodesian forces in the Battle of Chinhoyi.

1967   ZIPRA and Umkhonto we Sizwe armies join forces in the Wankie Campaign.

1968   UN imposes full mandatory sanctions on Rhodesia.

1969   Anglo-Rhodesian Agreement institutes a new constitution extending franchise to selected groups.

1971   Power struggle paralyses ZAPU; FROLIZI is formed.

New ANC formed under Muzorewa to oppose the Anglo-Rhodesian Agreement.

1972   Pearce Commission-initiated referendum to test the acceptability of the Anglo-Rhodesian Agreement results in a 'No' vote.

1973   Zambia closes its border with Rhodesia.

1974   Formation of the UANC through the amalgamation of ZAPU, ZANU, FROLIZI and the ANC under pressure from the Frontline States leaders.

Thousands of villagers are moved into 'protected villages' in Chiweshe and Madziwa Tribal Trust Lands as a counter-insurgency measure.

Nationalist leaders in detention are released in the spirit of détente.

Nhari Rebellion rocks ZANU.

1975   Herbert Chitepo assassinated.

Mozambique attains independence and immediately closes border with Rhodesia, at the same time allowing ZANLA use of its territory to infiltrate Rhodesia.

Sithole deposed as leader of ZANU and replaced by Robert Mugabe.

ZLC formed in an effort to unite ZAPU, ZANU, FROLIZI and the UANC.

ZIPA formed in an attempt to unite the ZIPRA and ZANLA fighting forces.

1976   Patriotic Front is formed as another Frontline States initiative to forge
       unity between ZAPU and ZANU.
       Geneva Conference to negotiate black majority rule fails.
       Massacre of over 1,000 Zimbabwean refugees by Rhodesian forces at
       Nyadzonia, Mozambique.
1977   Massacre of civilians and ZANLA guerrillas by Rhodesian forces at
       Chimoio and Tembwe camps in Mozambique.
1978   Disturbances in ZANU as the 'Vashandi' group accuses the leadership
       of bourgeois tendencies.
       Hundreds of Zimbabwean refugees are massacred by Rhodesian forces at
       'Freedom Camp' and Mkushi in Zambia.
       ZIPRA guerrillas shoot down a Kariba-bound civilian Air Rhodesia plane.
       ZANLA forces set on fire oil storage tanks in Salisbury.
       Internal Settlement to lead to majority rule elections agreed upon by
       Smith, Muzorewa, Sithole and Chirau.
1979   Muzorewa wins majority vote in the internal elections and Rhodesia
       becomes Zimbabwe-Rhodesia.
       Rhodesian passenger plane is shot down by the guerrillas killing 54
       passengers and five crew members.
       Lancaster House Conference reaches constitutional settlement to end the war.
1980   ZANU wins British-supervised elections. Independence of Zimbabwe
       with Mugabe as Prime Minister.
1982   Tensions mount following the arrest of a number of ZAPU leaders
       and ZIPRA commanders and the sacking of ZAPU leaders in the coalition
       government, including Joshua Nkomo, after the discovery of arms caches in
       ZAPU-owned properties around Bulawayo and Gweru.
1982-87   Gukurahundi Massacres. More than 20,000 civilians in
       Matabeleland and Midlands killed, mainly by government troops.
1982-1992   Government deploys around 15,000 troops to defend Zimbabwe's
       oil pipeline from Mozambique and to fight alongside FRELIMO soldiers
       against the South Africa-backed RENAMO.
1987   Constitution amended to abolish the separate voting roll for whites and
       introduce Executive Presidency to centralize political power and authority.
1987   Unity Accord and formation of ZANU(PF) bring an end to violence and
       effectively rid the country of the only major opposition party.
1988   Government commended by the World Health Organisation and
       UNICEF for progress in the provision of water and sanitation to rural
       households.

1989   University students demonstrate against abuse of state power and corruption in government resulting in the closure of the university for the first time since independence.

1990   Zimbabwe Unity Movement formed by former ZANU(PF) Secretary-General, Edgar Tekere.

1990   Indigenous Business Development Centre (IBDC) formed to press for greater black participation in the economy.

1991   Economic Structural Adjustment Programme (ESAP) introduced.

1992   First ZCTU protest march against the government's economic reform programme is poorly attended and brutally quashed by the police.

1992   Land Acquisition Act, empowering the government to compulsorily acquire land for resettlement.

1994   Affirmative Action Group (AAG) formed to spearhead a more aggressive campaign for local ownership of foreign-owned companies.

1996   Largest strike of civil servants in post-independence Zimbabwe.

1997   War veterans pressurise the government into paying them unbudgeted gratuities resulting in a crash in the value of the currency.

   General Strike forces government to abandon plans to introduce a new levy on workers.

1998   Widespread rioting in Harare and other cities follows a steep rise in food prices.

   Zimbabwe sends troops to the Democratic Republic of the Congo.

   ZCTU organises three national stay-aways.

   Formation of the National Constitutional Assembly.

1999   Formation of the Movement for Democratic Change.

   Government fails to make debt repayment to the Bretton Woods institutions.

2000   Government defeated in referendum on the draft constitution.

   Launch of the land occupations that become known as the 'Third Chimurenga'.

   General elections held against the background of state-led violence, in which the MDC gains nearly 50% of the parliamentary seats.

2002   Mugabe 'wins' highly contested Presidential election amidst high levels of violence.

   Introduction of the Public Order and Security Act (POSA) and the Access to Information and Protection of Privacy Act (AIPPA).

2002-08   Increasing levels of 'targeted' sanctions passed against selected ruling party officials involved in human rights abuses.

2007   Police beat and arrest leaders of the MDC and the civic movement.
       SADC mediation begins led by South African President Mbeki.
2008   MDC wins parliamentary majority in March election. Tsvangirai wins
       the first round of the Presidential election.

       Mugabe 'wins' the re-run of the Presidential election after the worst
       political violence since the mid-1980s.

       Global Political Agreement signed by ZANU(PF) and the two MDC
       formations to create the conditions for political and economic stabilisation.

       Cholera epidemic breaks out, deepening the humanitarian crisis in the
       country.
2009   Formation of the Inclusive Government.

Introduction

The Hard Road to Becoming National

Brian Raftopoulos and A. S. Mlambo

In his autobiography, the veteran Zimbabwean nationalist leader and 'father of the nation', Joshua Nkomo, thanked the settler colonial state for defining, 'once and for all, our national borders':

> The territories of each of the peoples in the land were defined only by custom: their vagueness led to raids and counter-raids in search of cattle, food or women. Now there was no reason why all of us should not unite and develop an unquestioned national identity.[1]

Nkomo's sentiments on the importance of territorial integrity for nationalist mobilisation were, by the late 1950s, the common position of most African nationalist elites on the continent who, eager to lead their states into the international system of nation-states, had concluded that any other form of territorial organisation, particularly on an ethnic basis, 'was not only entirely impracticable but politically explosive'.[2] However, as Nkomo's life was to prove, both during the anti-colonial struggle and in the era of post-colonial politics, the movement towards an 'unquestioned national identity' was to prove a dangerous fantasy, one that could not conceal the faultlines of ethnicity, class, gender and race that marked the terrain of Zimbabwean history. The idea of a pre-existing unified ideological or political subject that could quickly be mobilised against colonial rule was to come up against the complex processes of historical agency in which nationalist 'unity' and hegemony were always contingent, and were founded on the interplay of different identities, social forces and strategic alliances.[3]

Colonial power, as Cooper has written, was 'an object of struggle' within particular material, social and cultural conditions, in which the categories of 'coloniser' and 'colonised' were not 'immutable constructs'; they 'had to be

---

[1] Joshua Nkomo, *The Story of My Life* (London: Methuen, 1984), p. 7.

[2] Crawford Young, 'Nation, ethnicity and citizenship: Dilemmas of democracy and civil order in Africa', in S. Dorman, D. Hammett and P. Nugent (eds.), *Making Nations, Creating Strangers* (Leiden and Boston: Brill, 2007), p. 245.

[3] For an interesting theoretical discussion of these dynamics, see S. Hall, 'Gramsci's relevance to the study of race and ethnicity', in D. Morley and K-H. Chen, *Stuart Hall: Critical Dialogues in Cultural Studies* (London: Routledge, 1996), pp. 411-40.

reproduced by specific actions'.[4] Under white colonial rule, state coercion and assertions of racial and cultural differences were combined with the differential imposition of 'decentralised despotism'[5] in which 'custom' and 'traditional authority' became both modalities of administration and arenas of contestation and debate.[6] Moreover, the imposition of settler rule took place within the context of uneven settler capitalist development that dramatically changed the relations of production and land ownership, and led to the emergence of new social and economic forces.

This book offers an overview of the history of Zimbabwe from the pre-colonial era to the present day, and tracks the idea of national belonging and citizenship over this period. Within these broad parameters we also set out to explore the nature of state rule, the changing contours of the political economy, and the regional and international dimensions of the country's history. Thus, a central objective is to analyse the progress, challenges and continuing struggles over 'Becoming Zimbabwe'.

The pre-colonial period to the 1930s

In 1977 Robert Mugabe wrote an article on ZANU's view of pre-colonial Zimbabwe, in which he sought to argue the position of – in Bhebe and Ranger's words – 'a natural "Shona" nation which had always sought to defend its autonomy'.[7] According to Mugabe, drawing on his reading of the empire of Munhumutapa,

> The distinguishing features of our nation, cultural homogeneity, our biological and genetic identity, our social system, our geography, our history which together characterize our national identity, also combined in producing out of our people a national, vigorous and positive spirit which manifests itself in the consistently singular direction of its own preservation.[8]

Mazarire's opening chapter challenges such readings and proffers an alternative interpretation:

> The pre-colonial history of Zimbabwe is usually explained in terms

[4] F. Cooper, *Colonialism in Question: Theory, Knowledge, History* (Berkeley and Los Angeles: University of California Press, 2005).

[5] M. Mamdani, *Citizen and Subject: Contemporary Africa and the Legacy of Late Colonial Rule* (Princeton: Princeton University Press, 1996).

[6] D. S. Moore, *Suffering for Territory: Race, Place, and Power in Zimbabwe* (Harare: Weaver Press, 2005).

[7] N. Bhebe and T. O. Ranger (eds.), *The Historical Dimensions of Democracy and Human Rights in Zimbabwe, Volume One: Pre-Colonial and Colonial Legacies* (Harare: University of Zimbabwe Publications, 2001), p. xxv.

[8] Ibid., p. xxvi.

of the rise and fall of empires – the Great Zimbabwe, the Mutapa, the Torwa, the Rozwi and Ndebele states. These large states are interesting ... but it is misleading to think that nothing of significance happened before or afterwards, or outside their frontiers. Most autochthons lived in smaller units ...

Drawing on the work of historians like David Beach and Terence Ranger, Mazarire concludes that the 'Shona' – a term signifying linguistic, cultural and political characteristics of a people – did not even know themselves by that name until the late nineteenth century, and even then were variously described as 'vaNyai', 'abeTshabi', 'Karanga', or 'Hole'. In the case of the Ndebele who settled in the south-west of the Zimbabwe plateau after 1840, what began as the movement of a small Khumalo clan from the Zulu kingdom as a result of the nineteenth-century Mfecane in South Africa, developed into a more heterogeneous nation composed of Rozwi, Kalanga, Birwa, Tonga, Nyubi, Venda and Sotho, brought together through a combination of conquest, assimilation and incorporation.[9] In emphasising the need to move away from the conception of ethnicity as static and primordial, Ranger argued the importance of showing that 'tribal identity is not inevitable, unchanging, given, but a product of human creativity that can be re-invented and refined to become again open, constructive and flexible, subordinate to other loyalties and associations.'[10]

Under early colonial rule, in the aftermath of the brutal suppression of the Shona and Ndebele uprisings of the late nineteenth century, as emergent capitalism began to transform social and economic relations on the land and in the early mines and towns, new forms of social struggles and identities emerged. As Sabelo Ndlovu's chapter shows, these drew on the protean ethnic identities of the past, the ambiguities of missionary influences and imperial citizenship, the claims for a more respectable 'civilised' status from the tiny black elite, and the demands of early labour struggles. Michael West describes the difficulties of developing a 'national consciousness' by the 1930s:

> The emergence of an African identity specific to Southern Rhodesia, which is to say a Zimbabwean African national consciousness, as evidenced by the rise of anticolonial nationalism in the late 1950s, had been a long time in the making. The 'nationalising' of the African elite took an important turn in the mid-1930s, culminating in the establishment of the Bantu Congress, the first political

[9] S. Ndlovu-Gatsheni, 'Dynamics of Democracy and Human Rights among the Ndebele in Zimbabwe, 1818-1934' (Ph.D. thesis, University of Zimbabwe, 2003); T. Ranger, *The Invention of Tribalism in Zimbabwe* (Gweru: Mambo Press, 1985).

[10] T. Ranger, *The Invention of Tribalism in Zimbabwe*, p. 19.

formation that could claim to represent Africans throughout the colony, albeit largely in the urban centers. Even when they had the will, the quest for national representativity had eluded earlier protest groups, which essentially were organized on a regional or ethnic basis.[11]

From the Second World War to the 1960s

Alois Mlambo's chapter demonstrates that the emergence of mass nationalism had to contend with a range of competing and overlapping political and identity claims from the 1940s to the 1960s. In the rural areas, involvement in an array of organisations and institutions was the norm, with the political actors including teachers, farmers, chiefs, Christians, traditionalists and workers. As Jocelyn Alexander has argued, the multifaceted nature of rural politics underlines the need to avoid the view of a single African political culture, 'as well as the strict divisions between the customary and the modern, so often reified in official discourse and in social analysis, and which find their echo in the characterisa-tion of the state as technocratic and alien and rural society as bounded and traditional.'[12]

Similarly, in the urban areas, the process of imagining a 'named nation and its social boundaries' was part of a complex dynamic in which identities such as ethnicity, region, gender and labour consciousness competed with and comple-mented each other.[13] Such struggles also centred on the rights of Africans to urban citizenship, against the more selective, racialised claims of white ratepayers,[14] and combined local demands with broader claims to produce, in central figures like Charles Mzingeli, what Timothy Scarnecchia calls 'imperial working class citizenship'. Mzingeli 'fought for the rights of the poor and the working class in order to protect them both from the gross injustices of a settler racist society and misrepresentations by elite African politicians'.[15] This broader claim on political and land rights and citizenship, using one or another colonial ideology, was also deployed by trade unionists and nationalist politicians as they situated their

[11] M. West, *The Rise of an African Middle Class: Colonial Zimbabwe, 1898-1965* (Bloomington: Indiana University Press, 2002), pp. 33-4.

[12] J. Alexander, *The Unsettled Land: State-making and the Politics of Land in Zimbabwe, 1893-2003* (Harare: Weaver Press; Oxford: James Currey, 2006), p. 9.

[13] E. Msindo, 'Ethnicity and nationalism in urban colonial Zimbabwe: Bulawayo, 1950-1963', *Journal of African History*, 48, 2007, pp. 273-4.

[14] T. Ranger, 'City versus State in Zimbabwe: Colonial antecedents of the current crisis', *Journal of East African Studies,* 1(2), 2007, pp. 161-92.

[15] T. Scarnecchia, *The Urban Roots of Democracy and Political Violence in Zimbabwe: Harare and Highfield, 1940-1964* (Rochester, NY: University of Rochester Press, 2008), p. 14. See also T. Ranger, *Voices from the Rocks* (Oxford: James Currey, 1999).

claims within a more recognised universal referent. As Ann Stoler and Frederick Cooper write, the 'very universalism of the language gives subordinate groups a handle, outside of the immediate power relations in which they are immersed, to single out local tyrannies and to claim global rights'.[16] It was also clear, however, that the usefulness of such universal language depended on how grounded such discourse was in local or national political structures and mobilisation.[17]

Until the late 1950s many among the African elite held out some hope for the possibilities of multiracial politics and a meritocracy based on non-racial principles. Through organisations such as the Capricorn African Society and the Inter-Racial Association of Southern Rhodesia, they sought out the promise of multiracialism and the dream of inclusion in the politics of the settler state. After this period the limits of multi-racial politics became increasingly apparent in the face of more intransigent white settler politics. Against such a state, and within the context of a broader continental surge of African nationalism, the calls for nationalist 'unity' were combined with the demonisation of those considered 'sell-outs' or 'stooges' by the nationalist leadership. In the process, the unity of the nationalist movement became synonymous with the subordination of all other African associations.[18] In particular, it sought to enforce singular organisational loyalties and to undermine the autonomy of structures such as the trade union movement. As the emergent trade union federation reached out for broader international solidarity around labour rights, the nationalist leadership very quickly labelled this as the intrusion of outside interests into national concerns. This was to begin a long-term conflict between the nationalists and sections of the trade union movement that would culminate in a decisive rupture in the late 1990s.[19] Similarly, while African women 'sought to evade both male control and colonial subjugation',[20] an understanding of the 'central role of women in township life' in the politics of Mzingeli's Reformed Industrial and Commercial Union in the late 1940s and early 1950s gave way to the African nationalists'

[16] A. Stoler and F. Cooper, 'Between metropole and colony: Rethinking a research agenda', in F. Cooper and A. Stoler (eds.), *Tensions of Empire: Colonial Cultures in a Bourgeois World* (Berkeley and Los Angeles: University of California Press, 1997), p. 35.

[17] F. Cooper, *Decolonisation and African Society: The Labour Question in French and British Africa* (Cambridge: Cambridge University Press, 1996), p. 467.

[18] T. Ranger, 'Introduction to Volume Two', in T. Ranger (ed.), *The Historical Dimensions of Democracy and Human Rights in Zimbabwe, Volume Two: Nationalism, Democracy and Human Rights* (Harare: University of Zimbabwe Publications, 2001), p. 5.

[19] B. Raftopoulos, 'Labour internationalism and problems of autonomy and democratization in the trade union movement in Southern Rhodesia, 1951-75', in Ranger (ed.), *The Historical Dimensions of Democracy*.

[20] T. Barnes, *"We Women Worked So Hard": Gender, Urbanisation and Social Reproduction in Colonial Zimbabwe, 1930-1956* (Oxford: James Currey, 1999), p. 160.

stress on a 'rhetoric reflecting notions of male defense of women's honor, rather than greater equality.'[21] This had the long-term effect of entrenching a patriarchal nationalist politics.

As the nationalist movement grew in strength from the mid-1950s through the 1970s, it drew on a complex mix of local, continental and global ideologies. While the process of creating a national imaginary drew on clothing, food, music, drama, political slogans and ancestral prayers,[22] it also called upon broader repertoires. As Sabelo Ndlovu writes about this process, nationalism

> was fuelled by complex local struggles, histories and sociologies within the colonial environment that had a basis in the fading precolonial past, myth and memories. When talking about nationalism being shaped from 'above', we mean that the local formations and enunciations remained open to continental and global ideologies as they were seen as fitting and advancing the local agendas. It is within this context that nationalism incorporated such external ideologies as Garveyism, Negritude, Marxism, Ethiopianism, Christianity, Pan-Africanism, Leninism, Maoism and liberalism – mixing these with indigenous resources of entitlement to land for instance.[23]

The UDI years and the liberation struggle

While the UDI years appeared for the most part to be about 'conflicting visions of the desired nation' between blacks and whites, Joseph Mtisi, Munyaradzi Nyakudya and Terri Barnes argue in their chapter that this blanket interpretation generalises a decidedly 'more heterogeneous terrain of political opinion'. Thus, while race certainly became a central modality through which people lived and experienced their lives,[24] the development of white Rhodesian and African nationalist politics and identities was a complex and differentiated process.

In the case of the white settlers,[25] it is important to trace the formation of a

[21] T. Scarnecchia, *The Urban Roots of Democracy*, p. 85.

[22] T. Turino, *Nationalists, Cosmopolitans and Popular Music in Zimbabwe* (Chicago: University of Chicago Press, 2000), p. 174.

[23] S. Ndlovu, *Do Zimbabweans Exist? Nation-Building Violence and Citizenship* (Oxford: Peter Lang International Academic Publishers, 2009 [forthcoming]).

[24] This formulation is taken from Stuart Hall's seminal essay, 'Race, articulation and societies structured in dominance', in Unesco, *Sociological Theories: Race and Colonialism* (Paris: Unesco, 1980), pp. 305-43.

[25] This discussion of white identity is taken from B. Raftopoulos, 'Introduction: Unreconciled differences: The limits of reconciliation politics in Zimbabwe', in B. Raftopoulos and T. Savage (eds.), *Zimbabwe: Injustice and Political Reconciliation* (Cape Town: Institute for Justice and Reconciliation, 2004), pp. viii-xxii.

white community unified by race and a national identity 'founded on racialism and an idea of the nation that excluded the black majority',[26] but in which issues of class and different national origins made the emergence of such a Rhodesian identity an uneven and contingent construction. For, as Mlambo observes,

> despite the outward semblance of unity, the white Rhodesian community was deeply divided by, among other factors, racism and cultural chauvinism which emanated mostly from the settlers of British stock, evoking strong reactions from other white groups in the country such as Afrikaners.[27]

Mlambo also notes that the demography of white Rhodesians revealed them to be a 'society of immigrants and transients, most of whom did not stay long enough to establish roots in the country'.[28] Moreover, the fragility of this race-based unity had to contend increasingly with the different experiences of 'occupational groupings trying to protect their own interests'.[29] In attempting to build their 'raced' identity, an exclusionary notion of culture was deployed to justify positions of racialised political and economic dominance in the colonial period. This notion of culture had as one of its central features an 'etiquette of whiteness'. Thus, A. Shutt writes that becoming Rhodesian 'was not simply a matter of assuming a racially superior mode vis-à-vis the subordinate African peoples. Crude racism could not be defended and therefore newcomers had to be taught the nuanced world of racial etiquette.'[30]

An important feature of such racial etiquette was that 'inter-racial familiarity undermined whites' custom of social distance with blacks, which in turn threatened white solidarity'.[31] This white concern with social distance is power-fully evoked in Tstisi Dangarembga's novel, *The Book of Not*, in which she describes how some white schoolgirls loathed even the thought of contact with their black counterparts. Writing about the reaction of some white girls if a black child backed into her by mistake, Dangarembga describes with palpable pain that

[26] K. Alexander, 'Orphans of the empire: An analysis of elements of white identity and ideology construction in Zimbabwe', in Raftopoulos and Savage (eds.), *Zimbabwe: Injustice and Political Reconciliation*, p. 195.

[27] A. S. Mlambo, '"Some are more white than others": Racial chauvinism as a factor in Rhodesian immigration policy, 1890-1963', *Zambezia*, 27(2), 1998, p. 140.

[28] A. S. Mlambo, 'Building a white man's country: Aspects of white immigration into Rhodesia up to World War Two', *Zambezia*, 25(2), 1998, p. 124.

[29] P. Godwin and I. Hancock, '*Rhodesians Never Die*': *The Impact of War and Change on White Rhodesia, c.1970-1980* (Harare: Baobab Books, 1995), p. 19.

[30] A. Shutt, 'Manners Make a Nation: Citizenship in Southern Rhodesia, 1945-63', paper delivered in the Department of Economic History, University of Zimbabwe, May 2004, p. 6.

[31] Ibid., p. 6.

There was something they – a particular kind of girl – did when that happened. This was a pulling back of their very aura from contact with you, in a way that said not even your shadows that blocked the sun should intermingle. And looks of such horror flooded their face at this accidental contact that you often looked around to see what horrendous monster caused the expression, before you realised it was your person. The girls put up with going to school with us because the nuns gave them a prestigious education. But this did not at all mean these particular girls could bear the idea or the reality of touching us.[32]

Further in the novel, Dangaremba writes: 'You came to school where you frequently had to pinch yourself to see if you really existed. Then, after that was confirmed, you quite often wished you didn't. So you ducked away to avoid meeting people.'[33] It is easy to understand the sense of visceral African nationalism that would emerge from these experiences.

In the face of such tenuous white unity and the exclusive sense of Rhodesian identity that emerged, Ian Smith's Rhodesian Front sought what it perceived to be a more universal reference for its racist policies. Smith and his ideologues found this in the politics of the Cold War, which, as Onslow observes, became 'a battle fought on the home front', in which the combination of anti-communism, anti-liberalism, anti-socialism and anti-internationalism situated Rhodesia as the 'front line' against communism. Describing the effects of this discourse on Rhodesian politics, Onslow states that

The perception of Rhodesia at 'the cutting edge of the struggle against Communism, with its stalwarts trying to uphold Western civilized standards', went far beyond the Rhodesian Front politicians. Furthermore, anti-communist rhetoric and propaganda was used by RF politicians to undercut the democratic space of the liberal element of the white community. It was a means to maintain the solidarity of the European population, and was used as a tool to transcend race – thus vital glue to hold the Rhodesian Front together, for the RF as a mass movement was not as solid as it looked.[34]

In the face of this recalcitrant, though fragile, white settler politics, the

[32] T. Dangarembga, *The Book of Not* (Banbury: Ayebia Clarke Publishing, 2006), p. 58.
[33] Ibid., p. 114.
[34] S. Onslow, 'The Rhodesia/Zimbabwe Conflict, 1974-1980', paper presented at the Oral History Conference: Southern Africa and the Cold War, Post 1974, Monash University Johannesburg Campus, 29-31 January 2009.

African nationalist movement attempted to build an alternative unified vision of the nation that, at least in aspiration, would subsume all identities and politics below the national level. Ibbo Mandaza describes this optimistic view of the emergent nationalists as involving

> a conscious decision to put aside primordial loyalties, if there were still any, the burial of ... native and tribal associations, as had hitherto existed, and the conclusion of a Social Contract, albeit not explicitly stated, towards a nationalist coalition, of tribal leaders of yesterday, being born into nationalist leaders of tomorrow.[35]

However, such a transition was more a teleological hope than based on the multi-layered identities that combined to make up nationalist politics, which was a 'protean ideology, with variable content, different pathways, and varying reservoirs of symbolic resources'.[36] Thus, the discourse and politics of nationalism and ethnicity did not reside at opposite ends of the spectrum but overlapped, contradicted and drew their mobilisation resources from common historical ground. [37] Pre-colonial elements of culture, community and belonging were incorporated, reinterpreted and inscribed in the modernist vision of nationalist politics, and the instrumental manipulation of ethnic politics took place not on the basis of some primordial identity, but on the reconfiguration of past memories, symbols and moral economies.[38]

Masipula Sithole's work on ethnic struggles in Zimbabwe nationalist politics shows the continued importance of this factor describing the Ndebele, Kalanga and Zezuru struggles in ZAPU, and similar conflicts between the Karanga, Zezuru, Manyika and Ndau in ZANU in the 1960s and 1970s. Thus, writing about the struggles within Zimbabwean nationalism in the 1970s, Sithole observed: 'The Zimbabwe liberation movement has been torn apart by tribalism and regionalism, but rarely will this be admitted in public by the leadership and organizations in question, preferring distant Marxist ideological explanations.'[39] While Sithole's work did not explain the origins of such ethnic sentiments, it did point to its continued influence in nationalist politics and the ways in which, as

[35] I. Mandaza, *Race Colour and Class in Southern Africa* (Harare: SAPES Books, 1997), p. xxiv.

[36] Young, 'Nation, ethnicity and citizenship', p. 246.

[37] S. Dorman, D. Hammett and P. Nugent, 'Introduction: Citizenship and its casualties in Africa', in Dorman, Hammett and Nugent (eds.), *Making Nations*, p. 3.

[38] B. Berman, D. Eyoh and W. Kymlicka, 'Ethnicity and democracy in historical and comparative perspective', in B. Berman, D. Eyoh and W. Kymlicka (eds.), *Ethnicity and Democracy in Africa* (Oxford: James Currey, 2004), p. 3.

[39] M. Sithole, *Zimbabwe Struggles within the Struggle* (Salisbury: Rujeko Publishers, 1979), p. 10.

Ndlovu describes it, 'African nationalism was a terrain for the retribalisation of politics and identity'.[40]

In addition to the tensions between ethnicity and nationalism in Zimbabwe politics, mobilisation of the indigenous population around nationalist goals was not a self-evident proposition. For, while the violence and humiliation of settler rule and the injustices of colonial occupation provided a powerful basis for an alternative nationalist imaginary, the process of bringing people behind such an alternative projection was neither automatic nor built solely on a consensual basis. As the work of Norma Kriger has shown, Zimbabwean peasants participated in the war of independence not only because they wanted to remove the discriminatory policies of white settler rule: they also forged alliances with guerrillas to reconstruct oppressive village relations. Moreover, Kriger argues that an important part of this mobilisation by guerrillas involved coercion, because of the conflicting agendas of peasant communities, and, as T. K. Chitiyo has argued, the Second Chimurenga was as much a civil war as a national liberation struggle.[41]

While the experience of the liberation struggle differed according to geography, the political and religious institutions in the area, and the extent of incorporation into the colonial political economy, Kriger's work nevertheless pointed to a central problem of nationalist violence that would become a major characteristic of the post-colonial state. This violence in the liberation movements was also used to suppress dissenting voices, such as in the ideological and political struggles around the radical ZIPA grouping in ZANU in the early 1970s. According to David Moore, the challenge of ZIPA 'reached into the very core of the war of liberation's meaning' and 'had been developing ever since the formative stages of the Zimbabwe ruling class-in-the-making'.[42] Such violent confrontation within nationalist parties took place within the context of long-term enmity and struggles between the major liberation parties of ZANU and ZAPU, which was only temporarily put aside during the period of the Patriotic Front, patched together in the last years of the war. The violence against women in the liberation struggle also contributed to the long-term problems of

[40] S. Ndlovu, *Do Zimbabweans Exist?* p. 119.

[41] N. Kriger, *Zimbabwe's Guerrilla War, Peasant Voices* (Cambridge: Cambridge University Press, 1992); T. K. Chitiyo, 'Zimbabwe's military historiography', *Southern African Diaspora Review*, 1(Summer), 2006, pp. 117-21. For a discussion of the historiography of nationalism, see B. Raftopoulos, 'Problematising nationalism in Zimbabwe: A historiographical review', *Zambezia*, 26(2), 1999, pp. 115-34.

[42] D. Moore, 'The Zimbabwe People's Army: Strategic innovation or more of the same', in N. Bhebe and T. Ranger, *Soldiers in Zimbabwe's Liberation War* (Harare: University of Zimbabwe Publications, 1995), p. 5.

nationalist politics around gender issues. While women never constituted more than a small part of ZANLA forces, they were recruited into the liberation forces mainly as 'cooks, nurses and, above all, as porters and carriers'. In addition, while the chefs and veterans 'sexually exploited many women, the party sought to elaborate puritanical rules about sexual relations and marriage', drawing on 'customary law' and Christian teachings.[43]

However, even as nationalist politics was marked by coercion and violence, the promises and values of nationalism also became important reference points for community demands on the political parties and the post-colonial state. Drawing on their work in Matabeleland Alexander, McGregor and Ranger write:

> In the Shangani, moral debates over the nationalist practice of both local and national leaders constantly refer back to nationalist promises and ideals. The values of nationalism are regularly held up in a favourable light against what are seen as the corrupting and exclusive practices of 'tribalism'. In this context 'ethnicity' and 'nationalism' cannot be subsumed into each other or used interchangeably. Each has a separate history and evokes different meanings. By making this argument we are not suggesting that nationalism is intrinsically a positive force, simply that it can be used as a moral counterweight to much criticized post-colonial government practice.[44]

Thus, by the end of the 1970s, the legacies of the liberation struggle were broadly ambiguous, characterised by experiences of colonial rule that were marked by both commonality and difference, and by support for the national liberation struggle that bore the marks of coercion and consent.[45] The enormous hopes of building a post-colonial nation had to contend with these divisions and differences, as well as with the formidable challenge of transforming the colonial legacies of structural inequality.

---

[43] J. Nhongo-Simbanegavi, *For Better or Worse? Women and ZANLA in Zimbabwe's Liberation Struggle* (Harare: Weaver Press, 2000) p. xx.

[44] J. Alexander, J. McGregor and T. Ranger *Violence and Memory: One Hundred Years in the 'Dark Forests' of Matabeleland* (Harare: Weaver Press; Oxford: James Currey, 2000), p. 7.

[45] I. Phimister, 'The combined and contradictory inheritance of struggle against colonialism', in C. Stoneman (ed.), *Zimbabwe's Prospects* (London: Macmillan, 1988), pp. 8-27; C. Sylvester, *Zimbabwe: The Terrain of Contradictory Development* (Boulder, CO: Westview Press, 1991); S. Ranchod-Nilsson, 'Gender politics and the pendulum of political and social transformation in Zimbabwe', *Journal of Southern African Studies*, 32(1), 2006, pp. 49-67.

The post-colonial years[46]

The Lancaster House agreement, which ended the liberation war in Zimbabwe in 1979, and the constitution that emerged from it, together embodied a series of compromises over minority rights, in particular on the future of land ownership in the country and guaranteed white representation in parliament. In effect, the constitution gave white capital a decade-long period of consolidation, during which issues around the radical restructuring of the legacy of economic in-equality were effectively put on hold. The Lancaster House settlement was determined by a combination of national, regional and international pressures, in the parameters of which the policy of reconciliation was enunciated by Robert Mugabe. This policy embodied the fragile task of nation-building as it set out to allay the fears of the white minority and the international community while consolidating ZANU(PF)'s determination to control and extend the reach of the state, and to provide the resources for the improvement of the majority of the people.[47] The language of reconciliation was a generous and inclusive invitation for old antagonists to join the emerging nation. In Mugabe's words:

> Henceforth you and I must strive to adapt ourselves, intellectually and spiritually, to the reality of our political change and relate to each other as brothers bound one to the other by a bond of comradeship. If yesterday I fought you as an enemy, today you have become my friend and ally with the same national interests, loyalty, rights and duties as myself. If yesterday you hated me, today you cannot avoid the love that binds you to me and me to you. Is it not folly, therefore, that in these circumstances anybody should seek to revive the wounds and grievances of the past? The wrongs of the past must stand forgiven and forgotten.[48]

Yet, even as the new ruling party set out to place its mark on the Zimbabwean polity, it became quickly apparent that the policy of reconciliation would be based on the subordination of opposition political forces. As the violent birth of the Zimbabwean nation through the liberation struggle was represented as the central legitimising factor in national politics, the boundaries of 'insiders' and 'outsiders' to the nation became quickly apparent. The Gukurahundi massacres in Matabeleland and the Midlands in the mid-1980s displayed a number of traits

---

[46] Parts of this section are drawn from Raftopoulos, 'Unreconciled differences'.

[47] I. Mandaza, 'Introduction: The political economy of transition', in I. Mandaza (ed.), *Zimbabwe: The Political Economy of Transition, 1980-86* (Dakar: Codesria, 1986), pp. 1-20.

[48] R. Mugabe, 'Independence Message', *The Struggle for Independence: Documents of the Recent Development of Zimbabwe 1975-80*, Volume 7, December 1979 – April 1980 (Hamburg: Institute for African Affairs, 1984).

that would mark the authoritarian statism after 2000, namely the 'excesses of a strong state, itself in many ways a direct Rhodesian inheritance, and a particular interpretation of nationalism'.[49] This 'quasi-nationalism', as Richard Werbner refers to it, was 'energised by a myth of being prior to the nation-state' but nonetheless was 'made in and by the struggle for power and moral authority in the nation-state'.[50] The outcome of this conflict was the 1987 Unity Accord, which, while it ended the atrocities in Matabeleland, effectively emasculated the major opposition party at the time, PF-ZAPU, and confirmed the regional subordination of Matabeleland. Thus, while the ruling party used the language of reconciliation to structure its relations with the white elite and international capital, it deployed the discourse of a violently imposed 'unity' to control the political opposition. In summary, during the first decade of independence the new state set out to establish its sovereignty through the assertion of territorial control and monopolisation of the means of violence, and the introduction of a development programme that would begin to improve the livelihoods of the mass of the population.[51]

At the end of the period of economic liberalisation in the late 1990s, as James Muzondidya describes in his chapter, 'the unresolved questions of race and racial ownership of land and other resources became major talking points'. As the limits of the structural adjustment programme became increasingly clear, the political challenges to ZANU(PF)'s idea of the nation grew in intensity, first through the labour movement's intellectual and organisational challenges to the ruling party, and then through the demands for constitutional and demo-cratic reform of the state. These challenges set out explicit demands for more democratic citizenship stressing the centrality of popular sovereignty from which the state should derive its legitimacy. Both of these processes led to the emergence of a political opposition that for the first time in the post-colonial period threatened the ruling party's hold on state power and its majority support in the population.

As Brian Raftopoulos's chapter shows, these developments opened up

[49] Alexander et al., Violence and Memory, p. 6; S. Eppel, '"Gukurahundi": The need for truth and reparation', in Raftopoulos and Savage (eds.), Zimbabwe: Injustice and Political Reconciliation, pp. 43-62.

[50] R. Werbner, 'In memory: A heritage of war in south-western Zimbabwe', in N. Bhebe and T. Ranger (eds.), Society in Zimbabwe's Liberation War (Harare: University of Zimbabwe Publications, 1995), p. 197; R. Werbner, 'Introduction: Multiple identities, plural arenas', in R. Werbner and T. Ranger (eds.), Postcolonial Identities in Africa (London: Zed Books, 1996).

[51] For a useful discussion of the relationship between sovereignty and development, see T. Blom Hansen and F. Stepputat, 'Introduction: State of imagination', in T. Blom Hansen and F. Stepputat (eds.), States of Imagination: Ethnographic Explorations of the Post-Colonial State (Durham, NC: Duke University Press, 2001), pp. 1-38.

a vigorous debate on whatever 'social contract' ZANU(PF) thought it had 'negotiated' with the people of Zimbabwe in the proceeding years, and demanded a reopening of the terms of national belonging. Moreover, in confronting the legitimacy of the ruling party, these challenges also raised questions about the past of the liberation movements, by seeking both to reassert the agency of other social forces in the anti-colonial struggles and to question the monopolisation of this history by the ruling party. In an 'Introduction' to a history of the Zimbabwe labour movement produced in 1997, the then Secretary-General of the Zimbabwe Congress of Trade Unions, Morgan Tsvangirai, expressed the need for a 'more open and critical process of writing history in Zimbabwe' and to 'remind the victors in the political arena that the struggle for independence was a broad, uneven process, with many unsung heroes and unintended effects.' Moreover, he advised that the 'history of a nation-in-the-making should not be reduced to a selective heroic tradition, but should be a tolerant and continuing process of questioning and re-examination. We, in the Labour Movement, submit our history to such a process.'[52]

Between 1998 and 2008 Zimbabwean politics witnessed a range of political and economic convulsions in which new social relations emerged, the state was reconfigured in more authoritarian nationalist terms, and the 'production of sovereignty through the nation and the state'[53] produced a series of citizen exclusions from what was constructed as the 'authentic nation' by the ruling party. These exclusions were carried out through a combination of the law, the abuse of state institutions, and state-led and -supported violence. A key element of this state restructuring was a revived nationalist discourse located around a number of themes, namely the centrality of the land, a selective rendition of the history of liberation, and the collective branding of whites, the West, the Movement for Democratic Change, and the civic movement and their supporters as 'enemies of the state' and outsiders to the nation. Ranger dubbed this exclusive interpretation 'patriotic history' because it reduced a complex history of nationalism to a sequence of revolutionary resistance. Though Ranger sought to distinguish this new history from the older nationalist historiography that 'celebrated aspiration and modernization as well as resistance',[54] it is clear that,

[52] M. Tsvangirai, 'Introduction', in B. Raftopoulos and I. Phimister (eds.), *Keep on Knocking: A History of the Labour Movement in Zimbabwe 1900-1997* (Harare: Baobab Books, 1997), p. xi.

[53] T. Blom Hansen and F. Stpputat, 'Introduction', in T. Blom Hansen and F. Stepputat (eds.), *Sovereign Bodies, Citizens, Migrants, and States in the Postcolonial World* (Princeton: Princeton University Press, 2005), p. 36.

[54] T. Ranger, 'Nationalist historiography, patriotic history and the history of the nation: The struggle over the past in Zimbabwe', *Journal of South African History*, 30(2), 2004, p. 218.

while there are differences between the two, 'patriotic history' drew some of its symbolic resources from its predecessor. Nevertheless, as Ranger made clear, there are serious limitations with what he characterises as a 'dangerously one-sided, narrow and divisive' 'patriotic history':

> Its focus on the three episodes of violent struggle – the First Chimurenga of 1896-7, the Second Chimurenga of the late 1960s and 1970s, and the Third Chimurenga of land reclamation in the early 2000s – left out too much. It left out the towns, for instance, and the whole tradition of black worker struggle. It left out, or set aside, the greater majority of African women and their struggles for a better life. It left out, or played down, the contributions made by nationalists during the long years between the Chimurengas and the day-to-day history of survival and resistance. It carried over the terminology of 'heroes' and 'sell-outs' from the conflicts in which resistant Africans were fighting against an enemy with vastly more powerful firearms. In the Third Chimurenga the internal 'enemy' was not armed at all: nevertheless, public rhetoric sometimes defined almost half the nation as 'traitors'.[55]

In the course of 'the Zimbabwean crisis' and the series of population displacements that have been part of it, new identities and solidarities have emerged in the region that have raised further issues around the nation, citizenship and sovereignty. Even as the Zimbabwean state has asserted its pan-Africanist and anti-imperialist credentials, the MDC, labour and civic movements called for different forms of solidarity and sovereignty that have as their centre the democratic rights of citizens. While ZANU(PF) has stressed the importance of its version of colonial redress around the land question, the opposition has called for equal attention to the human rights legacies of the liberation struggle.[56] Where SADC has continuously reaffirmed its solidarity with the Zimbabwean state, labour and civic organisations in southern Africa have called for an expanded solidarity with the victims of repressive nationalism, and for limits to state authoritarianism that subjects its citizenry to increasing repression, exclusions and 'states of exception'.[57]

As Robert Mugabe, as Zimbabwe's first Prime Minister at independence in

[55] Cited in G. Mazarire, E. Chipembere and T. Ranger, 'What History for Which Zimbabwe?' (Harare and Oxford: Unpublished paper, 2008).

[56] For a recent discussion of the tensions between these issues, see S. Jacobs and J. Mundy (eds.), 'Reflections on Mahmood Mamdani's "Lessons of Zimbabwe"', *Concerned African Scholars Bulletin*, 82 (Spring), 2009.

[57] G. Agamben, *Homo Sacer: Sovereign Power and Bare Life* (Palo Alto, CA: Stanford University Press, 1998).

1980, called for national reconciliation at the end of the liberation war, so did Morgan Tsvangirai, the new Prime Minister of the Inclusive Government formed in 2009 after a decade of struggles between the opposition and the ruling party, make a new plea for national healing in a nation 'that has endured so much violence'.[58] Moreover, the 15 September 2008 Global Political Agreement, negotiated through SADC to end the political impasse in Zimbabwe, included a paragraph stating that the Inclusive Government would 'give consideration to the setting up of a mechanism to properly advise on what measures might be necessary and practicable to achieve national unity in respect of victims of pre- and post-independence political conflicts'.[59]

The insertion of this clause echoed the long-standing demands by civic groups for a 'credible and independent truth seeking inquiry into conflicts of the past'.[60] It also indicated the long-standing problems of violence and politics in Zimbabwe's colonial and post-colonial history that have marked the process of nation- and state-making in the country. As Zimbabweans, both inside the country and now in large numbers in the diaspora, struggle to find new, more democratic ways to become Zimbabwean citizens, they must confront the many and complex legacies of the country's history. The divisions of race, ethnicity and gender, as well as the intricately connected trajectories of rural and urban struggles, combined with the complex tensions and assimilations of the colonial past, remain part of the lived realities of Zimbabwe's present.

Truth commissions, which for the most part focus on individual human rights abuses and the victims and perpetrators of these abuses, tend to avoid the broader landscapes of historical process and structural economic violence.[61] Moreover, the methodology of such commissions – constrained by the need to distinguish between 'relevant and irrelevant truths', those deemed to fall within the human rights violation framework, and those removed from the 'debris of

---

[58] 'Tsvangirai calls for reconciliation', *Zimbabwe Times*, 23 Feb. 2009.

[59] 'Agreement between the Zimbabwe African National Union Patriotic Front (ZANU-PF) and the Two Movement for Democratic Change (MDC) Formations on Resolving the Challenges facing Zimbabwe', 15 Sept. 2008.

[60] Zimbabwe Human Rights Forum, 'Transitional Justice Options for Zimbabwe', 14 Oct. 2008. Also 'Civil Society and Justice in Zimbabwe', summary of proceedings of a symposium held in Johannesburg, 11-13 August 2003 (Pretoria: Themba Lesizwe, 2003). For a critical discussion of the transitional justice debate in Zimbabwe, see S. Eppel and B. Raftopoulos, *Prospects for Transitional Justice in Zimbabwe* (Pretoria: IDASA, 2008).

[61] M. Mamdani, 'Reconciliation without justice', *Southern African Review of Books*, Nov./Dec. 1996; M. Fullard and N. Rousseau, 'Uncertain borders: The TRC and the (un)making of public myths', *Kronos*, 34(November), 2009, pp. 215-39.

national history'[62] – is not suited to the broader reach of historical narrative. While such a commission is certainly necessary to deal with the central issue of human rights violations, there is also an urgent need to produce critical histories of Zimbabwe that 'seek to explore alternative and plural ways of conceiving its past'.[63] One of the most urgent tasks in this process remains a history of ZANU(PF) itself, which has had such a significant impact on the history of Zimbabwe. Perhaps not surprisingly, a party that has had to confront increasing criticism of its post-colonial performance has had to rely on a narrowly constructed view of the past, avoiding a critical confrontation with its history. In the absence of this historical engagement, Zimbabweans have had to be content with biographies of key members of the ruling party, which have begun to ask critical questions of the latter.[64] The opposition will also need to think critically about its past and the conflicting legacies that have shaped it in both positive and negative terms, remembering that there are no guarantees for good conduct in the future. It is our view that critically confronting the past, in all its dimensions in Zimbabwe, is an essential part of 'becoming better Zimbabweans' and of moving beyond what Horace Campbell refers to as an exhausted patriarchal model of liberation.[65] This book represents a small contribution to that process.

The history of the book

The idea for this book emerged in the early 2000s, when an attempt was made to form a Zimbabwe Historical Association at the University of Zimbabwe whose first task would be to write a new history of Zimbabwe. At that time, there was no single-volume history that could provide an accessible overview of the *longue durée* of the Zimbabwean past. The Association was short-lived, and the task of producing such a book remained to be done. The project was revived in 2006 when Brian Raftopoulos joined the Institute for Justice and Reconciliation in Cape Town, and he was able to engage with the Institute's own historical work around the *Turning Points* school history project in South Africa. When the project began in 2007, Zimbabwe was still in the midst of a dire political and economic crisis, to which there appeared little chance of an early resolution. By the time the project was completed in early 2009, there was new hope of

[62] L. Buur, 'The South African Truth Commission: A Technique of Nation-State Formation', in T. Blom Hansen and F. Stepputat (eds), *States of Imagination*, pp. 149-81.

[63] Mazarire, Chipembere and Ranger, 'What History'.

[64] E. Tekere, *A Lifetime of Struggle* (Harare: SAPES Books, 2007); F. Chung, *Re-living the Second Chimurenga: Memories from Zimbabwe's Liberation Struggle* (Harare: Weaver Press, 2006).

[65] H. Campbell, *Reclaiming Zimbabwe: The Exhaustion of the Patriarchal Model of Liberation* (Cape Town: David Philip, 2003).

such a resolution in the form a fragile political agreement mediated under the auspices of SADC in late 2008. This book ends with the entry of the MDC into the Inclusive Government in early 2009; while it originally set out to cover the period up to 2008, it was felt that it would be more historically appropriate to end it at the beginning of 2009, thus making it 'a long 2008'.

There are many people and organisations that have helped in bringing this book to fruition. Firstly, we would like to thank the contributors, who committed two years of their lives to the project. We would like to pay particular tribute to those authors who had to complete their chapters under the most difficult and stressful material and logistical conditions in Zimbabwe. We would also like to thank Professors Terence Ranger and Ian Phimister, two pioneers in the field of Zimbabwean history, who agreed to act as critical interlocutors throughout the process. Their comments and contributions to the various chapters were invaluable, and the different legacies of their work can be felt throughout the book. The Ford Foundation provided the generous grant for the project and we would like to thank Alice Brown and her team at the Ford Office in South Africa for their support and patience. The Institute for Justice and Reconciliation in Cape Town provided the administration of the project and we are grateful for the support of its new Director, Dr Fanie du Toit, and the Zimbabwe project officer, Shuvai Nyoni. Brian Raftopoulos would like to thank the Solidarity Peace Trust for supporting his role in the project and allowing him the time and space to carry it out. Finally, we would like to thank Irene Staunton and Murray McCartney of Weaver Press for their editorial work on the book and their un-wavering commitment to progressive publishing in Zimbabwe. We dedicate this book to the people of Zimbabwe and to the generations of historical actors who have contributed to the continuing process of 'Becoming Zimbabwe'.

1

Reflections on Pre-Colonial Zimbabwe, *c.*850–1880s

Gerald Chikozho Mazarire

Introduction

What we know about this period of Zimbabwean history has been under constant reinterpretation. Most of what today we call pre-colonial Zimbabwean history is a product of academic theories, and of ideas popularised during and since the nationalist struggle when it became necessary to debunk existing stereotypes of African identity, and to situate the struggle for independence within the ideals of self-determination and self-knowledge. This is as true of Zimbabwe as it is of many other African countries. Indeed, it can be argued that in its more recent assertions of sovereignty, reclamation, restitution, the return to tradition, and even anti-imperialism, the Zimbabwe state perceives the pre-colonial period as an important starting point for its own national reconstruction.

The pre-colonial history of Zimbabwe is usually explained in terms of the rise and fall of empires – the Great Zimbabwe, the Mutapa, the Torwa, the Rozvi and Ndebele states. These large states are interesting and important and will be discussed in this chapter, but it is misleading to think that nothing of significance happened before or afterwards, or outside their frontiers. Most autochthons lived in smaller units, and we have come to learn a lot more about life in those societies than we did twenty years ago. Many Zimbabweans feel proud that there were once large 'empires' that could fight against external invaders, but the story of the occupation of Zimbabwe's difficult landscape by many pioneering groups should be just as much a source of pride.

This chapter will consider several different groups of people inhabiting different kinds of environment – forests, river valleys, highveld and lowveld – and examine how societies emerged in them. The reader will encounter many of the same basic tools and ideas – about gender, livestock, rain, ancestors, crops, crafts and trade – but with important variations.

Small societies never existed in isolation. Pioneers came from and maintained links with 'parent' societies; people left the small society to trade or hunt or make pilgrimages to major rain shrines or oracular caves. When larger states emerged, the small societies had to come to terms with them, as we shall see with the Mutapa and Rozvi 'empires'. But before we turn to the peopling of the environment, it is necessary to make a further point: many writers have simplified Zimbabwean history by talking of distinct ethnic blocs – 'Shona', 'Ndebele', 'Venda', 'Tonga', etc. This chapter is not about the 'Shona' and their achievements. The term was not in use before the nineteenth century, and even then it was seen as an insult, a term used by one's enemies; no one thought of themselves as 'Shona'. Instead, there existed a large region of broadly similar languages, beliefs and institutions, larger than present-day Zimbabwe and stretching into areas now defined as South Africa, Zambia and Mozambique. Within that zone, there was a constant movement of people, goods, ideas, and a multitude of different self-identifications.

Academics have tended to depict pre-colonial Zimbabwe in fairly monolithic terms. One perspective they have popularised is a linear trajectory of states rising, falling and sometimes rising again. This is a general trend common throughout the world; it requires more specific revision within the Zimbabwean context. The transition of societies from what archaeologists often call 'primitive' to 'complex', i.e. exhibiting all forms of political economic and social sophistication, is a favourite theory. Yet 'complexity', viewed from any perspective, may not have been the ultimate aspiration of even the smallest of chiefdoms; it is more often the case that continuity has been achieved by fragmentation from these 'complex' state systems. This is true especially of the post-Great Zimbabwe period, where constituents of the political and social culture were disaggregated and spread across southern Africa through processes of replication and/ or modification. Archaeologists have tended to interpret this process as the 'decline of the Zimbabwe culture', but this can only hold true if one refers to the quality of the architecture, the stone walls or *zimbabwes*, and to nothing else.[1] Ideologically – and perhaps politically, it appears – these cultures became spatially more dynamic and sophisticated; the people associated with them were adventurous over a much wider area and, interestingly, they were linguistically experimental and innovative.

The pre-colonial history of Zimbabwe is best appreciated from 'breaking points' – those contexts of build-up and fragmentation already written into the larger narratives of the 'rise and fall' of states, when new identities emerged and old ones were transformed, negotiated or accommodated. This requires the revision of certain grand narratives about Zimbabwe's pre-colonial peoples. The first lies hidden in stories of 'abandoned' states. These have encouraged notions of a depopulated southern frontier, one that steadily moves northwards over

---

[1] 'Culture' in this sense is used to refer to group identities normally perceived by archaeologists to be represented through styles of ceramics.

centuries from the Limpopo region towards the Zambezi, until it is repopulated later by Rozvi and Karanga settlements of the eighteenth and nineteenth centuries. Certainly, no climatic or environmental data adequately supports such a theory, although it has been assumed that this pattern of settlement was dictated by changing trade routes.[2] Human evidence in the form of traditions, language and culture has not been given enough attention; interpretations have been based on the remains of pots and bones.[3] We know relatively little of the people who remained at Great Zimbabwe or Mapungubwe after the demise of these states, or indeed of those who drifted further south of them.

The second presumption concerns the term 'Shona', a collective noun which conflates the linguistic, cultural and political attributes of a people who did not even know themselves by that name until the late nineteenth century, and even then could still be variously described as 'vaNyai', 'abeTshabi', 'Karanga' or 'Hole'.[4] The Shona are perceived to be the descendants of the progenitors of the Zimbabwe tradition traceable to the Leopard's Kopje people (see below). In its modern sense Shona is no more than a reference to a dialect, and in its political context to the country's more populous ethnic group.

The 'Zimbabwean Plateau', its people and pots

Most pre-colonial activity has been understood to have taken place in a theatre defined by environment and topography as the 'Zimbabwean Plateau'. This term was popularised by David Beach to describe an area 'shaped like a giant "T" with one arm running towards the sea to the east, another towards Kariba to the west, and the stem going southwest.'[5] Later, it became an established notion that this region was inhabited by a 'huge crescent of population', cut apart by the Save valley, giving rise to Beach's much debated 'Great Crescent' theory.[6] Subsequent studies have discussed Zimbabwe as if it was just a plateau. Yet, even if the Great Crescent theory is accepted as it is, it shows that people became more important commodities of power than trade items or the environment. Archaeologists have tended to define both peoples and eras in pre-colonial Zimbabwe according to ceramic styles. Although the correlation between language and ceramic styles is still a subject of debate, it has enjoyed widespread application in southern African archaeology. In Zimbabwe, it has given rise to a phenomenon known

[2] G. Pwiti, 'Trade and economies in southern Africa: The archaeological evidence', *Zambezia*, 18, 1991.
[3] D. N. Beach, *Zimbabwe before 1900* (Gweru: Mambo Press, 1984), ch. 1.
[4] F. W. T. Posselt, *Fact and Fiction* (Bulawayo: Books of Rhodesia, 1935), p. 12.
[5] Beach, *Zimbabwe before 1900*, p. 7.
[6] D. N. Beach, *The Shona and their Neighbours* (Oxford: Blackwell, 1994), pp. 19-21.

as the 'Zimbabwe Culture', which also incorporates shared architectural, spatial and other symbolic features.[7] Its identity, traceable to the 'Leopard's Kopje Tradition', has been broadly associated with the ancestors of the speakers of modern 'Shona' with its numerous dialect clusters. This group of immigrants, variously linked to the movements of the Bantu people, replaced or transformed an already existing cluster of autochthons in the Limpopo region identifiable with the 'Zhizo Culture'. They, in turn, moved to the fringes of Kalahari desert to form the Toutswemogala culture.[8] The Leopard's Kopje people are presumed to have spoken an ancient Kalanga dialect and they developed into later phases of linguistic/ceramic correlates, which are striking in their general resemblance to each other. Thus they fit the generic description in archaeological circles as the 'Shona' or 'Zimbabwe' ceramic culture that is divided into subgroups such as Gumanye, Harare and Musengezi. This, it has been argued, can be taken to represent the spread of the Shona language family.[9]

The name Shona presents the modern historian with a number of challenges. It is not only an anachronism; the people in question were known to themselves and to outsiders mostly as Karanga.[10] There are also various theories accounting for the origins of the name Karanga itself: 'the people of the sun (*kalanga*)', 'sons of the junior wife (*mukaranga*)', etc.[11] However, 'Karanga' in its modern sense refers to a dialect of Shona spoken in the southern parts of Zimbabwe presently inhabited by people who migrated there in the eighteenth and nineteenth centuries from the northern and eastern sections of the so-called plateau. Their movements have been wrongly referred to as 'Karanga migrations' by interpreting their contemporary identity, which is both a misnomer and yet another anachronism.[12] While there is no doubt that the same people lived in a common area for a period after 900, it is almost certain that their identities mutated over time as a result of interactions within and beyond these regions. What were probably the 'Karanga' at Great Zimbabwe (1290-1450) could be 'Togwa' (1450-1690) in the north-west and part of the 'Mutapa' (1450-1902) in the Dande and Zambezi regions to the north, and later 'Rozvi' (1690-1830)

---

[7] For an accessible account of this culture, see I. Pikirayi, *The Zimbabwe Culture: Origins and Decline of Southern Zambezian States* (Walnut Creek: Altamira Press, 2001).

[8] Ibid., chs. 3 and 4.

[9] T. N. Huffman, *The Leopard's Kopje Tradition* (Salisbury: Trustees of the National Museums and Monuments of Rhodesia, 1974), p. 130.

[10] S. I. G. Mudenge, *A Political History of Munhumutapa* (Harare: Zimbabwe Publishing House, 1988), p. 21.

[11] G. M. Theal, *History of South Africa before 1795* (London: Swan Sonnenschein, 1910), III, p. 225; Posselt, *Fact and Fiction*, p. 137.

[12] For example, Pikirayi, *The Zimbabwe Culture*, ch. 8.

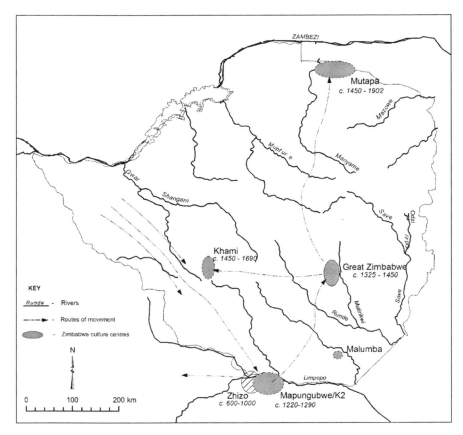

Map 1.1: Development of the Leopard's Kopje culture on the Zimbabwean Plateau.

[This and the other maps in this chapter were drawn by Seke Katsamudanga of the Archaeology Unit, History Department, University of Zimbabwe.]

in the south-west. The resurgence of the 'Karanga' populating the central and southern parts of Zimbabwe from around 1750 is just another stage in an unfolding process.

What is clear from both linguistics and archaeology is that the 'plateau' can never pass for an analytical concept that offers all the answers to the settlement patterns and distribution of these Zimbabwean peoples.[13] It was not the only preferred zone of settlement, nor was it necessarily the best. A new wave of archaeological enquiry has sought to use the concept of 'complexity' differently

[13] See the critique by I. Pikirayi, 'David Beach, Shona history and the archaeology of Zimbabwe', *Zambezia*, 26(2), 1999, pp. 135-44.

to discuss what are termed 'complex systems', a phenomenon that accepts an adaptive cycle of growth among prehistoric societies, allowing for their 'collapse, reorganisation, renewal and [or] re-establishment'.[14] In the Shashi-Limpopo basin where this concept has been convincingly applied, the end of the Leopard's Kopje culture may be said to have opened up new opportunities of re-organisation and innovation that allowed the valley to be continually inhabited. More than forty years after it first appeared, Chet Lancaster's study of the ethnic composition of pre-colonial Zimbabwe defined by geographical habitation still stands.[15] Although focusing on the Tonga of the middle Zambezi valley, his theory links the spread of the 'Shona' in this area to the development of distinct ethnic identities defined by settlement patterns. It is thus possible to distinguish between valley/lowland peoples and those settled in the high-altitude zones of the plateau.

Linguistically, the term 'Goba' or 'Gova' (wetland, or riverine valley) has been associated with a dialect cluster spoken by those Shona occupying the lowlands. The name has wide application in both the lowlands of the Zambezi in the north and those in the south around the Limpopo. Earlier work by Gilbert Pwiti on some of the Goba's locational choices in the Zambezi valley shows that their subsistence economy determined their choice of settlement and indicates a con-tinuity in their spatial behaviour since the fifteenth century.[16] The same may be true of the huge cluster of 'vaGova' people of the southern lowveld stretching into the Zoutpansberg area of South Africa. Later linguistic and ethnographic work, as demonstrated below, has revealed their common 'Shona' origins.

Similarly, the name 'Nyai' besides identifying a 'follower' implied a highland settler. It was commonly used in reference to those 'Shona' inhabiting the plateau environments. It is little wonder that the land that became the British colony of Southern Rhodesia was known to early hunters, travellers and missionaries as 'Banyailand'.[17] Such insights will require further ethnographic research about peoples long written out of their areas on the assumption that either the en-virons were unfit for human habitation or that their occupants needed only to be defined as 'Shona'. The first lead, suggested by this supposed continuity and

---

[14] M. Manyanga, *Resilient Landscapes: Socio-environmental Dynamics in the Shashi-Limpopo Basin, Southern Zimbabwe c.AD800 to the Present* (Uppsala: Studies in Global Archaeology, 2007), p. 15.

[15] C. S. Lancaster, 'Ethnic identity, "history", and tribe in the middle Zambezi valley', *American Ethnologist*, 1(4), 1974.

[16] G. Pwiti, *Continuity and Change: An Archaeological Study of Farming Communities in Northern Zimbabwe* (Uppsala: Studies in African Archaeology 13, 1996) pp. 140-1.

[17] See, for instance, F. Coillard, *On the Threshold of Central Africa* (London: Frank Cass, 1897), pp. 22-30.

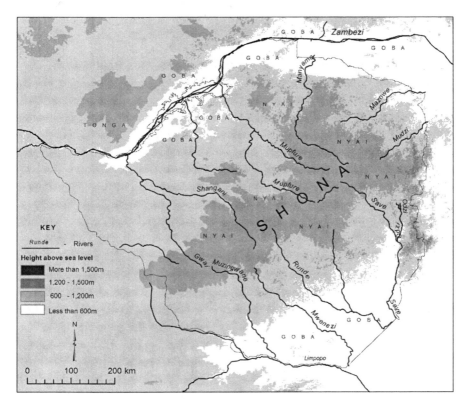

Map 1.2: Approximate settlement patterns of the Goba and Nyai.
[Modified from Lancaster, 'Ethnic identity', figs. 1 and 2, pp. 714 and 719.]

adaptability of settlement behaviour, evokes age-old environmentally determinist ideas, where the location of people in the highlands, lowlands, mountains, plains, riverine areas or dry lands earned them their ethnic labels.[18] The second concern is to explore the interactions between these people of varied environments and their consequences. Lastly, I seek to account for factors that bring about change, defining or reshaping these people's ideological, linguistic, political and social fabric. This analysis is clearer when it begins at Great Zimbabwe, to where most of the key concepts are easily traceable.

[18] W. Beinart and J. McGregor, 'Introduction', in W. Beinart and J. McGregor (eds.), *Social History and African Environments* (Oxford: James Currey, 2003).

The spatial dispersal in the lowlands from *c*.1450

The southern lowlands: The origins and spread of the Gova and Venda

Some rewarding results have derived from the combined use of oral tradition, linguistics, and the archaeology south of Great Zimbabwe. Together these have demonstrated the fate of populations to the south of the ancient city after its demise. Jannie Loubser found correlations between the ceramic sequence and oral traditions in the Mapungubwe area, which revealed continuity between two sets of 'Shona'-related settlements. There is evidence of movement into the area north of the Zoutpansberg by 'Shona' – chiefly lineages from Great Zimbabwe – around 1450. This was, however, an area already occupied by local 'Shona' and Sotho groups, so that by 1550 the interaction between them had produced the Venda language.[19]

Attempts to draw a link between the ethnography of the modern Venda and the ancient traditions of Great Zimbabwe have generated much scholarly debate, but all agree that Venda has its origins north of the Limpopo.[20] Venda oral traditions identify the aboriginal Ngona, Mbedzi and Rembetu groups who settled in the mountains and whose 'villages were built with great stones for fear of their enemies'.[21] In their fieldwork in the Zoutpansberg in 1969, Ralushai and Gray found the elusive Ngona still living within the reaches of the *zimbabwes* of their ancestors, but their oral traditions were 'disappointingly meagre'.[22] On closer analysis of their *mitupo* (totems), and considered in combination with the traditions of other autochthonous groups such as the Mbedzi, it became clear how central both the Ngona and Mbedzi were to the shaping of Venda identity and language as we know them today. As for the Rembetu, we know more from their language and locality. Linguists have accepted that Rembetu belongs to a Shona dialect cluster known as the 'Gova/Govha', spoken mainly in south-eastern Zimbabwe along the lower course of the Bubi river.[23] In its broader context this cluster incorporates more-recent dialects such as Twamamba and

---

[19] J. Loubser, 'Oral traditions, archaeology and the history of Venda *mitupo*', *African Studies*, 49(2), 1990, pp. 26, 28.

[20] T. N. Huffman, *Snakes and Crocodiles: Power and Symbolism in Ancient Zimbabwe* (Johannesburg: Witwatersrand University Press, 1996). See also the review of this book by various authors in *South African Archaeological Bulletin*, 53(166), 1997 pp. 125-43.

[21] M. M. Motenda, 'History of the Western Venda and of the Lemba', in N. J. van Warmelo (ed.), *The Copper Mines of Musina and the Early History of the Zoutpansberg* (Pretoria: Department of Native Affairs, 1940), p. 51.

[22] N. M. N. Ralushai and J. R. Gray, 'Ruins and traditions of the Ngona and Mbedzi among the Venda of the Northern Transvaal', *Rhodesian History*, 8, 1977, p. 3.

[23] P. J. Wentzel, *The Relationship Between Venda and Western Shona* (Pretoria: Unisa Press, 1983), vol. III, p. 40.

Romwe that have been understood by linguists such as J. P. Wentzel as 'lesser dialects [of Shona] falling into disuse'. Ethnographic evidence gathered in the 1950s by the Swedish missionary Harald von Sicard suggests that Twamamba is derived from 'ancient Rembetu'.[24] A recent reconstruction of Venda identity by the archaeologist Tom Huffman, based on pottery assemblages associated with the Ngona, suggests that some of them may have descended from Mapungubwe ancestors while some were of Sotho-Tswana origin.[25] This archaeological and linguistic pattern fits Huffman's own umbrella classification of the language spoken by the Leopard's Kopje people as being 'ancient Kalanga', as highlighted above.

Fig. 1.1: Lemba village scene in the Belingwe Reserve.
[Source: National Archives of Zimbabwe]

Further south-east of Great Zimbabwe the pattern of the spread of the Zimbabwe culture continues through the Save valley right up to the Mozambican coast where *zimbabwes* of various shapes and sizes can be traced even into Madagascar. Some of them have been identified with typical Karanga dynasties in the Portuguese records of the sixteenth century. One such was the chieftaincy of Gamba near the modern town of Sofala whose capital Manyikeni has been excavated by archaeologists to give results that suggest obvious parallels with

[24] H. von Sicard, 'The origin of some tribes in the Belingwe Reserve', *NADA*, 27, 1950, p. 10.
[25] T. N. Huffman, *Handbook to the Iron Age: The Archaeology of Pre-colonial Farming Societies in Southern Africa* (Scottsville: University of KwaZulu-Natal Press, 2007), p. 419.

Great Zimbabwe.[26] The other, Kiteve, is also well described in Portuguese records and is associated with a rebel chief of the Mutapa known as Nyamunda, of whom more is detailed below.[27]

The northern lowlands: Gova and 'Tonga'

To the north, the name 'Gova' once again draws our attention as it also applies to the inhabitants of the Zambezi lowlands on both banks of the river. The term 'Goba' has been used to refer to that portion of the Zambezi valley occupied by Shona-speakers.[28] It first occurs in the historical record before 1600 when the people associated with it moved west from the Zambezi towards its confluence with the Sanyati river.[29] Traditions from non-Goba people, such as the Tonga, considered the Goba refugees to be fleeing the depredations of the Shona kingdoms in the south induced by war and trade. The Tonga looked down upon these immigrants, who were also very poor because they settled in the region's harshest environments.[30] They may be seen as the first layer of immigrants from the southern Shona kingdoms, and judging by the time of their arrival in the northern lowlands may be considered migrants from Great Zimbabwe.

By the 1690s, they were fully integrated with the Tonga, and some historians call them Tonga/Shona. Our interest is not in the misleading collective noun 'Shona' but to account for these northern vaGova. Lancaster has shown that Shona traditions tended to refer to people living in river valleys, or those with no recognisable chiefs, as *tonga* or *gova*. He is quick to note, however, that these ethnic labels appear to have replaced one another, suggesting successive levels of ethnic homogeneity.[31] While the origins of the Tonga are still problematic, it is possible to identify what have been termed the proto-Tonga, who arose in the ninth century after building up herds in the grasslands around the Kafue river and progressed further down the Zambezi to populate the Gwembe valley 'absorbing smaller early iron age groups as they went'.[32] If the modern Tonga are a mixture of later 'Shona' settlers from the Mutapa and Rozvi periods and

---

[26] P. J. J. Sinclair, *Space, Time and Social Formation: A Territorial Approach to the Archaeology and Anthropology of Zimbabwe and Mozambique c.0-1700AD* (Uppsala: Societas Archaeologica Upsaliensis, 1987), p. 69.

[27] M. Newitt, *A History of Mozambique* (London: Hurst, 1995), pp. 41-4.

[28] Lancaster, 'Ethnic identity', p. 714.

[29] D. N. Beach, *The Shona and Zimbabwe* (Gwelo: Mambo Press, 1980), p. 72.

[30] Lancaster, 'Ethnic identity', pp. 715-16.

[31] Ibid., p. 709.

[32] T. Matthews, 'Notes on the pre-colonial history of the Tonga, with emphasis on the upper river Gwembe and Victoria Falls areas', in C. Lancaster and K. P. Vickery (eds.), *The Tonga-Speaking Peoples of Zambia and Zimbabwe: Essays in Honor of Elizabeth Colson* (Lanham, MD: University Press of America, 2007), p. 14.

these proto-Tonga, it is possible that earlier Shona-speaking people who settled in this area through a 'process dating back to the fifteenth century AD' were immigrants from Great Zimbabwe.[33]

A study of local spirits associated with the ownership of land and earth shrines in the Zambezi has shown that their origins are linked to the first wave of immigrants into the valley that came 'as early as the mid-fifteenth century' from (Great) Zimbabwe.[34] These *basangu*, or the royal spirits, are associated with the activities of the past kings, conquerors and traders of the valley Tonga. As with the Venda in the south, the Tonga recall two 'Shona'-induced movements into the valley. The first wave in the fifteenth century (see above), and the second coming largely from Korekore (i.e. Mutapa) country and the lower Zambezi induced by trade and slave-raiding.[35]

In summary, there is a distinct group of people related to the Leopard's Kopje culture who preferred to secure settlement in the lowlands and valleys, and they can be easily identified with the name Gova or Goba. They usually constitute the older autochthonous groups that are later supplanted by incoming groups who were not necessarily always Shona. However, where this process involved conquest by the immigrants, the autochthons frequently used the significance of being first in order to claim ownership of the land, spirits and rainmaking. This process unfolds in the lowlands as it does in the highlands.

Dispersal in the highlands and Plateau environs: Clientelism and the rise of the *Nyai*

The Nyai form another group of the 'Shona' associated with the highlands. The term 'Nyai' was frequently used to refer to soldiers of the Mutapa state, but in his account of the wars of succession in the 1760s pitting Mutapa Ganyambadzi and Prince Bangoma, Stanislaus Mudenge talks of 'Bangoma, as well as some of his Karanga and *vanyai* followers' being taken prisoner by a Portuguese force. He discusses this episode as though the *vanyai* and Karanga were different groups.[36] Beach, on the other hand, traces the use of the term to 1696, when it referred to young fighters in the Mutapa state, whereas later on in the southern parts of the plateau it simply referred to the subjects of the Rozvi Changamire.[37] Interestingly, Fritz Posselt writes of the vaRozvi:

---

[33] Pwiti, *Continuity and Change.*

[34] C. Lancaster, 'Spirits of the land among the BanaMainga on the Shona–Tonga frontier: Ethnohistory, mythology, and power in the easternmost Gwembe valley', in Lancaster and Vickery, *The Tonga-speaking Peoples of Zambia and Zimbabwe*, p. 38.

[35] Ibid.

[36] Mudenge, *A Political History of Munhumutapa*, pp. 134-5.

[37] Beach, *The Shona and Zimbabwe*, p. 150.

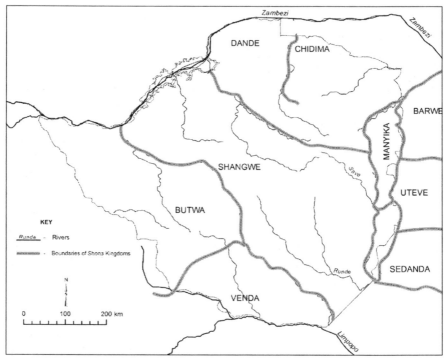

Map 1.3: Approximate distribution of Shona kingdoms in the seventeenth century.
[After Mudenge, *A Political History of Munhumutapa*]

they were also known as the Varozwi [*sic*], and sometimes called
'Banyai'. According to some Natives the name originated from a
quarrel between two sons of the Mambo respecting their claims
to the succession. The defeated party was called 'Banyai' (said to
mean inferiors or slaves). Other informants claim that the name
dates back to immemorial times and that it means 'messengers,' a
term generally exclusively applied to the messengers of a chief.[38]

Thus we have an interesting scenario, where an ethnic label runs through the
history of the plateau region over a long time. If we accept that the term Shona
is indeed an anachronism and that Karanga could have been used to refer to the
same people, it would suggest that the *vaNyai* were a different 'ethnic' group altogether, and this does not tally with the available evidence. It is necessary, after
accounting for its origins, to unpack the term itself. The last serious attempt to
do this remains Lancaster's work cited above. It locates the origins of the Nyai

---

[38] Posselt, *Fact and Fiction*, p. 135.

in the social systems of the people living on the plateau, particularly uxorilocal marriage arrangements made by 'big men' for dependent young men. Under the arrangements known in modern Shona as 'kutema ugariri', such wealthy men were able to offer their sisters and daughters as wives to young men in exchange for labour. The young men, in turn, established a dependent relationship with their hosts, expanding their activities to become henchmen, guards, errand runners, spies and, as the sphere of influence of their hosts expanded, councillors.[39]

I have discussed elsewhere the development of territorial defence structures in nineteenth-century southern Zimbabwe, where lineage heads transformed, through marriage alliances, their sons-in-law or vakuwasha, normally from un-related totemic groups, into councillors (makota) and their totemic kinsfolk into machinda, or governors. These could also double as territorial guards, nharirire, allocated land in the periphery to protect a political centre controlled by a lineage head.[40] When this arrangement was replicated more widely, it formed a hierarchy growing in scale from village to district to provincial level.[41] Lancaster's account of the origins of Nyai identity resembles a similar notion where the services of 'young men known locally as vanyai or kotakota' became critical beyond their general purpose in the domestic sphere. In the plateau region, where the control of people became increasingly more important than the control of material objects, these vanyai became, in addition to their usual duties, visible evidence of their patron's following. As they grew older, the vanyai could have been en-trusted with lands on the periphery of their patron's territory so that they in turn became headmen and slowly established themselves as leaders of their own vanyai. Lancaster writes of the Goba in the Kafue confluence region:

> From the level of the family compound elder and his small group of vanyai to the village headman, to the neighbourhood leader who might be a senior headman over several villages or a sub-chieftain, up through the level of the local chieftain or chief and his paramount, each subordinate group acted as vanyai to the next powerful neighbour, and there was sporadic conflict whenever dominance hierarchies appeared to be uncertain.[42]

---

[39] Lancaster, 'Ethnic identity', p. 718.

[40] G. C. Mazarire, 'Defence consciousness as way of life: "The refuge period" and Karanga defence strategies in the 19th century', Zimbabwean Prehistory 25, 2005, p. 23; see also R. M. G. Mtetwa, 'A Political and Economic History of the Duma' (D.Phil. thesis, University of Rhodesia, 1976), pp. 164-5.

[41] See, for example, J. G. Storry, 'The settlement and territorial expansion of the Mutasa dynasty', Rhodesian History, 7, 1976, pp. 24-5, and Mtetwa, 'A Political and Economic History of the Duma', p. 164.

[42] Lancaster, 'Ethnic identity', p. 718.

Among the Goba, where Lancaster worked, those in the confluence were known as *vaNyai*, or followers of highland southern chiefs, and somehow 'Nyai' was transmogrified to relate to a 'tribe', thanks to the work of early ethnographers and colonial administrators. Nevertheless, it is possible that the people south of the Zambezi could have been va*Nyai* in the Munhumutapa empire through the process elaborated above, but certainly these *vaNyai* had become an important force by the time the Rozvi rose in the 1690s. Let us consider this dispersal of these highland *vaNyai* each in turn.

The Mutapa/Korekore in the northern plateau

The Mutapa dynasty appears to have arisen out of the *nyai* process and went through at least three important phases of transformation.[43] The first, a period of political consolidation, was achieved through the gradual expansion and sophistication of the principle of clientship. The second was concerned with the dilemma of such a client state when confronted with the international versions of merchant capital that were being exported from Europe by the Portuguese and Spaniards to Latin America, Africa and Asia. The last stage deals with the effects of this confrontation on the 'dominance hierarchies' of such feudal clientelism and the sporadic efforts to reverse it that ultimately gave rise to the Rozvi, a class-based identity with warrior origins.

If indeed the northward movement of people from Great Zimbabwe can be accounted for in terms of the attraction of the 'good rock-salt north-east of Shangwe' as the Mutota legend would have us believe, then we must ask why this group never chose to settle in Gokwe, or why it ignored the richer, and more plentiful, salt deposits of the Save valley.[44] Be that as it may, the emergent Mutapa dynasty seems to have consolidated its power by taking advantage of the decentralised nature of northern Tavara/Tonga groups. Through intermarriage and economic relations, as well as calculated political intervention in the succession disputes of these groups, the Karanga were able to establish their control and spread their influence.[45] Thus, the *Nzou-Samanyanga* dynasty was established with a wide network of clients who transformed themselves into a formidable force expanding across the Dande hinterland through conquest and subjugation, plus the control of the all-important Muslim trade. The Mutapa figure (normally identifiable with Mutota) solidified his control by distributing

[43] It is important to state that the term Mutapa is used here in three ways, sometimes to refer to the Mutapa ruler, sometimes to the Mutapa people, but more often to the state itself.

[44] L. Mutema, 'Salt making, myth and conflict in Chireya', *Zimbabwea*, 4, 1996, pp. 44-53; Mudenge, *A Political History of Munhumutapa*, p. 39.

[45] Mudenge, *A Political History of Munhumutapa*, p. 39.

lands and creating an institution of divine kingship sanctified by an act of ritual incest. The interdependence of a political constitution and ideology was necessary when the transition had to be made to convert his kinsmen into his subjects. As the Mutapa's influence spread, so did the structures of society that became modelled along the lines of feudal clientelism. It is probably this trend that identified him and his followers as *vanyai*, a local term referring to highland peoples where this order of life had become commonplace. The Mutapa people could not easily have attracted any geographical stereotypes or labels, because successive Mutapa rulers frequently moved their capitals in and out of the valley. The Korekore dialect, however, became firmly a part of the Mutapa state.[46]

The expansion of the Mutapa's *nyai* occurs in a context where three distinguishable regions also emerge: the western Guruuswa/Butwa region dominated by the Togwa dynasty; the northern region in which the expansion was taking place by subjugating the Tavara/Tonga in the Zambezi valley; and the Barwe and Manyika further to the east. In the lands due south, the Mutapa took over Uteve, where he succeeded in imposing his own rulers. The troubles experienced within the Mutapa state in its early years are largely the product of the uneasy hierarchies of dominance that existed. Thus, around 1490, a Torwa ruler by the name of Changamire (not to be confused with Dombo of the 1680s) successfully usurped the Mutapa throne after killing the incumbent Mutapa Mukombero. He ruled for four years before he was similarly deposed by one of Mukombero's sons, Chikuyo Chisamarengu.[47] Likewise, a Mutapa appointee over Uteve made good his independence and began competing with the Mutapa to secure the as yet unconquered highlands of Manyika. This powerful lord of the south, known in the records as Nyamunda, launched a series of wars that effectively blocked any direct contact between the Mutapa state and the coast in the direction of Sofala.

By around 1515, the Mutapa had more powerful rebels than he could possibly have managed and he was soon forced to fight them on several fronts, some of them, as in the case of Sachiteve Nyamunda and the Torwa Changamire, managing to form a powerful coalition against him. The Portuguese were able to access the Mutapa state only after the fall of Nyamunda, around 1530, and even then only after they had supplanted the Muslim traders.[48] Further to the east, the Manyika kingdom, like Uteve, broke away from the Mutapa state in the late fifteenth century and controlled land north of the Buzi river, which was sandwiched between an expansionist Uteve neighbour and the powerful Makombe

[46] Pikirayi, *The Zimbabwe Culture*, ch. 6.
[47] Mudenge, *A Political History of Munhumutapa*, p. 49.
[48] Ibid., pp. 52–3.

rulers of Barwe to the north. Although tributary to the Mutapa, the Chikanga rulers of Manyika retained a degree of autonomy for much of the time.[49] Much of Manyika history has been recorded by a local historian, Jason Tichafa Machiwenyika, who traces the origins of the dynasty to Nyamubvambire, who overthrew an earlier dynasty known as Muponda. Beyond this, Manyika history is riddled with sagas of political intrigue and competition among pretenders to the throne in the late eighteenth century and most of the nineteenth.[50]

Meanwhile, in its nuclear zone to the north, the Mutapa state was defining an identity that would emerge as Korekore. The true Korekore, according to Michael Bourdillon, descend from Mutota and most are found in the Zambezi valley and north of the Mavhuradonha mountains, hence the name 'valley Korekore'.[51] After consolidating his position in the north, the Mutota successfully accommodated local Tavara/Tonga spirits Dzivaguru and Karuva, of the *Nhari Unendoro* totem, to emerge the superior of them all, thus adding a strong religious element to an already complex secular system that defined the Mutapa/Korekore identity. Indeed, when the Portuguese were eventually able to reach the Mutapa state, they had of necessity to confront this solid arrangement; their relations with the Mutapa state, whether in trade or politics, were virtually inseparable from religion. This is the background to the martyrdom of Fr Gonçalo da Silveira and subsequent punitive expeditions by the Portuguese to avenge his death and conquer the Mutapa state. The only way the Portuguese could penetrate the elaborate political and social system of the Mutapa state was through its nobility, specifically by converting the royal family to the Christian faith. A civil-war-ridden state and a court system bedevilled by conspiracies and coup plots is clearly vulnerable; attempts by the Portuguese to invade the Mutapa state between 1569 and 1577 failed because of shortcomings in the invading expeditions.

Soon, however, successive Mutapas began to accept Portuguese support in order to secure their hold on power. Mutapa Gatsi Rusere, who succeeded to the throne in 1586, suffered a number of setbacks, among them the Maravi invasions led by Kapambo and Chikanda. These had fuelled divisions in the Mutapa army and subsequently led to a revolt by its high-ranking staff, including the general, or *mukomohasha*. The rebellion was also supported by some members of the nobility. This Matuzianhe revolt marked a turning point in Mutapa-Portuguese

---

[49] H. H. K. Bhila, *Trade and Politics in a Shona Kingdom* (Harlow: Longman, 1982), pp. 10-13.
[50] D.N. Beach, 'Oral Tradition in Eastern Zimbabwe: The Work of Jason Tichafa Machiwenyika c.1889-1924', University of Zimbabwe, History Department Seminar Paper no. 99, 1997.
[51] M. F. C. Bourdillon, 'The cults of Dzivaguru and Karuva amongst the north-eastern Shona peoples', in J. M. Schoffeleers (ed.), *Guardians of the Land* (Gwelo: Mambo Press, 1979), p. 236.

relations: it not only deposed Gatsi Rusere but forced him to enlist the support of the Portuguese. Diogo Simões Madeira supported Gatsi Rusere in his three-year campaign in exile, between 1606 and 1609, and helped him win back the throne from Matuzianhe. In gratitude, Gatsi not only relaxed the conditions of Portuguese entry into his country but 'donated' gold, silver and copper mines to Madeira and allowed the Portuguese to build churches and promote Christianity. The succession crisis that followed Gatsi's death complicated issues further, with the wars between two contenders to the throne, Mavhura Mhande and Nyambo Kapararidze, drawing Mavhura closer to the Portuguese when he emerged victorious with their support. In return, the Portuguese demanded that Mavhura sign treaties of vassalage to the Portuguese crown. Indeed, in 1629, when he was appointed Munhumutapa, Mavhura signed the 'capitulations' that mortgaged the Mutapa state to the Portuguese crown, reducing him to a puppet who would sign away more concessions, mines and land to the Portuguese.[52] Before considering the dynamics of the reversal of this situation, however, let us look at the situation obtaining in neighbouring Butwa.

Butwa/Torwa in the west and the Kalanga traditions

We have already identified a Changamire personality from Togwa, who usurped the Mutapa throne for four years in the early 1490s. His son and successor continued intermittent wars with Mutapa Chikuyo Chisamarengu and ultimately disappeared into limbo. That was the last time we hear of the western rulers. Historians and archaeologists know a lot less about these Togwa people beyond that they built Khami, an ancient *zimbabwe* a few kilometres north of Bulawayo, which was abandoned after it was destroyed by fire in the early seventeenth century.[53] Portuguese documents referring to Khami suggest a civil war that involved a Portuguese warlord who was able to assist a Togwa aspirant to the throne before himself retiring to the north-east in 1644. There are no other clear references to any Togwa rulers, but we do know of some dominant Togwa houses, such as those of Tumbare and Chihunduru/Chiwundura, because of the power they subsequently wielded in the Rozvi state as part of the non-*moyo* Rozvi ruling elite. These houses, together with the Mavhudzi-*shava* and Nerwande-*shoko*, as will be shown below, were pivotal in the shaping of Rozvi class identity. The Togwa, however, seem to have a strong Kalanga connection, and in the seventeenth century Khami fell under the territory of the Kalanga ruler, Ndumba.[54] If we take Huffman's suggestion that the Leopard's Kopje

[52] Based on Mudenge, *A Political History of Munhumutapa*, chs. 6 and 7.
[53] Beach, *The Shona and Their Neighbours*, p. 94.
[54] Beach, *The Shona and Zimbabwe*, p. 193.

people spoke ancient Kalanga, it is possible that Togwa rulers were Kalanga if Togwa was the most immediate successor of the Great Zimbabwe state. However, historians have deliberately ignored Kalanga oral traditions of this period. Those collected by Masola Kumile reveal a lot more about Togwa/Kalanga history and its eventual fall to the *vaNyai*, who were later to become the Rozvi rulers of the region. It is interesting to note that in all his recordings the name Rozvi never features once.[55] These traditions trace the genealogy of Kalanga kings to Xamuyendazwa, interpreted as a predecessor to Munhumutapa or Malambodzibwa.

The Kalanga also traditionally claim that they came from as far away as the Zambezi. More concrete and datable references to this Mutapa connection relate to a later Kalanga ruler, Madabhale, or the legendary Chibundule, who 'broke away' from Mutapa after the wars of Gatsi Rusere and the ascension to the throne of Mutapa Mavhura. Chibundule had a number of followers who became his councillors, among them Nimale, Hungwe, Zwikono, Vunamakuni, Nkami, Nigwande and Ninhembwe. They are said to have settled in modern Matabeleland, which they found occupied by the 'bushmen', and then extended their rule to (Great) Zimbabwe before moving on to the Limpopo in Venda country and as far as the salt-pans of the Kalahari.[56] However, existing Kalanga traditions suggest that the continued interaction between the Togwa and Mutapa state may have led one section, either loyal to or with filial connections to the Mutapa, becoming the more dominant group among the Kalanga of Togwa. This is the group identifiable with Chibundule. Meanwhile, in the Mutapa state, the period of decline registered in the era of 'puppet' Munhumutapas was to come to an end with the rise of reformist forces in the Mutapa royal family itself.

Nyai transformation and the role of class in the making of Rozvi identity

The state of affairs on the plateau in general and the Mutapa state in particular presented a sorry picture by the 1650s. Portuguese influence had transformed itself into a form of indirect rule, with the Mutapa paying the *kuruva* tax to the Portuguese, through their Captain of the Gates, rather than vice versa. The Portuguese had been granted substantial land rights; their extensive estates, or *prazos*, expanded inland to the Mutapa centre and they treated its peoples as slave labour. This situation was reversed by the appointment of Kamharapasu Mukombwe as Mutapa in 1663. Between then and 1704, Mukombwe and his successors were able to launch an offensive against the Portuguese that success-

---

[55] P. J. Wentzel, *Nau dzabaKalanga: A History of the Kalanga* (Pretoria: Unisa Press, 1983), vol. 1.

[56] Ibid., pp. 11-16.

fully drove them off their *prazos*. He enlisted the support of the Tonga in the Zambezi valley, and subsequently the Chikanga of Manyika joined him.[57] Thereafter, Mukombwe's main accomplishment seems to have been the resettlement of various Mutapa families in the lands that he had freed. This was a way of consolidating his rule after nearly a century of civil war, and also of reviving the traditional *nyai* clientelism that had formed the foundations of the Mutapa state before it was disturbed by Portuguese mercantilism. This revival was accompanied by a transformation of the *nyai* ideal by a section of the *nyai* themselves, led by Changamire Dombo, giving rise to what would become the Rozvi state.

Dombo rose to prominence in June 1684 when he defeated the Portuguese in the battle of Maungwe after rebelling from Mutapa Mukombwe and defeating a punitive Mutapa force. Slowly, he consolidated his position in the western Butwa area, formerly dominated by the Togwa/Kalanga, as well as in the lands of Manyika and the trading centres of mainland Mutapa.[58] In the west, Kalanga tradition confirms Dombo's conquest in popular legends depicting the fall of chief Chibundule. Dombo is remembered as Chilisamhulu, or Nechasike, a leader of the *Nyai* who, strangely, 'came from Venda country'.[59] On a number of occasions, Nechasike – followed by a number of important councillors, among them Nhale and 'Ninembwe, the father of Tumbale and many headmen' – attempted to conquer Chibundule but was repelled by the magic believed to reside in his calabash. It was only after offering Chibundule his daughter that Nechasike and his *vaNyai* were able to learn the secret of this magic and eventually establish their rule over Chibundule's Kalanga.[60] Dombo was the first of seven successive rulers of the Rozvi dynasty; all those who followed were his direct descendants from the *moyondizvo* totemic group.

In his forthcoming book on the Rozvi, Mudenge offers some revisions that demonstrate that the foundations of the state rested on the military prowess of Changamire Dombo. When the conquest, subjugation and co-option of the people of Butwa and the western hinterland was complete and a civil administration had been established, it became necessary for the rulers to distinguish themselves from the ruled by shedding their *nyai* client/military identity and becoming a ruling elite, the 'Rozvi'. Because no one totemic group could lay claim to this, the Negwande *shoko*, Mavhudzi *shava*, Tumbare *Bepe-moyo* were, and still are,

[57] Beach, *The Shona and Zimbabwe*, pp. 133-4; Pikirayi, *The Zimbabwe Culture*, p. 230.
[58] Mudenge, *A Political History of Munhumutapa*, p. 287.
[59] Wentzel, *Nau dzabaKalanga*, pp. 51-77.
[60] Ibid.

equally accepted as Rozvi.[61] This practice is not uncommon, especially among conquest states such as those founded by Islamic jihads in West Africa: the Sokoto Caliphate, for instance, was founded by Usman dan Fodio when, after establishing a civil administrative structure, its ruling elite transformed itself into the Hausa ethnic group. Similarly, in contemporary African politics, it has been necessary for former liberation movements to demilitarise and assume civilian offices at independence. It is possible to argue therefore that a Rozvi ruling elite maintained political control of the central state and its peripheral territories occupied by their *nyai* subjects who themselves were not barred from becoming members of the 'Rozvi', as a social class.

We now need to examine this process, and the impact of Rozvi influence in the region. First, we are aware that, in Butwa, Dombo won over and incorporated some of the Torwa chiefs, who became important officers in the Rozvi hierarchy. Secondly, it should be acknowledged that Rozvi expansion was primarily effected by non-*moyo* nuclear Rozvi. Beginning with the north-western parts of Butwa, a Rozvi *shoko* dynasty advanced as far north as the Deka and Gwai rivers, then into the Zambezi valley where they established themselves as the Nambiya under Hwange. On the Sebungwe and Mafungavutsi (Mafungabusi) plateau, a *shava* dynasty led by Chireya took control of this zone at the peak of Rozvi power.[62] In the south, a section of the Togwa moved to the Limpopo valley to become the Thovela/Venda group which built the *zimbabwe* at Dzata.[63] Elsewhere in the country, it seems that the Rozvi ruling class maintained their *vanyai* under appointed regional 'governors or representatives' and kept them in check through periodic 'visits', particularly to those vassal chiefs who failed to pay their tribute.[64] Other non-*moyo* Rozvi spread out of the Butwa nucleus as part of this federalism, including most of the groups that settled on the southern edges of the central Zimbabwean watershed, such as the Nebgwine under Shindi, who eventually settled near the confluence of the Runde and Tugwi rivers, and Nyamhondo, who went to Mberengwa.[65]

[61] S. I. G. Mudenge, *A History of the Rozvi Empire*, forthcoming; see also Mudenge, 'An identification of the Rozvi', *Rhodesian History*, 5, 1974, p. 29. I am grateful to Dr Mudenge for sharing his vast knowledge on the subject and discussing with me his work in progress.

[62] Matthews, 'Notes on the pre-colonial history of the Tonga', pp. 16-18. A detailed account of individual Rozvi families that advanced north is in R. R. Tapson, 'Some notes on the Mrozwi occupation of Sebungwe district', *NADA*, 21, 1944, pp. 29-32. For a different version linking the expansion of the Nambiya to one of the Rozvi princes, Dhende, see G. T. Ncube, *A History of Northwest Zimbabwe* (Kadoma: Mond Books, 2004), pp. 8-11.

[63] Beach, *The Shona and their Neighbours*, p. 97.

[64] S. I. G. Mudenge, 'The role of foreign trade in the Rozvi empire: A reappraisal', *Journal of African History*, 15(3), 1974, p. 383.

[65] Beach, *A Zimbabwean Past*, pp. 138-43.

Thirdly, it must be appreciated that the greatest Rozvi accomplishment was certainly its enlargement of the scale of cliental structures. However, as more *vanyai* qualified to be Rozvi, their ambition grew to control their own *vanyai*. In this way, the same structures that defined Rozvi power became the very fissures through which the state cracked. This was possible when the cohesive mechanisms maintaining the Rozvi partrimonial system were compromised, or when the secular section of the Rozvi ruling elite fell out with their religious counterparts.[66] The dictatorship of Changamire Rupandamanhanga (the 'mad king') did further damage, disrupting Rozvi federalism to the extent that competition within and between factions became the order of the day. Thus, although Chirisamhuru was successfully able to assume the Changamire throne, he only narrowly escaped an attempt on his life engineered by the combined houses of Mutinhima, Mavhudzi and Nerwande. These, together with the Tumbare group, began moving away from the central Rozvi area, while others, apparently leaderless, roamed the plateau in search of new fortunes. Rozvi dispersal was hastened by the incoming Nguni, led initially by Ngoni and Swazi warriors in the 1820s.

I have discussed the northerly moves of the Nambiya and Shangwe chiefs; the more significant southerly migration of the eighteenth-century Rozvi gave rise to the Singo dynasty that occupied the Nzhelele valley and became a section of the Venda. Popular Singo tradition recalls this movement from an ancestral home, 'Matongoni' – presumably Manyanga, the new capital settled by the Changamire and his people when they left Danamombe. However, since these traditions are related from an Venda perspective there is much graphic detail concerning their struggles with *nyai* chiefs such as 'Tshivhi' [Chivi?], and the chronology is unreliable.[67]

The fourth issue relates to the challenge of managing the Rozvi cliental structures in peripheral zones when the centre could no longer hold. This is vividly illustrated in the south-east, between the Save and the Buzi rivers, where a distinct Ndau identity emerged. Four main Rozvi-related states are at the centre of this process, and, as noted above, the region was formerly under the Sachiteve Nyamunda, who blocked the coastal trade with the Mutapa state. By 1590, Nyamunda's son had assumed control of the southern part of Teve and ruled a new, semi-independent state known as Sedanda, or 'Danda'. It survived the demise of Teve and later became tributary to the Rozvi. However, when it pressed for independence during the time of Rozvi troubles, it was supplanted

---

[66] N. M. B. Bhebe, 'Some aspects of Ndebele relations with the Shona in the 19th century', *Rhodesian History*, 4, 1973, p. 32; for a fictional account based on Rozvi folklore, see N. M. Mutasa, *Misodzi, Dikita neRopa* (Gweru: Mambo Press, 1991).

[67] E. Mudau, 'Ngoma Lungundu', in Warmelo (ed.), *The Copper Mines of Musina*, pp. 109–32.

by the incoming Tsonga 'landims' who became the Hlengwe, and who are discussed below.[68]

The third state was an 'outrider', formed by and subject to the Changamire Rozvi during the early stages of their rule in the 1680s and 1690s. Known as Sanga, or Quissanga, by the Portuguese, it became independent in the eighteenth century, well before the Rozvi state began to break apart, and was ruled by Mutema, who established himself at Ngaone in the mountain fortifications a few kilometres north of the modern town of Chipinge. According to J. K. Rennie, it is from around the time that Sanga was formed that 'Ndau' emerged as an ethnic term. Further disintegration of Teve led to the formation of the fourth 'secondary' state known as Shanga, which perfectly exemplifies the administrative structures of this cluster of what essentially became Ndau states – rule by a series of territorial chiefs or *nyamasango* who maintained power, and more specifically ideology, through the administration of justice and the taxation of subjects on behalf of their overlords.[69]

These Ndau states exhibit a new addition to the Rozvi cliental concept where power ceased to reside within the people. With the unfolding process of fragmentation, 'power' increasingly assumed more territorial meanings, a trend that was to change once more under the Gaza Nguni chiefs. David Hughes has related this process from the point of view of an unfolding 'Kopytoffian' frontier. He traces a number of *moyo* totem clans leaving the central Rozvi state, steadily moving east, and conquering *dziva* and *soko* clans in the Save valley.[70] The most successful of these conquerors was Mutema, as we have seen, but he could not do without earlier settlers such as Nyamusetwa's Musikavanhu, who controlled an elaborate rain cult, or Mapungwana's *tembo* who appears to have been part of the migrations out of the Mutapa state immediately before or during the Mukombwean period. In time, however, the *moyo* dynasties completely colonised the Save valley, with Mutambara's Garwe north of the Nyanyadzi river and Newushoma's Muwusha further south.[71]

Rozvi factions become more visible as they moved about following *mfecane* disturbances after 1824. When the Ndebele arrived, according to Beach, it was enough to be identified as Rozvi to attract an attack. Most of the main Rozvi families seemed to have understood this and retreated. Thus, the house of Muti-

---

[68] J. K. Rennie, 'Ideology and state formation: Political and communal ideologies among the south-eastern Shona, 1500-1890', in A. I. Salim (ed.), *State Formation in Eastern Africa* (Nairobi: Heinemann, 1984), p. 168.

[69] Ibid., pp. 169-70.

[70] D. M. Hughes, *From Enslavement to Environmentalism: Politics on a Southern African Frontier* (Seattle: University of Washington Press, 2006) p. 24.

[71] Beach, *The Shona and Zimbabwe*, pp. 170-1.

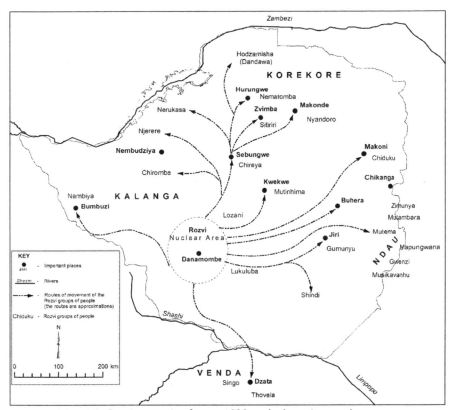

Map 1.4: Rozvi expansion from c.1690 to the late nineteenth century.

nhima, once dominant in the Malungwane hills near the centre of the state at Danamombe, became more active distributing land in the Kwekwe and Chirumhanzu regions.[72] Mutinhima, who was considered powerful enough to be a threat to the main Changamire dynasty, was viewed in the same light by the Ndebele who pursued him under instructions from King Mzilikazi to pluck out his heart and deliver it to him. He fled and exiled himself in the Mai yaVaHera hills in Buhera.[73] In another development, the once dominant Tumbare, Mavhudzi, Nerwande and Chihunduru houses retreated north-west, while other Rozvi houses sought refuge in the modern Makoni area to become the Chiduku and Tandi groups.[74] In the south, the Gumunyu and Jiri houses found a place among the Duma in Bikita. The

[72] Ibid., p. 240.

[73] Posselt, *Fact and Fiction*, p. 148; for an account of the Rozvi retreat, see Bhebe, 'Some aspects of Ndebele relations', pp. 32-3.

[74] T. O. Ranger, 'Tradition and travesty: Chiefs and the administration in Makoni District, Zimbabwe, 1960-1980', *Africa*, 52(3), 1982, p. 21.

credit for the last stand of the Rozvi goes to Tohwechipi, or 'Chibhamubhamu', who took over as Changamire and whose use of firearms allowed him to defeat the Nguni on many occasions until he was subdued in 1866; even then, he continued to win clients in the traditional fashion of parcelling out land.

In summary, the collapse of Rozvi federalism lay within its own unsustainable structures and the growing pressure from 'parasitic' *mfecane* groups, themselves in search of people to boost their numbers. It is arguable whether the Rozvi state would have survived had it maintained its patrimonial and structural balance; what is true is that, despite its fall, the 'Rozvi system' was emulated by all groups that followed, and was used frequently as the basis of political and social organisation by the emergent Karanga who followed them.

Emergent power vacuums and 'Karanga' settlement in the south

One notable development contemporaneous with the disintegration of the Rozvi was the resettlement of the central and southern regions of the country by newly established dynasties that came to occupy most of the areas now associated with the Karanga dialect. It can be argued that these groups were taking advantage of the power vacuum left by the retreating Rozvi, but such settlements had become a trend since Mutapa Mukombwe's activities in the late seventeenth century and it is prudent to examine these first. So far as the Mukombwean resettlement is concerned, the dynasties that were allocated land were in one way or another associated with the new sub-dynasties that repopulated the south as the Rozvi disintegrated. A case in point is the Nembire *soko-vhudzijena* dynasty; initially given the Gore area in the region of Ruya, they later gave rise to the Mbire YaSvosve cluster, a source of many dynasties that became dominant in the south in the later nineteenth century.[75] Another group, associated with the *tembo* totem, gave rise to dynasties in the eastern highlands and the modern Chirumhanzu area.[76] Contemporary Portuguese accounts suggest that the Mukombwean period is associated with some 'depopulation' in the central Mutapa area; however, it has been difficult to associate these movements with the resettlement initiative, although it must be said that they constituted an important phase of strategic relocation taking advantage of the Portuguese retreat.[77]

One way of capitalising on emerging power vacuums was to turn to predatory militarism. For groups that did not have the wherewithal to attract followers

---

[75] Beach, *The Shona and Zimbabwe*, pp. 135-7.

[76] I. M. Zvarevashe, *Dzinza ravaGovera vaChirumhanzu naMutasa* (Gweru: Mambo Press, 1998); traditions related in this text also claim descent from Mutapa Goveranyika (the distributor of land) who can be loosely linked to Mukombwe.

[77] Beach, *The Shona and Zimbabwe*, p. 137.

with economic rewards, in the traditional fashion of *nyai* clientelism, militarism was often a viable option. It would prove useful to many would-be powers in the plateau region after the mid-eighteenth century. The emergence of the Chikunda ex-slavemen in the Zambezi is perhaps the best example of the timing and sequence of this transformation.[78] In the south, the Hiya-*dziva* (pool) group represents this development. They had initially been a part of a larger cluster of *dziva* groups settled in Rutanga near modern Buhera, but, realising the damage caused by civil war in the Rozvi state, they attempted an invasion in 1768 that was successfully repelled. Undeterred, they continued their campaign under the leadership of Matema well into the 1790s, apparently targeting Rozvi peripheral agnates as they went.[79] The Hiya rampage possibly ended with the coming of the Nguni, who pursued a similar but militarily more sophisticated approach. By then, however, some Hiya had already secured land in between the Runde and Tugwi rivers to become the Ngowa-*dziva* dynasty.[80] In these regions, far away from points of trade, it was difficult to sustain a military culture without access to the guns and modern tactical innovations that became the trump card of the incoming Nguni, and this probably accounts for the demise of the Hiya.

The groups that emerged successful were those that either were able to mix superiority in numbers with charismatic leadership and celestial powers, or who were simply lucky. Mbire yaSvosve appears to have produced a number of leaders who were able to form dynasties that became dominant in the south this way. Although not part of one single migration (as suggested by more recent traditions), most *shumba* dynasties now dominant in the southern plateau, such as the Mhari, Jichidza, Nyakunhuwa and Charumbira, can claim origins in Mbire.[81] The second source of southern dynasties is VuHera, associated with several groups claiming descent from, or links with, the figure Mbiru Nyashanu. He is one of the founders of two *shava*-Hera totemic groups found in the area (the other being Marange's Bocha) who belong to the larger eland or *mhofu* category. Nyashanu was subordinate to the Rozvi but, like many others in his position, began to assert his independence as soon as Rozvi troubles surfaced. The Rozvi were keen to contain him and his successors with punitive raids or by supporting factions of incoming immigrants such as the Njanja to check on Hera expansion. If this was achieved in the long term, and probably assisted in

[78] See A. F. and B. S. Isaacman, *Slavery and Beyond: The Making of Men and Chikunda Ethnic Identities in the Unstable World of South-Central Africa, 1750-1920* (Portsmouth, NH: Heinemann, 2004); see also Lancaster, 'Ethnic identity', pp. 717-22.

[79] Beach, *A Zimbabwean Past*, pp. 152-3.

[80] M. M. Hove, 'Notes on the vaNgowa tribe', *NADA*, 20, 1943, pp. 41-5.

[81] C. Bullock, *The Mashona* (Cape Town: Juta, 1928) pp. 86-90; H. von Sicard, 'The Dumbuseya', *NADA*, 5, 1968, p. 25.

the break-up of VuHera, it did not prevent Nyashanu expansion by other means, specifically through the sheer numbers of his descendants. North of VuHera, the Masarirambi group established what later became known as the Mutekedza dynasty; further north, other groups descending from Nyashanu established the Hwata and Chiweshe dynasties, which were welcomed by their kinsfolk under Seke, a descendant of Bocha, who had preceded them in the region.[82]

In the south, the Nyashanu group's expansion appears to have been more dramatic. First, Nyashanu's son by his estranged rainmaker wife, Marumbi Karivara, founded the Munyaradzi dynasty under refuge in Mabwazhe Gutu's land in the regions of the Dewure river. They adopted a new totem, *shava-wakanonoka*, and gave rise to a powerful rain cult.[83] Others maintained the totem and laudatory name *mhofu/nhuka-musiyamwa* but ventured further south, as did Matenda, who found land near what is now Zvishavane. Two other sons, Mutunhakuwenda and Mutizira, encountered the *Shoko*-Rozvi dynasty of NeChishanga, south of Great Zimbabwe, and overcame it to give rise to the Mapanzure, Muchenugwa, Muchibwa and Gapare factions of a southern Hera federal structure that collapsed at the turn of the nineteenth century when it became dominated by a house descended from Mapanzure.[84] The last group to be considered from the VuHera area is Zimuto's *Ngara-Govere* dynasty, which was issued land in Chikato by the roving Rozvi Mambo Tohwechipi. Before long the dynasty had split into two factions, the Zimuto faction retaining the land around modern Gokomere and the other, led by Bamba, founding the Nemavuzhe dynasty further south next to Nyajena's vassals, described below.[85]

The politics of the south in the early nineteenth century were also being shaped by the rise of the Duma, who had emerged from Kiteve under Pfupajena. One of his descendants, Murinye, became dominant in the Mutirikwe region and distributed land to his sons Mugabe and Shumba-Chekai. The former entered into a perpetual conflict with the autochthonous Mamwa over control of the land around Great Zimbabwe, while the latter took over land left behind by Chinamhora's Shawasha with little resistance from the local *Shava-Nhire*.[86] The

[82] Beach, *The Shona and Zimbabwe*, pp. 74-7, 289-93.

[83] M. Daneel, *The God of the Matopo Hills* (The Hague: Mouton, 1970).

[84] G. C. Mazarire, 'A Social and Political History of Chishanga c.1750-2000' (Draft D.Phil. thesis, University of Zimbabwe, 2008), ch. 4; see also D. T. Rwafa, 'The Story of the Mapanzure People', *Masvingo Advertiser*, 1984.

[85] N[ational] A[rchives of] Z[imbabwe], File S2929/8/2 Delineation Report, Nemavuzhe Chieftainship and Community 1965.

[86] Mtetwa, 'A Political and Economic History of the Duma'; on the *Shava-Nhire*, see Mazarire, 'A Social and Political History of Chishanga', ch. 3.

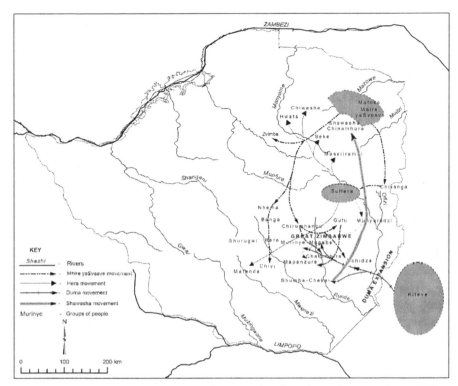

Map 1.5: Karanga migrations across the central and southern plateaux after c. 1750.

political puzzle of the south would be incomplete without reference to Nyajena, an equivalent of the Hiya, but operating on a much smaller scale and with perhaps less violence.

Nyajena was of *moyo* descent but not related to the Duma. He skilfully combined a system of Rozvi-style tributary networks and diplomacy to establish surrogate polities between the Runde and the Mukosi rivers. Nyajena's fame lies in his ability accommodate Rozvi refugees and newcomers to the south on his own terms. The Rozvi house of Nebgwine (Shindi) competed for land with another new group of Ndau origin led by Gororo. Their dispute played into Nyajena's hands when a defeated Shindi went into exile in Nyajena's country and concluded a marriage alliance. Nyajena had already been concluding such arrangements with other groups in Shindi's position, such as Madzivire, and found such alliances useful. As he gradually built up strength, his agnates competed for his favours; he first used them to repel an attack by marauding Dumbuseya mercenary warriors from Wedza, and remained the only recognisable power able to distribute land to each of them. Thus the Gororo, Shindi and Madzivire dynasties survived the turmoil of the 1820s to 1840s and kept their territories by eating out of Nyajena's hand.[87]

The VaRemba and Hlengwe

As the Karanga populated the areas south of the main watershed, two distinct groups augmented this exercise from either end of the plateau: the vaRemba, originating in the Zambezi around Sena country, and the Hlengwe of Tsonga origin in the Limpopo valley. Theories linking the vaRemba to Mediterranean cultures or to the Black Jews of Ethiopia (Abyssinian Falasha) have been put forward by such scholars as Leo Frobenius, Henri Junod and, more specifically for the Zimbabwean vaRemba, Harald von Sicard.[88] However, it has been proved that the Jewish element in Remba identity is fictitious; most vaRemba trace their ancestry to itinerant Muslim traders once dominant in the Mutapa state, the *vaMwenye* or *vaShambadzi*. Ephraim Mandivenga suggests that they are descendants of these Muslims traders who further penetrated inland when their links with the coast were severed by the arrival of the Portuguese.[89] In their migration southwards from Sena, the vaRemba broke into more than twelve different clans, settling as far north as Guruve and Wedza, in parts of Buhera, and further south of Great Zimbabwe. A section led by one Chamakofa apparently joined a Rozvi group moving from their capital at Manyanga ('Matongoni') to the Zoutpansberg, where they later became the Singo dynasty. Shortly thereafter, a Remba chief, Chinounda, decided to lead his people back to Sena, but in the event they were forced to settle in the Mberengwa area and thus the Mposi dynasty was born.[90] Most clans that claimed land in the south – the Chekure and Hamandishe in Gutu, the Chatora in Buhera, and the Majiri and Tadzembwa in modern Masvingo – are linked in one way or another to this Mposi nucleus.

If we accept that the region immediately north of the Limpopo river has remained a frontier in which the Venda have moved back and forth for centuries since the demise of Great Zimbabwe, it is possible to understand why, in Singo-

---

[87] NAZ, S2929/8/2 Delineation Reports for Nyajena, Gororo, Shindi, Madzivire and Mawadze 1965. For a fuller description of the role of women in this diplomacy, see G. C. Mazarire, 'Women, politics and the environment in pre-colonial Chivi, c.1830-1900', *Zambezia*, 30(1), 2003, pp. 45-6.

[88] H. A. Junod, 'The Balemba of the Zoutpansberg (Transvaal)', *Folklore*, 19(3), 1908, H. von Sicard, 'Lemba Clans', *NADA*, 34, 1962.

[89] E. Mandivenga, 'The history and "re-conversion" of the vaRemba of Zimbabwe', *Journal of Religion in Africa*, 9(2), 1989, p. 109.

[90] D. C. Chigiga, 'A Preliminary Study of the Lemba in Rhodesia' (University of Rhodesia, History Department Seminar Paper, 1972), p. 5.

based traditions, the VaRemba are always depicted as accompanying the Venda in their movements – 'carrying all the baggage of royalty' throughout their sojourn in the Zoutpansberg, and in the 'country of the vaNyai'.[91] This necessarily places Remba settlement in the area somewhere in the late eighteenth century during the troubles of the Rozvi state that led to the Singo migration. Most vaRemba ventured into areas that were being populated by the Karanga. There, using their famed magic – knowledge of medicine, or 'chiremba', and copper mining – they formed alliances with the emergent powers. So it was that most Remba enclaves in the lands around Great Zimbabwe, for instance, were facilitated by a long-standing alliance that they had established with the rulers of the Duma confederacy; today the vaRemba hold the honorific title of 'Mazodze', an office with the responsibility for crowning Duma chiefs.[92] The migrations of these VaRemba groups, and their relations with each other as well as with autochthonous and incoming groups, remain yet another area for further research.

The Hlengwe, who form part of the population, specifically the Tsonga, in the lower Limpopo region, have been described as a decentralised military people exhibiting most of the characteristics associated with the Nguni who emerged a century later. From the 1720s onwards, their activities interrupted coastal trade with Inhambane that successfully led to the collapse of the Ndau state of Sedanda. They established themselves along the Save river and moved north into the Zimbabwean plateau.[93] The original Hlengwe are associated with the *chauke* (fire) totem and appear to have been concentrated on the eastern banks of the Limpopo near the 'Shengane' river, from where they began their northward expansion.[94] They followed the courses of the Save, Runde, Chiredzi and Mutirikwi rivers, and much of their history is retold from the perspective of their competition for territory with groups already dominant in an area.

The first such group is the Sono, who were part of the major migrations from the Mutapa central state during its 'depopulation' period. This group was defeated and some of them were absorbed by the Hlengwe, while others left in the direction of the Indian Ocean coast. Hlengwe identity was to a large extent shaped by their confrontations with the vaNyai groups settled in the south. Continuous clashes led to the emergence of a charismatic figure, Zhari, who is

[91] Mudau, 'Ngoma-Lungundu', p. 19.

[92] Douglas Mudhosi, 'The Lemba People of Tadzembwa (Masvingo): An Investigation into their Beliefs and Practices and their Areas of Conflict with the Non-Lemba' (BA dissertation, Department of Religious Studies, University of Zimbabwe, 2003), p. 18.

[93] Rennie, 'Ideology and state formation', p. 168.

[94] J. H. Bannerman, 'Hlengweni: The history of the Hlengweni of the lower Save and Lundi rivers from the late 18th century to the mid-20th century', *Zimbabwean History*, 12, 1981, p. 6.

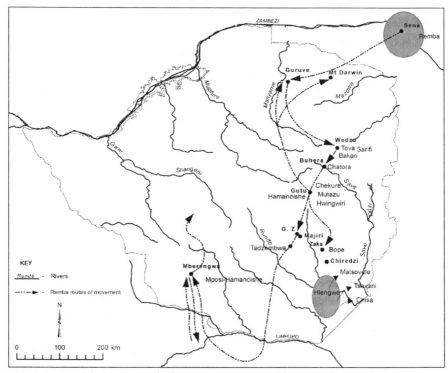

Map 1.6: Remba and Hlengwe migrations on the Zimbabwean Plateau
from the late eighteenth century.

known in local traditions as 'a great warrior always fighting the *Nyai*'. It was he
who conquered large tracts of *vaNyai* territory and was father to the progenitors
of the main Hlengwe dynasties throughout modern Zimbabwe and Mozambique:
the Chisa, Tsovani, Mavhuwe, Salani, Matsovele, Ximise and Makulunje.[95]
Unlike the Remba, the Hlengwe encounter with the Nyai involved a number of
conquests in their favour. Mhingo's Chisa, the most successful of all Hlengwe
dynasties, was able within a short space of time to subject the *moyo* clans of
Mujaki and Chivonja, as well as some autochthonous *shoko* dynasties, in a wide
sweep along the Save river that brought him into the region around Mkwasine,
near modern Triangle. Another dynasty, the Tsovani, proceeded through the
Chiredzi and Runde rivers to encroach on Duma territory. This expansion was
reversed only when these two Hlengwe factions clashed amongst themselves,
leading to the defeat of Chisa's group.[96] By the early nineteenth century the

---

95 Ibid., p. 8.
96 Ibid., pp. 10-11.

Hlengwe grip on these southern watercourses was confirmed, only to be altered slightly by the coming of *mfecane* migrants.

The *mfecane* and the settlement of the Ndebele and Gaza

Between 1826 and 1838 much of the region fell under the heavy pressure of migrants ejected from south of the Limpopo by the *mfecane* disturbances. This has led to speculation about the impact of these groups on local people, especially as it also gave rise to a local version of the *mfecane* characterised by sporadic movements of various 'Shona' dynasties. Given that at least five Nguni groups either passed through or settled in the region within this short period, there has developed a myth that these warring Nguni factions caused widespread devastation and depopulation, not only because each of them in turn attacked the Rozvi state but also because they transformed the way of life of the local people. Although the Nguni groups were well disposed to live off the land, when they were in transit and in the early years of settlement they needed people and cattle more than they needed land.[97] It was only the Ndebele and the Gaza who eventually settled permanently, at opposite ends of the Zimbabwean plateau; the other Nguni groups had crossed the Zambezi by 1838. Soshangane's Gaza also had a tremendous cultural impact on the Hlengwe, to the extent that they are often incorrectly referred to as the Shangani people.[98] This is intriguing, given that the Gaza capital was never in one place long enough to hold any significant control over its subjects. Not only was Soshangane vulnerable to attacks by fellow Nguni in the early stages of his rule but, after 1845, there was always the possibility of a joint attack by the Portuguese and Afrikaners. The atmosphere of anxiety to which this gave rise turned to a near crisis with the bitter conflict between two of Soshangane's sons, Mzila and Mawewe, that raged during the 1860s.[99] Gaza warriors did, however, raid and exact tribute as far inland as the Mutirikwi river, encroaching into what the Ndebele considered their own sphere of influence.[100]

The question remains: how were these immigrant states able to subject most of the 'VaNyai'/Karanga groups, despite the latter's complex social and political organisation? It is apparent that the Nguni introduced a new system of 'feudal parasitism', made possible by the threat of military force. None of these groups believed in total war against their subjects, nor was this feasible given their numbers, but violence became a useful means of fostering a new way of life, one

[97] S. J. Ndlovu-Gatsheni, 'Dynamics of Democracy and Human Rights among the Ndebele of Zimbabwe, 1818-1934', (D.Phil. thesis, University of Zimbabwe, 2003), p. 62.
[98] Beach, *Zimbabwe before 1900*, p. 57.
[99] G. J. Leisegang, 'Aspects of Gaza Nguni history', *Rhodesian History*, 6, 1975, pp. 3-5.
[100] Beach, *War and Politics*, p. 32.

Fig. 1.2: Shangaan dance during tax collection at Ndanga.
[*Source:* National Archives of Zimbabwe]

to which the old 'Nyai' structures needed to adapt to in order to survive. This was accomplished by building a new state along the same lines as its immediate predecessor, incorporating its people as far as possible as assets of its social fabric, and reinforcing class hierarchies upon them on the basis of ethnic origin. The Ndebele state resembled the Rozvi state in everything but the strategy of administration and the management of the class/ethnicity dichotomy. The Rozvi were essentially a class of VaNyai, who ruled those amongst them who were yet to achieve their status. They were not an ethnic entity. The 'Zansi' ruling elite of the Ndebele, on the other hand, were an ethnic coalition that sought to transform themselves into a class secured by guided inbreeding in favour of Zansi men. This is one reason that the argument for the Ndebele state organising according to 'castes' cannot be pushed too far in describing Ndebele social structures.[101]

Ndebele hegemony was established in a variety of ways. First, it must be appreciated that the Nguni traffic on the plateau between 1826 and 1838 left a lasting impression on local communities. The Nguni had not only dismantled the centre of the Rozvi ruling elite but scattered its factions widely and made any claimants to the throne fugitives among their own subjects. In essence, the 'Nyai' cliental structure had crumbled from the top. Some 'vaNyai' emulated the Nguni formula and imitated it with mixed success. The career of the Dumbuseya is

---

[101] B. Lindgren, 'The Politics of Ndebele Ethnicity: Origins, Nationality and Gender in Southern Zimbabwe' (Ph.D. thesis, Uppsala University, 2002), p. 80.

illustrative of this. Starting as a band of local warriors picked up in Nyajena and drafted into the army of Ngwana Maseko of the Ngoni, they were trained in Nguni fighting methods and broke away after Ngwana Maseko clashed with Zwangendaba's group in the Mazowe valley. Thereafter, they roamed the lands between the Tugwi and the Ngezi rivers, raiding some groups and offering their services as mercenaries to others. Eventually, after an illustrious career in banditry, they retired to the Wedza area of Zvishavane, like the Hiya before them.[102]

Secondly, it was necessary for the Ndebele to appreciate the existing modes of rule in order to thrive. Thus Mzilikazi's main preoccupation in the early years of the Ndebele state was simply to thwart or absorb the existing Rozvi ruling houses and any of those groups showing signs of replacing, or aspiring to replace, Rozvi power. The pursuit of Mambo Tohwechipi was launched simultaneously with campaigns to bring under control such emergent powers as Hwata and Chizema Chirumhanzu. By 1857, this task had been accomplished, as had the subjugation and/or incorporation into the Ndebele state of other Rozvi houses, such as those under Lukuluba and Svabasvi. The project was further extended in the 1860s to force Nyashanu and the Njanja into submission before turning their attention to smaller and less significant units.[103] In all instances, the Ndebele were careful not to disturb existing non-secular structures, and in some cases they invited back the defeated Rozvi as loyal subjects. Thus, even as they pursued their enemies up and down the plateau, this did not stop them from deferring to Shona spirit mediums of the Mupfure and Manyame valleys to whom they paid tribute. Similarly, in later years, Mzilikazi's son and successor, Lobengula, solidified his relations with the Mwari cult in order to become an important rainmaker himself.[104]

Thirdly, it was important for them to match the scale of the Rozvi empire in size and expose it to the new system, a strategy that had to be proven, particularly in areas further north of the state. The Nambiya at Bumbuzi were obvious targets, and they were forced to flee towards the Zambezi, seeking refuge amongst the riverine Tonga.[105] By the 1850s, Ndebele rule covered the Zambezi, the Mafungavutsi plateau and Gokwe, with such chiefs as Chireya, Tjabi, Pashu and Nkoka paying tribute to Ndebele.[106]

---

[102] Von Sicard, 'The Dumbuseya'.

[103] Beach, *War and Politics*, pp. 21-32.

[104] N. M. B. Bhebe, 'The Ndebele and Mwari before 1893: A religious conquest of the conquerors by the vanguished', in Schoffeleers (ed.), *Guardians of the Land*, p. 291.

[105] J. McGregor, 'Living with the river: Landscape and memory in the Zambezi valley, northwest Zimbabwe', in W. Beinart and J. McGregor (eds.) *Social History and African Environments* (Oxford: James Currey, 2003), pp. 89-92.

[106] J. R. D. Cobbing, 'The Ndebele under the Khumalos' (Ph.D. thesis, University of Lancaster, 1976), p. 139.

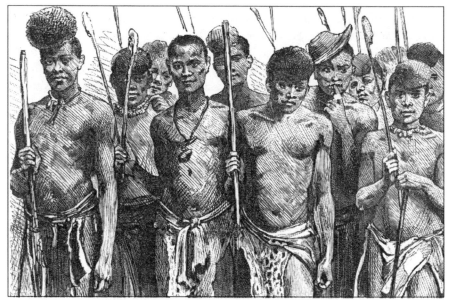

Fig. 1.3: Ndebele: Imbezi Regiment.
[Source: National Archives of Zimbabwe]

These three factors have led some historians to the conclusion that Ndebele policy towards their subjects may have been straightforward, in that they offered them the choice of paying tribute or being raided. But this, too, requires some revision, especially in the period after 1879, when Ndebele power came under serious threat in Shona country. Ndebele impis were being defeated owing to the gradual adoption of guns, and more sophisticated defence strategies, by most southern Shona groups. Raiding, however, was not a highly organised business in the Ndebele state. Emerging evidence shows cases of errant groups turning to banditry, and the Ndebele concept of *umhaso* (unsanctioned raids conducted by lesser chiefs) did not make proper administration of the tactic any better.[107]

The net effect of Ndebele presence in Zimbabwe was the change in the way of life, from that which existed in the federal cliental structures maintained during the time that the 'Nyai' ideal had flourished to one that was more security-conscious and individualistic. This need not imply a terrified subject population vulnerable to Ndebele raiding parties – a picture painted by early missionary and colonial literature – but rather a society conscious of the existing dangers and constantly working out means of dealing with them.

---

[107] I am grateful to Sabelo Ndlovu for making this suggestion to me in a debate in 1999; this argument was further developed in Mazarire, 'Defence consciousness as way of life'.

Economy and society in pre-colonial Zimbabwe

So far, I have tried to account for the origins and settlement of pre-colonial groups, and to show how their interactions shaped local politics. It is necessary, however, to make a few general remarks about the socio-economic conditions obtaining during this period. Early analyses of Zimbabwe's prehistoric states have depicted them chiefly as farming communities that adopted iron to modernise their agriculture and cultivate more extensively than their predecessors. They were also pastoralists who placed a lot of faith in livestock. Cattle occupied a central place in their economies because they were important indicators of wealth and a means of maintaining clients. Through a system of distributing herds to loyal followers on the basis of usufruct, or *kuronzera*, some cattle-owners were able to transform their wealth into power. Equally, cattle occupied a special place in ritual as abodes of departed spirits or objects of sacrifice in ancestral propitiation. They were also important commodities for bridewealth.[108]

From around the ninth century there is evidence that the Leopard's Kopje settlers came to dominate south-western Zimbabwe, 'absorbing' earlier Zhizo people. This process was facilitated by the build-up of herds – good cattle country stretched well into eastern Botswana. An economic base was established which allowed for the creation of a 'rank society', distinguishing the wealthy from the poor even in their settlement arrangements. In such a society, cattle were the measure of wealth, and areas with the largest concentrations, such as Toutswemogala in Botswana, became the first to exhibit characteristics of what we would call a 'state'.[109] There is much evidence indicating an increase in the number of cattle from the tenth century onwards, and with that we also see the gradual transformation and sophistication of this 'state' system. Certainly, cattle-owners became much more important than general cultivators and had the wherewithal to reward followers or pay for their labour. They could also pursue both agriculture and pastoralism, but this was usually at a local level. Mapungubwe, one of the early states associated with the Leopard's Kopje people in the twelfth and thirteenth centuries, shows signs of this diversification and an increasing tendency for its inhabitants to settle in one place for longer periods of time.[110]

However, archaeological evidence from some of these early states also indicates a shift from the general preoccupation with a subsistence-oriented economy servicing local needs to one that produced additional commodities for

---

[108] Mudenge, *A Political History of Munhumutapa*, p. 163.
[109] Pikirayi, *The Zimbabwe Culture*, p. 109-10.
[110] Ibid., p. 112.

exchange and sought greater participation in external trade.[111] Some scholars have argued that external trade was the key stimulus to growth among most of Zimbabwe's pre-colonial states.[112] This idea has long been challenged, although it is difficult to ignore the fact that, when evidence of external trade becomes available, there was a corresponding growth of new economic, social and political organisations.[113] Similarly, changes in trade arrangements on the Indian Ocean coast seemed to have had a spillover effect in the interior hinterland. There is, for example, a special relationship between Great Zimbabwe and Kilwa, the former being the supplier of goods destined for the coast and the latter being the port of entry for trade items. The collapse of Great Zimbabwe was linked in more ways than one to that of Kilwa.[114] The emphasis on the 'trade stimulus' hypothesis underplays alternative explanations, such as environmental factors. The Great Zimbabwe area still exhibits a variety of ecological zones: the tropical environment around present-day Morgenster Mission; the perennial water supplies draining the Mtirikwi watershed; the Zimbabwe granite creating micro-climates; and the alluvial gold deposits of the Tugwi fern spruit, as well as that of Nyajena. All of these may have contributed to the rise of such an important state as Great Zimbabwe. On the other hand, the state's development into a near-urban centre may have put pressure on the ecology, resulting in its collapse. There is an argument that these micro-environments are re-emerging because of the resurgence of rural communities, which, though densely populated, are sparsely distributed.[115] Similarly, Ian Phimister has shown that the Iron Age peoples of Great Zimbabwe worked alluvial and 'placer' gold deposits of the fern spruit around the town, whose viability was regulated by the Muslim coastal presence.[116]

I have shown the political developments that took place beyond the area of Great Zimbabwe and demonstrated that, in each of the population movements from this centre, groups occupied different environments and adapted to new socio-economic lifestyles. Beach has submitted that these movements went on to form a 'Great Crescent' of population, and that the ensuing settlement

---

[111] Pwiti, 'Trade and economies', p. 123.

[112] An extreme version of this argument in the historical period is D. Chanaiwa, 'Politics and long distance trade in the Mwene Mutapa empire during the sixteenth century', *The International Journal of African Historical Studies*, 5(3), 1972.

[113] Pwiti, 'Trade and economies', p. 125.

[114] Ibid., p. 127.

[115] J. H. Bannerman, 'Ecological and Other Factors in the Rise and Fall of the Zimbabwe State', Paper Presented to the Conference on Zimbabwean History, Progress and Development, University of Zimbabwe, 23-27 August 1982, pp. 4-5.

[116] I. R. Phimister, 'Ancient mining near Great Zimbabwe', *Journal of the South African Institute of Mining and Metallurgy*, 74(6), 1974, p. 236.

patterns followed the expanse of the gold belt that, in turn, formed a 'Golden Crescent' cutting across the plateau.[117] Indeed, it was gold that attracted the Portuguese to the Zimbabwean interior in the subsequent century and brought to life new trade patterns based on *ferias*, or fairs, where the Portuguese traded their goods for gold.[118] According to Mudenge, local gold-mining was influenced by the agricultural background of the people on the Zimbabwean plateau; they chose to work the gold mines in the months when they were not attending to their fields, or when there was little risk of mine-flooding by the rains.[119] Gold-washing, however, continued throughout the year and was the main source of the mineral. Local rulers tended to seek monopoly over the mining of gold and sought to regulate the trade; the Mutapa state provides a typical example of how control over gold and, later, silver, determined its local politics and the nature of its relations with external forces.

The agricultural base of the Zimbabwean plateau economy has led some historians to suggest that its sustenance revolved around the failure of local agriculture to provide economic security, i.e. people could not survive on just one branch of the economy but needed others, ranging from hunting and gathering, to fishing and external trade.[120] With time, such assertions have been questioned, especially given the growing evidence that economies did exist that could confidently rely on one or two branches of production: hunting amongst the Hlengwe; wild-vegetable gathering in the Zvishavane area; and gold-mining amongst the communities of Rimuka.[121]

More research is needed into the peculiarities of particular environmental zones and the detail of pre-colonial economies. In the northern lowveld, for instance, it is difficult to comprehend how the vaShangwe of Nyoka developed a lucrative tobacco industry just below the Mafungavutsi plateau. Heavily infested with mosquitoes and tsetse, it was not conducive to cattle, let alone human habitation, but the vaShangwe survived. There are reports that they did not cultivate any grain but bartered tobacco for the goods that enabled them to continue living there.[122] Similarly, although the pre-1890 Ndebele have largely

---

[117] Beach, *The Shona and their Neighbours*, p. 76.

[118] H. Ellert, *Rivers of Gold* (Gweru: Mambo Press, 1993), p. 41.

[119] Mudenge, *A Political History of Munhumutapa*, p. 170.

[120] D. N. Beach, 'The Shona economy: Branches of production', in R. Palmer and N. Parsons (eds.), *The Roots of Rural Poverty in Central and Southern Africa* (London: Heinemann, 1977), pp. 37-65.

[121] D. N. Beach, 'Second thoughts on the Shona economy: Suggestions for further research', *Rhodesian History*, 7, 1976, p. 4.

[122] B. Kosmin, 'The Inyoka tobacco industry of the Shangwe people: The displacement of a pre-colonial economy in Southern Rhodesia, 1898-1938', in Palmer & Parsons (eds), *The Roots of Rural Poverty*, pp. 271-3.

been characterised as surviving on a predatory economy dependent upon raiding cattle, grain and human beings, it has been convincingly demonstrated by
Julian Cobbing that 'the primary branch of production was cultivation and the
main part of Ndebele diet was grain rather than beef'.[123] In real terms, however,
the Ndebele do appear to have had the largest concentration of herds in the
region.[124] Tribute-collection augmented an already functioning economy and
was more a means of exerting political control over subjects than a mode of
survival.

Conclusion

No single chapter can do justice to a thousand years of a country's history, or be
a fitting tribute to all the scholars who have gone before. It has been the object
of this chapter to offer only a panoramic survey of pre-colonial Zimbabwe, its
people, places and ideas. It is an intervention based on sources old and new that
shed light on what is already known; but it is also a challenge to the canonic
myths that have made historians look through the prism of individual identities
when there is so much else to be found. Myths have made us look at these
people in monolithic terms, from the point of view of what others think of them
rather than what they thought of themselves. It is hoped that the fragmentation
of such meta-narratives will open up new fields for research that are sensitive to
all analytical categories, allowing a wide diversity of opinion and interpretation.

[123] Cobbing, 'The Ndebele under the Khumalos'.
[124] Beach, *The Shona and their Neighbours*, p. 135.

2

Mapping Cultural and Colonial Encounters, 1880s–1930s

Sabelo J. Ndlovu-Gatsheni

Introduction

This chapter attempts a broadly thematic and chronological account and analysis of the development of Western colonialism on the Zimbabwean plateau between the 1880s and the 1930s. It argues for a more nuanced understanding of the processes that characterised the imposition of European colonial rule and its subsequent consolidation rather than the somewhat simplistic, nationalist-inspired 'domination and resistance' paradigm that was popular in the 1960s.[1] Clearly, the processes were complex and mediated by contestations and conversations, rejections and acceptances, negotiations and complicity.[2]

The chapter begins with a discussion of the forces and agents of colonialism, particularly the activities of Christian missionaries, traders, concession-seekers and their empire-minded sponsors. Concession-seekers put pressure on African leaders to 'sign' the fraudulent Rudd Concession that was used to justify the occupation, conquest and colonisation of Zimbabwe in the 1890s. I then analyse events that led to the conquest of the African people, and their responses, between 1890 and 1897. This period saw the Ndebele resisting imperial forces at the Shangani River, Mbembesi River and at Pupu in what became known as the Anglo-Ndebele War of 1893, or simply as the Matabele War.

The 1890s also saw both Ndebele and the Shona reacting violently to the provocative interventions of early colonial rule in what became known as the Ndebele-Shona Rising of 1896-97: the *First Chimurenga* or *Umvukela Woku-qala*. The question of whether the reaction of the Ndebele to early colonial rule was co-ordinated or not, and the role of religion in it, provoked intense debate among scholars, pitting Terence Ranger's pioneering ideas of a united and co-ordinated uprising against revisionist perspectives of David Beach and Julian Cobbing that disputed the issues of unity, co-ordination and the centrality of religion.

---

[1] F. Cooper, 'Conflict and connection: Rethinking colonial African history,' in J. D. Le Sueur (ed.), *The Decolonization Reader* (New York: Routledge, 2003), p. 24.

[2] L. Russell, 'Introduction', in L. Russell (ed.), *Colonial Frontiers: Indigenous-European Encounters in Settler Societies* (Manchester: Manchester University Press, 2001), pp. 4-7.

The making of the early Rhodesian state became a complex enterprise with its own dynamics. These included the consistent attempt by the early white settlers to 'indigenise' themselves as well as the early Africans' various ways of making sense of their new position as a colonised people. Routinisation of early colonial rule became predicated on a delicate balancing of consent and coercion. The pre-colonial chiefly system of governance was reinvented to serve colonial interests, with African chiefs occupying the lowest echelons of the Native Affairs Department. At another level, the British South Africa Company administration pursued policies of social and spatial segregation based on race as part of colonial governance. The ambiguities and contradictions of colonial governance provoked equally ambiguous and contradictory African reactions that are analysed in this chapter.

Background to colonisation

The colonisation of Zimbabwe was part of the closing dramatic scenes of the European partition of Africa.[3] The push factors for colonisation included the dynamics taking place in the West, particularly the economic crisis in Britain that provoked the search for new markets, raw materials and job opportunities elsewhere. These dynamics were well analysed by John A. Hobson, who advanced the thesis of 'overproduction' punctuated by 'underconsumption'.[4] The key colonial actors in the territory now known as Zimbabwe were the Portuguese, Afrikaners and the British. The discovery of diamonds, and later gold, south of the Limpopo River set the stage for aggressive expansionism in southern Africa; it also facilitated regional linkages as Africans from the Zimbabwean plateau were attracted to the mines.

The Cape Colony acted as the staging post for colonial expansionism into the interior of South Africa and, later, north of the Limpopo River. The contest pitted the British against the Afrikaners. The Portuguese were also threatening British interests; their presence dated back to their relations with the Mutapas in the fifteenth century, but they had failed to establish an effective colonisation of the Zimbabwean plateau. David Beach argued that the Portuguese had succeeded the Muslims and 'yet the Portuguese were different from the Muslims in one significant way: from 1560 some of them planned to conquer the Zambezi goldfields rather than simply trade with them.'[5]

In summary, the colonisation of Zimbabwe was a complex affair that involved the capitalist interests of the Cape, Natal, the Rand and London, the British

---

[3] R. Blake, *A History of Rhodesia* (London: Eyre Methuen, 1977).

[4] J. A. Hobson, *Imperialism: A Study* (London: Allen and Unwin, 1948).

[5] D. N. Beach, *The Shona and Their Neighbours* (Oxford: Blackwell, 1994), p. 108.

Foreign Office, the Colonial Office and the Governors and High Commissioners of the Cape, as well as missionary interests and those of the Afrikaners and Portuguese.[6] The Afrikaners and the Portuguese were eventually thwarted, and the British emerged as the colonisers in the 1890s.

But the drama of colonisation was not just a white affair. It was an encounter between human beings, both white and black. The key preoccupation of each was to make sense, and take advantage, of the other. In Diana Jeater's words: 'There was a mutual lack of recognition and understanding, expressed through both goodwill and hostility. The "other" was potentially a fellow but potentially an enemy or savage. There was room for uncertainty. Interactions succeeded or failed; people learned from their interactions.'[7] Studies that relied heavily on colonial records tended towards a Eurocentric interpretation of African affairs, in which white agency was privileged over the agency of the black people.[8] In this interpretation Africans were objects of white civilisation rather than rational and active historical actors.

Christian missionaries were the earliest representatives of the imperial world that would eventually conquer the Ndebele and the Shona in the late 1890s. John and Jean Comaroff argued that missionaries were not just the bearers of a hegemonic Christian ideology but were also human vehicles of a Western worldview. Their mission was to engage African communities in a web of symbolic and material transactions that was to bind them ever more securely to the colonising culture.[9]

The London Missionary Society (LMS) was among the earliest Christian groups that sought to convert Africans to Christianity. It was active in Matabeleland because the founder of the Ndebele state, King Mzilikazi Khumalo, had established a personal friendship with Robert Moffat in the 1820s. Moffat was one of the first missionaries to enter southern Africa, establishing a mission station among the Sotho-Tswana in a place called Kuruman.[10] When the Ndebele

[6] A. Keppel-Jones, *Rhodes and Rhodesia: The White Conquest of Zimbabwe, 1884-1902* (Pietermaritzburg: University of Natal Press, 1983).

[7] D. Jeater, *Law, Language and Science: The Invention of the 'Native Mind' in Southern Rhodesia, 1890-1930* (Portsmouth, NH: Heinemann, 2007), p. 2.

[8] L. H. Gann, *A History of Rhodesia* (Salisbury: Books of Rhodesia, 1965).

[9] John L. Comaroff and Jean Comaroff, *Of Revelation and Revolution: The Dialectics of Modernity on a South African Frontier: Volume Two* (Chicago: University of Chicago Press, 1997); Jean Comaroff, *Body of Power, Spirit of Resistance: The Culture and History of a South African People* (Chicago: University of Chicago Press, 1985).

[10] J. P. R. Wallis (ed.), *The Matabele Journals of Robert Moffat, 1829-1860* (London: Chatto and Windus, 2 vols., 1945); R. Kent Rasmussen, *Migrant Kingdom: Mzilikazi's Ndebele in South Africa* (Cape Town: Rex Collings, 1978); N. Etherington, *The Great Treks: The Transformation of Southern Africa, 1815-1854* (London: Pearson Education, 2001).

settled on the south-western part of the plateau, Moffat visited them in 1854 and established the first LMS mission in Inyathi in 1859.[11]

Mashonaland had been exposed to Christianity by the Portuguese in the sixteenth century.[12] Fr Gonçalo da Silveira, a Portuguese Jesuit, managed to convert one of the Mutapas to the Christian faith before his murder in the 1560s.[13] However, it was later missionaries, including Charles D. Helm and John Smith Moffat (son of Robert Moffat), who played a more significant role in the events leading to the colonisation of Zimbabwe.

Missionary activities did not directly challenge the autonomy of the Ndebele and Shona polities. But 'Christianisation' by its very nature was dangerous, as it entailed the 'colonisation' of the Ndebele and Shona people's consciousness with the axioms and aesthetics of western culture.[14] Ngwabi Bhebe has shown how the Ndebele resisted conversion throughout the 1880s and 1890s, prior to the violent conquest of the Ndebele state.[15] Christian teachings emphasised individual accountability to God alone, thus undermining African ideologies of divine leadership that combined political, judicial and religious powers;[16] they promoted the idea of the equality of all people before God, including captives of the Ndebele – a society that was organised in a hierarchy of the superior Zansi aristocracy, a middle-social stratum of the Nhla, and the despised Hole, as well as captives.[17] They dismissed African ways of worshipping God as nothing but paganism while at the same time belittling *amadlozi/vadzimu* (ancestral spirits) as demons and evil spirits.[18]

But African responses to missionary activities remained ambivalent, because they came with advantages as well as hazards. The Ndebele wanted guns and

---

[11] N. M. Bhebe, *Christianity and Traditional Religion in Western Zimbabwe* (London: Longman, 1979).

[12] Blake, *A History of Rhodesia*, pp. 11-12.

[13] H. H. K Bhila, *Trade and Politics in a Shona Kingdom: The Manyika and Their Portuguese and African Neighbours, 1575-1902* (Harlow: Longman, 1982); S. I. G. Mudenge, *A Political History of Munhumutapa c.1400-1902* (Harare: Zimbabwe Publishing House, 1988); D. N. Beach, *The Shona and Zimbabwe, 900-1850* (Gweru: Mambo Press, 1980).

[14] S. J. Ndlovu-Gatsheni, 'Re-thinking the colonial encounter in Zimbabwe in the early twentieth century', *Journal of Southern African Studies*, 33(1), 2007, pp. 173-91.

[15] Bhebe, *Christianity and Traditional Religion*.

[16] S. J. Ndlovu-Gatsheni, 'The Dynamics of Democracy and Human Rights among the Ndebele of Zimbabwe, 1818-1934' (Ph.D. thesis, University of Zimbabwe, 2004), pp. 230-50.

[17] S. J. Ndlovu-Gatsheni and F. J. Ndhlovu, 'Twilight of patriarchy in a southern African kingdom: A case study of captives and women in the Ndebele state of Zimbabwe', *UNISWA Research Journal*, 19, 2005, pp. 59-71.

[18] *The London Missionary Record*, xxviii, 1864. The missionaries resident in the Ndebele state began to ignore Ndebele 'holy-days' like *inxwala*.

the missionaries were able to secure these.[19] Modern medicine cured diseases such as gout, which troubled both Mzilikazi and Lobengula. Those Africans who were experiencing oppression and exploitation within African societies found the Christian gospel appealing. Many people within both Ndebele and Shona communities were executed after being accused of witchcraft; missionaries dismissed witchcraft, making them attractive to those accused. Thus the first few Christian converts came from people who were critical of some of the customs and traditions of their own societies or who were finding themselves culturally oppressed.[20] Some women, for instance, did not like arranged marriages, child-pledging and the practice of killing twins; for them, mission stations were the best place of refuge.[21]

White traders also indirectly prepared people for the coming of colonialism. 'Commodities of the empire' – intoxicating spirits, sugar, mirrors, teas and trinkets – transformed the tastes of the African communities and drew them closer to the nexus of the imperial cash economy. Traders included the Arab-Swahili, Portuguese, Boers and British.[22] These were followed by the more dangerous concession-seekers, sponsored by imperialists such as Cecil Rhodes, bent on exploiting Africans' human and natural resources. Those who had come in earlier – John Smith Moffat, Frederick Selous, Charles Helm and others – became 'experts' on the Ndebele and the Shona. For instance, John Smith Moffat had this to say about the Ndebele: 'an army of warmongers ... a nation of murderers whose hand is against every man.'[23] Some missionaries abused African trust and confidence by conniving with the concession-seekers. Thomas Morgan Thomas's *Eleven Years in Central Africa* described Africans in derogatory terms and characterised their systems of governance as nothing but manifestations of barbarism, autocracy and a long night of savagery.[24] Colonisation was justified

---

[19] B. Mahamba, 'Women in the History of the Ndebele' (MA thesis, University of Zimbabwe, 1996).

[20] Ndlovu-Gatsheni, 'The Dynamics of Democracy and Human Rights among the Ndebele'.

[21] Mahamba, 'Women in the History of the Ndebele', pp. 20-5, and L. Decle, *Three Years in Savage Africa* (Bulawayo: Books of Rhodesia, 1974).

[22] H. H. K Bhila, *Trade and Politics in a Shona Kingdom*; Mudenge, *A Political History of Munhumutapa*; Beach, *The Shona and Zimbabwe*; N. Bhebe, 'Ndebele trade in the nineteenth century', *Journal of African Studies*, 1(2), 1974; Bhebe, *Christianity and Traditional Religion*.

[23] O. Ransford, *The Rulers of Rhodesia* (Bulawayo, Books of Rhodesia, 1968), p. 102. See also N[ational] A[rchives] [of] Z[imbabwe] Historical Manuscripts MO5/1/1, John Smith Moffat to Mary Moffat, August 1854.

[24] T. M. Thomas, *Eleven Years in Central South Africa* (London: Routledge, 1971 [1873]). For a different view on pre-colonial governance, see S. J. Ndlovu-Gatsheni, 'Quarrying African indigenous political thought on governance: A case study of the Ndebele state in the 19th century', *Indilinga: African Journal of Indigenous Knowledge Systems*, 4(2), 2005, pp. 449-70.

as a 'civilising mission' in a 'dark continent'. The pre-literate Africans could not 'write back' and their views on the early whites are missing as a public record.

Concession-seekers and colonial agents

Karl Mauch and Henry Hartley's discovery of gold near the Umfuli (Mupfure) River in the 1860s was followed by a flurry of local gold-rushes in the area between the Zambezi and the Limpopo rivers.[25]

These culminated in Lobengula's signing of the Tati Concession in 1870, giving gold-mining rights to the London and Limpopo Mining Company, represented in Matabeleland by Sir John Swinburne. Lobengula later granted a similar concession in the north to the South African Goldfields Exploration Company represented by the explorer, Thomas Baines.[26]

Meanwhile, the Berlin Conference, hosted by German Chancellor Otto von Bismarck in 1884-85 with the purpose of dividing Africa among European powers, galvanised what became known as the 'scramble' for Africa.[27] The Ndebele and the Shona could not survive these invigorated colonial manoeuvres as Cecil Rhodes endeavoured to gain concessions from African leaders and secure signed treaties.[28] During the same period, prospectors, traders and adventurers intensified their search for mineral concessions on behalf of companies, individuals and governments.

Fig. 2.1: Lobengula: From a photograph in *Life* taken in 1893.
[*Source:* http://tbn0.google.com/hosted/images/c?q=0567a9a0f4c8133f_large]

In 1886 gold was discovered on the Witwatersrand, and a year later Lobengula was under pressure from an emissary of Transvaal president Paul

---

[25] Karl Mauch made a lot of publicity about his discovery of gold, and his high-blown nonsense about the Land of Ophir were captured by the *Transvaal Argus*, which spread rumours of rich goldfields in Zimbabwe.

[26] Blake, *A History of Rhodesia*, pp. 24-6.

[27] P. Nugent and A. J. Asiwaju (eds.), *African Boundaries: Barriers, Conduits and Opportunities* (London: Pinter, 1996).

[28] According to the Berlin Conference those imperialists with no evidence of agreements and actual activities in the claimed spheres of influence risked these being taken away by others.

Kruger for a treaty of 'friendship' with the Transvaal. The emissary, Piet Grobler, had personal ambitions to be Transvaal's ambassador in the Ndebele state, and the treaty signed in 1887 became known as the Grobler Treaty. When it became public, Rhodes was ready to clip the wings of Afrikaner imperialist ambitions.[29]

Rhodes sent John Smith Moffat, by then an Assistant Commissioner to Sir Sidney Shippard in Bechuanaland, to negotiate with Lobengula. This was a clever choice because Lobengula and Moffat knew each other well. Lobengula called Moffat 'Joni' as their fathers were friends, but was not aware that 'Joni' was working against the interests of the Ndebele state.[30] Unwittingly, Lobengula trusted 'Joni' and it was easy for the latter to secure the signature of the Ndebele king on what became known as the Moffat Treaty. Under the terms of the treaty, signed on 11 February 1888, Lobengula was expected not to give any further concessions or to enter into any further treaties 'without the previous knowledge and sanction of her Majesty's High Commissioner in South Africa'.[31]

Why did the Ndebele king sign these treaties and grant these concessions? This question is commonly asked in relation to the Rudd Concession, which was signed a few months after the Moffat Treaty and became a justifying document for the colonisation of the Ndebele and the Shona. John Smith Moffat and Charles Helm influenced Lobengula to sign by giving him the impression that he was going to get British protection, like his neighbour Khama of the Ngwato, and that no more than ten white men would be mining in Matabeleland – a verbal assurance that was never written into the concession. Lobengula was under extreme pressure from various groups of concession-seekers and thought the British were the most powerful and best able to provide protection.[32]

Beach has suggested that

> The reason why Lobengula agreed to the treaties and concessions
> that he did, in spite of the fact that most of those with whom
> he dealt were trying to cheat him, was in order to keep foreign
> capitalist influence in and around his state to a minimum. He
> tried nearly every possible means to avoid outright war with the
> whites, because he did not think he could win.[33]

As Bhebe has noted, by the 1880s Ndebele society was bifurcated into

---

[29] S. Samkange, *The Origins of Rhodesia* (Heinemann, London, 1968).

[30] Ransford, *Rulers of Rhodesia*, p. 156; Blake, *A History of Rhodesia*, p. 39.

[31] P. R. Warhurst, 'Concession-seekers and the scramble for Matabeleland', *Rhodesiana*, 29, 1973, pp. 55-64.

[32] Samkange, *The Origins of Rhodesia*; R. Brown, 'Aspects of the scramble for Matabeleland', in E. Stokes and R. Brown (eds.), *The Zambesian Past: Studies in Central African History* (Manchester: Manchester University Press, 1966), pp. 63-93.

[33] Beach, *The Shona and their Neighbours*, pp. 166-7.

inflexible conservatives and militarists and a minority of pacifists (those who wanted change). The former group of *amajaha* (young soldiers) wanted war against the whites, while the pacifists wanted negotiations and peace. This put Lobengula in an invidious position, and he could do little but use delaying tactics.[34] A pre-literate king who relied on interpreters and who could not read and write for himself was almost bound to be cheated.

Also important at this time were the exaggerated accounts about the economic endowments of the continent that were doing the rounds in Europe, including that of the legendary riches of Ophir lying between the Limpopo and the Zambezi rivers, which galvanised the imperialists into colonial action.[35] The myth of the Second Rand, which was linked directly to the discovery of rich gold deposits in the Rand in 1886, in particular, spoke of the Zimbabwean plateau as being 'one vast gold-reef'.[36]

Despite Lobengula's protests the British government granted a Royal Charter on 29 October 1889, authorising Rhodes to create the British South Africa Company (BSAC). Modelled on the British and Dutch East India companies, the BSAC was a commercial-political entity with a mandate to focus on the exploitation of economic resources such as gold and diamonds as well as on political powers to clear the way for British finance capital. It had the power to raise its own police force, fly its own flag, build roads, railways, telegraphs and harbours, establish banks, conduct mining operations and settle territories that it acquired.[37] In short, it had full imperial and colonising powers. Even if Lobengula had refused to sign, colonisation could not have been avoided. By this time many parts of Africa had been colonised, and by the First World War, only Ethiopia and Liberia had survived it.[38]

What had started as a cultural encounter, characterised by mutual trading and attempts to covert Africans to Christianity, was taking on a violent colonial dimension. The creation of the BSAC, together with the raising of an armed invasion force, was indicative of how Western powers were prepared to destroy African social, economic and political formations. The Maxim gun in particular played a decisive role in tilting the balance of power in favour of the whites. Gerald Mazarire rightly argued that the relations between indigenous people

---

[34] R. Brown, 'Aspects of the scramble for Matabeleland'; T. Ranger, *Revolt in Southern Rhodesia, 1896-7: A Study in African Resistance* (London: Heinemann, 1967).

[35] I. Phimister, *An Economic and Social History of Zimbabwe, 1890-1948: Capital Accumulation and Class Struggle* (London: Longman, 1988), p. 5.

[36] Rose Blennerhassett and Lucy Sleeman, *Adventures in Mashonaland* (Bulawayo: Books of Rhodesia, 1969 [1893]), p. 26.

[37] Blake, *A History of Rhodesia*, p. 54.

[38] A. A. Boahen, *African Perspectives of Colonialism* (London: Currey, 1989), pp. 38-45.

and the Boers were initially confined to trade in guns, and that this trade 'subsequently gave rise to a gun culture in the interior evident in the increase in incidence and fatality of local wars'.[39]

The Pioneer Column and the occupation of Mashonaland

The invasion of Mashonaland by the Pioneer Column marked the beginning of white settler occupation of the Zimbabwean plateau. Military-style forts marked the trail between the Limpopo and Zambezi rivers, many of which still mark the 'Road to the North' that runs from the Limpopo to modern Harare.[40] The forts were symbolic of the advance of colonisation; Fort Victoria, for instance, eventually became a military staging post for attacks on the Ndebele state in 1893.

The Shona communities delayed in responding because many of them perceived the Pioneer Column as simply a trading and gold-seeking party that would go away once its commercial desires had been fulfilled, as had Portuguese and other traders before it. This absence of immediate resistance led Arthur Keppel-Jones to argue that white settlers 'occupied' Mashonaland and then 'conquered' Matabeleland,[41] a view that ignores scattered Shona resistance to labour impressments and tax collection.[42] Shona communities could see no logic to these BSAC demands, but, as Ranger has written,

> In Mashonaland, the Company could and did see its main role as support for the extension of white economic activity. In the early years the Company presented itself to the Shona merely as an extension of settler power; its activities were confined to supporting settlers through punitive expeditions and through the compulsion of labour ... Given the weakness of the Company administration and the fact that the Shona paramounts regarded themselves as unconquered and still possessed arms, it was bound to lead to serious disorder.[43]

The construction of BSAC governance in Mashonaland happened in tandem

[39] Gerald C. Mazarire, 'Memories and contestations of the scramble for Zimbabwe: Chivi (Mashonaland) c.1870-1892', in F. J. Kolapo and K. O. Akurang-Parry (eds.), *African Agency and European Colonialism: Latitudes of Negotiations and Containment* (Lanham, MD: University Press of America, 2007), p. 62.

[40] Ibid. p. 63.

[41] A. Keppel-Johns, *Rhodesia and Rhodes* (Kingston: McGill-Queens University Press, 1984), p. 389.

[42] Ranger, *Revolt in Southern Rhodesia*, ch. 2, provides details on how the BSAC made great efforts to treat the Shona as subjects and how the Shona resisted this treatment throughout the 1890s.

[43] Ibid. p. 87.

with accelerated commoditisation as some communities responded to the new markets brought about by white settler demand for crops and cattle.[44] These were exchanged for cloth, beads, whisky, salt, guns and sugar. Colonisation was not characterised only by violence and loss; it also introduced new modes of capital accumulation and led to the emergence of some very rich African communities.[45] However, as Phimister argues,

> Merchant capital's patchy advance had modified existing social relations without decisively altering them, while neither the interests of speculative capital nor the extremely limited resources of the Chartered Administration required or permitted the profound transformation of indigenous social formations. Primitive accumulation was largely confined to looting, leaving the struggle to separate direct producers from the means of production very much to the future.[46]

All of this reveals the complexities of colonial encounters as well as the uneven reach of colonial frontiers.

Violent colonial conquest and African response, 1893–97

By 1893, following the pioneers' failure to find rich gold deposits in Mashonaland, the BSAC decided to extend into Matabeleland, where some thought the 'Second Rand' lay. But Rhodes reacted to this failure by granting farming land to settler pioneers, part of the original promises to those who participated in the occupation of Mashonaland.[47]

The 'effective colonisation' of the Ndebele and the Shona took place only after the Anglo-Ndebele War of 1893 and the Ndebele-Shona uprisings of 1896-97. Preparations for the former included encouraging Shona communities to stop paying tribute to the Ndebele. Lobengula's forces, under the command of Mgandani Dlodlo and Manyewu Ndiweni, invaded Fort Victoria, crossing the border created by the BSAC as they pursued two Shona chiefs accused of stealing Lobengula's cattle.[48] This event was seized upon by those, such as Leander Starr

[44] P. Fitzpatrick, *Through Mashonaland with Pick and Pen* (Johannesburg: Argus, 1892 [Harper, 1973 reprint]), p. 45.

[45] R. G. M. Mtetwa, 'The Political and Economic History of the Duma People of South-Eastern Rhodesia,' (Ph.D. thesis, University of Rhodesia, 1976).

[46] Phimister, *An Economic and Social History of Zimbabwe*, p. 17.

[47] A. Leonard, *How We Made Rhodesia* (Bulawayo: Books of Rhodesia, 1896), p.20.

[48] Jameson had regarded the 'border' as roughly the line of the Munyati and Shashe Rivers. The two chiefs were Bere and Gomani; for details, see S. J. Ndlovu-Gatsheni, 'The Dynamics of Democracy and Human Rights among the Ndebele', and J. R. D. Cobbing, 'The Ndebele under the Khumalos, 1820-1896' (Ph.D. thesis, University of Lancaster, 1976).

Jameson and Captain Lendy, who desired to attack the Ndebele. The incident confirmed missionary reports that the Ndebele were 'bloodthirsty' destroyers of human life who survived by plundering their neighbours.[49] Blake noted that, before attacking the Ndebele, 'the truth would seem, rather, to be that Rhodes and Jameson were waiting upon events. They were not going to start a war'.[50]

Using the 'Victoria Incident' as a pretext, the settler pioneers and some Shona groups that had scores to settle with the Ndebele combined to destroy the Ndebele state.[51] The conquest was swift and brief due to the superior arms in the hands of the pioneers. The Ndebele resisted at the battles of Mbembesi and Shangani rivers, but after defeat there Lobengula set fire to his capital and fled north, never to be seen again. At Pupu – the last theatre in the Matabele War – the Ndebele forces wiped out Allan Wilson's Patrol that was pursuing their king. The tragedy was that the Ndebele won a battle and lost the war.[52] Bulawayo was already occupied by the invading forces and the king had disappeared. But Julian Cobbing has argued that the Pupu victory was an important indicator that in 1893 the Ndebele forces were not completely defeated; their state, and particularly its military institutions, remained intact, and they were able to mobilise for another war in March 1896.[53]

The Ndebele and the Shona rose violently against the BSAC in March and June 1896 in an uprising that eventually formed the basis of mass nationalism and future imaginings of an independent Zimbabwe.[54] There is some consensus among scholars on its causes: the outbreak of natural disasters like rinderpest, drought and locusts that were easily blamed on the presence of the whites; settler brutalities, including forced labour, rape, looting and early colonial impositions such as the 1894 hut tax.[55] By 1895, the country was under police

---

[49] J. D. Omer-Cooper, *The Zulu Aftermath: Revolution in Bantu Africa* (London: Longman, 1966).

[50] Blake, *A History of Rhodesia*, p. 102. See also Ndlovu-Gatsheni, 'The Dynamics of Democracy and Human Rights among the Ndebele', ch. 6.

[51] Anne Dorey, *The Victoria Incident and the Anglo-Matabele War of 1893* (Salisbury: Central African Historical Association, Local Series No. 16, 1966).

[52] The latest study of these events is by B. Lindgren, 'Power, education, and identity in post-colonial Zimbabwe: Representations of the fate of King Lobengula of Matabeleland', *African Sociological Review*, 6(1) pp. 46-67. See also P. Nyathi, *Mthwakazi: Imbali YamaNdebele 1820-1894* (Gweru: Mambo Press, 1995).

[53] Cobbing, 'The Ndebele under the Khumalos', pp. 340-5.

[54] The Anglo-Ndebele War of 1893 is remembered well in Matabeleland as *Imfazo Yokuqala (Mfazo1)* and is part of Ndebele memory of their past. This is because it was a Ndebele affair to preserve their Ndebele kingdom, which even some Shona wanted to see destroyed.

[55] M. Tsomondo, 'Shona reaction and resistance to the European colonisation of Zimbabwe', *Journal of Southern African Affairs*, 2, 1977, pp. 11-31.

rule, characterised by oppression, lawlessness and extreme aggression towards the Ndebele and the Shona.[56]

Because of its importance, a summary follows of the three dominant analyses of the Ndebele-Shona uprising: by Terence Ranger, Julian Cobbing and David Beach.

Terence Ranger on the uprisings as the first national war of liberation

Ranger's book, *Revolt in Southern Rhodesia*, constituted the first comprehensive study of the Ndebele-Shona uprisings.[57] He summarised his argument in a review article:

> The book asserts that the risings of 1896 drew upon the creative strengths of Shona and Ndebele culture. The risings were led by Shona chiefs and Ndebele *indunas* but at the same time the influence of remarkable religious figures enabled prophetic and innovative modifications of 'tradition'. The risings 'summed up' African pre-colonial history; at the same time they contained elements which remained constant to mass protest throughout the colonial period. The continuities between the risings of 1896 and the protest movements of the early 1960s were to be found mostly in the recurrent manifestations of mass emotion and enthusiasm, which did not take the form of armed confrontation but which deployed those idioms which had been crucial to the commitment of the fighters of 1896.[58]

Ranger provided a detailed analysis of early colonial administration in Matabeleland and Mashonaland and of how BSAC rule provoked both the Ndebele and the Shona to rebel against colonialism. Beach called the book 'a magnificent account of the colonisation process itself', concluding that 'Ranger's insights into white society, illustrated by quotations from the colonisers themselves, are thoroughly convincing.'[59] Ranger also provided an overview of the pre-colonial

[56] Ranger, *Revolt in Southern Rhodesia*, analysed deeply what he termed the 'administration' of Mashonaland and Matabeleland and revealed all the issues that caused the risings of 1896-97.

[57] *Revolt in Southern Rhodesia* was written and published in 1967. The 1960s were characterised by 'winds of change' that resulted in decolonisation of Africa. In Rhodesia the 1960s were not only the years of the rise of mass nationalism, but were also a time of bitter and violent clashes between supporters of ZAPU and ZANU. Terence Ranger was a member of the National Democratic Party (NDP) and the Zimbabwe African National Union (ZAPU).

[58] T. Ranger, 'The people in African resistance: A review', *Journal of Southern African Studies: Special Issue on Protest and Resistance*, 4(1), 1977, pp. 125-6.

[59] D. N. Beach, 'Review article: *Revolt in Southern Rhodesia*', *International Journal of African Historical Studies*, 13(1), 1980, p. 108.

past, showing that Ndebele-Shona relations were by no means as bad as colonial historiography presented them.

He noted how the Ndebele and the Shona were able to achieve almost complete tactical surprise in their attacks on the white settlers in March and June 1896, although he acknowledges that the Ndebele rose first, in March, and the Shona in June. To Ranger, the Shona uprising was essentially an extension of what was started by the Ndebele. The latter broke out at an opportune moment, occasioned by the absence of many settler forces owing to the Jameson Raid.[60]

The most controversial element in Ranger's analysis concerns the role of traditional African religious authorities, which were said to have provided unity and co-ordination across Ndebele-Shona ethnic divides. He identified two major operational centres, Ntaba zikaMambo and Mashayamombe. Two religious figures, Mkwati of the Mwari cult and Kaguvi of the Shona *mhondoro* religious system, co-ordinated the secular and other lesser religious figures as both Ndebele and Shona battled the white colonists in 1896 and 1897.[61]

Ranger brought the issue of ideology into the Ndebele-Shona uprising. Religion became the unifying ideology within a context of serious crisis. In 1978, *Revolt in Southern Rhodesia* was reprinted with a new preface by Ranger in which he conceded some of the criticisms levelled at his book but emphasised that 1896 was a year of crisis that made people resort to religious-prophetic leadership. In short, Ranger maintained his ideas about the role of religious authorities in the Ndebele-Shona upising.[62] According to Ranger, religious leaders appropriated the African pre-colonial past and promised a new society without the white people based on millenarian transformation. It is within this terrain that Murenga or Mulenga came into the picture with his administration of war medicine to make Ndebele and Shona fighters invulnerable. Murenga was a spirit medium who promised immunity from bullets to those who were fighting against white settlers.[63] Within nationalist historiography, the African resistance of 1896-97 became popularly known as *Chimurenga*, taking inspiration from Murenga.

Considering how religious leaders like Mkwati co-ordinated both the Ndebele and the Shona to fight against white settlers, Ranger pointed to the

[60] S. J. Ndlovu-Gatsheni, 'The First Chimurenga, 1896-1897: Considerations of Ndebele Military Strategy and Tactics' (BA thesis, University of Zimbabwe, 1992). The Jameson Raid was a disastrous military adventure ranged against the Transvaal Boer Republic.

[61] Ranger, *Revolt in Southern Rhodesia*, pp. 212-18.

[62] T. Ranger, *Voices from the Rocks: Nature, Culture and History in the Matopos Hills of Zimbabwe* (Harare: Baobab Books, 1999) is in fact a restatement of the centrality of religion in politics.

[63] Ranger, *Revolt in Southern Rhodesia*, pp. 217-20.

use of messengers like Tshihwa and Bonda, sent to Mashonaland to encourage the spreading of the rising into the central Shona country by Mkwati.[64] Mwari cult 'officers' and *mhondoro* mediums provided missing links in spreading the rising from Matabeleland to Mashonaland to the extent that the Charter district ended up as the 'nursery of the Mashona rebellion'.[65] Mbuya Nehanda emerges in Ranger's account as another important religious leader who spread the rising in areas around Mazowe. Nehanda has dominated both historical and fiction writing as a renowned spirit medium who was deeply opposed to colonialism. She was hanged at the end of the Ndebele-Shona rising and is said to have prophesied during her trial that her bones would one day arise to fight against colonialism once more.[66]

Ranger's interpretation of the events of 1896-97 inaugurated a nationalist historiography. He provided nationalists of the 1960s with a rich mosaic from which to draw heroes and heroines as they imagined a post-colonial nation.[67] Ranger's book was published at a time in which nationalism had taken root, making it easy for nationalists seeking to unite the Ndebele and the Shona in a struggle against colonialism to appropriate. David Beach, in his review of Ranger's *Revolt*, posed the following question:

> What did *Revolt* offer its African readers? In the first place, they learned that they had a rich and proud past: Ranger brought into play much of the available evidence on Great Zimbabwe, Mutapa and Changamire states, and showed how their heritage lived on in the Shona 'paramountcies', which were far from being the harassed remnants depicted by Rhodesian historians. The Ndebele past was described sympathetically and it was shown that, in spite of certain unpleasantness, relations with the Shona were by no means as bad as had been thought.[68]

---

[64] Ibid., pp. 202-5.

[65] Ibid., p. 202.

[66] S. Mutswairo, 'The Picture of Nehanda and Kagubi', in P. Halsey, G. Morlan and M. Smith (eds.), *If You Want to Know Me* (New York: Friendship Press, 1976), pp. 18-19; L. Vambe, *From Rhodesia to Zimbabwe* (London: Longman, 1976). Yvonne Vera also wrote a novel on Nehanda emphasising her heroism: Y. Vera, *Nehanda* (Harare: Baobab Books, 1993).

[67] B. Raftopoulos, 'Problematising nationalism in Zimbabwe: A historiographical review', *Zambezia*, 26(2), 1999, pp. 115-34. The important books informed by nationalist historiography include: T. O. Ranger, *The African Voice in Southern Rhodesia* (London: Heinemann, 1970); N. Sithole, *African Nationalism* (Oxford: Oxford University Press, 1959); E. Mlambo, *The Struggle for a Birthright* (London: C. Hurst, 1972); L. Vambe, *An Ill-Fated People* (London: Heinemann, 1972).

[68] D. N. Beach, *War and Politics in Zimbabwe, 1840-1900* (Gweru: Mambo Press, 1986), p. 119, where he quotes at length his 1979 review of *Revolt in Southern Rhodesia* (see fn. 59).

While Ranger provided African readers with a proud, heroic history, he also sowed the seeds of what he later criticised as state-supported ascendancy of 'patriotic history'.[69] It was Ranger who provided the Ndebele-Shona uprisings of 1896-97 as a respectable foundation myth for nationalist imaginations of Zimbabwe. As an actor within the early nationalist politics of the 1960s, Ranger tried to make connections between 'primary resistance' and the later mass nationalism of the 1960s.[70] His achievement in nationalist circles was that he managed to unearth the necessary heroes and heroines for the imagination of the nation. These include Mkwati, Nehanda, Mashayamombe, Makoni, Kunzvi-Nyandoro, Mlugulu, Siginyamatshe, Mpotshwana and others. However, by the 1970s Ranger's arguments on the events of 1896-97 were subjected to severe criticism from revisionist scholars.

Absent priesthood: Julian Cobbing on the Ndebele rising of 1896

Julian Cobbing was the first revisionist scholar to question the central thesis of Ranger's book based on his extensive study of the Ndebele history. Cobbing has challenged and rejected the centrality of the Mwari cult in the organisation and co-ordination of the rising in Matabeleland. His critique begins with a pertinent question:

> Is it necessary to postulate this 'co-ordinating factor' or to rummage
> for a 'secret history' of the wars ... when in most respects the nature
> of the risings and the manner in which Africans fought reflected
> very closely the structures of participating political units?[71]

Cobbing is not convinced by Ranger's argument that the Ndebele state had seriously disintegrated following the Matabele War of 1893 to the extent that the Ndebele people and their leaders succumbed to Mwari cult blandishments.[72] Of course the Ndebele had lost their *inkosi* (king) and *isigodlo* (capital), but the other political structures manned by *izinduna* (chiefs) were still functional, enabling the Ndebele aristocracy to mobilise once more for another war in March 1896. While it is not true that 'in all probability the pattern of Ndebele

---

[69] T. Ranger, 'Historiography, patriotic history and the history of the nation: The struggle over the past in Zimbabwe', *Journal of Southern African Studies*, 30(2), 2004, pp. 215-34.

[70] Ranger, 'The people in African resistance: A review'; and T. O. Ranger, 'Connexions between "primary resistance" movements and modern mass nationalism in east and central Africa', *Journal of African History*, 9(3/4), 1968.

[71] J. Cobbing, 'The absent priesthood: Another look at the Rhodesian rising of 1896-1897', *Journal of African History*, 18(1), 1977, p. 63.

[72] T. Ranger, 'The Organisation of the Rebellion of 1896 and 1897: Part One: The Rebellion in Matabeleland', Paper presented at the History of Central Africa People's Conference, Rhodes-Livingstone Institute, Lusaka, Zambia, 1963.

settlement was in 1895 very much as it had been before the 1893 war', there is
sense in arguing that the Ndebele kingdom's military system was not completely
de-militarised.[73] Cobbing is right in pointing out that BSAC power was very weak
beyond Bulawayo and the main roads.[74] The gist of Cobbing's analysis is that
the rising in Matabeleland was initiated, led and organised by secular *izinduna*
(chiefs), utilising their pre-colonial powers and influence on *izigaba* (provinces).
This argument is justified by the fact that the first attacks on scattered white
settlements on 20 March 1896 in the Godlwayo-Filabusi area were initiated by
chief Maduna Mafu and Chief Mahlahleni Mafu. These realities led Cobbing to
conclude that

> the Ndebele state had not expired in 1893 and lived to fight again.
> The monarchy had not expired either, and there is little doubt that
> the Ndebele began the war impressively united for a Nguni people,
> where disputes over succession were often acrimonious, behind a
> monarch-elect, Nyamanda, one of the elder sons of Lobengula.[75]

Rather than Mwari cult priests dominating the instigation and organisation of
the rising as argued by Ranger, the Ndebele chiefs like Mlugulu Khumalo, Fezela
Khumalo, Dliso Mathema, Sikombo Mguni, Mpotshwana Ndiweni, Manyewu
Ndiweni of Nyamandlovu *isigaba*, Mayeza of the Kalanga, and Nyamanda
Khumalo (the monarch-elect) were active and commanding the fighters in
Matabeleland.[76] The surviving queens of Lobengula, including the influential
Lozikheyi Dlodlo, even joined the rising and she distributed ammunition at the
beginning of the war.[77]

Cobbing is of the opinion that Ranger's emphasis on religion as a central
issue in the organisation of the Ndebele rising was probably due to his being
influenced by the 'witchdoctor' propaganda that was spread by the BSAC, with
its focus on 'mystical fanaticism', including a belief in bullets turning into water
as a result of divine intervention.[78] On the participation of the Shona in the
rising, Cobbing argues that the 'tributary zone' that has always been influenced
by Ndebele developments was mobilised by leading Ndebele *izinduna*, and
some Shona shared the same grievances as the Ndebele against the BSAC

---

[73] Cobbing, 'The absent priesthood', p.63.

[74] NAZ, Historical Manuscript C. 8547, Report of Sir Richard Martin on the Native Administration of the British South Africa Company, 1897.

[75] Cobbing, 'The absent priesthood,' p. 65.

[76] Cobbing, 'The Ndebele under the Khumalos', pp. 80-5. See also NAZ, Historical Manuscript
Lo5/6/2, Report of W. E. Thomas from Nyamandlovu, 18 July 1896.

[77] NAZ Historical Manuscript Lo5/6/6, Gielgud to Chief Native Commissioner, 19 October
1896, who described Lozikheyi as the most dangerous woman because of her active role.

[78] Cobbing, 'The absent priesthood', p. 62.

colonial rule. Considering that the rising extended to the central Shona peoples, Cobbing argues that 'the kingdom was not a direct co-ordinating factor in the part of Mashona country which rose in June, despite the frequent allegations of the Company.'[79] The major Shona groups to rise outside the 'tributary zone' were concentrated mainly in Salisbury, Charter and Hartley districts. The distinguishing feature of these groups was that they had acquired guns from the Portuguese, which they had used to resist Ndebele raids. Cobbing adds two crucial points on the rising in Mashonaland. The first is that about 30 per cent of the Shona who rebelled in 1896-97 had been exposed to severe European pressures. Secondly, he notes that

> The Shona entered the fighting when it appeared the British had been sufficiently weakened for an assertion of independence. At the end of April, Mashonaland had been denuded of white police and soldiers as Colonel Beal's column went to the relief of Bulawayo.[80]

This is an important observation, as it departs from Ranger's idea of a Mwari cult-connected epicentre located in Mashayamombe's chieftaincy in the Mupfure valley as being responsible for the rising spreading to Mashonaland under the influence of Mkwati. Cobbing concluded that the pervasive co-ordinating role of the Mwari cult was illusory, adding that

> A major theme of the risings is disunity and fragmentation, with the Ndebele fighting a civil war, and some important Shona chiefs collaborating with the British South Africa Company. The Ndebele fell short of a united strategy, as to an even greater extent did the Shona: there was certainly no strategic linkage of the two risings.[81]

To Cobbing, religious figures like Mkwati, Kaguvi and Nehanda were local figures subordinate to local Shona political structures rather than supra-ethnic purveyors of a forward-looking millenarianism.[82]

Zvimurenga not *chimurenga*: David Beach on the Shona rising of 1896-97

Like Cobbing, Beach was very critical of the central arguments of Ranger on the Ndebele-Shona rising, particularly with regard to the role of traditional religious leadership as a factor in bringing the Ndebele and the Shona together in a united African national front. Beach introduces two important ideas that

[79] Ibid., p. 77.
[80] Ibid., p. 78.
[81] Ibid., p. 84.
[82] Ibid., p. 84.

run counter to Ranger's thesis. Firstly, the concept of gradual *chindunduma*, the rising spreading with a ripple effect from area to area. For example, Kaguvi and Mashayamombe were drawn to the rising while on a journey to 'get medicine from Mkwati to combat the locust threat to the economy and only then responded to news of Ndebele victories'.[83] Secondly, Beach introduced the idea of *zvimurenga* (plural) rather than *chimurenga* as the proper historical characterisation of what took place in Mashonaland during this period. Starting with Kaguvi and Mashayamombe, Beach argues that they 'were disunited and sometimes rivals rather than joint commanders'.[84] From these two standpoints Beach severely criticises Ranger's thesis, stating that

> The rising was not 'simultaneous', or 'almost simultaneous' even within the limitations of Shona communications and technology, and it had not been predetermined and co-ordinated in the way that had been previously assumed. Consequently, the need for a 'religious' or 'political' overall organisation falls away, and our understanding of the social and political situation among the central Shona in 1896 must undergo a sharp revision.[85]

Beach added the important preliminary events to the rising between 1890 and 1896 that included various forms of Shona resistance to colonial rule, ranging from desertion from work, abandonment of homes in the face of tax and labour demands, and cattle-maiming, etc. Based on this approach Beach provides a new chronological account of the rising. He provides complex details of Shona resistance, beginning with Charter district where, in 1895, Native Department police collecting taxes were attacked by gunfire and sjambokked by the Njanja, putting the whole central Shona country into an 'exceptionally tense state' portending full-scale war between March and June 1896. This tense atmosphere was characterised by unco-ordinated and isolated attacks on the colonial police, a refusal to pay tax, and threats of violence.[86] Locust attacks on crops in the summer of 1895/6 created a real threat of the feared *shangwa* among the Shona and increased tension. To Beach, the Shona rising of 1896-97 'had been a local war fought by each ruler in his territory – until he was driven out of it.'[87] Beach concluded: 'In short, the history of the 1896 central Shona

---

[83] Beach, 'Review Article: *Revolt in Southern Rhodesia*', p. 107.
[84] Ibid., p. 107.
[85] D. N. Beach, '"Chimurenga": The Shona Rising of 1896-97', *Journal of African History*, 20(3), 1979, p. 401.
[86] Ibid., pp. 403-4.
[87] Ibid., p. 416.

chimurenga promises to be the history of many local *zvimurenga* with their similarities, differences and connexions – or lack of them.'[88]

In view of the manner in which both the Ndebele and the Shona were eventually defeated by the white settlers, it makes sense to accept Cobbing's and Beach's issues of disunity rather than unity in the Ndebele-Shona uprising. This is confirmed by the Ndebele making a separate settlement with the whites at Matopos during the course of the Shona rising. Superior technology played a major role in the defeat of the rising, as did disunity among the Africans.

By the 1990s Beach was still criticising 'nationalist'-inspired narrations of history to the extent of portraying Mbuya Nehanda, a revered spirit medium within nationalist circles, as an ordinary 'innocent woman, unjustly accused'.[89] What Beach wrote about Nehanda qualifies as 'unpatriotic' history, although ironically it stands in opposition to his portrayal of Mapondera as a hero.[90] Ranger had not emphasised the role of the latter in the politics of the 1890s. Until his untimely death in 1998, Beach continued to write what increasingly sounded like dynastic histories of Mashonaland; a pre-colonial history of Zimbabwe dominated by 'tribal' stories of witchcraft, succession disputes, inter- and intra-ethnic hatreds, migrations, inter-marriages, kinships and *mutupo* (clan names).[91]

Beach's and Cobbing's revisionist criticisms of Ranger advanced our understanding of what they termed 'resisters' and 'collaborators' in the wars of 1896 and 1897. In Matabeleland, Gampu Sithole emerged as a leading 'collaborator' who enabled the white relief forces' entry to help their colleagues besieged by the Ndebele forces inside the Bulawayo laager. One of the weaknesses of the historiography of the Ndebele-Shona resistance of 1896-97 is that it remains interpreted mainly from the perspective of those considered as patriots; no one has attempted to understand the logic of those who fought on the 'side' of the whites. There is need for further fresh research into local conditions and circumstances that made Africans fight on different sides in a seemingly 'white-black conflagration'.

---

[88] Ibid., p. 419.

[89] The writings of Beach seemed to have been aimed at subverting African heroism. This agenda was openly manifest in D. N. Beach, 'An innocent woman, unjustly accused: Charwe, medium of the Nehanda Mhondoro spirit and the 1896-1897 Shona rising in Zimbabwe', *History in Africa*, 25, 1998, 27-54.

[90] D. N. Beach, *Mapondera: Heroism and History in Northern Zimbabwe, 1840-1904* (Gweru: Mambo Press, 1989).

[91] Beach, *The Shona and Zimbabwe*; D. N. Beach, *A Zimbabwean Past* (Gweru: Mambo Press, 1994).

What is beyond doubt is that Ranger's interpretation flourished in the popular imagination of Zimbabweans faster than the revisionist interpretations of the Ndebele-Shona uprising. Zimbabwean history is still permeated by a nationalist perspective, and Ranger's perspectives are comfortably 'in synch' with the rendition of Zimbabwean history into successive *chimurengas*. The 1896-97 rising constitutes the First Chimurenga, the nationalist liberation struggle of the 1960s and 1970s was the Second Chimurenga, and the controversial Fast Track land reform programme of 2000s was first defined as the Third Chimurenga by ZANU(PF).

The early Rhodesian colonial state

The occupation of Mashonaland and Matabeleland constituted the required 'right of conquest' to justify white rule over the African people. The first issue to be settled was the name for the newly found colony. Cecil John Rhodes had preferred 'Zambesia'. Leander Starr Jameson suggested 'Charterland'. But these two names did not gain sway. Instead, the first newspaper to be found in Salisbury (now Harare) in 1892 called itself the *Rhodesia Herald*. It was in May 1895 that the BSAC officially adopted the name Rhodesia, but it was not recognised by the British government until the Southern Rhodesia Order-in-Council of 1898.[92] The 1898 Order-in-Council became the governing instrument of Rhodesia until the time of Responsible Government in 1923. It was a compromise between imperial and BSAC interests.[93] What was being constructed was a settler colony whose major characteristics, as in Australia and Canada, were land seizures, the arrival of a settler population, segregated internal colonial governance, and political and economic privileges for the white community.[94] Caroline Elkins and Susan Pedersen correctly noted that settler colonialism was marked by ongoing negotiation and struggle among four key groups – an 'imperial metropolis' where sovereignty formally resided, a 'local administration charged with maintaining order and authority, an indigenous population significant enough in size and tenacity to make its presence felt and an often demanding and well-connected settler community' – that were expecting to reap dividends from their domination of the African population.[95]

The major task of the BSAC administration was to construct a stable colonial

[92] Blake, *A History of Rhodesia*, p. 114.

[93] C. Palley, *The Constitutional History and Law of Southern Rhodesia, 1898-1965* (Oxford: Oxford University Press, 1966), pp. 10-16.

[94] Russell, 'Introduction', pp. i-x.

[95] C. Elkins and S. Pedersen, 'Introduction: Settler colonialism: A concept and its uses', in C. Elkins and S. Pedersen (eds.), *Settler Colonialism in the Twentieth Century: Projects, Practices, Legacies* (New York: Routledge, 2005), p. 4.

form of government to satisfy imperial designs and the local demands of the settler population without provoking further violent African resistance. The BSAC state was a very weak and vulnerable colonial formation. It was compromised by staffing issues, threats of African resistance, remote-control from London and by shareholders, and was forced to depend on very complex alliances with local African authorities and a rather impatient and disgruntled white population.[96] For the BSAC administration to establish colonial hegemony, it had to fulfil many tasks, quickly learning local languages, and understanding indigenous cultures and the broader African worldview over which it had to inscribe its hegemony. Diana Jeater had this to say about the difficulties of creating colonial hegemony in Africa in general:

> Hegemonic projects in a colonial context normally required
> the participation of a ruling class within the colonised society,
> supporting the benefits of capitalist enterprise and the values of
> investment in industry, rationalism, and progress. Such indigenous
> capitalist classes were thin on the ground in nineteenth-century
> central Africa.[97]

Despite this weakness the BSAC began to construct a colonial state permeated by a 'caste' division between the settler (white Rhodesians) and the indigene (Ndebele and Shona). This 'caste' division proceeded through the construction of a separation of races in the economy, the political system and law. At an economic and political level, this process manifested itself in terms of privileging the rights of whites over land and the denial to Africans of the right to participate in the evolving political system. From the beginning, race and racial difference were articulated and institutionalised within the colonial state institutions. The net effect of this was that citizenship was racialised and the population of Rhodesia bifurcated into 'citizens and subjects'.[98] The population was delineated into racial and ethnic groups of Europeans, Asians and Coloureds, and Natives. Natives were further bifurcated into 'aboriginal natives' and 'colonial natives'; the 'Mashona natives' and the 'Matabele natives'.[99]

The settlers had a clear idea of what they wanted to construct but had no clear idea of how to achieve it. Every step they took had to take into account

[96] Jeater, *Law, Language and Science*, p. 4.
[97] Ibid.
[98] M. Mamdani, *Citizen and Subject: Contemporary Africa and the Legacy of Late Colonialism*, (Princeton: Princeton University Press, 2006); R. Holland, 'Introduction', in R. Holland (ed.), *Emergencies and Disorder in the European Empires after 1945* (London: Frank Cass, 1994), pp. 210-19.
[99] Southern Rhodesia, *Statute Law of Southern Rhodesia: Volume 7* (Salisbury: Government Printer, 1963).

the reactions of the Ndebele and the Shona, who were not only factored in as a source of cheap labour but also as potential enemies who could easily react against the foreign interventions into their lives.[100] Thus turning the Ndebele and the Shona into a productive labour force was a process rather than an event. Throughout its life, the BSAC state was governed in an *ad hoc* manner through police patrols and patriarchal Native Commissioners tasked to construct a local government. In addition to the 'pacification' of pockets of resistance, the early colonial state had to buy the loyalty of Ndebele chiefs to use them in local governance. This included returning some looted cattle, including to those who had fought fiercely against the settlers in 1896.[101] Throughout his last years, from 1898 to 1902, Rhodes masqueraded as a peace-maker at the Matopos Indaba, making promises to the Ndebele that the colonisers would lay down their arms, resulting in some Ndebele describing him as *umlamlankuzi* (one who separated fighting bulls).[102]

Fig. 2.2: Ndebele chiefs and Native Police, Matabeleland.

[*Source:* National Archives of Zimbabwe]

[100] A. J. Wills, *An Introduction to the History of Central Africa* (Oxford: Oxford University Press, 3rd. edn., 1973), p. 225.

[101] Ibid.

[102] S. J. Ndlovu-Gatsheni, 'Grappling with the ambiguities of the colonial encounter and the nationalist paradigm in Zimbabwe', *Association of Concerned African Scholars (ACAS) Bulletin: Special Issue on Race in Africa – Past and Present*, 72, 2005/2006, pp. 14-20. Available at <http://acas.prairienet.org/bulletin/bull72-04-Ndlovu-Gatsheni.html>; Ndlovu-Gatsheni, 'Re-thinking the colonial encounter in Zimbabwe', pp. 177-81.

Allison K. Shutt wrote that the 'challenge was to govern with creative authority. This proved more difficult than the political and military power of settlers would suggest.'[103] The broader search for a cheaper but exploitative mode of governing Africans became known as the 'native question'. The 'native question' entailed the definition and fashioning of a relationship between white settlers and indigenous people and the consequent problem of the equality and inequality of races within a colonial society. As early as 23 June 1887, Rhodes had told the Cape Parliament that his colonial policy was one of treating Africans a 'subject race' that lived under pass laws and peace preservation acts. Rhodes urged white settlers to 'be lords over' Africans 'as long as they continue in a state of barbarism and communal tenure'. He even prescribed that Africans were not to be allowed to drink liquor.[104]

The philosophy underlying white conceptions and thinking on the 'native question' was permeated by what Ronald Weitzer termed a settler 'superordinate position vis-à-vis native inhabitants'.[105] In the earlier settler colonies in America and Australia, the 'native question' was settled through 'final solutions' involving outright elimination and forcible displacement to open the way for the establishment of settler communities.[106] In Zimbabwe, the settlers went for what Mahmood Mamdani termed the bifurcation of the colonial state. In this scheme of things, 'direct rule' took the form of urban civil power that excluded Africans from civil liberties and freedoms. Africans were confined to 'indirect rule' premised on what was considered to be African customary order.[107] While Mamdani provides a picture of a neatly dichotomised bifurcation of the colonial state into 'citizens' and 'subjects', the evidence from the Ndebele and Shona interactions with the early settlers indicates a contested boundary that was porous and exploitable by Africans as well as whites. The early colonial state introduced many measures in its endeavour to create a racially bifurcated colony, dotted with white cities.

---

[103] A. K. Shutt, '"The natives are getting out of hand": Legislating manners, insolence and contemptuous behaviour in Southern Rhodesia c.1910-1963', *Journal of Southern African Studies*, 33(3), 2007, p. 655.

[104] S. Samkange, *What Rhodes Really Said About Africans* (Harare: Zimbabwe Publishing House, 1982), pp. 15-25.

[105] R. Weitzer, *Transforming Settler States: Communal Conflict and Internal Security in Northern Ireland and Zimbabwe* (Berkeley and Los Angeles: University of California Press, 1990), p. 25.

[106] 'Final solution' includes individual and genocidal killings of indigenous people such as Native Americans and Australian Aborigines.

[107] M. Mamdani, *Citizen and Subject: Contemporary Africa and the Legacy of Late Colonialism* (Princeton: Princeton University Press, 1996). p. 18.

Early urbanisation and urban struggles

Raftopoulos and Yoshikuni have rightly characterised early urban colonial centres as 'sites of struggle'.[108] The forts established by the Pioneer Column – Fort Tuli, Fort Victoria, Fort Charter and Fort Salisbury – became nurseries of colonial towns. As such, early urban settlements had characteristics of expanding 'settler laagers' permeated by surveillance as well as the colonial politics of control, segregation and exploitation.[109] Another feature of early urban development was the continued interactions of town and country. This rural-urban connection was facilitated by the movement of people, flows of money, the exchange of goods, and the circulation of ideas and values. This is a theme that Yoshikuni dealt with effectively in his impressive studies of urban social history.[110]

The key tension that made urban settlements 'sites of struggle' lay between the racial pressures that urban areas be 'white cities' and the imperatives of using cheap African labour. The net effect of this was a myriad of often conflicting problems that were accentuated by the mapping of urban areas along racial, class, ethnic and gender lines. [111] It was within this terrain that such problems as miscegenation and inter-racial sexualities emerged and were criminalised.

Criminalisation of inter-racial sexualities

The majority of the early white settler population was young and male, which had implications for the evolution of sexual politics in the colony. By as early as March 1895, there were 1,329 white men and 208 white women in Bulawayo. In Salisbury, by November 1897, there were 505 white men and 134 white women.[112] Robert Blake noted that this imbalance was almost bound to cause trouble, as white men sought sexual satisfaction (forced or voluntary) among the indigenous population.[113] Both Ndebele and Shona complained about the harassment and rape of women by white police officers.[114]

---

[108] B. Raftopoulos and T. Yoshikuni (eds.), *Sites of Struggle: Essays in Zimbabwe's Urban History*, (Harare: Weaver Press, 1999).

[109] Ibid., p. 3.

[110] T. Yoshikuni, 'Notes on the influence of town-country relations on African urban history, before 1957: Experiences of Salisbury and Bulawayo', in Raftopoulos and Yoshikuni (eds.), *Sites of Struggle*, pp. 113-28. This theme is further developed in Yoshikuni's book, *African Urban Experiences in Colonial Zimbabwe: A Social History of Harare Before 1925* (Harare: Weaver Press, 2007).

[111] Ibid.

[112] B. A. Cosmin, 'The Pioneer Community of Salisbury in November 1897', *Rhodesian History*, 2, 1971, pp. 25-37.

[113] Blake, *A History of Rhodesia*, p. 119.

[114] Chief Makoni complained to the Anglican missionary, Frank Edwards, that there were white raiders who abused Shona women: NAZ Historical Manuscript WE3/2/5, Weale's Reminiscences.

The early Rhodesian state wanted to avoid what had happened at the Cape Colony, where most of the early Dutch settlers developed illicit sexual unions with Khoisan and Malay slaves imported to supply cheap labour. These unions created a large Coloured community in Cape Town. The few pioneer white women regarded sexual relations between white men and black women with contempt if not jealousy. At a broader level, miscegenation was a threat to the philosophy of separate development.[115] Since early Rhodesian society was male-dominated, white males could not tolerate any sexual relationship between white women and black men. They quickly criminalised such relationships, arguing that there was no excuse for its existence, insisting that such sexual encounters could only occur as a result of *force majeure* by black men or immorality on the part of white women. [116]

In 1903 the colonial Legislative Council approved two measures that governed issues of sexual relations between black and white races. One was the Immorality Suppression Ordinance, which made extra-marital sexual intercourse between a black man and a white woman illegal. The punishment was five years with hard labour for the black man and two years for the white woman. However, there was no corresponding penalty for a white man found guilty of having sexual relations with a black woman. The Rhodesia Women's League fought to amend the ordinance but failed.[117] In the end, white men retained the right to have affairs with black women, as it was never made illegal. But white women tried to prevent such relationships from developing by, for example, making sure that domestic servants were African men rather than women.[118] The ordinance prohibiting sexual affairs between black men and white women was immediately followed by another, which imposed the death penalty for attempted rape.[119] This obsession with protecting white women from being sexually attacked by black men became known as the 'black peril'.[120]

The social history of the early colonial state has attracted interest in recent years. Shutt has demonstrated that some Africans adopted the strategy of

---

[115] S. J. Ndlovu-Gatsheni, 'African Criminality in Southern Rhodesia, 1900-1923' (MA thesis, University of Zimbabwe, 1995).

[116] Blake, *A History of Rhodesia*, p. 158.

[117] *Rhodesia Herald*, 20 June 1913.

[118] Ndlovu-Gatsheni, 'African Criminality', pp. 10-15.

[119] This ordinance did not discriminate between black and white, but it was based on the assumption that black men would try to rape white women since they worked as domestic servants. If the rape was committed by a white man, it was taken lightly and no sentence of death or imprisonment was ever passed. But many black men suffered under this law. Numerous black men were charged on the thinnest evidence with the rape or attempted rape of white women.

[120] Ndlovu-Gatsheni, 'African Criminality', pp. 16-22.

'insolence' to 'disrupt the image of natural and just domination that settlers and their government projected'.[121] Timothy Burke, Michael West and other scholars have written on etiquette, manners and respectability as social means used by early whites to separate themselves from Africans.[122] Legislation such as the Southern Rhodesia Native Regulations of 1910, the Native Affairs Act (1927) and the Masters and Servants Act (1901) were introduced to enable colonial officials to police civility, and to protect the racial boundaries and settler prestige that was assumed to be threatened by insolent Africans.[123]

Dispossession and forcible proletarianisation

In *Chibaro: African Mine Labour in Southern Rhodesia*, Charles van Onselen analysed how the Ndebele and the Shona were forced to provide labour to the mining sector. Such means included the restriction of Africans' access to land in order to undercut peasant agricultural production and increasing taxation as a way to force Africans to sell their labour cheaply to mine-owners.[124] Van Onselen added that there were two fundamental aims of the mining sector during early colonial period: output maximisation and cost minimisation. The latter had to be achieved by ensuring that African workers received starvation wages. In addition, forced labour was built into the exploitative Masters and Servants Ordinance under which labour contracts were defined. What became known as *isibalo* (Ndebele) or *chibaro* (Shona) referred to the system of forced recruitment of African people, who were required to sign long work contracts that obliged them to remain under the compound conditions at their place of work. The terms *isibalo* or *chibaro* implied a form of slavery that was practised by the Rhodesia Native Labour Bureau.[125] Van Onselen commented that

> Through changes in the structure of the political economy between
> 1903 and 1912 Ndebele and Shona tribesman were becoming
> increasingly proletarianised. The structural determinants of the

[121] Shutt, '"The natives are getting out of hand"', pp. 653-4.

[122] T. Burke, *Lifebouy Men, Lux Women* (Durham, NC: Duke University Press, 1996), pp. 99-104; M. O. West, *The Rise of an African Middle Class: Colonial Zimbabwe, 1898-1965* (Bloomington: Indiana University Press, 2002); C. Summers, *Colonial Lessons* (Portsmouth: NH, Heinemann, 2002); D. Kennedy, *Islands of White: Settler Society and Culture in Kenya and Southern Rhodesia, 1890-1939* (Durham, NC: Duke University Press, 1987).

[123] Shutt, '"The natives are getting out of hand"', p. 655. See also Alison K. Shutt, 'The settlers' cattle complex: The etiquette of culling cattle in colonial Zimbabwe, 1938', *Journal of African History*, 43(2), 2002, pp. 263-86.

[124] C. van Onselen, *Chibaro: African Mine Labour in Southern Rhodesia, 1900-1933* (London: Pluto Press, 1976), p. 91.

[125] G. N. Burden, *Nyasaland Native Labour in Southern Rhodesia* (Salisbury: [n.p.], 1938).

process of proletarianisation, such as access to land, taxation and the inroads made by an increasingly competitive white commercial agricultural industry, were supplemented by the techniques used by mine managers to produce these features.[126]

A combined deployment of such legislation as the Masters and Servants Ordinance, the Pass Laws, the Native Regulations Ordinance provided mine-owners with semi-feudal powers over the lives of African labourers that were close to those of the slave-owners of the nineteenth century.[127] The development of both white agricultural and mining sectors in Rhodesia took the form of undermining the Africans' means of livelihood. Only when Africans had been dispossessed of their land and cattle would they depend on selling their labour cheaply to the mines and farms. The 1920s and 1930s witnessed the settler colonial state becoming increasingly interventionist on behalf of white settlers but against the interests of Africans. As noted by Phimister, the wanton under-cutting of African peasant production was sowing the seeds of underdevelopment in the reserves of Rhodesia.[128] Land expropriation was part of a broader strategy of creating property-less natives dependent on selling their labour. The unsteady development of white commercial agriculture was a tale of destruction of African peasant agriculture, a tale of the monetisation of the economy, a tale of dispossession and forced proletarianisation.

Spatial segregation and the roots of land problems

The early white settlers made clear drives for the accumulation of wealth ahead of the indigenous black people. Besides looting cattle in a primitive accumulation style and levying taxes on Africans, the BSAC government, as well the successor Responsible Government that came to power in 1923, made open moves to parcel out land to white settlers.[129]

As early as 1894, the British government announced the appointment of a Land Commission to deal with issues of Ndebele settlement following the defeat of the Ndebele in the Anglo-Ndebele War of 1893. That same year the British government promulgated an Order-in-Council which put pressure on

---

[126] Van Onselen, *Chibaro*, p. 100.

[127] D. G. Clarke, *Contract Workers and Underdevelopment in Rhodesia* (Gwelo: Mambo Press, 1974); D. G. Clarke, 'Settler ideology and the African underdevelopment in post-war Rhodesia', *Rhodesia Journal of Economics*, 8(1), 1974, pp. 17-38.

[128] I. R. Phimister, 'Peasant production and underdevelopment in Southern Rhodesia, 1890-1914', *African Affairs*, 73(291), 1974, pp. 217-28; J. M. Mackenzie, 'Colonial labour in the chartered company period', *Rhodesian History*, 1, 1970, pp. 43-58.

[129] R. H. Palmer, *Aspects of Rhodesian Land Policy, 1890-1936* (Salisbury: Central Africa Historical Association, Local Series No. 22, 1968), pp. 10-21.

the BSAC to assign Africans land sufficient for their occupation and suitable for agriculture.[130] The first reserves for Africans were designated in 1894 by the BSAC, and these were the arid Gwai and Shangani areas. Even the British Deputy Commissioner, Sir Richard Martin, found these reserves to be 'badly watered, sandy and unfit for settlement'.[131] Prior to the conquest, the Ndebele occupied 21 million hectares, but by 1894 they had been pushed into only two reserves that measured one million hectares. The seeds for future land struggles were sown between the white settler community and the Ndebele and the Shona, and their resonance rebounded through the nationalist phase and into the post-colonial period.

By 1905, the BSAC had created about 60 reserves that occupied only 22 per cent of the new colony; the settler community appropriated the bulk of the land for themselves. In 1907, for example, the BSAC established its first Agricultural Research Station near Salisbury.[132] These initiatives were followed in 1914 by the establishment of a Reserves Commission with the mandate to complete the delimitation of the reserves. By 1922, a year before Responsible Government, 64 per cent of all Africans were required to live in reserves.[133] Moreover, if land expropriations were not enough to push people into formal employment, the Hut Tax introduced in the 1890s was doubled in 1904.

Initiatives for total spatial segregation were formalised with the appointment in 1924 of the Morris Carter Commission to inquire into views about land segregation. Its conclusions were that the overwhelming majority of Africans expressed a desire for land segregation.[134] The recommendations of the Commission were incorporated into the Land Apportionment Bill that sought to legalise land segregation. The Bill became an Act in 1930, and its provisions were implemented in 1931. Under this Act land was divided into European Areas, Native Reserves, Native Purchase Areas and Forest Areas; there were also about seven million hectares of 'unassigned land'. Native Reserves were increased to 98 and this was considered to be adequate for the needs of a fast-growing African population.[135]

Besides legally instituting racial segregation, the Land Apportionment Act introduced differential tenure categories for the apportioned land areas. In European areas, land was considered private property and was accompanied

[130] V. Moyana, *The Political Economy of Land in Zimbabwe* (Gweru: Mambo Press, 2nd. edn., 2002), p. 4.

[131] Ibid., p. 2.

[132] Phimister, *An Economic and Social History of Zimbabwe*, p. 68.

[133] Ibid., p. 67.

[134] Ndlovu-Gatsheni, 'Re-thinking the colonial encounter in Zimbabwe', pp. 188-90.

[135] Moyana, *The Political Economy of Land*, p. 43.

by title deeds, whereas in the Native Reserves, land was held under what was termed 'communal tenure' without title deeds. Africans were granted usufruct rights to use specific land for cultivation, building homesteads, and grazing cattle as part of communal property. African chiefs were given rights to allocate land under the supervision of Native Commissioners.[136]

Native Purchase Areas were kept as 'middle' land between the races within which Africans with money could purchase land. A small African rural middle class began to purchase this land, which was adjacent to Native Reserves but offered personal privacy. Native Purchase Areas were unfortunately characterised by poor-quality soils.[137] When the Great Depression of the 1930s hit the nascent settler economy, the government took drastic measures to curtail African peasant agriculture that had been successfully competing with the emerging settler commercial agriculture. These measures included the enactment of the Maize Control Act, the Cattle Levy Act, the Reserve Pool Act, the Market Stabilisation Act and a whole array of Marketing Boards, and the Farmers' Debt Adjustment Act – all of which were introduced in quick succession between 1930 and 1937.[138] The Maize Control Act of 1931 resulted in the establishment of a state-run marketing board that directly regulated sales of maize within Rhodesia and to foreign markets. By 1934, through an amendment to the Maize Control Act, European farmers were allocated 80 per cent of the domestic market and prices for maize produced by Africans were low. These measures had the desired consequences of forcing Africans to participate in wage labour market.[139]

When African agricultural production dropped, the colonial state blamed poor farming methods on the part of Africans instead of taking blame for deliberately destroying peasant agriculture. Instead of increasing land allocated to the Reserves, the colonial state introduced some modernisation initiatives. These included opening two government schools at Domboshawa in Mashonaland and Tjolotjolo (Tsholotsho) in Matabeleland where modern methods of farming

[136] This is a clear case of the 'invention of tradition' as the colonial state was of the belief that communal tenure accorded with African traditional life and customary law. See T. Ranger, 'The invention of tradition in colonial Africa', in E. Hobsbawn and T. Ranger (eds.), *The Invention of Tradition* (Cambridge: Cambridge University Press, 1983), pp. 211-62; T. Ranger, 'The invention of tradition revisited: The case of colonial Africa', in T. Ranger and O. Vaughan (eds.), *Legitimacy and the State in Twentieth-century Africa* (London: Macmillan, 1993).

[137] S. Moyo, *The Land Question in Zimbabwe* (Harare: SAPES Books, 1988); T. O. Ranger, *Peasant Consciousness and Guerrilla War in Zimbabwe* (Harare: Zimbabwe Publishing House, 1988); J. Alexander, J. McGregor and T. Ranger, *Violence and Memory: One Hundred Years in the Dark Forests of Matabeleland* (Harare: Weaver Press, 2000).

[138] Phimister, *An Economic and Social History of Zimbabwe*, pp. 171-218.

[139] Robin Palmer, *Land and Racial Domination in Rhodesia* (London: Heinemann, 1977), p. 213.

were taught. A former American missionary, E. D. Alvord, became one of the leading agriculturalists responsible for teaching Africans new farming methods, including the use of fertiliser and improved seeds.[140] Of course, new skills in farming were required but what was needed more was adequate fertile land for Africans to increase their food production. The difficulties created by early colonialism provoked contestations from the African population.

African responses to early colonisation

Terence Ranger's *African Voice in Southern Rhodesia* provided the first comprehensive study of the African protest movements that emerged in the aftermath of the Ndebele-Shona Risings of 1896-97.[141] He documented and read all the religious, agrarian, political, labour and social agitation that took place during the early colonial period as an aspect of African resistance to colonisation. He presented his theory of 'domination and resistance' in the 1960s, which included such concepts as primary and secondary resistance.[142] However, recent scholarship has shown that African responses to early colonisation were an admixture of complicity, resistance and other reactions that do not fit easily into this paradigm, which ignores issues of mimicry, syncretism, hybridities, negotiations and alienations that were also central within encounters between the colonised and the colonisers.[143] The works of post-colonial theorists have succeeded in reorienting and reinvigorating imperial and colonial encounters, taking them in new directions that conventional historiography has hardly began to consider.[144] Frederick Cooper used insights from post-colonial theorists to deal with questions of how colonial power was constructed and deployed, how the Africans engaged, contested, deflected and appropriated this same power to push forward their own various agendas.[145]

[140] M. Drinkwater, 'Technical development and peasant impoverishment: Land use policy in Zimbabwe's Midlands province', *Journal of Southern African Studies*, 15(2), 1989, pp. 287-305.

[141] T. O Ranger, *The African Voice in Southern Rhodesia, 1898-1930* (London: Heinemann, 1970).

[142] Ranger, 'Connexions between "primary resistance" movements'.

[143] F. Cooper, 'Conflict and connection', pp. 20-45; Ndlovu-Gatsheni, 'Re-thinking the colonial encounter in Zimbabwe', pp. 173-91. See also Ndlovu-Gatsheni, 'Grappling with the ambiguities of the colonial encounter', pp. 14-20.

[144] Leading post-colonial theorists include H. K. Bhabha, *The Location of Culture* (London: Routledge, 2nd. edn., 2004); E. Said, *Orientalism* (London: Routledge, 1978); G. Spivak, 'Can the subaltern speak?', in P. Williams and L. Chrisman, (eds), *Colonial Discourses and Post-Colonial Theory: A Reader* (New York: Columbia University Press, 1994), pp. 66-111; A. Mbembe, *On the Postcolony* (Berkeley and Los Angeles: University of California Press, 2001).

[145] Cooper, 'Conflict and Connection', pp. 24-5.

Thus, beneath what Ranger called the 'African voice' subsisted complex African reactions and responses ranging widely from outright resistance to taking full part in the colonial economy as labourers; deploying pre-colonial doctrines of political legitimacy, entitlement and inheritance to contesting colonial dispossession; imbibing colonial claims of civility and fighting for inclusion in the sphere of liberal rights and democracy that were a preserve of white settlers. Others intensified the struggle to critique the colonial state and expose its iniquities and hypocrisy using imperial notions of a civilising standard together with Christian ideologies that emphasised equality. When the colonial state and mainstream European churches remained unresponsive, some African Christians broke away to develop African Christianity, which itself became a haven for the critical African imaginations of freedom.[146] Robert Blake was right when he wrote that 'The African voice in the country, dumb since the rebellions, began in the early 1920s to become audible, but the sound was faint and far away, the message confusing and obscure.'[147]

The critical voice came from the traditional elites of Matabeleland, including the sons of Lobengula. This was made possible by the fact that Ndebele aristocracy had not been altogether crushed, as happened in Mashonaland. Lobengula's eldest surviving son, Nyamanda Khumalo, together with certain chiefs reacted to colonisation by forming the Matabele Home Movement. Ideologically, this movement was largely backward-looking, justifying its claims and demands on the basis of Ndebele pre-colonial ideas of rights, legitimacy and entitlements to land and cattle.[148] However, Nyamanda and his group used modern forms of protest, including deputations and written petitions. What the Matabele Home Movement wanted was a form of protectorate status for the Ndebele under the direct supervision of the British Crown. They were inspired by the protectorate arrangements that Khama of Bechuanaland (Botswana), Lewanika of Barotseland (Zambia) and Moshweshwe of Basutoland (Lesotho) were granted. In 1919, they petitioned the Crown for the return of alienated Ndebele land to the family of King Lobengula in trust for the Ndebele community according to Ndebele customs and traditions.[149] Despite some contradictions and ambiguities manifest in Nyamanda's fight for Ndebele land, the return of King Lobengula's cattle and the restoration of Ndebele monarchy, the Movement remained one of the earliest representatives of Ndebele concerns and aspirations at a time when

---

[146] Ndlovu-Gatsheni, 'Re-thinking the colonial encounter in Zimbabwe', pp. 173-91.
[147] Blake, *A History of Rhodesia*, p. 196.
[148] Ndlovu-Gatsheni, 'Re-thinking the colonial encounter in Zimbabwe', pp. 183-4.
[149] NAZ, N3/18/10 Nyamanda's Land Protests.

the colonial state expected acquiescence from Africans.[150] Nyamanda managed to secure the support of the South African Native African Congress, formed in 1912, and the Aborigines Protection Society in Great Britain.

By 1923, African politics had become more complex to the extent that a national organisation called Southern Rhodesia Bantu Voters' Association (SRBVA) was formed in Gwelo (now Gweru). Its formation coincided with the Responsible Government referendum. Unlike the Matabele Home Movement, the SRBVA was informed by modernist issues of African voting rights. Its immediate task was to get Africans onto the electoral register to bargain votes for Responsible Government in the hope of some concessions to African demands.[151] Its founder was Abraham Twala, who had come from South Africa and was a teacher by profession. Its membership and leadership included what one would call elite Ndebele and Shona men and women. But, like all early African organisations, it developed into a bizarre mixture of various traditions including Fingo modernist politics, Bulawayo township tradition, Ethiopianism, and the Matabele Home Movement.[152] Its modernism was even demonstrated by its having a Native Women's League, and it ended up being led by a woman, Martha Ngano, an electrifying speaker and determined politician who represented African opinion before the Morris Carter Commission.[153]

In ideological terms, the SRBVA remained conservative, fighting mainly for the right to full participation in the economic and political life of the colony for those Africans able to compete with Europeans. For instance, in its 1924 annual conference, it bought into the imperial propaganda of a British political system that was based on justice, freedom and commerce, proclaiming its desire to come under magistrates and not Native Commissioners.[154] On many occasions, the SRBVA manifested its elitist origin and tendencies by uncritically embracing colonial and imperial ideologies of civilisation to the extent of criticising some Africans as old-fashioned, contradicting its drive for popular African support. It scorned those Africans that sought the improvement of Africans outside the bounds of open competition.[155]

---

[150] R. S. Roberts, 'Traditional paramountcy and modern politics in Matabeleland: The end of the Lobengula royal family – and of Ndebele particularism?', *Heritage of Zimbabwe*, 24, 2004, pp. 4-38.

[151] Blake, *A History of Rhodesia*, p. 197.

[152] Ndlovu-Gatsheni, 'Re-thinking the colonial encounter in Zimbabwe', p. 189.

[153] Ranger, *The African Voice*, pp. 45-50.

[154] *Rhodesia Herald*, 3 Feb. 1928.

[155] S. Thornton, 'The struggle for profit and participation by an emerging petty-bourgeoisie in Bulawayo, 1893-1933', in Raftopoulos and Yoshikuni, *Sites of Struggle*, p. 36.

The SRBVA advocated individual ownership of property and the unlimited right of Africans to buy land. It had a vibrant Women's League that voiced the concerns of urban African women who had remained an unwelcome constituency in European cities. The Women's League concerned itself with the question of beer-brewing and, in 1934, organised a successful boycott of the beer hall when women were being prosecuted for brewing beer in the Location of Bulawayo.[156] Its leadership was composed of what Stephen Thornton correctly terms 'emerging petty-bourgeoisie'.[157] The majority of the members of the SRBVA were those few Africans who had achieved the qualification to vote and a few others who aspired to the right to vote.

Another significant urban political phenomenon was the extension of the South African Industrial and Commercial Workers Union into Rhodesia in 1927 by Clements Kadalie, who came from Nyasaland (Malawi). It took advantage of the Shamva mine strike – the first serious instance of African workers' strike action in Rhodesia – to announce its presence.[158] Worker politics and trade unionism were weakened by the simple fact that there were no permanent workers with a mature worker consciousness in the 1920s. Africans kept on moving between the mines, farms and their rural homes. What was developing was a blend of rural and urban grievances, coalescing into one common protest movement.[159]

A third phenomenon was that of African religious responses to early colonisation. Many of those who had believed or hoped that Mwari and the mountain cults were powerful and took their advice seriously were disappointed when the 1896-97 risings were crushed by the Europeans. Christian missionaries took advantage of the situation in Matabeleland and Mashonaland to introduce Christianity and the Christian God as the only hope for Africans. Indeed, many Africans flocked to the churches, attracted by spaces for critical imagination and a doctrine of the equality of all human beings before God.[160] Some missionaries, like John White of the Methodist Church, became openly critical of colonial

---

[156] NAZ File S138/22, Sergeant Clark to Assistant Superintendent, CID, Salisbury, 28 Oct. 1929.

[157] Ibid., p. 36. See also NAZ File S138/22, Detective Sergeant Chubbock to Chief Superintendent, CID, Bulawayo, 28 Oct. 1928.

[158] I. Phimister, 'The Shamva Mine strike of 1927: An emerging African proletariat', *Rhodesian History*, 2, 1971, pp. 65-88; B. Raftopolous and I. Phimister (eds.), *Keep on Knocking: A History of the Labour Movement in Zimbabwe, 1900-1997* (Harare: Baobab Books, 1997).

[159] Ndlovu-Gatsheni, 'Re-thinking the colonial encounter', pp. 189-90.

[160] T. O. Ranger, 'Early History of Independency in Southern Rhodesia', in W. Watt (ed.), *Religion in Africa* (London: University of Edinburgh, 1964).

abuses of Africans and in the process made a professed ideology of a 'Christian Civilising Mission'.[161] Christianity became a promising emancipatory religion in the aftermath of the risings.

However, the failure of Christian missionaries to mitigate the impact of early colonisation, together with the arrogance of some missionaries, led to the growth of African independent churches; the Christian solution was now appropriated to advance African issues. The first independent churches to emerge included M. D. Makgatho's American Episcopal Church. Makgatho was a Sotho who came to Rhodesia in 1890 and bought a plot at Riverside in 1904. He was a successful farmer as well as a minister of religion. His independent church was formed in 1904 and drew its ideology from Black-American struggles against racism.[162] It was followed by the establishment of the African Home Mission in 1914 by P. S. Ngwenya and later by the Christian Catholic Apostolic Church in Zion. These independent churches emphasised Holy Spirit possession, healing and prophecy, aspects of Christianity considered politically dangerous by the colonial state, which believed that, through possession, Zionist men and women could spread propaganda.[163]

Independent churches represented what I call 'dissenting Christianity' and offered a haven to the Ndebele and Shona who were still trying to make sense of their previous world as well as the new one.[164] Colonial authorities refused to grant permission to preachers like Makgatho to preach in the areas where the majority of Africans lived, and for twenty years Makgatho was under close colonial surveillance, as the police declared that

> Some of the ministers are active members of the movement termed Africa for Africans, whose leaders are American and West Indian Negroes and whose object is to form an independent African republic with Martin [sic] Garvey as President, and it would be advisable to refuse them access to Rhodesia.[165]

---

[161] T. O. Ranger, 'Protestant missions in Africa: The dialectics of conversion in the American Methodist Episcopal Church in eastern Zimbabwe', in T. D. Blakely, W. E. A. van Beek and D. L. Thompson (eds.), *Religion in Africa: Experience and Expression* (London: Currey, 1994); T. Ranger, *Are We Not Also Men? The Samkange Family and African Politics in Zimbabwe* (Harare: Baobab Books, 1995), pp. 10-20.

[162] M. Daneel, *Quest for Belonging* (Gweru: Mambo Press, 1987), pp. 90-5.

[163] A. Mazrui, 'Seek Ye First the Political Kingdom', in A. Mazrui (ed.), *UNESCO General History of Africa: Volume VIII* (California: Heinemann, 1993), pp. 117-19.

[164] Ndlovu-Gatsheni, 'Re-thinking the colonial encounter in Zimbabwe', p. 188.

[165] NAZ File TCINB23/3/3R 5892: Superintendent CID to Town Clerk, 26 Sept. 1924.

Regarding the impact and appeal of Garveyism to Africans opposed to early colonisation, Michael O. West argued that the attraction was its 'ideological malleability, its capacity to be all things to all Africans with grievances against the colonial regime – pan-Africanists, nationalists, trade unionists, Ethiopianists and ethnic mobilisers alike.'[166] By 1934, Africans had formed the Bantu Congress of Southern Rhodesia that was based in Bulawayo. It was an elitist and moderate political organisation led by mission-educated leaders adhering to colonial modernist ideas of progress and civilisation. The spirit underpinning the Bantu Congress was that of 'Are We Not Also Men?', a powerful statement made by the Revd Thompson Samkange and reflecting the development of an African national political consciousness.[167] Being a man here meant resisting colonial abuses and fighting for one's rights. Like all proto-nationalist organisations, the Bantu Congress was reformist rather than radical.

Conclusion

This chapter has traced the gradual consolidation of Western colonial rule in the territory between the Zambezi and the Limpopo Rivers in the period from the 1880s to the 1930s. This period witnessed the meeting of two worlds – one African and the other Western – and was marked by complex interactions involving domination and resistance, and negotiations and contestations between the colonisers and the colonised.

African responses to colonial rule were complicated by the fact that there was no clear-cut ideological unity that could have enabled both the Ndebele and the Shona to develop a combined African front against colonial rule, even in 1896-97 when Africans finally rose violently against the British South Africa Company's colonial excesses. Even traditional African religion, including the much-written-about Mwari cult, failed to provide such a pan-ethnic, unitary African front to engage the early colonial state. The lack of unity and a co-ordinated military strategy, embraced by both the Ndebele and the Shona, together with poor weaponry accounted for the defeat of both the Ndebele in 1896 and the Shona in 1897.

The construction of the early colonial state was characterised by ambiguities and contradictions as it tried to prevent the further provocation of active African resistance while at the same time going ahead with its social and spatial segregation and dispossession of Africans. The imperative of indirect rule as

---

[166] M. O. West, 'The seeds are sown: The impact of Garveyism in Zimbabwe in the interwar years', *International Journal of African Historical Studies*, 35(2-3), 2002, p. 341.
[167] Ranger, *Are We Not Also Men?*

a governing colonial strategy involved the reinvention of pre-colonial chiefly institutions to serve colonial interests. The ambiguities of early colonisation and its contradictory policies provoked equally ambiguous and contradictory African responses. This led Michael O. West to conclude that the dynamics of African political consciousness never followed a linear or direct route. It took the form of ambiguous, contradictory and numerous struggles that were a response to the concrete challenges posed by early settler colonialism in Rhodesia.[168]

[168] West, 'The seeds are sown', p. 362.

3

From the Second World War to UDI, 1940-1965

A. S. Mlambo

Introduction

The period between the outbreak of the Second World War and the Unilateral Declaration of Independence (UDI) by Rhodesian Prime Minister Ian Douglas Smith in 1965 was a significant one in Zimbabwe's history. In these years, Rhodesia experienced far-reaching economic, demographic, social and political changes, and a gradual process of transformation in the political consciousness and self-perception of the African population was reflected in a change of attitude towards white colonial rule – from an earlier position of asking for fair governance to one of wanting self-rule.

This period has attracted the attention of many scholars, who have written on a variety of topics ranging from the history of the labour movement, the growth of African nationalism, the rise of an educated African middle-class, the quest for respectability and gender, to economic relations and political developments leading to UDI.[1] This chapter will highlight some of the major themes and debates that have emerged from such scholarship in order to contextualise the historical forces that helped shape the trajectory of Zimbabwe's experience.

[1] Among the numerous studies focusing on this period are: T. Barnes, 'We Women Worked So Hard': Gender, Urbanization, and Social Reproduction in Colonial Harare, Zimbabwe, 1930-1956 (Portsmouth, NH: Heinemann, 1999); N. Bhebe, Benjamin Burombo: African Politics in Colonial Zimbabwe, 1945-1958 (Harare: College Press, 1989); A. S. Mlambo, E. S. Pangeti and I. Phimister, Zimbabwe: A History of Manufacturing, 1890-1995 (Harare: University of Zimbabwe Publications, 2000); B. Raftopoulos and T. Yoshikuni, Sites of Struggle (Harare: Weaver Press, 1999); I. Phimister and B. Raftopoulos, '"Kana sora ratswa ngaritswe": African nationalists and black workers: The 1948 general strike in colonial Zimbabwe', Journal of Historical Sociology, 13(3), 2000, pp. 289-324; B. Raftopoulos, 'Gender, nationalist politics and the fight for the city: Harare 1940-1950s', Safere: Southern African Feminist Review, 1(2), 1995, pp. 30-45; T. Scarnecchia, 'Poor women and nationalist politics: Alliances and fissures in the formation of a nationalist political movement in Salisbury, Rhodesia, 1950-56', Journal of African History, 37(3), 1996, pp. 283-310; M. O. West, The Rise of an African Middle Class: Colonial Zimbabwe 1898-1965 (Bloomington and Indianapolis: Indiana University Press, 2002); A. S. Mlambo, White Immigration into Rhodesia: From Occupation to Federation (Harare: University of Zimbabwe Publications, 2002); Eshmael Mlambo, Rhodesia: The Struggle for a Birthright (London: C. Hurst, 1972); T. H. Mothibe, 'Zimbabwe: African working class nationalism, 1957-1963', Zambezia, 23(2), 1996, pp. 157-80; Iden Wetherell, 'Settler expansionism in central Africa: The imperial response of 1931 and subsequent implications', African Affairs, 78, 1979, pp. 210-27. There are many others.

Overview

The Second World War and its impact on the Rhodesian economy, in combination with specific economic policies and strategies adopted by the colonial state to deal with the economic challenges posed by the war, resulted in the relatively rapid growth of the country's manufacturing sector, which transformed the economy from heavy dependency on agriculture and mining to a diversified one.[2] Industrial expansion during and after the Second World War was fuelled by a combination of import-substitution, war needs and increasing domestic demand.

On the heels of the war-time boom came the establishment of the Federation of Rhodesia and Nyasaland, which expanded the domestic market, improved the creditworthiness of the three countries, and encouraged considerable inflows of foreign currency. The immediate post-war years also witnessed a large influx of white immigrants,[3] considerably boosting the country's settler population, and providing the economy with the necessary skilled labour and a larger domestic market. White immigration, however, also fuelled inter-racial tensions and hastened the rise of militant African nationalism, especially since the arrival of large numbers of white settlers resulted in the displacement of African communities from the so-called 'European areas'. According to Nyambara, some of the people who were affected by this policy

> were the Rhodesdale inhabitants who were to be moved to Gokwe
> and Sanyati. About 7 to 10 thousand Africans lived on Rhodesdale
> but ex-servicemen were taking up farms there under the Govern-
> ment Settlement Scheme. The new white land owners strongly
> resented the continued residence of Africans on Rhodesdale and
> they wanted them evicted immediately.[4]

Meanwhile, because of its relatively strong industrial base, Southern Rhodesia became the industrial heartland of the Federation and benefited most from both the investments and enlarged market, as well as from the Federal and Southern

---

[2] Phimister and Raftopoulos, caution against exaggerating the pace and size of secondary manufacturing growth in this period, pointing out that the industrialisation that occurred at this time was 'limited in scale', with the country boasting only '382 industrial establishments employing a grand total of 20 439 black workers'. Phimister and Raftopoulos, '"Kana sora ratsva ngaritsve"', p. 294.

[3] Mlambo, *White Immigration into Rhodesia*.

[4] Rhodesdale was a ranch owned by the giant British conglomerate Lonrho in the Southern Rhodesian Midlands. After the Second World War, this land was bought by the government and was surveyed into farms and ranches and the Africans living on them were moved away. See P. Nyambara, 'Land Acquisition, Commercialisation and Socio-Economic Differentiation in the Gokwe District of Zimbabwe, 1945-1990' (Unpublished.)

Rhodesian governments' policies of promoting the manufacturing sector through tariffs, trade agreements and direct state investments in select sectors.

The emerging manufacturing sector demanded an increasingly larger pool of workers that could be built up only through a combination of policies: those intended to push Africans off the land into the cities, and those – such as the provision of better family accommodation for workers in the urban areas – aimed at stabilising labour. Indeed, the question of urban housing became more important and contentious, with larger numbers of Africans migrating to the towns and cities as rural livelihoods were eroded by overcrowding, environmental degradation and hostile colonial land policies.

The gradual inflow of indigenous African workers into the urban centres changed the ethnic and cultural face of Southern Rhodesian towns and cities. Hitherto, as Tsuneo Yoshikuni has documented, Salisbury was dominated by 'foreign' or migrant workers from neighbouring countries such as Nyasaland (Malawi), Northern Rhodesia (Zambia) and Portuguese East Africa (Mozambique).[5] Indeed, as late as the 1950s, 'alien' Africans still comprised a sizeable proportion of the country's urban population.[6] However, the local African population gradually dominated the country's urban centres.

Also significant was the rise of an African middle class of educated professionals – teachers, nurses, lawyers and entrepreneurs – whose concerns and aspirations did not, at first, always coincide with those of the ordinary people and who sought to distance themselves from the 'masses'.[7] The tensions emerging from the interaction of these groups and between trade union activists and the nationalists were to help shape the trajectory of the development of African political growth and activity in the subsequent two decades. Thus, while towards the end of the period an African political consensus eventually emerged, initially the anti-colonial struggle took different and sometimes conflicting forms, as each social grouping – alien and indigenous urban workers, the rural population, the emerging middle class – sought to advance its own interests.

Differences also existed within the dominant white settler society, particularly between the so-called 'Old Rhodesians', those who had been in the country for a long time and who wanted to maintain the status quo to safeguard their interests, and the post-Second World War immigrants from Europe who tended to be more liberal in their attitudes towards the Africans and argued that the only

[5] Tsuneo Yoshikuni, *African Urban Experiences in Colonial Zimbabwe: A Social History of Harare before 1925* (Harare: Weaver Press, 2007).

[6] Between 40 and 60 per cent of the urban African population at the time were designated 'alien natives', see Phimister and Raftopoulos, '"Kana Sora Ratsva Ngaritsve"', p. 295.

[7] West, *The Rise of an African Middle Class*.

way to avert the threat of militant African nationalism was to make some limited concessions to the educated elite. The latter group argued for the co-option of the African middle class into colonial society and governance, albeit as junior partners, in order to blunt the potential for militant nationalism that was likely to emerge from the larger uneducated African population.

Through such organisations as the African Association and the Capricorn Africa Society, these liberals, led notably by Garfield Todd, the Rhodesian Prime Minister in the 1950s, pushed this agenda, often in the face of strong hostility from the rest of the white community.[8] Growing opposition to these 'integrationist' policies led to the removal of Todd from office in 1958 through a Cabinet coup because members of his government perceived him as being too partial to the Africans and, therefore, potentially dangerous to the Rhodesian cause. This effectively marked the eclipse of liberal tendencies and the ascendancy of right-wing policies that were to find full expression in the Rhodesian Front Party under Ian Smith and culminated in UDI and the fratricidal war that followed.[9]

The Second World War and its impact

The Second World War was a watershed in the history of modern Western imperialism in Africa and elsewhere, fundamentally changing the relationship between European colonial powers and the colonised peoples and making it impossible for the status quo to continue. Africans participated in the war in large numbers, with an estimated 370,000 and 80,000 African soldiers serving in the British and French armies, respectively, while colonial populations contributed immensely to the war effort in other ways.[10] In the case of Southern Rhodesia, thousands of Africans participated in the fighting, while those left at home contributed to the war effort through the production of foodstuffs and essential minerals such as chrome, and by 'building military bases for use by the British Air Force'.[11]

The African people's involvement in the war was to have profound psychological and political effects that would change their attitude towards colonisation thereafter. For example, Africans were struck by the contradiction of their defending their colonisers from German and Italian tyranny while they themselves continued to labour under the tyranny of Western colonialism. The decision by Franklin Roosevelt and Winston Churchill to limit the coverage of the 1941

---

[8] Hardwicke Holderness, *Lost Chance: Southern Rhodesia 1945-58* (Harare: Zimbabwe Publishing House, 1985).

[9] Ian Smith, *The Great* Betrayal (London: Blake, 1997); H. Holderness, *Lost Chance*.

[10] Kevin Shillington, *History of Africa* (New York: Macmillan, 2nd. edn., 2005), pp. 371-2.

[11] West, *The Rise of an African Middle Class*, p. 155.

Atlantic Charter, which proclaimed the right of peoples to self-determination, only to Europe made the contradiction of the war's aims even more glaring.

This contradiction was not lost on one Rhodesian African soldier, Lance Corporal Masiye:

> A denial was published in the *Bantu Mirror* as to whether Africans should be included in the New World Order through the Atlantic Charter. This did not only surprise me, but I took it for granted that whatsoever faithfulness and devotedness we might show the Europeans, we must never dream of comparative human rights ... It must be a very shameless sort of ruler who exploits people under his thralldom at ease and yet he never dreams of their release nor allows them to have privileges to race for comparative human rights. The African has served his rulers with admirable devotedness. What is he to receive for this? A continual exclusion from human rights? If so, our rulers must be quite shameless to blame the enemy for his brutality and assumed racial superiority.[12]

At the front, African soldiers had interacted with poor whites from Europe who were little different from themselves and who treated them as equals, unlike the whites they had grown accustomed to at home. Waruhui Itote recalled how, at the Burma front during the war, African and white soldiers were unified by the ever-present threat of death and treated each other as equals because 'the white heat of battle had blistered all [racial differences] away and left only our common humanity and our common fate, either death or survival'.[13]

Africans had also come into contact with Indian soldiers whose country was already agitating for independence from British rule and who inspired them to struggle for their own freedom once the war ended.

After the war, Africans were incensed by the fact that their sacrifices and efforts were neither recognised nor rewarded, most receiving a mere 'pat on the back' before being shoved back to their pre-war impoverishment, while demobilised white soldiers were fêted and given farms and other material rewards. These factors contributed to the rise of militant African nationalism that was to demand not the reform of colonial rule, as in the past, but freedom from it, and – what became the rallying call throughout the continent – majority rule, or 'one man, one vote'.

Given the carnage that had characterised the Second World War, the colonial powers emerged from it with the confidence of the superiority of their civilisation

---

[12] *Bantu Mirror*, 17 June 1944. I am grateful to Terence Ranger for drawing my attention to this letter.

[13] Waruhui Itote, *'Mau Mau' General* (Nairobi: East African Publishing House, 1967), pp. 9-15.

somewhat dented. They had been very dependent on the help of the colonised peoples and could no longer continue their relationships with them as if nothing had happened: new strategies were necessary to deal with the colonies in the changed and changing post-war world. Moreover, the war affected the future of Europe in a very fundamental way as it gave rise to the Cold War which was to define relations between East and West for almost half a century. The rise of African nationalism thus coincided with the emergence of a communist bloc of countries which became its natural allies against the Western colonial powers.

In Southern Rhodesia, the immediate post-war years saw a large influx of white immigrants, mostly from Britain. Some were demobilised British soldiers, attracted, in part, by the incentives offered by the Rhodesian government's post-war settlement scheme; some were returning to the country that they had fallen in love with during their brief sojourn as trainees at the Royal Air force training centre in Salisbury during the war.[14] Yet others were fleeing the difficult post-war conditions in Britain and hoped to benefit from the promising economic prospects in a country that, because of institutionalised discrimination against the employment of Africans in skilled trades, provided great prospects for self-advancement.

The influx was such that the Rhodesian European population rose from 82,000 to 135,000 between 1946 and 1951, the highest increase for over thirty years.[15] Of these, some 17,000 entered the country in 1948 alone, the largest one-year inflow ever.[16] Not surprisingly, this impacted on the African population in several ways, the most obvious of which was the displacement of over 100,000 Africans from their lands, now re-classified as European areas, to the already overcrowded African reserves.[17]

---

[14] Frank Clements, *Rhodesia: The Course to Collision* (London: Pall Mall Press, 1969), p. 78.

[15] Julius Isaac, *British Post-War Migration* (Cambridge: Cambridge University Press, 1954), pp. 132-4.

[16] Harold D. Nelson *et al.*, *Area Handbook for Southern Rhodesia* (Washington, DC: American University, Foreign Area Studies, 1975), p. 73.

[17] An example of late colonial forced removals is the relocation of the Gwebo Chieftaincy from the Charter Estates in Gweru to the malaria-infested and arid area of Gokwe. See P. S. Nyambara, 'Madheruka and Shangwe: Ethnic identities and the culture of modernity in Gokwe, northwestern Zimbabwe, 1963', *Journal of African History*, 42, 2002, pp. 287-306; P. S. Nyambara, 'Immigrants, "traditional" leaders and the Rhodesian state: The power of "communal" land tenure and the politics of land acquisition in Gokwe, Zimbabwe, 1963-1979', *Journal of Southern African Studies*, 27(4), 2001, pp. 771-91; P. S. Nyambara, 'The politics of land acquisition and struggles over land in the "communal" areas of Zimbabwe: The Gokwe region in the 1980s and 1990s', *Africa*, 71(2), 2001, pp. 54-108. See also Robin Palmer and I. Birch, *Zimbabwe: A Land Divided* (Oxford: Oxfam, 1992), p. 8.

Table 3.1: Sources of European population increase, 1901-1969

Period	Net immigration	Natural increase	Total increase	Average annual rate of growth (%)
1931-1941	11,025	8,019	19,044	3.3
1941-1951	50,066	16,576	66,642	7.0
1951-1961	47,097	38,811	85,908	4.0
1961-1969	13,914	20,706	6,792	0.3

Source: Rhodesia, Census of Population, 1969 (Salisbury: Central Statistical Office, 1969), p. 3.

The war brought about significant changes in the Rhodesian economy, the most prominent of which was the shift away from the country's traditional dependence on agriculture and mining to a more diversified economy in which manufacturing became increasingly prominent. The growth of the manufacturing sector was spurred by the attitude of the colonial state towards the desirability and feasibility of government support for manufacturing. Until the war, the government was not keen to encourage secondary industrialisation since it was felt that private capital was quite capable of developing 'worthwhile industries as opportunity occurred'.[18] It was contended that local manufacturing would not be viable because of the landlocked nature of the country, the very small domestic market, the lack of local skills and the absence of domestic capacity to manufacture capital equipment.[19]

By 1940, however, the difficulties of international trade caused by the war had persuaded the authorities that a policy of import-substitution industrialisation was necessary if the country's economy was to develop. Proponents of this pointed out that the country enjoyed a number of advantages that would make industrialisation possible: the abundance of undeveloped mineral resources, such as iron, coal and chrome; the cheapness of the land for building factories; the rapidly growing domestic market provided by an expanding population; and the availability of a large 'cheap native labour force' which had the advantage of being particularly 'suited to work of a repetitive nature'. Moreover, Southern Rhodesia's isolation from the industrial powerhouses of Europe and America meant that 'its industries would enjoy natural protection from crippling competition from the factories in those countries'.[20]

[18] Report of the Economic Development Committee (Salisbury: Government Printers, 1939), pp. 38-40, cited in Alois Mlambo and Ian Phimister, 'Partly protected: The origin and growth of colonial Zimbabwe's textile industry', Historia, 51(2), 2006, pp. 120-44.
[19] N[ational] A[rchives] of Z[imbabwe] F295/51/26/51 Import Controls: Piece Goods – Department of Trade and Industrial Development, 'Secondary Industry in Southern Rhodesia', May 1953 [W. A. E. Winterton – Minister of Trade and Industrial Development].
[20] Ibid.

The result was that, while government preferred to leave the establishment of industries to private enterprise whenever possible, it was no longer averse to assisting with the establishment of secondary industries, 'particularly those based on the processing of raw materials produced in the country' in 'the national interest'.[21] This thinking led to the setting up of an Industrial Development Advisory Committee, later renamed the Industrial Development Commission, to assist with the establishment of secondary industries in the country.

Several factors contributed to the growth of the Southern Rhodesian manufacturing sector in this period: the increasing availability of skilled labour and the expanded domestic market owing to post-war European immigration; the booming tobacco and base-minerals industries and the foreign currency that they earned; access to the foreign-currency earnings of Northern Rhodesia's copper-mining industry following the establishment of the Central African Federation in 1953, as well as the expanded domestic market made possible by the Federation; favourable fiscal policies, and customs agreements with South Africa which gave Rhodesian industry access to that country's market.[22] Under these stimuli, the industrial economy expanded rapidly, with the number of manufacturing units rising from 299 in 1939 to 724 in 1952.[23]

Inevitably, the expansion of the manufacturing sector meant greater demand for a permanent urban-based labour force, rather than seasonal migrant labour that had largely serviced the pre-war urban economy. The African population of Salisbury, for instance, is estimated to have increased from 22,126 in 1936 to 45,993 in 1946 and to 75,249 in 1951.[24] Given the increase in the number of Africans in urban areas and the demand for more dependable labour, it is not surprising that the authorities felt the need to implement measures that would 'stabilise' African labour. This was in line with mainstream thinking in the imperial world, for, as Cooper has argued, in the 1940s the British and French colonial authorities were re-imagining African workers as industrial men to be governed by laws and administrative institutions similar to those used in their own countries rather than as temporary wage earners who belonged to the rural areas and were called upon only as and when needed by the modern economy;[25] measures to 'stabilise' such labour were necessary in order to both

---

[21] Ibid.

[22] Ian Phimister, 'From preference towards protection: Manufacturing in Southern Rhodesia, 1940-1965', in A. S. Mlambo, E. S. Pangeti and I. Phimister, *Zimbabwe: A History of Manufacturing, 1890 to 1995* (Harare: University of Zimbabwe Publications, 2000), p. 34.

[23] Raftopoulos and Yoshikuni, *Sites of Struggle*, p. 131.

[24] Cited in ibid.

[25] Frederick Cooper, *Decolonization and African Society: The Labour Question in French and British Africa* (Cambridge: Cambridge University Press, 1996), p. 2.

Table 3.2: Gross output and average growth rate of Rhodesian industry, 1946-53

Sector	Gross output (£m)		Average growth rate (%)
	1946	1953	
Food manufacturing	5.6	18.8	19.0
Beverages	1.2	3.4	16.5
Tobacco manufacturing	1.3	4.0	17.5
Textiles and clothes	2.4	8.8.	20.8
Wood manufactures (except furniture)	0.6	1.9	18.3
Furniture and fixtures	0.3	1.3	22.3
Paper, printing, publishing	0.6	2.4	21.6
Rubber	0.1	0.2	15.3
Chemicals	1.0	3.9	21.9
Non-metallic minerals	0.8	3.8	24.4
Metal manufacturing	1.9	6.8	20.3
Transport (manufacture and repair	1.1	4.8	24.1
Miscellaneous	0.5	1.7	17.7
Total manufacturing	17.3	61.9	20.0

Source: C. Stoneman, 'Industrialisation and Self-Reliance in Zimbabwe', in M. Fransman (ed.), *Industry and Accumulation in Africa* (London: Heinemann, 1982), p. 279.

increase its productivity and gain greater control over it. In post-war Rhodesia, such measures were introduced to stabilise African labour for the benefit of the rapidly growing urban economy.

The increasing demand for urban labour, coupled with the push from post-war colonial land policies, such as the Native Land Husbandry Act (NLHA) of 1951, de-stocking, and the more rigorous implementation of the 1930 Land Apportionment Act and its subsequent amendments, resulted in increasing rural-urban migration and, consequently, greater urbanisation. This, and the dictates of 'labour stabilisation', demanded more and better housing. The 1939 Ibbotson Report on 'Housing, Wages and Living conditions of Africans in Bulawayo District', for instance, reported that there was 'serious overcrowding everywhere' and that living conditions were 'scandalous' in some cases. In 1943, the Howman Commission reported that 'African housing was appalling and that overcrowding was common' and that these conditions were fuelling outbreaks of disease, such as tuberculosis and pneumonia.[26]

[26] P. Ibbotson, *Report on a Survey of Urban African Conditions in Southern Rhodesia* (S.R.: 1943), 13; E. G. Howman Commission, 'Committee to Investigate the Economic, Social and Health Conditions of Africans Employed in urban Areas (1943-4)', cited in E. Chipembere, 'Colonial Policy and Africans in Urban Areas, with Special Focus on Housing, Salisbury, 1939-1964' (Unpublished, 2007), pp. 30-3.

Commenting on the housing problem in Salisbury at the time, Chipembere noted how the country's rapid industrialisation, African migration into Salisbury in search of employment and increased European immigration had 'put a strain, not only on available accommodation, but also on the construction industry' and how

> 'Temporary' accommodation for Africans, which ended up being permanent, was erected, but demand still outstripped available stands. Overcrowding became evident in the locations, resulting in many negative consequences, such as juvenile delinquency, alcohol and sexual abuse, and generally, unhealthy living conditions.[27]

Africans in urban areas had other grievances against the colonial authorities. Among these were the provisions of the Urban Areas Act of 1947, which was designed to enable the authorities to exercise greater control by, among other things, denying housing to the unemployed and making employers responsible for their workers' rents. Other control measures included the authorities' use of registration and pass laws to control African residence and mobility, and the treatment of single females as legal minors who could not access urban housing except through marriage.[28]

Furthermore, the authorities imposed stringent liquor laws that monitored what Africans drank, and when and where, and closely supervised their recreational activities in sports clubs, women's clubs and other social organisations. Finally, municipal police conducted regular night raids in the townships to root out those without official passes to be there.[29] These grievances contributed to the growth of African dissatisfaction with colonial rule and control, which manifested itself in various forms of organisation and protest in the post-Second World War period.

From the proto-nationalist to the nationalist moment[30]

In his study on the rise of the African middle class in Zimbabwe, Michael West has suggested a useful way of tracking the development of African organisational politics and political activism prior to the 1960s by dividing it into three periods: the proto-nationalist period between the two World Wars; the national moment from 1945 to 1948; and the nationalist moment from the late 1950s onwards. He has argued that, in the proto-nationalist period, the sense of nationalism was as yet underdeveloped, with the merging African elite tending to be narrow and

---

[27] E. Chipembere, 'Colonial Policy and Africans in Urban Areas', p. 4.
[28] Ibid., p. 5.
[29] Ibid.
[30] Expressions borrowed from West, *The Rise of an African Middle Class*.

'socially specific' in the pursuit of policies that would improve their lot. Thereafter, the scope of mobilisation and interaction broadened.

Thus, the nationalist moment emerged at the end of a long process in which African protest and mobilisation were targeted not at overthrowing the colonial dispensation but only at encouraging the provision of a fairer colonial governmental environment. It was the failure of these early campaigns and the growing disillusionment with the colonial system's unwillingness to deliver, particularly its failure to extend the benefits of political, social and economic participation to the educated middle class, that gave birth to militant nationalism that then demanded self-government or 'one man, one vote'.

Indeed, the two decades after the outbreak of the Second World War were a period of intense political and organisational activity among the Africans of Southern Rhodesia. This activity revolved around several issues, among which were opposition to the establishment of the Federation of Rhodesia and Nyasaland, the emerging African elite's experimentation with multiracialism; trade unionism concentrating on bread-and-butter issues affecting the urban working classes; opposition to the colonial state's rural initiatives such as de-stocking, soil conservation and land reform; and, ultimately, by the end of the decade, the question of self-determination.

Featuring prominently in the proto-nationalist period were African grievances over the land question and the colonial state's African agricultural policies. As Phimister has argued, state policies affecting African peasant farmers since the 1930s had fuelled growing resentment. These included measures designed to subsidise European agriculture at the African farmers' expense, such as the Cattle Levy Acts of 1931 and 1934 which charged a slaughter levy on cattle for domestic consumption as a means of subsidising stock for export which was owned by white farmers; the 1934 tax of 3d. per head and, subsequently, a 10s. slaughter levy; and the Maize Control Acts of 1931 and 1934.[31]

African agricultural producers' grievances were compounded during and after the war by increasingly strained conditions of overcrowding and over-grazing, and accelerated environmental degradation through soil erosion. The result was the colonial state's urgent search for corrective measures which would increase the capacity of the land to carry more Africans and become more productive.

For instance, in order to accommodate the large numbers of displaced Africans, the state introduced a number of measures to improve the carrying capacity of the existing African reserves. These included a policy of centralisation which

---

[31] I. Phimister, *An Economic and Social History of Zimbabwe, 1890-1948: Capital Accumulation and Class Struggle* (London: Longman, 1988), pp. 171-218.

sought to reconfigure land usage patterns in order to maximise carrying capacity, resulting in approximately 13 million acres being subjected to this process by 1954, as well as a ruthless de-stocking campaign that decimated African cattle herds in a bid to reduce overstocking. These measures failed to fully resolve the problems of overcrowding in the countryside.

The state's determination to find a long-lasting solution, coupled with growing demands for cheap and more permanent industrial labour, resulted in the 1951 Native Land Husbandry Act. This Act was the outcome of enduring efforts to design a strategy that would not only increase the productivity of the Reserves but also ensure that those who could not be accommodated in the countryside would be transformed into cheap permanent labour for the emerging manufacturing sector. Indeed, as early as 1947, the Chief Native Commissioner had recommended the establishment of a Commission of Inquiry that would make appropriate recommendations on how to resolve the problem of overcrowding in the Reserves, enabling the state to take measures that would present Africans with a choice of either becoming 'a peasant farmer only, adopting proper agricultural and soil conservation methods, or ... an industrialised worker'.[32] The NLHA proved to be highly unpopular. Not surprisingly, militant African nationalist movements received considerable support in the Native Reserves during and after the 1950s; indeed, the armed struggle of the 1960s and beyond was anchored mainly in the countryside, where African peasant support was pivotal to its success.

The Central African Federation
The idea of a larger political and economic entity in which Southern Rhodesia would be combined with another European-dominated colony had long exercised the minds of sectors of the Southern Rhodesian settler community.

As early as 1915, the British South Africa Company (BSAC) had proposed amalgamating Northern and Southern Rhodesia, citing the advantages of an enlarged African labour market and the opening up of commerce through the removal of trade barriers. Furthermore, it was argued, 'such unification would be of value in securing the effective recognition of Rhodesian interests in any re-settlement of political boundaries in Africa which might follow the conclusion of the European War'.[33] The idea was shot down by the Southern Rhodesian legis-

[32] Report of the Secretary for Native Affairs, Chief Native Commissioner and Director of Native Development, for the Year 1946, p. 2.

[33] Report of the Rhodesia-Nyasaland Royal Commission [Chairman: Viscount Bledisloe] (Cmd. 5949, 1939), (London: HMSO, 1939), 108. [Hereafter called the *Bledisloe Commission Report*].

lature for fear that it would permanently scupper the settlers' hope of attaining self-government in the future.

In 1929, the Hilton Young Commission which was set up to consider the future not only of the East African territories of Kenya, Uganda, Tanganyika and Zanzibar but also of Nyasaland and Northern Rhodesia, since the acceptance by the United Kingdom of a mandate for Tanganyika had created an unbroken stretch of territory under British control extending from the Zambezi to the Nile'.[34]

The United Kingdom government eventually decided that the time had not yet come for taking any far-reaching step in the direction of formal union of the East African dependencies. In any case, whatever interest the Northern Rhodesian whites might have had in closer political arrangements with the East African territories was dissipated by the publication of the Passfield Memorandum in 1930, which gave paramountcy to African interests in any such arrangements. In 1931, the British rejected amalgamation of the Rhodesias but indicated their willingness to reconsider the idea 'should circumstances in their opinion justify it at a later date'.[35]

Another attempt to promote the amalgamation cause was made in the Northern Rhodesia legislature in 1933 when a motion urging amalgamation of the two Rhodesias was rejected. The idea was also opposed by the Ndola Native Welfare Association, which passed a resolution stating that

> while this Association would welcome amalgamation with Nyasaland where laws and conditions are similar to those of this country, it humbly asks that the Government will not agree to the amalgamation of Northern Rhodesia and Southern Rhodesia. Such a step would, in the opinion of this Association, be greatly to the detriment of the interests and legitimate aspirations of the Native population of this country, who number 100,000 to 10,000 Europeans. [36]

In January 1937, leaders of the amalgamation lobby in Southern Rhodesia, members representing Southern Rhodesia's three political parties, and members of the Northern Rhodesian Legislative Council met at Victoria Falls to debate the amalgamation question, and passed a resolution in support of the idea. The

---

[34] *Bledisloe Commission Report*, 109-10; *Report of the Commission on Closer Union of the Dependencies in Eastern and Central Africa* (Cmd 3234, 1929), cited in Wetherell, 'Settler expansionism in central Africa'.

[35] D.O. 35/424/11969/24, SS to Gov SR, 1 July 1931, cable, cited in Wetherell, 'Settler expansionism in central Africa', 222.

[36] *Bledisloe Commission Report*, 112.

resolution was subsequently supported by the Southern Rhodesian Legislative Council and the Southern Rhodesian Prime Minister. Thereafter it was presented to the Governor of Southern Rhodesia with a request for the British authorities to convene a conference to discuss the issue of amalgamation. The request was turned down.

In 1937, a Commission of Inquiry was appointed but recommended against federation between the Rhodesias and Nyasaland, citing disparities among them in matters of governance, as Southern Rhodesia was self-governing, while the other two were controlled by the Secretary of State for the Colonies. Moreover, it was noted that Africans in the northern territories were strongly opposed to amalgamation owing to their dislike of 'some features of the native policy of Southern Rhodesia' and that this factor could not be ignored.[37] In the end, the Commission proposed the setting up of an Inter-Territorial Council to be made up of the Prime Minister of Southern Rhodesia and the Governors of Northern Rhodesia and Nyasaland whose role would include co-ordinating services and promoting economic development.

Then, in 1939, the Bledisloe Commission was set up to report 'whether any, and if so what, form of closer co-operation or association between Southern Rhodesia, Northern Rhodesia and Nyasaland is desirable and feasible'. It re-commended amalgamation of Northern Rhodesia and Nyasaland but did not 'consider that the conditions are yet present for the extension of the policy to Southern Rhodesia partly because of its different native policy'.[38]

The next, and decisive, initiative came from Southern Rhodesia after the Second World War, when economic prosperity prompted growing interest in certain quarters for a bigger market and more African labour than were available in the country itself. Amalgamation with Northern Rhodesia would provide these advantages while, at the same time, enabling Southern Rhodesian settlers to access the considerable foreign currency earnings from Northern Rhodesia's copper exports, especially in the light of the copper boom of the immediate post-war years, which saw the value of Northern Rhodesia's copper output rising from £7,990,000 in 1939 to £51,475,000 in 1953.[39]

For Britain, the advantages of a larger British-controlled central African territory included a bigger market for British goods, a counter to the rising Afrikaner political influence in South Africa, especially in the light of the National

[37] Ibid., p. 218.
[38] *Bledisloe Commission Report*.
[39] Martin Loney, *Rhodesia: White Racism and Imperial Response* (Harmondsworth: Penguin, 1975), p. 84.

Party's ascent to power in 1948, [40] and a possible check to the growing threat of African nationalism. What emerged in the end was not an amalgamated territory of Northern and Southern Rhodesia as proponents of the idea had hoped but a Federation, including Nyasaland which was 'thrown in' by the British and accepted by the other two territories unenthusiastically because it was economically poor and had only a very small settler population.

African opposition to the Federation, especially in Northern Rhodesia and Nyasaland, was strong from the beginning. As early as 1950, African organisations expressed their opposition to the proposed Federation. The Nyasaland African Protectorate Council argued that 'promises made by the British Government would not be fulfilled and that the Africans would not realize their hopes of self-government'. The Nyasaland African Congress stated that they would not send representatives to a proposed conference at Victoria Falls 'as they had already announced their rejection of Federation as an obstacle to their ultimate aim of "all-African self-government"'.[41]

Similarly, the Northern Rhodesia Trade Union Congress denounced amalgamation as an 'act of injustice' and 'a breach of the Atlantic Charter' which 'would lead to increased immigration from South Africa' and thus undermine 'the security of the Native land ownership' and threaten 'Native political and economic development'. Meanwhile, a meeting called by the Southern Rhodesian African National Congress (SRANC) decided that, 'whilst the creation of a Central African Federal Dominion was economically desirable, it would not be in the Natives' interest at the present stage of political development'. [42]

In 1951, African representatives from the three territories met at Fort Jameson and denounced the Federation. Representing Rhodesia were three prominent organisations, the African Workers Voice Association (the Voice), founded by Benjamin Burombo in 1947, the Reformed Industrial and Commercial Workers' Union (RICU), under Charles Mzingeli, and the SRANC. Thereafter, Africans set up the All-African Convention to mobilise opposition to federation. Although African objections failed to prevent its creation, the Federation faced African opposition throughout its ten years of existence from 1953 to 1963, with the staunchest opposition coming from the two northern territories, where nationalists were angry at the fact that their views had not been solicited. They were also worried that the openly discriminatory racist legislation and culture

---

[40] R. Hyam, 'The geopolitical origins of the Central African Federation: Britain, Rhodesia and South Africa, 1948-1953', *Historical Journal*, 30(1), 1987, pp. 145-72.

[41] *Keesing's Contemporary Archives*, 8 (Cambridge: Keesings Worldwide, 1950-52, June 30 – July 7, 1951), p. 11,770.

[42] Ibid.

Fig. 3.1: Charles Mzingeli.
[*Source:* National Archives of Zimbabwe]

of Southern Rhodesia would be imported into their own comparatively more liberal colonial system.[43]

Despite the SRANC's public opposition, and more outspoken denunciations – such as that by Robert Mugabe, who accused the proposed organisation of being little more than 'an instrument that will be wielded to suppress our self determination and progress'[44] – Southern Rhodesian African opposition to federation increasingly became ambivalent, as some leaders went on to participate in Federal Government structures through their membership of the white-led United Rhodesia Party. Thus, public posturing against federation notwithstanding, Joshua Nkomo and Jasper Savanhu went on to participate in the 1952 London talks that paved the way for the Federation. Subsequently, Jasper Savanhu and Mike Hove stood for election to the Federal Parliament under the auspices of Godfrey Huggins's Federal Party. Explaining why the Southern Rhodesian African elite accepted federation, Nathan Shamuyarira wrote that the establishment of the Federation was

> regarded by Southern Rhodesian Africans as full of promise: the new policy of partnership, which was to be inscribed in the federal constitution, would bring to a speedy end the segregation, humiliation and indignation which we had suffered for 40 years ... the Northern territories would help to break down the racial barriers and the southern Rhodesian whites would even of their own accord, inspired by partnership, pass laws which would let us share political power and economic privileges and enjoys social justice.[45]

This optimism was, of course, misplaced. Little improved in the lot of the

---

[43] John Day, *International Nationalism* (London: Routledge, 1967), pp. 61-2.
[44] *Bantu Mirror*, 27 June, 1953.
[45] Nathan Shamuyarira, *Crisis in Rhodesia* (London: Deutsch, 1965), pp. 15-16.

Africans under colonial rule because, as Eshmael Mlambo observed, Federation notwithstanding, in all three territories a form of petty apartheid prevailed in which 'Africans continued to be denied the right to use hotels, restaurants, public lavatories and public facilities on the railways. Up to 1957, they were not allowed that dangerous liquid, European beer'. Discriminatory practices continued, and by the end of 1950s 'even the so-called African "moderates" were expressing their misgivings about the Federation'.[46]

Administered from Salisbury in Southern Rhodesia, the Federation operated a two-tier system of government in which Federal administrative posts and structures, such as Governor and Parliament, were replicated at territorial level. The constitution provided for a division of power and responsibility between the territorial and Federal governments, with the former retaining autonomy over local matters, including African affairs, and the latter being responsible for pan-territorial issues such as defence and foreign policy.

Economically, the Federation was a notable success. The period 1953 to 1963 was one of such rapid economic development that the region soon became the most industrialised bloc in sub-Saharan Africa, outside South Africa, while its agriculture, mining and service industries also expanded and prospered. Investment increased notably, amounting to £805m between 1954 and 1959, £224m of which came from overseas. National income rose from £303m in 1954 to £440m in 1959, while exports increased by 74 per cent in the first six years of Federation, as compared to 56 per cent in the six years preceding its establishment.[47] The region also witnessed impressive infrastructural improvements, epitomised by the construction of the Kariba hydroelectric plant and the establishment and commissioning of the University College of Rhodesia and Nyasaland in 1957. Meanwhile, the Federation's cities and towns grew rapidly, as Africans sought employment in the emerging industries.

Being the most industrialised, and having the most diversified economy, Southern Rhodesia benefited from the Federation at the expense of its partners. Nyasaland remained, essentially, a supplier of cheap labour to Southern Rhodesian farms and mines, while Northern Rhodesia contributed its copper exports' earnings, most of which were invested in Federal projects which largely benefited Southern Rhodesia. Apart from these advantages, Southern Rhodesia also enjoyed increased foreign investment and an expanded local market. The

---

[46] Mlambo, *Rhodesia: The Struggle for a Birthright*, p. 114.

[47] 'Federation of Rhodesia and Nyasaland: Report of the Monckton Commission', in *Commonwealth Survey*, 6(22), 25 October 1960, pp. 997–1006 [Hereafter called the *Monckton Commission Report*].

inequalities of economic benefits created resentment against Southern Rhodesia in the other territories and fuelled anti-Federation sentiment.

By the end of the 1950s, however, the economy of the Federation was not as vibrant as in the early years, as world demand for copper declined and foreign investment inflows also fell.[48] In any case, as noted, the Federation had never been popular among the Africans, especially those in Northern Rhodesia and Nyasaland, whose opposition to it finally led to its collapse. Opposition stemmed partly from the fact that Africans remained politically marginalised: although the African population of the Federation was three million and the European population only 300,000, Africans were allocated only six representatives, two for each territory, in a Federal Legislative Assembly of 35 members.

Moreover, racist policies and practices persisted, with African workers continuing to be paid lower wages than their European counterparts and being barred from patronising service facilities used by Europeans. These and other grievances fuelled militant African nationalism in all three territories, giving rise to the Malawi Congress Party under Kamuzu Banda and the United National Independence Party under Kenneth Kaunda, in Northern Rhodesia. In Southern Rhodesia, nationalists founded several political parties in succession to oppose continued white rule and the Federation. In December 1958, nationalist leaders from the three territories met at the All-African People's Conference in Accra, Ghana, and resolved to campaign for the dissolution of the Federation and independence for their respective countries.

According to the Monckton Commission Report of 1960, opposition to Federation was 'widespread, sincere and of long standing. It is almost pathological.' This was, partly, the result of the fact that 'in the Africans' view, "partnership" had been a sham' and also because Africans in Northern Rhodesia and Nyasaland regarded the Federation as a stumbling block to their political independence and the attainment of self-determination. In the words of the Commission,

> It now appears to many Africans that only the presence of the European community politically entrenched behind the Federal constitution stands between them and the form of freedom already granted to their fellow Africans in most other parts of the continent. So long as Federation seems to them to block their way to rapid political progress, so long will their hostility to it continue to grow.

The Monckton Commission concluded that although Europeans in all three territories and some Africans in Southern Rhodesia wanted the Federation to

---

[48] Mothibe, 'Zimbabwe: African working class nationalism', p. 160.

continue, 'the strength of African opposition in the Northern Territories is such that Federation cannot, in our view, be maintained in the present form'.[49]

As anti-Federation pressure mounted, particularly in Northern Rhodesia and Nyasaland, on the eve of the two countries' independence, right-wing elements in Southern Rhodesian also began to demand an end to the Federation, fearing that the African population, infected by the fever sweeping the continent since Ghana's independence in 1957, might prevail upon Britain to grant them independence under African majority rule as it was about to do in the other two territories. Under the banner of the Rhodesian Front Party, these elements took power in Southern Rhodesia in 1962, and thus brought to office an anti-federalist party which, like its counterparts in Northern Rhodesia and Nyasaland, but for different reasons, was committed to ending the Federation. The following year, the Federation collapsed, as Northern Rhodesia became independent as Zambia and Nyasaland as Malawi, and Southern Rhodesia drifted inevitably towards a unilateral declaration of independence .

Multiracialism and the African elite

As Shamuyarira suggested, the African elite were buoyed by a naïve optimism in the ability and willingness of the dominant white population to reform itself; they led themselves to believe that it was sensible for them to participate in the country's multiracial liberal experiment of 'partnership' in the 1950s. This is clear evidence that they were not, as yet, seeking to overthrow colonial rule in order to replace it with 'one man, one vote' but were merely asking to be governed well and to be accorded rights and privileges that they thought were due to them as 'civilised' men and women. It is, therefore, conceivable that had the white establishment opened its doors more widely to the educated elite, the rise of militant African nationalism might have been delayed considerably. It is partly because of the establishment's refusal to promote, in Cecil John Rhodes's conception, 'equal rights for every civilised man' that the African educated elite became more radicalised and turned to militant nationalism by the end of the Federation.

As Michael West has ably documented, the African elite that were to participate in the multiracial experiment of the 1950s had been long in the making in Southern Rhodesia, the process of middle-class formation having begun in earnest between 1914 and 1933. This group included 'clerks, teachers, preachers, social workers, journalists, nurses, lawyers and doctors' who, because of their education, saw themselves as being different and of a higher status than other

---

[49] *Monckton Commission Report.*

Africans.[50] Determined to attain Western standards of 'respectability', the members of this class, who defined themselves according to their level of education, the social institutions that they belonged to and their levels of sophistication,[51] saw themselves as being better than the generality of the 'poor and the uneducated in the townships'.[52]

Bent on acquiring a respectable bourgeois culture of domesticity and determined to distance themselves from the uneducated African population,[53] this class demanded to be treated differently from the 'untutored African sitting by the fire in the reserve'.[54] T. Scarnecchia documents how, in the 1940s and early 1950s, there were evident tensions 'between married and single workers and among married people between migrant workers, those who aspired to middle class status, and those who remained tied to rural ways of living' and how those desiring to attain spatial respectability were at the forefront of condemning the informal live-in relationships between men and women commonly referred to as *mapoto* and were behind the campaign for better married housing in Salisbury and other places. [55]

It was this middle class that participated in the multiracial experiment of the 1950s in which various liberal white organisations, the most prominent being the Inter-Racial Association (IRA) and the Capricorn Africa Society (CAS), attempted to co-opt the educated elite in order to forestall the rise of militant African nationalism. According to one of the founder members of the IRA, Hardwicke Holderness, the organisation rejected both South African apartheid and African nationalism as racist, and championed a politically moderate regime that would recognise African freehold tenure in the cities, operate a colour-blind franchise, and promote labour stabilisation. Subscribers to Cecil Rhodes's 'equal rights for all civilised men', they felt that some privileges should be extended to the 'civilised' among the Africans, but only as they demonstrated their sense of political responsibility.

White liberal organisations of the time were thus composed of paternalists who believed, without question, in the superiority of Western culture and civilisation and regarded Africans as junior partners in the political, economic and

---

[50] West, *The Rise of an African Middle Class*, p. 2.

[51] Raftopoulos and Yoshikuni, *Sites of Struggle*, p. 137.

[52] T. Scarnecchia, 'The mapping of respectability and the transformation of African residential space', in Raftopoulos and Yoshikuni, *Sites of Struggle*, p. 161.

[53] For a good discussion of the cultural pretensions of the African middle class in this period, see West, *The Rise of an African Middle Class*, pp. 68-98, and Scarnecchia, 'The mapping of respectability'.

[54] West, cited in Raftopoulos and Yoshikuni, *Sites of Struggle*, p. 137.

[55] Scarnecchia, 'The mapping of respectability', p. 151.

social advancement of the society. Consequently, they believed that African political participation would emerge gradually as a middle class 'consisting of Africans who, through the skill and responsibility they had learned, would come to feel an identity of interests with whites and therefore be no longer a threat to them as voters'. As junior partners in this enterprise, Africans would, of course, have to prove themselves and work their way up.[56]

Among those who bought into the idea of respectability and privileged treatment for the educated Africans were several individuals who were to become prominent in the subsequent struggle against colonial rule, including Nathan Shamuyarira, Herbert Chitepo, Lawrence Vambe, Jasper Savanhu and Chad Chipunza, who, at one time, became a full-time employee of CAS.[57] Similarly, Joshua Nkomo was then a 'member and Bulawayo chairman of the white-led Federation of African Welfare Societies', whose membership also included Professor S. T. J. Samkange, the lawyer E. Dumbutshena, the trade union leader L. S. [sic] Mzingeli, and others'.[58]

The multiracial enterprise eventually collapsed when the African elite became frustrated by the unwillingness of the establishment to advance their interests beyond a certain point and they realised that they were being taken for a walk down the proverbial garden path. As West notes, all they had to show for their hobnobbing with white liberals was the repeal of the laws forbidding them to drink European liquor. The futility of their approach became even more evident when the one white political leader they thought was sympathetic to their aspirations, Garfield Todd, was toppled from power by members of his Cabinet who felt that he was too sympathetic to African interests and was promoting African advancement too rapidly for their liking, even though his harsh handling of the Wankie Colliery strike in 1954 showed that, when it came to the crunch, he could be just as ruthless as the rest of them. It was then that they turned their backs on white liberals and joined hands with the masses that they had spurned in the past to build a militant African nationalist movement that was now demanding 'one man, one vote'.

For much of the 1950s multiracialism had succeeded in alienating the African elite from their potential power base, the workers and peasants, and whites were able to maintain 'a division between the rural and urban African masses, and the African elite', as the elite sought 'to obtain the best terms that they could for themselves' and were encouraged to do so by the white purveyors of the doctrine of equal rights for all civilised men. This separation of the elite from the

---

[56] Holderness, *Lost Chance*, p. 107.
[57] Ibid., p. 170.
[58] Mlambo, *Rhodesia: The Struggle for a Birthright*, pp. 123-4.

people was only bridged towards the end of the decade. In the meantime, the elite remained ambivalent in their attitudes towards European colonialism so that,

> faced with the prospect of federation, the elite equivocated; faced with the promise of partnership, they responded by joining the United Federal Party and later the Central African Party. Only with the defeat of Todd; with the framework of Federation crashing about their ears; with the rebirth of the mass nationalist movement; and with the growing strength of the white backlash reflected in the Dominion Party, did they finally come to terms with the reality that there would be no solution to the problems of the African elite without a solution to the problems of the African masses.[59]

Workers' struggles

In the period between the two World Wars, Africans had established a number of organisations to promote their interests and to defend their rights. While these organisations had contributed to the development of African political consciousness and workers had sometimes resorted to strike action, the African voice was relatively muted and marginalised prior to the 1940s. Thereafter, African mobilisation and agitation for political and economic betterment quickened so that, by the time that the African elite were attending tea parties and public lectures featuring paternalistic white liberals in the 1950s, the workers were demanding improved working and living conditions and better wages, employment opportunities, housing, and social services, as well as fairer colonial governance. Throughout the 1940s, they participated in workers' organisations and organised strikes, as did their counterparts elsewhere on the continent, a period that John Lunn has described as 'a watershed decade in the evolution of African labour'.[60]

The first major protest was the 20 October 1945 railway workers' strike, inspired by rising inflation and stagnant wages that were eroding the workers' living standards.[61] Accommodation was poor and overcrowded; in one case, 2,173 African men and women packed into accommodation that was designed for only 1,450.[62] When Bulawayo-based workers, including those represented

---

[59] Loney, *Rhodesia: White Racism and Imperial Response*, p. 97.

[60] J. Lunn, 'The meaning of the 1948 general strike in colonial Zimbabwe', in Raftopoulos and Yoshikuni, *Sites of Struggle*, ch. 7.

[61] West, *The Rise of an African Middle Class*, p. 159.

[62] Tredgold Commission Report, cited in B. Raftopoulos, 'The labour movement in Zimbabwe', in B. Raftopoulos and I. Phimister (eds.), *Keep on Knocking: A History of the Labour Movement in Zimbabwe, 1900-97* (Harare: Baobab Books, 1997), pp. 58-9.

by the Rhodesia Railways African Employees Association (RRAEA), established a year earlier to represent railway workers' interests, pressed for better working conditions, they were rebuffed by management.[63]

In response, they began a strike that was to spread to Broken Hill in Northern Rhodesia and to involve approximately 10,000 workers by its end on 29 October. Apart from economic grievances, there was also unhappiness at the provisions of the Industrial Conciliation Act of 1934, which excluded Africans from the definition of worker and thus prevented them from forming trade unions and engaging in collective bargaining. The strike ended only after government promised to set up a Commission of Inquiry to investigate the workers' grievances and related matters.

Although the workers did not attain their objectives immediately, the Commission of Inquiry recommended the establishment of Native Labour Boards. Subsequently, a Railways Native Labour Board was established and, in January 1948, recommended a controversial new wage structure with an entry point of 35 shillings per month, a figure that was far below what the workers were demanding.

The 1945 strike signalled the determination of workers to improve their lot through organised action and, more importantly, had a 'demonstration effect',[64] showing the potential power of organised workers. Consequently, in the subsequent two years, new workers' organisations were established: the Federation of Bulawayo African Workers Union (FBAWU, otherwise known as 'the Federation') under Jasper Savanhu, the African Workers Voice Association (the Voice), led by Benjamin Burombo, and the Salisbury-based Reformed Industrial and Commercial Workers' Union (RICU) led by Charles Mzingeli.[65]

The period between the 1945 strike and the next major strike in 1948 was, therefore, one of African organisational ferment as these unions sought to address a wide array of issues and build a broad coalition that would cut across class. For instance, the Voice represented both urban and rural constituencies and campaigned for, among other issues, annual paid vacations, advancement into skilled positions, overtime wages and sick leave,[66] as well as opposing the conservation measures imposed by the colonial authorities in the rural areas. The RICU, on its part, although confined to Salisbury, attempted to build a mass organisation that would speak to the interests of both workers and the emerging African business classes. Among the issues it fought against was the Native

[63] Scarnecchia, 'The mapping of respectability', pp. 151-62.
[64] Lunn, 'The meaning of the 1948 general strike'.
[65] Raftopoulos, 'The labour movement in Zimbabwe'.
[66] West, *The Rise of an African Middle Class*, p. 166.

(Urban Areas) Accommodation and Registration Act of 1946, which tightened
the state's control over African urban areas by, among other measures, denying
accommodation to the unemployed and making employers responsible for paying the rent for their workers. It also demanded the recognition of African trade
unions, as well as state attention to 'the problems of African business people, the
rights of women in the city, the sale of liquor to Africans, the housing crisis and
participation in local government'.[67]

This period also saw the revival of the Southern Rhodesian Bantu Congress,
now renamed the Southern Rhodesian African National Congress, and the
establishment of the Voters League, both of which defended Africans' voting
rights, as well as promoting workers' interests. Other manifestations of African
protest were the creation of the African Methodist Church by Reverend Esau
Nemapare in 1947. Rising out of the ashes of the earlier Ethiopian Churches,
such as the African Methodist Episcopal Church of the 1920s, Nemapare's new
church was an African revolt against European religious and racial domination
and stemmed from the same Africanist protest sentiment as the student strike
at Dadaya Mission in the same year.[68]

These years 'witnessed a rapprochement, indeed an evolving political alliance
across the social divide between the African middle and working class', as efforts
were made to build multi-interest coalitions that would bridge the gap between
the emerging elite and the workers.[69] West identifies this confluence of interests
and concerns as constituting the 'national moment':

> To be sure, the years between the 1945 and the 1948 strikes
> were bedevilled by jockeying for political supremacy by various
> formations ... These battles were, however, neither ideological
> nor strategic. ... there was broad agreement on objectives and
> goals during this period, with each faction claiming that it best
> represented the African consensus. In sum, a new dispensation
> had dawned – the national moment.[70]

This was not yet a *nationalist* moment, however, because Africans were still
thinking in terms of the amelioration of white rule rather than sovereignty and
independence.[71]

[67] Raftopoulos, 'The labour movement in Zimbabwe', pp. 60-2.

[68] West, *The Rise of an African Middle Class*, pp. 169-70. For a detailed discussion of the
religious dimension of the African protest in this period, see Terence Ranger, *Are We Not Also
Men? The Samkange Family and African Politics in Zimbabwe, 1920-64* (Harare: Baobab
Books, 1995).

[69] West, *The Rise of an African Middle Class*, p. 167.

[70] Ibid., p. 168.

[71] Ibid.

The multi-interest group approach unravelled with the next major workers' action, the 1948 General Strike, when the African elite broke ranks with the workers. The build-up began with an October 1947 strike by the Bulawayo Municipal African Employees Association protesting cuts in food rations. The dispute was eventually resolved following negotiations with management. In February 1948, matters again came to a head when, during wage negotiations, the Municipal authorities offered a paltry 10 per cent increment when workers were demanding more. They rejected the offer and demanded the establishment of a Labour Board, a demand which the Council turned down. Consequently, on 9 April, workers voted for a strike.

Fig. 3.2: General Strike: Crowds assembled at the Bulawayo Location.
[*Source:* National Archives of Zimbabwe]

Strike action was delayed because of a recommendation from a joint meeting of the SRANC, the Federation of Bulawayo African Workers Union (FBAWU) and the RICU to allow the government more time to set up the desired Labour Boards. By 13 April, workers were no longer willing to wait and went on strike in defiance of their leadership.

What had started as a Bulawayo strike soon spread throughout the country, as workers in Umtali, Salisbury, Gwelo, Gatooma, Selukwe and other small towns also downed tools. However, while the strike in the various parts of the country lasted for a little longer, in Bulawayo it fizzled out on 15 April after Benjamin Burombo persuaded the workers to return to work by misleading them into believing that the government had agreed to a wage increase of £5 per month for single workers and £7 10s per month for married men. As all commentators on this issue agree, Burombo's statement was, for reasons that remain unclear, a deliberate misrepresentation meant to break the strike.

The 1948 strike has generated debates about its character and significance and the role of the African elite in the events surrounding it. One issue is whether the strike was, as is claimed by some scholars, a militant industrial workers' initiative which was ultimately betrayed by the African elite[72] or a well-organised action in which the elite played a successful role in directing the workers' actions towards the desired goal. Representing the latter view are Ngwabi Bhebe and Enoch Dumbutshena, who regard the leadership of the elite, in general, and Benjamin Burombo, in particular, in a very positive light, seeing them as able leaders who astutely played the system in order to best advance the cause of worker's action and nationalism.[73]

If the leaders appeared sometimes to be ambivalent about the strike in public, these authors argue, it was only because they wanted to mislead the authorities about their real role as instigators and leaders of the strike in order to avoid arrest. Thus, according to Bhebe,

> It was in the context of the leaders' taking care not [to] be seen
> by the law enforcement agents as advocating for a strike that we
> have to look at their behaviour on 13 April and during the strike.
> The ordinary people had to be seen as if they were acting on their
> own accord. This, as Burombo had said earlier, would make it im-
> possible for the colonial regime to throw everybody in Bulawayo
> jail.[74]

What Bhebe does not adequately address is why Burombo deliberately lied to the workers when he knew that no such undertaking had been made by the authorities. He argues that, once the authorities had agreed to 'appoint Labour Boards within seven days after the strikers returned to work' and had put this promise in writing, the leaders were satisfied that the workers had 'won a big victory' and should return to work. [75] This, however, still does not explain away the lie.

Some scholars are not persuaded by this interpretation of events. Stephen Thornton and John Lunn,[76] among others, maintain that the 1948 strike was a

---

[72] O. Pollak, 'The impact of the Second World War on African labour organisation in Rhodesia', *Rhodesian Journal of Economics*, 7(3), 1973; S. Thornton, 'The Patterning of Industrial
Conflict: African Working Class Assertion and a Collective Employer Response' (Unpublished,
1979); J. Lunn, 'The Political Economy of Protest: The Strikes and Unrest of 1948 in Southern
Rhodesia', (BA(Hons.) thesis, University of Manchester, 1982).

[73] Bhebe, *Benjamin Burombo*; E. Dumbutshena, *Zimbabwe Tragedy* (Nairobi: East African
Publishing House, 1975).

[74] Bhebe, *Benjamin Burombo*, p. 65.

[75] Ibid., p. 70.

[76] Thornton, 'The Patterning of Industrial Conflict'; Lunn, 'The Political Economy of Protest'.

radical and united industrial action that was ultimately betrayed by the leading elites who, either consciously or unconsciously, collaborated with capital and the state in suppressing worker militancy. With respect to Burombo in particular, West questions his *bona fides* as a supporter of the workers' interests and charges him with being a traitor to the workers' cause:

> despite his role as articulator of proletarian and other grievances in the period leading up to the 1948 strike, Burombo, in the end, misled the urban masses, privileging the British over the Blacks, the Whites over the workers, and the coloniser over the colonised.[77]

In any case, West contends, the strike had taken place 'against the pleadings, even without the knowledge, of the elite black leadership'. In his view, 'the working class ... had been betrayed by the elite leadership'.[78] This betrayal destroyed any chances of harnessing the joint efforts of the elite and the masses to make African mobilisation an irresistible force.

Some of Burombo's own contemporaries also dismissed the claim that he led the strike. For instance, Mkushi Khumalo, then President of the National African Federation of Unions, and Grey Bango, then Deputy President of the FBAWU, pointedly commented that Burombo was not a worker but a petty businessman who had no business posing as a workers' leader. They characterised him as an opportunist who had jumped on the bandwagon of workers' protests to advance his own economic interests.[79]

The other issue is the extent to which the events of 1948 amounted to a *general* strike. Ian Phimister and Brian Raftopoulos have disputed this characterisation, arguing that, while secondary industry had grown relatively rapidly in the post-war years, it had not developed to such an extent by 1948 that one could identify a national industrial working class sharing a common class ethos and capable of undertaking concerted class action against capital. They point out that in 1945 the country had only 382 industrial establishments employing a mere 30,439 black workers, that a large percentage of these were transient 'alien natives', and that parochial rather than national perspectives informed worker action. It was impossible for such disparate forces to stage a general strike. The eruptions which gave the impression of being part of one movement were, in fact, a series of separate actions, some of which, as in the Salisbury case, were effectively lockouts imposed by government forces.[80]

---

[77] West, *The Rise of an African Middle Class*, pp. 174-6.
[78] Ibid.
[79] Raftopoulos and Phimister (eds.), *Keep on Knocking*, pp. 69-71.
[80] Phimister and Raftopoulos, '"Kana sora rikatsva ngaritsve"'.

A further question concerns the relationship between workers' movements and nationalism in this period. According to Philip Warhurst, with the rise of African nationalism in the 1950s, the urban working classes were marginalised, or subordinated to politics, by the elite, especially following the formation of the SRANC. This subordination of the trade union movement to politics and the problems emanating from it have, in his view, not yet been resolved.[81]

Tension between workers' movements and nationalism became apparent in the 1960s, particularly in the period of exile politics and the armed struggle, but it is doubtful that the process of the marginalisation of urban workers and trade unions in the anti-colonial struggle began this early. It can be argued that, while the African elite did publicly distance themselves from the workers in the heyday of the tea-party politics of multiracialism, there was considerable co-operation between the two groups. Indeed, according to Raftopoulos, in the 1950s 'trade unionists played an active role in the growth of the nationalist movement by providing leadership to the emerging nationalist parties as well as through the organisational experience that trade unionists brought to the growth of nationalist structures'.[82]

Similarly, T. H. Mothibe has contended that, up to the start of the armed struggle in the 1960s, 'organised labour was not subordinated to petit bourgeois nationalism, rather it was an integral part of the nationalist upsurge' and that 'organised labour and nationalism were intimately connected'.[83] Evidence of the close linkage is the fact that some of those who were at the forefront of efforts to establish the Southern Rhodesia Trade Union Congress (SRTUC) in 1954, such as E. Nkala, J. Z. Moyo and J. Nkomo, were also to feature prominently in the nationalist parties when they were established.[84]

Marginalisation occurred later, with the birth of the armed struggle and the theatre of confrontation between the colonial state and African nationalism shifting from the urban areas to the countryside.[85] Thus was born the misleadingly self-serving post-independence view propagated by Zimbabwe's ruling party that the urban population did not fight for the liberation of the country and that the rural people were the only real fighters for independence. Until the guerrilla war took off in the 1960s, therefore, it is not entirely accurate to speak of urban

[81] Philip R. Warhurst, 'African Trade Unions in Southern Rhodesia, 1948-56: Prelude to Mass Nationalism?', p. 1, cited in Mothibe, 'Zimbabwe: African working class nationalism', pp. 157-80.

[82] Raftopoulos, 'The labour movement in Zimbabwe', pp. 55-6.

[83] Mothibe, 'Zimbabwe: African working class nationalism', pp. 157-8.

[84] Ibid., p. 159.

[85] Ibid., p. 158.

workers being 'marginalised' by or 'subordinated' to petit bourgeoisie politics or nationalism; trade unionism was 'an integral part of the nationalist upsurge'.[86]

The tensions that did arise emerged, in part, from the local unions' involvement with the international trade union movements which, at the height of the Cold War, were competing for influence in developing countries. Those that became involved in Rhodesian labour politics were the Europe-based International Confederation of Free Trade Unions (ICFTU), the American Federation of Labor and Congress of Industrial Organizations, and the Communist World Federation of Trade Unions. Disagreements over which, if any, of these African workers should align themselves to contributed to the disagreement that eventually resulted in the split of the labour movement in 1962.

At the centre of the disagreement was Jamela's perceived closeness to the ICFTU and his unwillingness to co-operate with the nationalist movement. Josiah Maluleke, the Secretary-General under Reuben Jamela, broke away to form the Southern Rhodesian African Trade Union Congress (SRATUC). When the nationalist movement split in 1963 between the Zimbabwe African People's Union (ZAPU), under Joshua Nkomo, and the Zimbabwe African National Union (ZANU), under Ndabaningi Sithole, SRATUC became closely linked to the latter, while a new labour movement calling itself the Zimbabwe African Congress of Unions (ZACU) aligned itself with the former.[87]

As African workers were not recognised under the 1934 Industrial Conciliation Act, they continued to be governed by the 1901 Masters and Servants Act, which forbade them from forming trade unions or engaging in collective bargaining. In the face of growing restlessness and organisation, however, the government was compelled to revisit its labour legislation and eventually came up with a revised Industrial Conciliation Act in 1959 which allowed African workers to form and join trade unions. Excluded were agricultural and domestic workers, public servants and employees of the Rhodesia Railways.[88] Until then, white unions had used their influence to exclude African workers from certain skilled categories of work to protect them from competition in the workplace.

The 1959 act was designed to enable the government to better control the increasingly restive African workers by recognising only skills-based unions, which tended to be predominantly white in membership. This perpetuated the traditional practice of favouring European over African workers. Moreover, the 1959 Act provided for a weighted voting system that privileged skilled workers

---

[86] Ibid., p. 157.

[87] Raftopoulos, *Keep on Knocking*, pp. 78-87.

[88] Peter Harris, 'Industrial workers in Rhodesia, 1946-1972: Working class elites or lumpen-proletariat?', *Journal of Southern African Studies*, 1(2), 1975, pp. 139-61.

and ensured that white unions continued to dominate the country's labour movements.

The advent of mass African nationalism

What West has referred to as the 'Nationalist Moment' began with the formation of the City Youth League (CYL) in 1955 by Salisbury-based young activists George Nyandoro, James Chikerema, Edson Sithole and Duduza Chisiza. The CYL soon eclipsed the multiracial politics of the elite with its domination of the Harari Township Advisory Board and its overshadowing of the leadership of Charles Mzingeli.[89] Reflective of this new militancy was the CYL's sponsorship of the Salisbury Bus Boycott in August 1956 in protest at fare increases by the United Transport Company.

This well-organised boycott, which encompassed most of Harare's African townships, became violent and led to the unfortunate incident in which several women were raped at Carter House in Harari Township (now Mbare) as retribution for breaking the boycott by riding on buses. As several comment-ators have pointed out, this clearly revealed the gender tensions in the urban African community at the time, as young working women sought to assert their independence and the patriarchal urban males, in turn, sought to reassert their control. While Terri Barnes seems to suggest complicity of the leaders of the boycott in the events, it is more likely that unruly elements took advantage of the boycott to pursue their own ends to the possible embarrassment of the leadership; there is no evidence that CYL leaders 'sanctioned violence, especially sexual violence'.[90]

As the work of Barnes has shown, women were active members of the African urban community throughout this period. They participated, with their male counterparts, in the demand for better housing, in the search for respectability, and in demands for political representation. Although they did not establish a militant women's political organisation, as did their counterparts in South Africa during the anti-apartheid struggle in that country, they did join anti-colonial organisations, participate in anti-colonial demonstrations, and lent their voices to the demand for African freedom and human rights. In any case, as Barnes points out, male workers' strikes in the 1940s were influenced by 'how the prevailing economic system affected their females' and the implications of their status as workers for 'issues of family viability and social reproduction';[91]

---

[89] Raftopoulos and Yoshikuni, *Sites of Struggle*, p. 38.

[90] West, *The Rise of an African Middle Class*, p. 206.

[91] T. A. Barnes, '"We Women Worked So Hard": Gender, Labour and Social Reproduction in Colonial Harare, Zimbabwe, 1930-1956' (D.Phil. thesis, University of Zimbabwe, 1993).

the role that women played in the anti-colonial struggle went beyond just their public participation in the activities of labour and political organisations of the time.

Women also had to deal with patriarchy within their own societies and handled that struggle in many subtle ways that defy easy classification and labelling.[92] Clearly there were unresolved tensions between the women's determination to assert their independence and the men's desire to control women's activities. This ambivalence was evident from the fact that, in some instances, women were regarded by men as partners in the struggle, while in others, such as in the Carter House incident, they were seen as enemies.[93]

In September 1957, the CYL came together with the Bulawayo-based African National Council to form the first national political party, the SRANC (later called, simply, the ANC) under the leadership of Joshua Nkomo. Other members of the executive included J. Chikerema, G. Nyandoro, J. Z. Moyo, J. W. Msika, Francis Nehwati, P. Mutandwa and P. Mudikwane.[94] The party proved so popular that, within a relatively short time, it had established no less than 39 branches around the country and boasted a membership of 6,000 by May 1958.[95] The African elite who were later to play a prominent role in nationalist politics were not yet willing to identify themselves with the masses at this point; they still clung to the partnership illusion of the Federation. According to Mlambo, they still believed that the Federation would deliver on its 'partnership' promise, especially since 'most of them were voters, and gained preferential treatment as "emergent" Africans'. Consequently, they 'rejected the leadership of the ANC' and 'preferred to go along with the Federalists'.[96]

The birth of the CYL, and of the ANC and subsequent nationalist political parties, has to be seen within the context of the quickening of post-war nationalism that culminated in the independence of Ghana in 1957, an event which – in the age of the radio and growing international air travel – inspired nationalist struggles elsewhere on the continent, including in Southern Rhodesia.[97]

The ANC challenged the Native Land Husbandry Act, de-stocking, and the

---

[92] T. Barnes and E. Win, *To Live a Better Life: An Oral History of Women in Harare, 1930-70* (Harare: Baobab Books, 1992); T. Barnes, '"So that a labourer could live with his family": Overlooked factors in social and economic strife in urban colonial Zimbabwe, 1945-52', *Journal of Southern African Studies*, 21(1), 1995, pp. 95-113; Barnes, '"We Women Worked So Hard"'.

[93] Scarnecchia, 'Poor women and nationalist politics'.

[94] Mlambo, *Rhodesia: Struggle for a Birthright*, p. 117.

[95] Ngwabi Bhebe, 'The nationalist struggle, 1957-1962', in C. Banana (ed.), *Turmoil and Tenacity* (Harare: College Press, 1989), pp. 66-7.

[96] Mlambo, *Rhodesia: Struggle for a Birthright*, p. 123.

[97] Raftopoulos and Yoshikuni, *Sites of Struggle*, p. 139.

unpopular government-sponsored soil-conservation policies, gaining growing mass support in the process.[98] As discussed above, the NLHA was based on the premise that production in the African reserves would be boosted through a system of private ownership of land rather than the communal or customary rights to land that had existed hitherto. Its implementation, which included reducing the size of land units and the number of cattle that individuals could hold, undermining the chiefs' control of the land and, thus, their power, as well as the enforcement of various conservation measures, such as de-stocking and contour-ridging, antagonised the African rural population and provided a fertile recruiting ground for the nationalist movement. In the end this attempt to change African land tenure through the privatisation of land ownership failed, mainly because of the bitter opposition that it engendered, evident in widespread 'attacks on officials and the spread of nationalist parties into rural areas'.[99]

The ANC also took every opportunity to subvert the authority of the Native Affairs Department in the Reserves, and denounced the policy of partnership as a sham, but it was rather ambiguous on the issue of African self-determination, demanding 'self-government for all the inhabitants', instead.[100] Meanwhile, NLHA policies were displacing large numbers of Africans from the land and leading to a growing flow of people into the urban areas. Thus, it provided the link between the rural and urban African population that was to be such an important support base for the ANC and subsequent nationalist movements in the country.[101]

The African elite were becoming disillusioned with partnership and multiracial tea-party politics which were not leading to racial equality and better respect for African human rights. A major shock came when the leading white liberal whom the Africans regarded as a champion of their interests, Garfield Todd, fell from power in 1958 following a Cabinet revolt against his 'pro-African' policies. White sentiment regarding what was perceived as Todd's softness towards Africans is reflected in Ian Smith's autobiography, where he notes that, during the Federation, things 'went well right from the beginning ... resulting in new investment and economic expansion' but that the one fly in the ointment was Garfield Todd, 'the new Southern Rhodesian Prime Minister, advocating policies

---

[98] For a discussion of the ANC's influence in the rural area of Matopos, see, T. Ranger, *Voices from the Rocks* (Harare: Baobab Books, 1999), ch. 6.

[99] Jocelyn Alexander, *The Unsettled Land: State-making and the Politics of Land in Zimbabwe, 1893-2003* (Harare: Weaver Press; Oxford: James Currey, 2006), p. 59.

[100] Mlambo, *Rhodesia: Struggle for a Birthright*, pp. 118-19.

[101] West, *The Rise of an African Middle Class*, p. 215.

which were not only out of step with public opinion [i.e, white opinion], but which would play into the hands of extremist black politicians'.[102]

The message that multiracialism was a dead end was reinforced by the results of the 1958 general election, which pitted Todd's new party, the United Rhodesia Party, against the United Federal Party (UFP), now under Edgar Whitehead, the Independent Labour Party under Jack Keller, and the Dominion Party, headed by Sir Ray Stockil. The UFP's victory demonstrated support for racial separation rather than Todd's partnership approach, and it became clear to some that the African people's future could no longer be entrusted to the whims of benevolent white liberals and that Africans had to take control of their own destiny.

Not surprisingly, many people abandoned multiracial organisations such as the UFP and the Inter-Racial Society and joined the ANC. It was not until 1960, however, that the elite really embraced African nationalism and abandoned flirting with multiracialism. It was then that the anti-colonial struggle gained some of the names that were to feature prominently in struggle politics for decades to come. Among these were Herbert Chitepo, Bernard Chidzero, Enock Dumbutshena, Ndabaningi Sithole and Robert Mugabe. Not all members of the elite abandoned multiracialism, of course. Some continued to participate in white-led organisations, such as the UFP and Garfield Todd's Central Africa Party.[103]

In February 1959, Whitehead declared a national state of emergency, banned the ANC under the newly enacted Unlawful Organisations Act, confiscated most of the party's assets,[104] and detained over 500 African political leaders. On 1 January 1960, African nationalists[105] launched the National Democratic Party (NDP), whose aims were similar to those of the banned ANC with the exception that it now contained an explicit demand for majority rule under universal suffrage. Other objectives were the abolition of the Land Apportionment Act and improved social conditions and better housing in the urban areas. According to Mothibe, support for the new party was overwhelming, with the NDP attracting no less than 7,000 people to its meetings within a few months of its establishment.[106]

---

[102] Smith, *The Great Betrayal*, pp. 33, 34.

[103] Mlambo, *Rhodesia: Struggle for a Birthright*, p. 129.

[104] According to Lawrence Vambe, *From Rhodesia to Zimbabwe* (London: Heinemann, 1976), p. 281, the government confiscated property to the value of £15,000.

[105] Among the founder members were Michael Mawema, E. J. Zvobgo, T. G. Silundika and E. Nkala.

[106] Mothibe, 'Zimbabwe: African working class nationalism', p. 168.

Fig. 3.3: NDP officials, 1960. *Left to right:* J. Z. Moyo, Moton Malianga, Joshua Nkomo, Enos Nkala, Robert Mugabe.

[*Source:* National Archives of Zimbabwe]

Fig. 3.4: Policing urban violence, 1960.

[*Source:* National Archives of Zimbabwe]

Like its predecessor, the NDP enjoyed both rural and urban support. The NLHA and the de-stocking campaign were wreaking havoc on rural lives, leading to declining agricultural incomes, landlessness and urban drift. In the urban areas, an economic recession resulted in growing unemployment, declining wages and a rising cost of living.[107] The NDP's militancy, particularly the nation-wide protests from late 1960 that resulted in widespread destruction of property and some deaths of protesters,[108] eventually led to the party being banned in December 1961. Africans responded by establishing yet another party, the Zimbabwe African People's Union (ZAPU), also under Joshua Nkomo's leadership. ZAPU was to split a few years later when a new party, the Zimbabwe African National Union (ZANU) was established.

Important to any understanding of the rise of militant African nationalism in this period is the influence of independence struggles elsewhere on the African continent. The Mau Mau uprising in Kenya in the 1950s, in which people took up arms in a bid to drive white settlers off the land, fired the imagination of African nationalists in other countries and demonstrated the potential for challenging white colonial domination. The independence of Ghana in 1957 also served as an inspiration for those struggling for their freedom, and the subsequent independence of many African countries in the early 1960s, particularly of the neighbouring countries of Zambia, Malawi and the Congo, further spurred African nationalist efforts in Zimbabwe.

Towards UDI

Contributing to the 1963 split in ZAPU was Nkomo's alleged weakness as a leader, based on his handling of the 1961 constitutional talks. These talks were held at Southern Rhodesia's insistence, as the Whitehead government hoped that a new constitution would pave the way for Southern Rhodesia's independence from Britain, in line with developments in other British colonies such as Northern Rhodesia and Nyasaland. The resultant 1961 constitution provided for the widening of the franchise in order to include more Africans on the voters' roll by creating a 'B Roll' with lower qualifications, ostensibly because Africans could not meet the higher standards required for the 'A Roll'. It also provided for the enlargement of the Rhodesian Parliament from 30 to 65 members, 15 of whom would be elected by 'B Roll' voters.

White voters approved the new constitution in a referendum on 26 July 1961. However, there were groups within the white community who believed that it

---

[107] Ibid.
[108] Ibid., p. 172.

made too many concessions to African nationalism and was too liberal on racial matters. Patrick Bond points out that political alignments among the white population were shaped by their economic position and interests *vis-à-vis* those of the African. For the industrial and financial capitalists, it was important to nurture the development of a black middle class that would provide a domestic market as well as help to reduce social unrest, while mining and agricultural capital, as well as 'white wage earners and petty bourgeois elements', worried about the implications of political concessions to Africans for labour costs and competition in the workplace. It was 'this coalition of white reaction' that sabotaged the political reforms proposed by the United Federal Party and co- alesced around, first, the Dominion Party and, subsequently, the Rhodesian Front (RF).[109] It was this coalition under the leadership of the RF that won the December 1962 general elections, with Winston Field becoming Prime Minister and Ian Smith his Deputy Prime Minister and Minister of the Treasury.

Winston Field's rule was short-lived, however. He was unable to advance the cause of Rhodesian independence in the face of an intransigent Britain, which insisted that Africans should participate more in the country's political affairs before independence could be considered. Unwilling to declare independence unilaterally, he was forced to resign in April 1964. According to W. Gale,

> Since it was obvious that Britain would not grant Rhodesia independence except on her own terms, which were unacceptable, the whisper grew that Rhodesia would have to take it for herself. Mr. Field shrank from the possible consequences of a unilateral declaration of independence and found himself at loggerheads with his more impatient colleagues, who considered that he was not taking a tough enough line. He accordingly resigned as Prime Minister.[110]

Ian Douglas Smith, the first Rhodesian-born Prime Minister, took over.[111] When negotiations with Britain for independence made little headway, Smith opted for a unilateral declaration of independence on 11 November 1965, thus setting the Rhodesian white population on a collision course with the African majority.

The decision to break away from Britain must be understood also in the context of the tide of decolonisation that was sweeping across the continent. The

---

[109] Patrick Bond, *Uneven Zimbabwe: A Study of Finance, Development, and Underdevelop- ment* (Trenton, NJ: Africa World Press, 1998), p. 111.

[110] W. Gale, *The Years Between, 1923-1973: Half a Century of Responsible Government in Rhodesia* (Salisbury: H. C. P. Andersen, 1973), p. 49.

[111] The story of Field's ouster is told in detail in Smith, *The Great Betrayal*.

Fig. 3.5: Ian Smith signs the Unilateral Declaration of Independence.
[*Source:* National Archives of Zimbabwe]

military revolt in the Congo just a few days after that country's independence led to a mass exodus of whites into Rhodesia and South Africa, confirming local fears about what African majority rule might hold for them unless they could pre-empt it by taking their independence from Britain. Thus, while the attainment of independence elsewhere in Africa was an inspiration to the African nationalists, its significance for the whites was just the opposite.

Meanwhile, in 1963, African nationalists had split into two major movements, ZAPU under Joshua Nkomo and ZANU under Ndabaningi Sithole, following dissatisfaction by some nationalist leaders who claimed that Joshua Nkomo had sold out by accepting the fifteen African seats at the 1961 Constitution. However, as Mlambo demonstrates, the entire NDP team – including some, such as Robert Mugabe, who were to lead the breakaway in 1963 – had concurred with the decision. They were to repudiate the Constitution only later, when they came under fierce criticism from party supporters.[112]

Masipula Sithole argues that the split was caused mainly by personality and temperamental differences among the leaders rather than any fundamental strategic differences on the way forward. He wrote:

[112] Mlambo, *Rhodesia: Struggle for a Birthright*, pp. 151-64.

both Nkomo and Sithole, as well as other leaders, had begun to see the need for radical approaches to the problem of decolonisation (or more correctly, the problem of de-settlerisation) ... However, the difference became that of temperamental disposition ... the temperamental question deals with whether one is 'afraid' or 'courageous' ... It has nothing to do with whether one sees 'what needs to be done' but has everything to do with whether one will 'do what needs to be done'.[113]

Nathan Shamuyarira, a founder member of ZANU, claims that the differences were mainly over Nkomo's decision to establish a government in exile in order to conduct the anti-colonial campaign from outside Rhodesia. He maintains that the split came because 'Nkomo wanted to circumvent the situation at home and organise international support in the hopes of bringing effective pressure to bear', while Sithole and Mugabe believed that it was vital that the party leadership concentrate on 'more organisation at home to crystallise the situation there'.[114] These and other views notwithstanding, the debate on why the split occurred, and who was to blame, remains unresolved.

The split within the nationalist movement ushered in a sad chapter in the history of African nationalism in Rhodesia, as supporters of the two parties fought pitched battles against each other in the streets, diverting attention from the anti-colonial struggle itself. This gave the Rhodesian authorities a convenient excuse to ban both parties in August 1964. Nkomo, Sithole, Mugabe and other leaders were detained or imprisoned. Those who evaded arrest went into exile in neighbouring countries, from where they organised the armed struggle.[115] With the coming of UDI in November 1965, the country entered another phase of its turbulent history.

---

[113] M. Sithole, *Zimbabwe: Struggles within the Struggle* (Harare: Rujeko Publishers, 2nd. edn., 1999), pp. 52-3.

[114] Shamuyarira, *Crisis in Rhodesia*, p. 177. See also Sithole, *Zimbabwe: Struggles within the Struggle*. For another insightful interpretation of the background to Nkomo's ouster by a participant in nationalist politics at the time, see M. Nyagumbo, *With the People* (Salisbury: Graham Publishing, 1980).

[115] For a history of the early efforts to organise the armed struggle, see D. Dabengwa, 'ZIPRA in the Zimbabwe war of liberation', in N. Bhebe and T. Ranger (eds.), *Soldiers in Zimbabwe's Liberation War* (Harare: University of Zimbabwe Publications; London: Currey, 1995), pp. 24-35; J. Tungamirai, 'Recruitment to ZANLA: Building up a war machine', in Bhebe and Ranger (eds.), *Soldiers in Zimbabwe's Liberation War*, pp. 36-45.

Conclusion

African organisation and political activity took various forms in the period under review, ranging from workers' strikes, and elite experimentation with multiracialism, to the rise of militant nationalism. Similarly, the conception of nationalism changed over time. Until the mid-1950s, Africans generally accepted their place as citizens of the British Empire and asked only that they be governed fairly and well. Some, like the elite, aspired to be incorporated into the imperial system as equals of the Europeans. It was only when the mirage of multiracial partnership disappeared that they turned their backs on white paternalism and began to demand self-government and independence. By the end of the 1950s, therefore, the tone and goals of the African political movement had become more radicalised under the leadership of the emerging nationalists.

There were tensions along class, gender and ethnic lines in the anti-colonial movement. Class tensions had surfaced in the cleavage between the elite and the workers in the era of multiracialism, and continued into the 1960s between the nationalist leaders and the workers. Meanwhile, the Carter House incidents and the marginalisation of women in male-led nationalist parties and trade unions spoke to the gender tensions that existed and which, arguably, were never resolved. Ethnicity surfaced after 1963 when ZAPU and ZANU became constituted on broadly tribal lines, notwithstanding the fact that each had members of other ethnic groups within its leadership and following. Thus, while the anti-colonial struggle coalesced in the late 1950s behind the banner of nationalism, there was by no means a common view of how the envisioned nation would look.

As for the whites, their perception of their role as members of the Empire also underwent change. With roots in Britain or its dominions and regarding Rhodesia as a British colony, most white settlers proudly considered themselves to be fully-fledged members of the British Empire and embodying the spirit of those who occupied the country in 1890. Indeed, Rhodesians of British origin had consistently discriminated against non-British groups such as Afrikaners, Jews and Poles and marginalised them in national affairs while keeping their numbers small by applying stringent immigrant criteria. [116]

Rhodesians helped to establish the Central African Federation, partly to counterbalance Afrikaner nationalism, but their confidence was shaken when Britain refused to grant them independence in the early 1960s, insisting on the principle of 'no independence before majority rule'. Thereafter, Rhodesian white identity seems to have taken on a very contradictory character; they regarded

[116] Mlambo, *White Immigration into Rhodesia*, pp. 49-67.

themselves as the upholders of true British values and defenders of such values against the twin threats of African nationalism and Communism, as well as, ironically, against the decadence of Britain itself. Their often repeated claims to defend 'civilisation' and 'standards' reflected these beliefs. Such claims were often backed by appeals to the 'pioneering spirit' of their Rhodesian ancestors. The irony was that 'most of the 1965 UDI rebels who appealed to the free and proud spirit of their Pioneer ancestors to mobilise domestic support for their defiance of the world were, in fact, not descendants of the Pioneers at all'.[117] Only 27 per cent of the Rhodesian Front leadership sampled by B. Schulz were Rhodesian-born; 33 per cent had been born in South Africa, and 26 per cent in Britain.[118]

[117] Ibid., p. 2.
[118] Barry M. Schulz, 'Homeward bound? A survey study of the limits of white Rhodesian nationalism and permanence', *Ufahamu*, 5(3), 1975, p. 605.

4

Social and Economic Developments during the UDI Period

Joseph Mtisi, Munyaradzi Nyakudya and Teresa Barnes

Introduction

The trajectory of events in Zimbabwe's history between 1965 and 1980 differed from that of most countries in Africa in a number of ways. Whereas a number of them attained their independence in the 1950s and 1960s, developments in Southern Rhodesia took a different turn. While Britain claimed she was committed to the attainment of black majority rule, white Rhodesians were determined to safeguard their economic and political privileges and move towards consolidating Southern Rhodesia as a 'white man's country'. To this end, 'one of the most centrally controlled capitalist economies in the world' was created,[1] which Herbst aptly describes as 'Socialism-for-the-Whites'.[2]

For their part, Africans sought to gain independence, as was the case in many other countries. These conflicting visions of the future led to a complex, and often violent, power struggle as various forces sought to define and redefine the political, social and economic boundaries of the desired nation. This chapter attempts to unravel these complex struggles and discuss how they found expression in the various spheres of Rhodesian life during the period following UDI in 1965.

Background

As has been shown in the previous chapter, the years after the Second World War were marked by an upsurge of African nationalism throughout the continent.[3] This expressed itself in increased confrontation with the state, mainly through industrial action, and a proliferation of organised political parties that challenged colonial rule. Southern Rhodesia was not spared these developments. The 1945

---

[1] E. S. Pangeti. 'The State and the Manufacturing Industry: A Study of the State as Regulator and Entrepreneur in Zimbabwe, 1930-1990' (D.Phil. thesis, University of Zimbabwe, 1995), p. 117.

[2] J. Herbst, *State Politics in Zimbabwe* (Harare: University of Zimbabwe Publications, 1990), p. 22.

[3] For a detailed study of the Africa-wide process of decolonisation, see R. W. M. Louis, *Decolonization and African Independence: The Transfers of Power, 1960-1980* (New Haven: Yale University Press, 1988).

Railway Workers Strike and the 1948 General Strike,[4] whose magnitude and organisation were unprecedented in the colony, exemplify this confrontation. Michael West observed that 'although a sense of African nationhood began to take hold among Africans in Southern Rhodesia between 1945 and 1948, this nation was not imagined as a sovereign and independent entity'.[5] The focus of political agitation in the immediate post-war period was directed at European misrule rather than at removing it altogether. However, 'by the early 1960s the black elite, as a social category, had moved to an African nationalist stance, with its leadership demanding transfer of political power from the white minority to the African majority'.[6]

Although the idea of racial partnership had been put forward in order to push for the Federation of Rhodesia and Nyasaland in 1953, in reality very little had changed in terms of the political and economic status of the Africans. Despite the efforts to achieve some degree of African advancement, developments since 1953 confirmed Huggins's description of the Federation as the relationship 'between the horse and the rider'.[7] From the late 1950s, it became apparent to the Africans that their interests were not going to be addressed through the Federal arrangement. Their reaction is succinctly captured in the declaration by Michael Mawema, president of the National Democratic Party (NDP), that 'the [colonial] Government [is] wasting time "on small things", instead, we feel we should get control of the Government itself'.[8]

Africans in Southern Rhodesia thus turned increasingly to confrontation with the colonial authorities in the tumultuous 1960s. Urban areas such as Harare and Bulawayo were rocked by the 'Zhii Riots' in July 1961, in which 18 people were killed by police.[9] Inspired by nationalist sentiment as well as by their opposition

---

[4] See L. W. Ndlovu, 'The 1945 African Railway Strike' (BA(Hons) dissertation, University of Zimbabwe, 1983); B. M. Zulu, 'The History of Railway African Workers Union' (BA(Hons) dissertation, 1985); Shi Xiuchun, '1948 Strike in Salisbury and Bulawayo' (BA(Hons) dissertation, University of Zimbabwe, 1986).

[5] M. West, *The Rise of an African Middle Class: Colonial Zimbabwe, 1898-1965* (Bloomington: Indiana University Press, 2002), p. 168.

[6] Ibid., p. 203.

[7] T. R. M. Creighton, *The Anatomy of Partnership: Southern Rhodesia and the Central African Federation* (London: Faber, 1960).

[8] Quoted in A. Megahey, *Humphrey Gibbs: Beleaguered Governor* (London: Macmillan, 1998), p. 72.

[9] See T. O. Ranger, 'The Meaning of Urban Violence: *Zhii* in Bulawayo, July 1960', paper presented in the Economic History Department Seminar Series, University of Zimbabwe, 2000.

to the Native Land Husbandry Act, rural residents also demonstrated their own anger over Rhodesian rule(s).[10] In the Sabi North reserve in 1961, for example,

> An LDO [Land Development Officer charged with implementing the Land Husbandry Act] who was trying to measure boundaries of arable plots was stopped by a crowd of thirty people. When he returned to his car he found that he could not move it because logs had been put in front of the wheels. 150 villagers forced him to attend a meeting during which he was interrogated about the Land Husbandry Act and destocking issues. Following the interrogation, the LDO was forced to write down: 'No allocation and no destocking.' Finally the headman told the LDO that he would be beaten up if he tried to return to the reserve.[11]

There was similar resistance to the Native Land Husbandry Act in the Honde Valley. Heike Schmidt states that villagers in Chief Mandeya's area often refused to dip their cattle and threatened the lives of government officials such as extension workers and demonstrators in open protest against the Act. Resistance against land pegging and soil conservation lessons was also not uncommon.[12]

The Southern Rhodesian government was, however, determined to crush any form of African nationalism. The NDP was banned in 1961, but was quickly replaced by ZAPU, which was itself banned in September 1962, leading to the formation of the People's Caretaker Council. It is important to note, however, that the early establishment of an organisational presence in townships and rural areas when nationalist activity was still legal would have important legacies in the guerrilla war era of the 1970s.

In the context of this increasingly militant resistance to colonial rule, the United Federal Party government led by Garfield Todd, and later by Sir Edgar Whitehead, made a number of legislative changes that were designed to give

[10] It is important to note that the impact of the NLHA was uneven. In some areas in the eastern highlands, it was not possible to implement it owing to the terrain. However, where it was implemented, the NLHA attracted resistance. For a fuller discussion of the NLHA, see I. Phimister, 'Rethinking the reserves: Southern Rhodesia's Land Husbandry Act reviewed', *Journal of Southern African Studies*, 19(2), 1993, pp. 225-39; J. Alexander, *The Unsettled Land: State-making and the Politics of Land in Zimbabwe, 1893-2003* (Harare: Weaver Press; Oxford: James Currey, 2006); N. Bhebe, *Benjamin Burombo: African Politics in Zimbabwe, 1947-1958* (Harare: College Press, 1989); V. E. M. Machingaidze, 'Agrarian change from above: The Southern Rhodesia Native Land Husbandry Act and African responses', *International Journal of African Historical Studies*, 24(3), 1991, pp. 557-88.

[11] N. Bhebe, 'The nationalist struggle', in C. Banana (ed.), *Turmoil and Tenacity: Zimbabwe, 1890-1980* (Harare: College Press, 1989), p. 97.

[12] H. Schmidt, 'The Social and Economic Impact of Political Violence in Zimbabwe, 1890-1990: A Case Study of the Honde Valley' (D.Phil. thesis, Oxford University, 1996), pp. 178-80.

Africans a limited degree of advancement.[13] Larry Bowman argues that these concessions were granted in the hope that the colony would attain Dominion status.[14] Under pressure, the Whitehead government further pushed for a new constitution in 1961. This constitution facilitated progress towards majority rule, provided for changes to the hated system of land tenure, and granted more concessions on the issue of rights.[15] These concessions, however, caused a stir among the right-wing elements in the government, who preferred a much slower pace of change. Among the dissenting voices was Ian Douglas Smith, who opposed the 'liberal' provisions of the 1961 constitution. The displeased elements formed a new party, the Rhodesian Front (RF), headed by Winston Field, to contest in the 1962 elections.[16] The RF won the elections convincingly with Field as Prime Minister, sounding the death knell to the moderate liberal period that had started in the early 1950s. At the same time, Africans felt that their progress towards majority rule was being impeded. Consequently, there was increased agitation, some of it violent.[17]

Two other developments in the early 1960s had an important bearing on the course of events. The first was the end of the Federation in 1963. On the eve of its dissolution, a central issue related to the future of the colonies and, in particular, how Southern Rhodesia would develop. Britain was unwilling to grant independence without a sign of commitment to black majority rule on its part. The second development, closely linked to the first, related to the political changes that were occurring in Southern Rhodesia itself. In 1964, Winston Field was ousted as Prime Minister because some in his party felt that he had failed 'to bring [back] an assurance of independence on terms acceptable to them'.[18] He was replaced by Ian Smith, who led the country until 1979.

[13] For a more detailed discussion on the liberal drift in Rhodesian politics, see K. M. Thornton, 'The Liberalism of Garfield Todd' (BA(Hons) dissertation, University of Zimbabwe, 1984).

[14] L. W. Bowman, *Politics in Rhodesia: White Power in an African State* (Cambridge, MA: Harvard University Press, 1973), pp. 442-6. A Dominion was a self-governing colony in the British Empire, such as New Zealand, Australia, Canada and South Africa.

[15] R. Welensky, *Welensky's 4000 Days: The Life and Death of the Federation of Rhodesia and Nyasaland* (London: Collins, 1964), pp. 275-82. Africans were, however, opposed to the constitution as they were holding out for a majority-rule settlement, which was now on the cards for Northern Rhodesia.

[16] The support base of the RF lay in the 'domestic white classes', including farmers, white workers and the petit bourgeoisie. However, the alliance was not a solid one and became increasingly fractured; see P. Godwin and I. Hancock, *'Rhodesians Never Die': The Impact of War and Political Change on White Rhodesia, c.1970-1980* (Oxford: Oxford University Press, 1993).

[17] N. Shamuyarira, *Crisis in Rhodesia* (London: Deutsch, 1965); N. Sithole, *African Nationalism* (London: Oxford University Press, 1968).

[18] Ibid.

The political changes of 1964 ignited a series of diplomatic visits between Salisbury and London meant to resolve the impasse over the political future of the colony.[19] The British position was encompassed in 'Five Principles', the conditions for granting Rhodesian independence: unimpeded progress to majority rule as enshrined in the 1961 constitution, guarantees against retrogressive changes to the constitution, improvement in the political status of Africans, an end to all forms of racial discrimination, and the acceptability of any agreement to the Rhodesian people as a whole. The addition of a sixth principle, NIB-MAR: No Independence Before Majority Rule, was critical in leading to UDI in November 1965.

White intransigence inadvertently supported the further development of the nationalist movement. The nationalists' response to the banning of the NDP and ZAPU was twofold. Some members of ZAPU, citing their impatience with the party's sluggish response to the end of unsuccessful constitutional talks in London, broke away and formed ZANU in August 1963, with Ndabaningi Sithole as the first president. Secondly, the two political parties began to send young recruits, who included Dumiso Dabengwa, for military training to Soviet bloc countries. Dabengwa recalled:

> I was among one of the first groups that left the country for Zambia in 1963. Towards the end of 1963 we left Zambia for Tanzania en route to various countries in the then socialist bloc. My group, for instance, went to train in the Soviet Union. After training, most of the groups assembled in Zambia toward the end of 1964 and in early 1965.[20]

The early objective of these fighters was to carry out acts of sabotage, rather than conduct guerrilla warfare.[21] However, following UDI there was a gradual shift towards establishing a larger-scale military offensive. After sending the first small group out to China to be trained in 1963, the armed wing of ZANU, the Zimbabwe African National Liberation Army (ZANLA), carried out its first attack in April 1966. Seven ZANLA guerrillas died on their way to the Charter area when they encountered Rhodesian troops outside Chinhoyi (then called

---

[19] Meetings after the UDI included the ill-fated meetings on HMS Tiger and HMS Fearless in 1966 and 1968, respectively. See J. R. T. Wood, *So Far and No Further!: Rhodesia's Bid for Independence during the Retreat from Empire, 1959-1965* (Victoria, BC: Trafford, c.2005).

[20] D. Dabengwa, 'ZIPRA in the Zimbabwe war of national liberation', in N. Bhebe and T. O. Ranger (eds.), *Soldiers in Zimbabwe's Liberation War* (Harare: University of Zimbabwe Publications; London: James Currey, 1995), p. 26.

[21] Ibid., p. 27; Bhebe, 'The nationalist struggle', pp. 13-16.

Sinoia).[22] This early phase of the armed struggle included activities such as the 1967-68 Wankie Campaign, in which the Zimbabwe People's Revolutionary Army (ZIPRA) guerrillas based in Zambia joined forces with members of Um-khonto we Sizwe (MK), the armed wing of the African National Congress in South Africa. The objective of the campaign was 'to fight the common settler enemy to the finish, at any point of encounter as they make their way to their respective fighting zones'.[23] Ironically, the ZIPRA and MK forces fought initially against other Africans, soldiers of the Rhodesian African Rifles (RAR),[24] who were later reinforced by further ground and air forces.[25]

Envisioning the nation, defining citizenship

The political struggles of the UDI period were most visibly about the political, social and economic interests of blacks and whites, i.e. conflicting visions of the desired nation. On the whole, the white population sought to maintain its interests and hegemony, and Africans were determined to challenge the status quo. This would seem to support the interpretation of the UDI period as being characterised by two rigidly opposed racial camps; however, there existed a more heterogeneous terrain of political opinion: race did not always inform the actions of the members of the different interest groups. It is also worth remembering in this context that a small Coloured community evolved in Rhodesia, developing a largely reformist set of responses to these political developments.[26] The racial line was sometimes crossed, either because of political and economic exigencies, or for personal interests.

As early as 1923, when the colony attained Responsible Government status, the white section of the Rhodesian population demonstrated that it was able to assert its own interests in its relationship with foreign capital, as well as to take control of the state as an instrument for realising those interests. By 1965, it had gone a long way towards bringing into existence its vision of the nation. West observes that a long-standing goal of the whites in Rhodesia since 1923

[22] D. Martin and P. Johnson, *The Struggle for Zimbabwe* (Harare: Zimbabwe Publishing House, 1981), p. 10.

[23] Oliver Tambo, 1968, quoted in N. Bhebe, *The ZAPU and ZANU Guerrilla Warfare and the Evangelical Lutheran Church in Zimbabwe* (Gweru: Mambo Press, 1999), p. 19.

[24] The RAR was a military unit that consisted of black soldiers led by white officers. It had been originally raised to fight in the Second World War.

[25] E. Sibanda, *The Zimbabwe African People's Union, 1961-87: A Political History of Insurgency in Southern Rhodesia* (Trenton, NJ: Africa World Press, 2005), p. 106. For further reading on the liberation struggle, see the next chapter in this book.

[26] J. Muzondidya, *Walking a Tightrope: Towards a Social History of the Coloured People of Zimbabwe* (Asmara: Africa World Press, 2004), pp 217-22.

was to achieve 'outright independence'.[27] Successive Rhodesian leaders made it clear that their prime aim was to ensure that the settler community remained comfortable; what differed, however, were the strategies by which they intended to achieve this. The founding principles of the RF, which dominated white politics in the UDI period, clearly communicated this vision:

> the RF promised to preserve each community's right to maintain its own identity, to preserve proper standards by ensuring that advancement must be on merit, to uphold the principle of the Land Apportionment Act, to oppose compulsory integration, to support the government's right to provide separate amenities for the different races, and to protect skilled workers against cheap labour. Above all, the party promised 'that the Government of Southern Rhodesia will remain in responsible hands', and that it would ensure 'the permanent establishment of the European'.[28]

This same thinking drove whites in their fight against the African nationalists. The position of some Rhodesian whites was described in a pamphlet:

> We must know what we are defending. This is nothing less than the survival of what is left of Christian Civilization and its values and standards, the belief in right and wrong, which Communism exists to destroy.[29]

Rhodesian rhetoric sometimes hit the heights of historical fantasy. It was claimed, for instance, that

> Seldom in the history of mankind has a gallant little country such as ours, with so many virtues and so little fault, been so grievously beset by enemies as we are. The Russian colossus is on the march to subjugate and enslave all of Africa and we, like the Spartans at Thermopylae, are a major stumbling block in their path.[30]

Essentially, the RF notion of the nation was that whites would dominate it, and that citizenship would be assigned primarily on the basis of race.

But the aspirations of the white community were significantly more complex. Admittedly, race was a useful political resource for mobilising support for particular agendas as well as for marking out the lines of exclusion. However, it was not as powerful in inspiring loyalty to 'the nation', however defined, nor in

---

[27] West, *The Rise of an African Middle Class*, p. 233.

[28] Godwin and Hancock, *'Rhodesians Never Die'*, p. 57.

[29] 'Rhodesian Christian Group pamphlet, March 1977', quoted in Bruce Moore-King, *White Man, Black War* (Harare: Baobab Books, 1988), p. 51.

[30] P. K. van der Byl, Minister of Foreign Affairs, 1977, speaking at the top national rehabilitation centre for the war-wounded. Quoted in J. Frederikse, *None but Ourselves: Masses vs Media in the Making of Zimbabwe* (Harare: Zimbabwe Publishing House, 1982) p. 157.

Fig. 4.1: Whites demonstrate against Ian Smith in Salisbury.
[*Source:* National Archives of Zimbabwe]

determining the actions of the different groupings involved in the contests of the period. The settler community itself was divided on a number of lines such that a sense of nationhood had to be, in the words of Godwin and Hancock, 'manufactured'.[31] In essence, factors other than race also influenced white opinion. J. A. McKenzie sees a significant degree of heterogeneity among whites in Rhodesia and thus cautions that 'while in the 1960s, the dominant social pressures among the whites were for political conformity [and] racial solidarity ... it would be a mistake to stress the unity of opinion too strongly. Not all white Rhodesians were the same; not all white Rhodesian farmers were the same.'[32] In the first instance, the roughly 200,000 white settlers in the colony could not speak confidently of a common history, as 'the overwhelming majority were either immigrants or had been born in the country since the Second World War'.[33] In addition, a significant number already had – or could easily obtain – foreign citizenship, a factor which served to divide white loyalty to the 'nation'.

[31] Godwin and Hancock, *'Rhodesians Never Die'*, p. 17.
[32] J. A. McKenzie, 'Commercial Farmers in the Governmental System of Colonial Zimbabwe' (D.Phil. thesis, University of Zimbabwe, 1989), p. 21. This argument is also made by Godwin and Hancock, *'Rhodesians Never Die'*.
[33] Ibid., p. 7. See also A. S. Mlambo, *White Immigration into Rhodesia: From Occupation to Federation* (Harare: University of Zimbabwe Publications, 2000).

Other factors dividing the white community included ethnicity, locality, occupation and class. These acted as sources of identity as well as division, and they 'emerged more naturally' than the largely invented idea of nationhood.[34] At face value, the successive RF electoral victories between 1962 and 1980 would seem to point to a high degree of consensus within the settler community.[35] However, closer analysis of white politics reveals an uneven success of the RF in manufacturing this sense of nationhood. Godwin and Hancock suggest that political opinion among Rhodesian whites was divided into three major views. One third, they argue, consisted of 'supremacists and segregationists' who believed that blacks would always be unable to rule themselves; a quarter was made up of liberals who supported African independence, while the balance 'did not oppose African advancement but hoped to delay its passage into majority rule for as long as possible'.[36] The RF was thus an uneasy alliance of right-wing and moderate elements in white society.

The 1969 constitution exposed these differences by extending the franchise to selected groups and allowing for a slow progress towards majority rule. Minority groups such as Asians and Coloureds were also included on the 'A' voters' roll,[37] although, as Muzondidya points out, this was more of a political gimmick than anything else, given the exclusion of Asians and Coloureds from European land in the 1969 Land Tenure Act, and the continued call for segregation in schools and hospitals.[38] Underpinning these apparent concessions was the strategy of 'inclusive exclusion' spearheaded by Smith and his wing of the RF: the incorporation of other racial groups (Africans, Coloureds, and Asians) in the structures of government in such a way as to prevent them from effectively influencing policy. Thus, the changes were indeed cosmetic. It was hoped that co-opting the African middle class would help in stemming the tide of African nationalism. In addition, the appearance of accommodating Africans was deemed useful in securing a settlement with Britain. The extremist wing, however, chose the hard-line stance of excluding Africans and considered the attempts by Smith to engage with Britain as irrelevant.

The 1969 constitution meant that the line dividing citizens from subjects became progressively more porous;[39] it qualified the binary conception of colo-

[34] Godwin and Hancock, 'Rhodesians Never Die', p. 21.
[35] Ibid., p. 56.
[36] Ibid., p. 46.
[37] The 'A' roll was previously reserved exclusively for the white electorate.
[38] Muzondidya, Walking a Tightrope, p. 201.
[39] For a detailed discussion of the citizen–subject divide in colonial society, see M. Mamdani, Citizen and Subject: Contemporary Africa and the Legacy of Late Colonialism (Princeton, NJ: Princeton University Press, 1996).

nial society as constituting white citizens and black subjects.[40] To understand society and politics under UDI through the prism of the citizen/subject binary, one needs to take into account the changes in the political situation and the concessions that were granted over time. With increasing nationalist resistance, it became clear that Smith's original vision of the nation could not be realised. From an initial stance of denying the possibility of black majority rule 'in a thousand years', the RF government was forced to retreat significantly. It not only conceded that majority rule was a possibility, but also engaged in a number of conferences in a bid to broker a deal with the nationalists.[41] The political aspirations of the RF were thus altered by circumstances, leading to a shift from the ideal to the possible.

African politics during the UDI period were quite as complex as those obtaining in the white community. The dominant voice amongst the Africans was that of the nationalists. By the late 1940s and early 1950s, the African middle class in Southern Rhodesia, as in many African countries, had assumed the leadership of the nationalist cause. West and Mandaza concur that such leaders aspired to acquire 'a proper share in the economic, social and political privileges enjoyed by the colonialists', and to inherit the privileged position of the minority whites.[42] The nationalist vision of the new nation tended to emphasise issues of equal opportunity and racial equality without critiquing the exploitative system and the class differences. In essence, it was not so much a new nation that the middle class envisioned as a change in the mode by which citizenship was assigned in order to enjoy the associated benefits. In constructing their idea of the nation, the nationalists drew heavily on discourses of race and origin.[43] The ideas of origin and indigeneity were clearly communicated in the often-used phrase *mwana wevhu* (child of the soil). On the one hand, the phrase communicated a claim to citizenship on the basis of origin; on the other, it de-legitimised the claims of other groups on the basis of their being 'settlers' on the land. As with the case of white society, race was stronger as a tool of exclusion than as a source of loyalty to the 'nation'.

[40] For a critique of Mamdani's work, see J. Alexander, *The Unsettled Land*, pp. 1-14.

[41] These conferences included those at Geneva and Victoria Falls, as well as at Lancaster House; such political repositioning was a significant feature of UDI political struggles.

[42] West, *The Rise of an African Middle Class*; I. Mandaza, *Race, Colour and Class in Southern Africa: A Study of the Coloured Question in the Context of an Analysis of the Colonial and White Settler Racial Ideology and African Nationalism in Twentieth Century Zimbabwe, Zambia and Malawi* (Harare: SAPES, 1997), p. 528.

[43] See J. Muzondidya, '"Zimbabwe for Zimbabweans": Invisible subject minorities and the quest for justice and reconciliation in post-colonial Zimbabwe', in B. Raftopoulos and T. Savage, *Zimbabwe: Injustice and Political Reconciliation* (Cape Town: Institute for Justice and Reconciliation, 2004), p. 214.

As Alexander *et al.* have pointed out, however, the middle class did not hold a monopoly over the concept of nationalism. The rural masses also had agency and 'redefine[d] issues of local concern within the framework of a nationalist project'.[44] In their view, the basic goal of local nationalism in the Shangani area, for example, was to 'replace what was from their viewpoint a bad state – one which removed people from a viable environment and dumped them in wild forests, one which commanded and demanded – by what they dreamt of as a good state, which would cease discrimination, provide services, restore markets and be accountable to them as citizens.'[45] This basic goal, held in common with other communities, was not a static nationalism. Alexander *et al.* further point out that

> In the Shangani, the pioneers of nationalism were Christian modernizers. But as the confrontation with the state intensified, many teachers, preachers and storekeepers became identified as at best 'moderates' and at worst 'sellouts'. Furthermore, the need to develop a [wider] nationalism ... meant an appeal to multiple histories and to multiple religious legitimations. Local nationalism became less Christian and more 'traditionalist' over time.[46]

Notwithstanding this contention, it is clear that the idea of the 'nation' had to compete for loyalty with other more parochial interests related to class, gender, religion and ethnicity.

The numerous examples of Africans who served on the side of 'white Rhodesia' in various capacities as policemen, soldiers and informers are evidence that racial antagonism was not always the overriding factor in determining political loyalties. For example, while white men were conscripted into the Rhodesian army, black soldiers were volunteers until early 1979, when the first 'national service' intake for black men was instituted.[47] The Rhodesian African Rifles had white officers and black soldiers; the one battalion that had been raised to fight in the Second World War was doubled in size in the 1970s; the counter-insurgency Selous Scouts had black members, as did the police and other security forces. There are a number of possible explanations for the phenomenon of blacks who risked (and lost) their lives in the service of white hegemony. The recollections of an African member of the Rhodesian police force gives an indication of the attraction of joining the forces of 'law and order'. G. A. Chaza reminisces:

---

[44] J. Alexander, J. McGregor and T. O. Ranger, *Violence and Memory: One Hundred Years in the Dark Forests of Matabeleland* (Harare: Weaver Press; Oxford: James Currey, 2000), p. 85.

[45] Ibid., p. 86.

[46] Ibid., p. 87.

[47] Frederikse, *None but Ourselves*, p. 235. She records that 'the initial turn-out ... was a pitiful 300 out of over 1,500 blacks called up to fight'.

there, in the streets of the big city who should I meet but a former classmate of mine at Domboshava Government School – one Solomon Dzviti. I just met him by chance in the big city whilst he was on beat-patrol dress in the uniform of a Native Town Policeman – a branch of the B.S.A.P. [British South Africa Police] force ... This native police branch was for the educated elite only, during those days ... There was Solomon – transformed and dazzling in police uniform, *doing a man's job!* Did I stand a chance of joining the police force too? Of course I had, Solomon assured.[48] [Emphasis added.]

The approach of Ron Reid-Daly, a commander of the infamous 'pseudo' Selous Scouts, in recruiting African soldiers for the Scouts highlighted both social status and economic factors as influencing the decisions of those who joined:

I ... reminded them forcibly that we were looking for *men to do men's work ... very tough men ...* then showed them promotion posts available to men in the Selous Scouts. After they had digested this I casually lobbed in another bombshell. From the day a man passed the selection course and became a Selous Scout proper, he would draw an additional one dollar and twenty cents per day, special unit allowance, which would put their pay on a par with that of sergeant majors in a rifle battalion ... Suddenly they were all keen volunteers once more.[49] [Emphasis added.]

This notion of participation in violent acts as a way not only to retain or contest political power but to define and redefine gendered norms was a recurring theme in the 15-year period of the war waged between the nationalists and the Rhodesian state.

Extension of state power and economic reorganisation

Britain responded to UDI by severing diplomatic ties with Salisbury and placing official economic sanctions on Rhodesia. The sanctions included the cessation of trade with Rhodesia, her removal from the sterling area and Commonwealth

---

[48] G. A. Chaza, *Bhurakuwacha: Black Policeman in Rhodesia* (Harare: College Press, 1998), pp. 10-11. Chaza joined the police force in 1936 but left it in 1957, disillusioned by Rhodesian racism.

[49] Ron Reid-Daly, as told to Peter Stiff, *Selous Scouts: Top Secret War* (Alberton: Galago, 1982), p. 107. Black Scouts were known as 'pseudos' because they acted as *agents provocateurs* in rural communities and when infiltrated into the guerrilla armies. White Scouts were notorious for painting their faces black and committing atrocities which Rhodesian propaganda then blamed on the guerrillas.

Fig. 4.2: Demonstrators appeal to Harold Wilson for support.
[*Source:* National Archives of Zimbabwe]

preference system, and denying the country access to London's capital markets.[50] On the trade front, Britain banned the purchase of Rhodesian sugar and tobacco, stopping a net 71 per cent by value of Rhodesian exports to Britain.[51] In December 1965, Britain extended the ban to all minerals and foodstuffs, which made up 95 per cent of Rhodesian exports to Britain. In January 1966, it imposed an embargo on Rhodesian trade, making the purchase of any of its products a violation of British law. For its part, the United Nations imposed an oil embargo in April 1966, followed by comprehensive mandatory sanctions on 29 May 1968.

At the time, it was hoped that sanctions would achieve the intended goal of pressuring the Smith government to quickly reverse the declaration of independence. The British Prime Minister, Harold Wilson, believed that the sanctions would bring the rebellion to an end 'within a matter of weeks rather than months'.[52] This optimistic assessment was based on knowledge of the Rhodesian economy's dependence on external economic relations, particularly with Britain. In 1965, the country was essentially an exporter of primary products, the most important being tobacco, whose revenue contributed a third of the total export

[50] H. R. Strack, *Sanctions: The Case of Rhodesia* (Syracuse, NY: Syracuse University Press, 1978), pp. 16-20.
[51] Ibid.
[52] Pangeti, 'The State and the Manufacturing Industry', p. 110.

value. Minerals represented another 22 per cent.[53] Britain was Rhodesia's largest market for tobacco. Rhodesian exports contributed 45 per cent of national income, of which 34 per cent was, in turn, spent on imports. Rhodesia also relied on imports for virtually all its machinery, transport, equipment, chemicals and spare parts, and all of its petroleum. Added to this list were capital, technical skills and management capability.[54] The fact that Rhodesia was a landlocked country rendered it seemingly even more vulnerable to international economic sanctions.

The RF government was determined to cushion the white section of the population, on whose endurance the UDI scheme was dependent, from the effects of sanctions through economic reorganisation and the extension of state power. In the agricultural sector, this reorganisation came in the form of a drive to reduce the production of tobacco in order to diversify the type of crops produced. McKenzie points out that 'the area devoted to flue-cured tobacco in 1965/66 was 24,000 acres less than in 1964/65'.[55] The government announced a scheme to limit the next year's crop to 200 million pounds at a guaranteed price of 28*d.* per pound.[56] This was meant, in part, to reduce dependency on tobacco while ensuring that those white farmers who continued to grow the crop would remain solvent.

Simultaneously, the state sought to encourage large-scale production of maize, cotton, wheat, soya beans and beef. Besides reducing the farmers' exposure to the impact of sanctions, this was also aimed at national food self-sufficiency, thus reducing the food import bill, and its success was evident in the levels of production of maize, cotton and wheat. In 1972, maize production totalled 18 million bags valued at R$26,250,000, with an average yield of 62 bags per hectare. This was a marked improvement from the 5.2 million bags valued at less than R$10,000,000 that were produced in 1965, with an average of 30 bags per hectare.[57] However, the greatest success came in cotton production, which expanded by 800 per cent to over 200 million pounds between 1965 and 1972.[58] This success was expensive, however; European agriculture was able to survive largely because of increased state subsidies and loans. The successes achieved in

[53] W. Minter and E. Schmidt, 'When sanctions worked: The case of Rhodesia re-examined', *African Affairs*, 87(347), 1988, p. 20.

[54] Ibid.

[55] McKenzie, 'Commercial Farmers in the Governmental System', p. 97.

[56] Ibid.

[57] Strack, *Sanctions*, p. 94.

[58] Ibid.

agricultural diversification and the expansion of production were characterised by a number of problems. In the case of tobacco, while a significant reduction of production was achieved, its marketing remained problematic.[59] Where wheat was concerned, the expansion of local production in the absence of an export market translated to an oversupply in the domestic market and falling prices, which ultimately meant lower profit margins for farmers.[60] A similar problem emerged in the case of sugar production, where the expansion of production coincided with falling world prices and a shrinking export market.[61]

Another problem faced by farmers related to their access to inputs (in particular, nitrogenous fertiliser) and credit,[62] which led to competition among farmers for limited resources; it was in such situations that the fault lines in the 'white alliance' tended to appear. Fertiliser shortages led tobacco farmers to argue that they deserved more ammonium nitrate than maize farmers, as tobacco had a higher fertiliser conversion rate.[63] Similarly, the higher grain prices which maize farmers lobbied for were opposed by ranchers, who would then face increased production costs. Combined with the fact that the farming community was one of the most affected by guerrilla attacks,[64] it is understandable that many of the farmers felt that the RF government was not protecting their interests effectively.[65] This led to a political repositioning among some of the white farmers and the adoption of strategies to protect themselves, their families and their investments.

One such strategy involved entering into 'arrangements' with guerrillas to secure their protection from attacks. While it is difficult to quantify the extent of these, there is reason to believe that this practice existed in many areas of

---

[59] J. Kurebwa, 'The Politics of Multilateral Economic Sanctions on Rhodesia during the Unilateral Declaration of Independence period, 1965-1979' (D.Phil. thesis, University of Zimbabwe, 2000), p. 384.

[60] Between 1977 and 1978, for instance, the price of class 'A' wheat fell from 12.3 cents to 11 cents per kg: ibid., p. 387.

[61] Ibid., p. 385.

[62] Ibid., p. 403.

[63] Ibid., p. 406.

[64] Selby notes that 'Approximately 300 farmers or members of their immediate families were killed between 1972 and 1980, which amounted to more than half the civilian deaths.' This disproportionate number owed much to the fact that farmers often lived in outlying areas, a precarious position that necessitated a variety of survival strategies. See A. Selby, 'Commercial Farmers and the State: Interest Group Politics and Land Reform in Zimbabwe' (D.Phil. thesis, Oxford University, 2006), p. 78.

[65] Ibid., pp. 75-124.

the country;[66] assistance to the guerrillas included providing food, medicines and clothing.[67] These actions by the farmers must be understood in the context of their vulnerability to attacks owing to their location in rural areas, and the fixed nature of their investments which made it difficult for them to emigrate. In essence, for many farmers, such actions constituted an 'insurance policy'. However, in the cases of farmers such as Garfield Todd of Hokonui Ranch and Guy Clutton-Brock of Cold Comfort Farm, support for the nationalist forces was a matter of conviction. In pursuit of their interests, a 1975 Rhodesia National Farmers' Union delegation of P. Strong and S. Fircks told Kenneth Kaunda, the Zambian president, that the farming community was prepared for majority rule and would work with a black government.[68] They pointed out that at least 70 per cent of the leadership of the farming community shared this view. What is important in all these farmers' efforts at rapprochement is how the attempt to construct a racially exclusive nation was challenged by other more concrete interests.

With respect to African agriculture, the picture was marked by contradictory policies. Importantly, the basic goal of promoting European interests informed both neglect and improvement of African areas. Where funding was concerned, for example, expenditure on African agriculture fell from 2.8 per cent of total spending between 1966 and 1969 to 1.2 per cent between 1975 and 1976.[69] Even the farmers in the African Purchase Areas, who had received token support from previous governments since the 1930s, began to be removed from their land.[70] There was widespread discrimination in terms of the allocation of credit facilities. In 1977, for instance, 6,000 white farmers had access to 100 times more credit than an estimated 600,000 African Purchase Area farmers;[71] the difference was even greater for those in the Tribal Trust Lands (TTLs). As the

[66] K. Manungo, 'Collection, Management and Dissemination of Oral Evidence from Zones of Conflict: A Post-mortem of the Liberation War in Concession and Chiweshe, North-eastern Zimbabwe', paper presented at T. O. Ranger's Valedictory Lecture, University of Zimbabwe, 1999. Interviews conducted in rural Zimbabwe under a regional research programme on liberation struggles in southern Africa have revealed various instances of white farmers assisting the guerrillas. In the Chimanimani area, for instance, a white farmer named Hains was particularly noted for his assistance to the guerrillas.

[67] This observation is also made by D. Caute, *Under the Skin: The Death of White Rhodesia* (London: Allen Lane, 1983), pp. 299 and 384.

[68] Selby, 'Commercial Farmers and the State', p. 90.

[69] A. Astrow, *Zimbabwe: A Revolution that Lost Its Way?* (London: Zed, 1983), p. 65.

[70] A. Shutt, '"We are the Best Poor Farmers": Purchase Area Farmers and Economic Differentiation in Southern Rhodesia, c.1925-1980' (D.Phil. thesis, University of California, 1995), pp. 190-237.

[71] Ibid. See also S. S. Mushunje, 'The Development of Agricultural Credit Systems in Zimbabwe, with Special Reference to the Agricultural Finance Corporation, 1971 to 1986' (MA dissertation, University of Zimbabwe, 1988).

liberation war intensified, the state deliberately suffocated peasant agriculture, particularly food production. The rationale behind this was to prevent peasants from generating a surplus that could be used to feed the guerrillas. Officials even proposed that peasants living near border areas be encouraged to produce cash crops to foreclose the possibility of cross-border food raids by the guerrillas.

The state's interest in developing certain African areas reflected its awareness that there was a limit to the extent to which the exploitation of the Africans could be pursued without undermining European interests and, indeed, the whole UDI project. The state realised that total neglect of the TTLs would lead to their implosion, to heightened social unrest, and ultimately to increased competition between black and white workers on the job market. It was also conscious that production in the rural areas would aid the overall efforts of the country to achieve a measure of economic self-sufficiency. In 1967, for instance, 50 irrigation schemes were established in African areas, 42,000km of road and 10 high-level bridges were constructed, 5,000 farmers were resettled in Gokwe, and Chisumbanje was established as a pilot project in TTL development.[72] In addition to these efforts, a statutory body, the Tribal Trust Land Development Corporation (TILCOR) was established in 1968 to 'promote rural participation in the national economy and to create employment'.[73] From 1972, TILCOR spearheaded Growth Point development in areas such as Sanyati and Seki. The overall picture, however, was the promotion of European agriculture, and the systematic undermining of its African counterpart.

The efforts at improving African rural areas were part of a raft of measures meant to curb the rise of African nationalism. One strategy which gained prominence in the UDI period was the ploy to use traditional rulers. As early as the 1950s, senior civil servants in the colony had suggested the need to counter the influence of African nationalists in the reserves by 'increasing' the power of chiefs.[74] In line with this advice, the RF government began according token power to the chiefs. The state hoped to present these 'traditional' leaders, as opposed to the nationalists, as the legitimate representatives of the Africans.[75] This policy, however, had mixed results.

---

[72] Kurebwa, 'The Politics of Multilateral Economic Sanctions', p. 412.

[73] Ibid. p. 413.

[74] A. K. H. Weinrich, *Chiefs and Councils in Rhodesia: The Transition from Patriarchal to Bureaucratic Power* (London: Heinemann, 1971), p. 20.

[75] See: P. S. Nyambara, 'Immigrants, "Traditional" Leaders and the Rhodesian State, 1963-1979', paper presented to the Department of Economic History Seminar Series, University of Zimbabwe, October 2000; Alexander, *The Unsettled Land*. Other efforts to enhance the status of chiefs included the passing of laws such as the Tribal Trust Lands Act of 1967, which was meant to shore up the power of chiefs.

Under the challenges of sanctions, the Rhodesian economy became more centralised in order to harness and utilise scarce resources profitably. A number of committees were set up to regulate affairs in different sectors of the economy, including the Industrial Tariff Committee, which considered all requests for tariff changes, and the National Export Promotion Council (NEPCO), which handled all exports, and GENTA, which was responsible for all oil imports.[76] The allocation of foreign currency was placed under a regulatory board in the Ministry of Commerce and Industry. The state was also directly involved in investment in the economy: for example, the government nationalised the Rhodesia Iron and Steel Company, in which it invested about R$60 million.[77] For similar strategic reasons, the state invested about R$30 million in abattoirs and meat-freezing industries through the Cold Storage Commission.

An important aspect of the history of Rhodesia after 1965 is the development of import-substitution industries. The industrialisation of the country had begun during, and continued after, the Second World War such that, on the eve of federation in 1953, Southern Rhodesia had better developed industries than Northern Rhodesia and Nyasaland. The sanctions period saw increased government commitment to import-substitution industries as well as to the diversification of existing ones. J. J. Wrathall, the Rhodesian Minister of Finance, spelt out the government's commitment towards this policy. In his economic policy blueprint in 1967, he indicated that, 'government would intensify its efforts in support of manufacturing industry, giving emphasis to growth industries, to those which can effect import substitution, to those producing raw materials for local manufacturers and to those which have good export prospects.'[78] This was part of a wider economic policy reorientation aimed at reducing Rhodesia's dependency on, firstly, the agricultural sector, especially tobacco, and, secondly, on external sources of manufactured goods.

A large measure of success was achieved in these objectives during the early UDI period. Manufacturing industries, for example, registered impressive growth figures, averaging 12 per cent per annum, while gross fixed capital formation in the sector grew by 524 per cent during the same period. Diversification led to a 212 per cent growth in secondary industries between 1966 and 1974, and

---

[76] C. Stoneman, 'The economy: An overview', in C. Stoneman (ed.), *Zimbabwe's Inheritance* (London: Macmillan, 1981), p.

[77] Cheap steel was a crucial raw material in the import-substitution industries, as well as to reduce dependence on the international market. See Pangeti, 'The State and Manufacturing Industry, pp. 175-7.

[78] Quoted in A. Mseba, 'Money and Finance in a Closed Economy: Rhodesia's Monetary Experience, 1965-1980' (MA dissertation, University of Zimbabwe, 2007), p. 52.

production volume rose by 160 per cent. In addition, there were more than 400 infant industries by 1969.[79]

Throughout the UDI period, Rhodesia invested a significant amount of energy into evading sanctions. A strategy used to achieve this was the formation of quasi-state bodies that oversaw the export of specific goods. One of these was the Joint Marketing Organisation (JMO), which was formed to oversee the export of tobacco as well as minerals such as chrome, lithium and aluminium through its two subsidiaries, Tobacco Corporation and UNIVEX.[80] The JMO operated separately from government, allowing it the necessary freedom and secrecy to engage in its activities. Rhodesia also made use of international middlemen despite the high costs involved. Some of the transnational corporations operating in Rhodesia also provided assistance in accessing goods from the outside world. Finally, the state suspended local laws that hampered the resistance to sanctions, especially those relating to the transportation of petroleum products.[81]

An important factor in the survival of the UDI government under sanctions was the general lack of commitment within the international community to their effective implementation, especially in the early part of the period. A combination of ideological, political and economic factors led certain countries to maintain trade relations with the RF government. Three months after the imposition of sanctions, the *New York Times* commented,

> At the United Nations, support for Britain seemed unanimous ... but on closer inspection, support for Britain was never as great as might have been thought. Some industrialised countries have done nothing to curtail their trade with Rhodesia. Rhodesia's severest critics, including some African states, were among the quickest to jump into the trading vacuum left by the departing British.[82]

A number of 'neutral' countries such as West Germany, Switzerland, China, Bangladesh and North Korea did not ratify the sanctions on Rhodesia, while others like Denmark and the Netherlands took a non-interventionist policy.[83] In addition, political rivalry led some countries to refuse 'to assist Britain in solving what they considered to be her problem'. Notable examples were France and Spain, which begrudged Britain's intervention in Tunisia and Gibraltar, their

---

[79] Pangeti, 'The State and Manufacturing Industry', p. 110.
[80] Kurebwa, 'The Politics of Multilateral Economic Sanctions', p. 365.
[81] Ibid., p. 399.
[82] Quoted in L. Kapungu, *The United Nations and Economic Sanctions against Rhodesia* (Lexington, Lexington Press, 1973), pp. 9-10.
[83] Ibid., pp. 86-8.

respective areas of interests.[84] Thus, Charles de Gaulle, the President of France, presided over the passing of Decree Number 65-759 of 1968 that listed 93 French products for exemption from sanctions. France continued to import Rhodesian tobacco and ferro-chrome under various guises.[85] The fact that Rhodesia possessed strategic minerals such as chrome worked in its favour. Kurebwa observes that Rhodesia was a major producer of high-quality chrome, producing 14 per cent of total world production outside the communist bloc.[86] Rhodesia's importance in the global strategic mineral supply chain was underlined by the United States of America's passing the Byrd Amendment to ensure that it could still access chrome from Southern Rhodesia, sanctions notwithstanding.[87] The amendment lifted the prohibition on the importation into the USA of any strategic and critical material from any non-communist country so long as the importation of such material from communist countries was not prohibited.[88]

South Africa and Portuguese Mozambique also refused to honour the UN-sponsored mandatory sanctions, creating important 'lifelines' for Rhodesia. Until the 1970s, these countries issued certificates of origin for goods in their own names to disguise Rhodesian exports. Mozambique was particularly notorious for smuggling Rhodesian tobacco.[89] Pangeti states that South Africa was 'the lifeline for the beleaguered Rhodesian economy, becoming the main source of investment finance, the main market for both primary and secondary exports and the transit route for much of the trade traffic of Rhodesia.'[90] Minter and Schmidt take the argument further by stating that 'without the full-fledged support of its southern neighbour, Rhodesia would not have withstood sanctions for as long as it did.'[91] This camaraderie was nurtured by the need for the three white-ruled southern African countries to unite against what they perceived as a black communist onslaught engulfing the region. Jorge Jardim, however, shows that economic considerations also loomed large. For example, the disruption of trafficking of Rhodesian goods through Mozambique's railways and harbours would have had severe repercussions on Mozambique's trading economy: at

---

[84] Ibid. France, for example, was aggravated by Britain's continued supply of firearms to Tunisia, despite complaints that these were being re-transported to Algerian nationalists.

[85] Ibid., p. 88.

[86] Kurebwa, 'The Politics of Multilateral Economic Sanctions', p. 314. In addition, southern Africa possessed 97 per cent of the world's chrome reserves outside the Communist bloc. This partly explains America's sustained interest in the region during the Cold War period.

[87] Ibid., p. 315.

[88] N. Chimhete, 'The Impact of UDI Sanctions on the Mining Industry in Rhodesia, 1965-1980' (BA(Hons) dissertation, University of Zimbabwe, 2001), p. 27.

[89] Ibid., p. 301.

[90] Pangeti, "The State and the Manufacturing Industry', p. 109.

[91] Minter and Schmidt, 'When sanctions worked', p. 228.

that time, Rhodesian traffic averaged about four million tonnes per annum and yielded foreign currency revenues of over £18m.[92]

Economic exigencies also limited Malawi, Zambia and Botswana from implementing full sanctions against Rhodesia. All three had a long history of dependence on Rhodesia's manufactures, energy, capital and railways. In 1965, Zambia received 42 per cent of its mining industry energy requirements and 95 per cent of its rail shipments from Rhodesia. In addition, 40 per cent of the energy requirements of other sectors were

Fig. 4.3: Demonstrators thank South Africa for petrol supplies.
[*Source:* National Archives of Zimbabwe]

supplied by Rhodesia in the form of coal from Wankie Colliery, oil from the Central African Petroleum Refinery in Umtali, and hydroelectricity from Kariba Dam.[93] Likewise, Malawi was almost entirely dependent on Rhodesian meat and meat products, sugar, manufactures, coal and capital; in addition, there were over 300,000 Malawian migrant labourers working in Rhodesia. Botswana's beef industry also depended on export routes provided by Rhodesia Railways. Malawi and Zambia informed the UN Secretary-General that 'they would apply economic sanctions against Rhodesia only to the extent that they did not disrupt their economies and impose economic hardship on them.'[94]

However, the relationship between Rhodesia and the countries that, for whatever reasons, continued trading with her, was not altogether happy. Countries and middlemen who were involved in under-the-counter dealings with Rhodesia

[92] J. Jardim, *Sanctions Double Cross: Oil to Rhodesia* (Bulawayo: Books of Rhodesia, 1979), p. 14. A. de Roche, in his book, *Black, White and Chrome: The United States and Zimbabwe, 1953-1998* (Trenton, NJ, and Asmara: Africa World Press, 2001), demonstrates how economic interests played an influential role in determining American policy on Rhodesia in the 1970s.

[93] Kapungu, *The United Nations and Economic Sanctions*, pp. 94-5.

[94] Ibid., p. 95.

took advantage of her desperate need for foreign currency to get Rhodesian goods at low prices. Eddie Cross, an economist for the government's Agricultural Marketing Authority from 1969 to 1980, expresses this point succinctly:

> The South Africans were totally mercenary about the sanctions against Rhodesia ... They exploited the situation from the word go. They exploited their monopolistic control over our transport routes. They exploited their favourable position as a supplier of spares and critical things that we couldn't buy internationally because of sanctions. We owe the South Africans nothing for the 14 years of sanctions busting ... They were making a good business out of it.[95]

It should thus be borne in mind that sanctions-busting came at a cost to Rhodesian business in general, and to the economy at large.

As with most of its policies, the RF government used labour laws in an attempt to ensure a degree of stability for the white population. The dismissal of European workers, for example, was prohibited, forcing firms to continue paying white employees even if they became redundant.[96] Measures were also put in place to restrict the vocational training of African workers. Job reservation for whites was also common. In addition, various barriers prevented Africans from rising up the job ladder, such as the 1968 Apprenticeship Training and Skilled Manpower Development Act, which stated that skilled occupations were open only to those who had completed a formal apprenticeship or passed a recognised trade test; although there was no stipulation that blacks could not qualify, the prerequisites effectively sidelined the vast majority of them.[97]

The state's efforts to ensure white comfort did not mean, however, that white workers were always in agreement with it. White unions often found themselves in conflict with the state and capital during the UDI period over two key issues: the erosion of salaries by inflation, and the trend towards fragmentation and Africanisation of formerly white jobs.[98] The state had to keep a balance between maintaining economic, social and political stability and ensuring a certain standard of living for semi-skilled and unskilled whites. This balance proved difficult to achieve, as witnessed by the 1968 strikes of the Rhodesia Railway Workers'

---

[95] Quoted in Minter and Schmidt, 'When sanctions worked', p. 228.

[96] P. Sutcliffe, 'The political economy of Rhodesian sanctions', *Journal of Commonwealth Political Studies*, 7(July), 1979, p. 119; Stoneman, 'The economy', p. 155.

[97] For more on the labour dynamics of the period, see B. Raftopoulos and I. Phimister (eds.), *Keep on Knocking: A History of the Labour Movement in Zimbabwe 1900-1997* (Harare: Baobab Books, 1997), p. 99. See also M. Majonga, 'The Struggle Continues: African Trade Unions and Workers' Responses in Rhodesia, 1965-1980' (MA dissertation, University of Zimbabwe, 1998).

[98] Godwin and Hancock, *'Rhodesians Never Die'*, p. 25.

Union (RRWU) and the Amalgamated Engineering Union (AEU) over a cost-of-living adjustment. The unions were forced to return to work with less than their full demands by the Minister of Transport, Brigadier T. Dunlop.[99] In some cases, white workers who felt that the state was not supporting their interests formed opposition political parties. In 1970, for example, disgruntled members of the RRWU and the AEU helped to form the right-wing Republican Alliance.[100]

In general, the balance of power in industrial relations was in favour of employers.[101] African unionisation bore the brunt of increasing state repression, with 68 union leaders being in detention by 1973.[102] The number of reported work stoppages declined from 138 in 1965 to 57 in 1966, and to only 19 in 1971.[103] While black workers generally faced the brunt of state repression, migrant workers were even more vulnerable. In April 1965, for instance, Smith warned that, 'If, through British government action, the Rhodesian economy was to suffer, even for a short time, an inevitable first step would be the necessity for Rhodesia to consider the repatriation of foreign workers and their families to Zambia and Malawi.'[104] This threat was fulfilled in 1965 when thousands of migrant workers of Zambian origin were repatriated. Those who remained were restricted to employment in the eastern districts of Rhodesia. Smith was not only putting pressure on his neighbours, he was also ensuring the availability of jobs for local Africans in the context of an economy under sanctions. In 1976, alien migrant workers were prohibited from seeking employment anywhere in Rhodesia except in mines and on farms. Local Africans, it was thought, would take up the employment, in the process depriving nationalists of recruits. The thinking in official circles was that nationalists were recruiting from the pool of the unemployed Africans. However, the government was never really able to close its borders to foreign African workers because of labour shortages and the influence of the agricultural and mining lobbies.[105]

By the late 1970s, however, the economy had taken a turn for the worse. Several reasons have been given to explain the slump. The cost of the war rose

[99] In justifying his action, Dunlop asserted that he refused to allow the nation to be held at 'pistol point' for the benefit of 'a few'; see ibid., pp. 23-5.

[100] Ibid., p. 25.

[101] The enforcement of laws such as the Law and Order Maintenance Act and the Emergency Powers Act of 1960 was tightened and there was an increase in police surveillance of trade unions. The 1967 Industrial Conciliation Amendment Act further restricted the conditions under which labour operated.

[102] P. Bond, *Uneven Zimbabwe: A Study of Finance, Development and Underdevelopment* (Trenton, NJ: Africa World Press, 1998), p. 123.

[103] Ibid., p. 123. See also Majonga, 'The Struggle Continues'.

[104] Astrow, *A Revolution that Lost Its Way?*, p. 109.

[105] Strack, *Sanctions*, p. 204.

phenomenally as the conflict escalated, by 1979 accounting for 40 per cent of GDP. The war also led to skills losses, through the recruitment of white workers for military service as well as emigration. In order to finance vital oil and other requirements regarded as essential to the success of UDI, the government cut the importation of non-petroleum import allocations drastically from the mid-1970s, creating a shortage of goods that had formed the basis of the Rhodesian daily life.[106] There was also a series of poor agricultural seasons, notably in 1972/73. The rise in the international oil prices in 1973 sparked a world economic recession and reduced the demand for primary commodities, making Rhodesia's position even more precarious, given that she had already been selling her commodities cheaply as a way of busting sanctions.[107] Stoneman argues that discrimination against the rural population and the low level of black wages had the effect of restricting the size of the internal market, leading to a problem of under-consumption.[108] Smith's counter-insurgency strategies did not make the situation any better. His decision to close the Zambian border in 1973, for example, backfired as it resulted in the loss of a considerable amount of revenue as Zambian copper was re-routed through Tanzania. It also earned Rhodesia the ire of her closest allies, South Africa and Mozambique, who disliked this 'unnecessary' escalation of the conflict.[109]

The combination of all these factors was critical. From 1974 to 1978, manufacturing production declined by 27 per cent, capacity utilisation fell by 38 per cent, and there was a net loss of 50,000 urban private-sector jobs, mainly in the manufacturing and construction industries. Even government officials who had taken a self-congratulatory tone since 1965 admitted in 1976 that the general picture in the economy was 'indicative of an economy feeling the effects of international recession, sanctions and the strains of anti-terrorist operation'.[110] In addition, the economy struggled under the weight of expensive petroleum imports. Fuel had to be rationed and its purchase was controlled through the use of coupons.[111] In the mining sector, export earnings began to fall owing to low international prices, and mines began to experience liquidity problems[112] as

[106] See Minter and Schmidt, 'When sanctions worked', p. 226.

[107] Ibid.

[108] Stoneman, 'The economy', pp. 95-6.

[109] M. Meredith, *The Past Is Another Country: Rhodesia UDI to Zimbabwe* (London: Pan Books, 1980), p. 113.

[110] Rhodesia. Ministry of Finance, *Economic Survey of Rhodesia, 1976* (Salisbury: Government Printers, 1977).

[111] Rhodesia. Ministry of Finance, *Economic Survey of Rhodesia, 1979* (Salisbury: Government Printers, 1980).

[112] See B. Ngwenya, 'The Rise and Fall of Copper Mining at Mhangura, c.1957-2000' (MA dissertation, University of Zimbabwe, 2007).

Fig. 4.4: Mangula Mine, 1974. *[Source: National Archives of Zimbabwe]*

well as transport bottlenecks, which particularly affected low-value, high-bulk goods,[113] and shortages of skilled labour.

In the rural areas, the escalating war disrupted the pattern of peasant production, and not only because of labour problems but also because of the general lack of certified seed.[114] The seed shortages are explained in two ways. Firstly, the road network was reported to have been badly damaged and 'was impassable due to landmines'.[115] Thus the local traders found it increasingly difficult to find new supplies from their traditional sources. Secondly, the increased requests by guerrillas for food and clothing taxed the local businessmen, making the accumulation of capital increasingly difficult.

In the northern and eastern districts, measures meant to curtail further guerrilla incursions by settling the civilians in 'protected villages' worsened the situation. In the first instance, the policy was meant to deprive the guerrillas of food and other essentials. Thus, as Michael Bratton observes, 'the state accordingly adopted a form of "scorched earth" policy at the frontline whereby, at the time of resettlement, existing villages and crops [were] put to the torch or poisoned. Cattle [were] summarily sold.'[116] Commenting on the effects of 'protected villages' on the lives of peasants in Honde Valley, Schmidt argues that the dehumanising practice of forced removals went against the official policies

[113] Rhodesia. Ministry of Finance, *Economic Survey of Rhodesia, 1977* (Salisbury: Government Printers, 1978).

[114] P. Makaye, 'The Underdevelopment of Matsai Communal Area before and after the Second Chimurenga' (MA dissertation, University of Zimbabwe, 2000), p. 38.

[115] Ibid.

[116] M. Bratton, 'Settler state, guerrilla war and rural underdevelopment in Rhodesia', *Issue: A Journal of Opinion*, 9(1/2), 1979, p. 61.

of winning the hearts and minds of rural Africans.[117] Protected villages placed curfews on villagers, who were often killed if they broke them, and shelter in the fenced camps was often poor. Usually, peasants' property that had been left outside was destroyed. In order to limit food supplies to guerrillas, the amount of food that any given family was allowed at a time was limited to less than 7 kg and a ban was placed on carrying food to the fields.[118]

Alexander *et al.* also note the possibility of the use of chemical and biological warfare by the Rhodesian forces in Shangani in the late 1970s, when anthrax was believed to have been used 'to hit at civilians and hence guerrillas' means of sustenance'.[119] Such outbreaks of anthrax and other animal diseases could be attributed to biological warfare as well as to the breakdown of veterinary services as a result of the war. Whatever the real causes, the peasants' losses were significant.

Conclusion

Given Rhodesia's historical background and its racial and ethnic heterogeneity, a sense of nationhood had to be manufactured: to whom should Rhodesia belong and who belonged to Rhodesia? More often than not, race was a key ingredient in these efforts to construct national identity. However, its significance was limited largely to mobilising certain constituencies and marking the lines of exclusion, i.e. defining whose nation it was not. In fostering loyalty to the 'nation' and determining political outlooks, race was not always as influential as economic interests. In white society, for example, as the political and economic hardships of the UDI period began to bite, groups such as farmers also began to reconfigure their political outlook.

The state's actions in the economy during the UDI period were guided by the need to ensure stability for the white population. The state attempted to diversify agriculture, implement measures to evade sanctions and restructure the financial system. To this end, regional and international politics that informed individual countries' foreign and economic policies with regard to Rhodesia assisted in sustaining the UDI project. The economy stood its ground until the mid-1970s when several crises combined to cause its collapse. Overall, Africans were the biggest losers in the economic reorganisation that followed UDI. While the state made token efforts to stimulate production in certain African areas, they fell far short of what was required to meet Africans' needs. The overall picture remained one of entrenched and uneven development.

[117] Schmidt, 'The Social and Economic Impact of Political Violence', p. 254.
[118] Ibid., pp. 254-6.
[119] Alexander, *et al.*, *Violence and Memory*, p. 145.

5

War in Rhodesia, 1965-1980

Joseph Mtisi, Munyaradzi Nyakudya and Teresa Barnes

Introduction
The attempts by the Rhodesian Front (RF) government to cushion the white population against the 'winds of change' were complicated by the intensifying social, economic and political crises in the country. The nationalists, however, also faced hard challenges as their united stance frayed under many pressures. This chapter discusses the civil war/liberation struggle that developed from political and economic changes both within and beyond the borders of Rhodesia, and how these were perceived and interpreted by the contending forces in the country.

The escalating crisis
The year 1971 has been identified as marking 'the peak of white fortunes in Rhodesia'.[1] By this date, the most prominent nationalist leaders and trade unionists were either in detention or exile, or had been silenced. Years of negotiations with Britain had culminated in the signing of the 1969 Anglo-Rhodesian Agreement which ensured the continuation of white rule with only very slow concessions to the concept of majority rule.[2] At the front, the two ZANLA and ZIPRA armies were bedevilled by logistical and operational problems such as poor and unco-ordinated strategies, as well as lack of ammunition. Sanctions notwithstanding, the RF was adamant that they had the situation well under control. However, the circumstances in Rhodesia began to change significantly, both politically and economically.

This declining state of affairs had the effect of shaking white confidence in the UDI project. The early 1970s were marked by invigorated resistance to white rule in the urban areas, complemented by the escalation of the war in the countryside. An important benchmark in the race relations of the country was the 1972 Pearce Commission, which was set up to test the acceptability of the Anglo-Rhodesian Agreement. To a large extent, the findings of the Commission were representative of the class and racial divides that existed in the country.

[1] M. Meredith, *The Past Is Another Country: Rhodesia UDI to Zimbabwe* (London: Pan Books, 1980), p. 82.
[2] Ibid.

On the one hand, most Africans, in both the urban and rural areas, opposed the proposals. These included Purchase Area farmers, who were ostracised by both the RF government and the nationalists; not even chiefs, despite efforts to make them state agents, supported to the proposals.[3] In the urban areas, 'the emotional discontent, frustration and bitterness about the fate of the African people, bottled up for seven years',[4] found an outlet in the violent demonstrations that followed the Pearce Commission in cities such as Salisbury, Umtali and Gwelo. The build-up to the Pearce Commission saw the rise of Abel Muzorewa, a United Methodist Church Bishop, into mainstream nationalist politics. In the absence of most nationalist leaders, Muzorewa was one of those who spearheaded the campaign for a 'No' vote in the Pearce Referendum.[5]

Opposition to white rule became increasingly militant as the execution of the guerrilla war escalated in the early 1970s. David Caute claims that between 1967 and 1972, 'not a single white person died as a result of guerrilla action'.[6] This was soon to change, however. In 1971, ZANLA guerrillas began infiltrating into the north-east corner of the country in order to recruit peasants as porters to assist in stockpiling weapons caches. In December 1972, these methodical endeavours came to fruition with an attack on Altena Farm.[7]

Table 5.1: Rhodesian government estimates of deaths in the war, 1973–74

	European civilians killed	Rhodesian security forces killed	Guerrillas killed	African civilians killed
1973	12	44	179	52
1974	16	96	345	118

Source: Martin and Johnson, The Struggle for Zimbabwe, p. 145.

From 1972 to 1974, ZANLA forces made contact with peasants and engaged in guerrilla operations in the northern districts of the country. At the same time,

---

[3] See J. Alexander, The Unsettled Land: State Making and the Politics of Land in Zimbabwe (Harare: Weaver Press; Oxford: James Currey, 2006), pp. 83-99, for more on state efforts to co-opt traditional leaders.

[4] Meredith, The Past Is Another Country, p. 93.

[5] For more on the Pearce Commission, see J. Todd, The Right to Say No (London: Sidgwick and Jackson, 1972), and A. T. Muzorewa, Rise Up and Walk: An Autobiography (London: Evans Brothers, 1979).

[6] D. Caute, Under the Skin: The Death of White Rhodesia (Evanston, IL: Northwestern University Press; London: Allen Lane, 1983), p. 40.

[7] See P. Godwin and I. Hancock, 'Rhodesians Never Die': The Impact of War and Political Change on White Rhodesia, c.1970-1980 (Harare: Baobab Books, 1995), pp. 85-6, and D. Martin and P. Johnson, The Struggle for Zimbabwe (Harare: Zimbabwe Publishing House, 1981), pp. 1-3, 73-4.

Fig. 5.1: Saying 'No' to the Pearce Commission.
[*Source:* National Archives of Zimbabwe]

Fig. 5.2: Bulawayo workers demand consultation.
[*Source:* The Standard]

ZIPRA organised in Zambia, regrouping after a political split within the ZAPU leadership in 1971 had resulted in the formation of a short-lived group, the Front for the Liberation of Zimbabwe (FROLIZI).

Added to the economic problems as a result of the war and the world economic recession, there was also some opposition to the RF from the white population, who criticised the government's failure to chart a racially inclusive programme.[8] More disturbing to the white loyalists was the steadily rising European emigration rate and the effect that the war had on intending immigrants.[9] The majority of emigrants were professionals and younger Rhodesians who had no family or financial commitments.

At no time were the military developments in the country solely a Rhodesian affair. Until 1975, Portuguese Mozambique and, especially, South Africa played an important part in the political and economic fortunes of Rhodesia. In addition, the Rhodesian state continued to be supplied with goods, including materiel, from countries such as the United States, which covertly manoeuvred around the UN sanctions. The Rhodesian army also gladly accepted white mercenaries into its ranks. With regard to the African nationalists' efforts, Tanzania and Zambia, among others, provided the nationalist forces with support and links to the African, Third World and European-based anti-colonial movements of the day. Finally, the Rhodesian conflict constituted a chapter in the global Cold War, with the Soviet bloc and China supporting the two guerrilla armies and the United States and its allies backing white Rhodesia and South Africa as strategic, resource-laden bastions of anti-communism.

The attainment of independence by Mozambique in 1975 had a seismic impact on the course of events in Rhodesia. In the first instance, Mozambique implemented the UN sanctions. In addition to closing its borders, it confiscated all Rhodesian property and assets; consequently, a significant amount of Rhodesia's railway rolling stock was locked in Mozambique. This necessitated 80 per cent of Rhodesia's foreign trade being redirected through South Africa, where the extra distances increased import costs and decreased export earnings, aggravating the already severe foreign currency shortages. This problem was exacerbated by severe railway and port congestion in South Africa. At the political level, Mozambique's independence had two significant implications: first, it

---

[8] Leading these critics were a diverse range of individuals, including Bishop Lamont, Judith and Garfield Todd, Allan Savory and Sam Putterill. Members of the farming community also became increasingly opposed to the RF's political strategies.

[9] In September 1973, migration figures showed a net loss of 118, 'the first such loss since 1966'. See Godwin and Hancock, 'Rhodesians Never Die', pp. 137-8.

meant the opening up of 764 miles of border to guerrilla incursions;[10] second, it meant that Smith lost a key ally and inevitably found himself having to rely more on South Africa, thereby making him more vulnerable to the will of its President, John Vorster, who himself 'quickly grasped the significance of an independent Mozambique'.[11]

Much like Smith, the nationalist camp was also afflicted by problems, in particular the increasing jostling for power both within and among the African nationalist parties. In ZANU, for example, Ndabaningi Sithole's position as president was challenged by a group of ZANU detainees, who appointed Robert Mugabe as the new leader of the party.[12] Besides the division between the military and political leaders, the political leaders themselves were divided along age, educational, ideological and even personal lines.[13] The divisions in ZANU went beyond the leadership and extended to its rank and file. An example of this was the Nhari Rebellion of December 1974, in which ZANLA guerrillas accused the High Command led by Josiah Tongogara of indifference and incompetence in the provision of ammunition, food and clothing while it continued to live lavishly in Lusaka.[14]

The independence of Mozambique and Angola marked the beginning of a new era in Rhodesia's relationship with her neighbours. With regard to South Africa, it became increasingly evident to Vorster that an early settlement of the Rhodesian crisis was imperative to the survival of apartheid. Henceforth, Vorster's prime strategy was to establish better relations with black-ruled southern African states. Kenneth Kaunda was also keen to see a resolution of the crisis so as to direct Zambia's attention back to its own pressing domestic problems.[15]

This coincidence of interests led to the 'détente' period, which began in earnest in late 1974 and witnessed protracted efforts by Kaunda and Vorster to arrange a negotiated settlement between Smith and the African nationalists. The leftist influence – seen in the links between ZIPRA and ZANLA, as well as

[10] Meredith, *The Past Is Another Country*, p. 150.

[11] A. De Roche, *Black, White and Chrome: The United States and Zimbabwe, 1953-1998* (Trenton, NJ: Africa World Press, 2001), p. 204.

[12] See Martin and Johnson, *The Struggle for Zimbabwe*, p. 202, and F. Chung, *Re-living the Second Chimurenga: Memories from Zimbabwe's Liberation Struggle* (Harare: Weaver Press, 2007), pp. 114-15.

[13] E. Sibanda, *The Zimbabwe African People's Union, 1961-87: A Political History of Insurgency in Southern Rhodesia* (Trenton, NJ: Africa World Press, 2005), p. 167.

[14] The section entitled 'Untangling the struggle(s)', below, attempts to unpack these conflicts within the nationalist movement by putting them in the context of other factors such as ethnicity, ideology and class.

[15] Sibanda, *The Zimbabwe African People's Union*, p. 207.

Mozambique and Angola, with the socialist bloc countries – was perceived to be a threat to western interests in the region. Consequently, Henry Kissinger, the US Secretary of State, sought to win the support of the African states by committing the US to resolving the Rhodesian crisis.[16] De Roche argues that the Kissinger policy was an attempt 'to remove potential battlefields' and avoid the embarrassing military approach that had been used unsuccessfully in Angola.[17] Kissinger's use of a combination of financial incentives and direct pressure from South Africa resulted in Smith's grudging release of the imprisoned African nationalists in 1974. South Africa was pressured into withdrawing most of its personnel who had been assisting Rhodesian forces. Other subtle pressure was exerted through planned South African railway delays, which seriously affected Rhodesian imports and exports.

If arm-twisting Smith into negotiation was one side of the détente coin, drawing the nationalist parties to the same table as a united force formed the other. One major task of the Frontline States (FLS) after 1975 was to try to bring unity among the nationalist parties.[18] This was made more difficult as ethnic tensions and power interests surfaced. Inevitably, the attempt to bring ZANU, ZAPU, FROLIZI and Abel Muzorewa's[19] African National Council (ANC) together was short-lived. By April 1975, the umbrella union was facing problems as Muzorewa and Nkomo battled for leadership of the party.[20] Neither ZANU nor ZAPU recognised Muzorewa, who was regarded as nothing more than a figurehead.[21] The ANC initiative was soon followed by yet another effort, in September 1975, to unite the parties under the Zimbabwe Liberation Council (ZLC), which was to be comprised of ZAPU, ZANU, FROLIZI and the ANC.[22]

The FLS leaders felt that ZANU and ZAPU disunity was an obstacle to achieving a national settlement as each party constantly sought to out-manoeuvre

[16] De Roche, *Black, White and Chrome*, p. 210.

[17] Ibid. For details on what happened in Angola, see J. Hanlon, *Beggar Your Neighbours: Apartheid Power in Southern Africa* (London: Catholic Institute for International Relations, 1986).

[18] The FLS included Zambia, Botswana, Tanzania and Mozambique.

[19] Abel Muzorewa, a United Methodist Church bishop, rose to prominence in the nationalist struggle during the run-up to the Pearce Commission's visit after both ZANU and ZAPU recognised him as the 'spokesperson for blacks'. See Chung, *Re-living The Second Chimurenga*, p. 87.

[20] See N. Bhebe, *Simon Vengayi Muzenda and the Struggle for and Liberation of Zimbabwe* (Gweru, Mambo Press, 2004), p. 170. Muzorewa, who was in Maputo, expelled Joshua Nkomo and took control of the external wing, while Nkomo took its internal wing at a congress in Harare in September 1975.

[21] J. Nkomo, *The Story of My Life* (Harare: SAPES Books, 2001), p. 155.

[22] E. Mnangagwa, 'The formation of the people's army: ZIPA', in C. Banana (ed.), *Turmoil and Tenacity* (Harare: College Press, 1989), pp. 146-9.

the other. Threats which sought to 'persuade' the nationalists into unity included being thrown off Zambian soil and losing their ammunition supplies.[23] The result was the formation of the Marxist-inspired Zimbabwe People's Army (ZIPA) in November 1975, an ill-fated attempt to bring about unity between the two armies, ZANLA and ZIPRA.[24] The ZIPA period was also the expression of a 'purist' aspiration among a generation of younger guerrillas who desired a more ideologically grounded approach to the struggle.[25] These aspirations were captured in the Mgagao Declaration, submitted to the Organisation of African Unity's Liberation Committee, which proposed the unification of ZANLA and ZIPRA. The 'old guard' in both ZANU and ZAPU treated the new formation with suspicion. Eventually, the young cadres who spearheaded ZIPA were 'eliminated' by the senior nationalists in a typically authoritarian manner. However, as David Moore observes, ZIPA 'ensured the legacy of the Zimbabwe liberation struggle includes a strong component of Marxism'.[26]

Continued pressure by the independent African nations led to the formation in October 1976 of a joint front (not a merger) between ZANU and ZAPU, named the Patriotic Front. Differences continued to exist between the two parties, however. ZANU, for example, openly demonstrated its resentment of détente, which it interpreted as an arrangement to deprive it of its imminent military victory.[27] Most nationalist leaders in ZANU were also suspicious of Kaunda, who they believed wanted to form a united African front under Nkomo's leadership.

The efforts at settlement during the détente period were, however, unsuccessful. Over and above the disunity within the African nationalists, Smith's antipathy towards proposed majority rule was an impediment: amidst talks to prepare for a constitutional conference, he continued to promise his electorate that there would be no deviation from, or lowering of, Rhodesia's standards of civilization.[28] He remained adamant that he would neither accept racial parity in government, nor majority rule in five years. Instead, he proposed the option he

---

[23] Bhebe, *Simon Vengayi Muzenda*, p. 196.

[24] See D. B. Moore, 'The Contradictory Construction of Hegemony in Zimbabwe: Politics, Ideology and Class in the Formation of a New African State' (D.Phil. thesis, York University, 1990), ch. 5, for a more nuanced analysis of the circumstances that brought about the emergence of ZIPA.

[25] W. Z. Sadomba, 'War Veterans in Zimbabwe's Land Occupations: Complexities of a Liberation Movement in an African Post-Colonial Settler Society' (D.Phil. thesis, Wageningen University, 2008), pp. 41-9.

[26] Moore, 'The Contradictory Construction of Hegemony in Zimbabwe', p. 310.

[27] This should be seen in light of the military superiority that ZANU believed itself to be enjoying since 1973. See Bhebe, *Simon Vengayi Muzenda*, p. 168, and Chung, *Re-living the Second Chimurenga*, p. 87.

[28] Meredith, *The Past Is Another Country*, p. 163.

euphemistically termed 'Responsible Majority Rule', by which he meant a slowly progressing multiracial state in which whites would remain at the helm. The ensuing conferences were characterised by accusations and counter-accusations of negotiating in bad faith, resulting in the failure of the Victoria Falls Conference in August 1975.[29]

The crisis of unity in the African nationalists' camp that had been exposed with détente did not subside thereafter. In October 1975, ZANLA guerrillas denounced Sithole, Muzorewa and Chikerema as collectively 'hopeless and completely ineffective' in leading the liberation movement.[30] Wary of the various pressures closing in on Rhodesia, Smith sought to negotiate with an African nationalist who was 'moderate' in his eyes yet acceptable to the majority of the Africans. He eventually settled on Joshua Nkomo, with whom he met secretly in Lusaka with Kaunda's assistance.[31] Smith's political objective was a power-sharing arrangement which would leave whites in a dominant role. Nkomo's acceptance of it served to heighten the distrust already existing among the nationalists. Most leaders in ZANU had held as a fact Kaunda's preference for Nkomo as the first leader of independent Zimbabwe and saw the secret negotiations as a plan to bring Nkomo to power. However, like the Victoria Falls Conference, the talks with Nkomo broke down on one irreconcilable difference: the question of when majority rule would be attained.

Despite the failure of his strategic objectives, Kissinger had succeeded in making Smith concede, for the first time, to the idea of majority rule. Renewed efforts were made at the Geneva Conference of 1976, which was meant to involve Britain more in the resolution of the situation in Southern Rhodesia, a grievance that had led to resentment of the Kissinger arrangements by both the nationalists and the FLS presidents. Like previous settlement talks, the Geneva Conference highlighted the disparate interests of the various nationalist groups. The four nationalist delegations led by Nkomo, Mugabe, Muzorewa and Sithole arrived with a common purpose: to arrange for the transfer of power to a black government. Beyond that, they differed greatly about the tactics to be employed.[32] Political machinations amongst the nationalists also caused discord in the negotiation process. For example, Muzorewa, who was particularly concerned with undermining the Patriotic Front's political dominance, called for

---

[29] Martin and Johnson, *The Struggle for Zimbabwe*, pp. 158-65, and Meredith, *The Past Is Another Country*, p. 194.

[30] Meredith, *The Past Is Another Country*, p. 202.

[31] See ibid., pp. 196-215, for detailed insights into the relationship between Smith and Nkomo during the period November 1974 to March 1976, and Kaunda's role.

[32] Meredith, *The Past Is Another Country*, pp. 277-8.

greater involvement of the British High Commissioner in the interregnum period as well as the immediate inclusion of the guerrillas into a national army.[33] Under these pressures, the Geneva talks also failed.

Meanwhile, the war escalated. Particularly bloody atrocities featured in the last phase of the war. The Rhodesian attacks on ZANLA camps in Mozambique at Nyadzonia in 1976 and Chimoio in 1977, and on ZIPRA camps in Zambia at Mkushi Training Camp and Freedom Camp in 1978, were perhaps the worst examples of the state's no-holds-barred warfare. Selous Scouts infiltrated into Mozambique and were responsible for the slaughter of 600 refugees at Nyadzonia. On 23 November 1977, also in Mozambique,

> planes began to drop napalm and fragmentation bombs over the school near Chimoio. Some teachers and children were instantly killed. Soon after the bombings paratroopers parachuted down. They followed the fleeing children and their teachers towards the hospital where they encountered the nurses and the sick and injured. Those who could not flee in time were killed. After a day of carnage, the paratroopers left. In their wake they left 85 dead, 55 of whom were children. Most of the adults killed were women, as many women worked as teachers and nurses. ... Those injured by napalm and gunfire numbered over 500, 200 of them [injured] very seriously.[34]

Chung argues that these attacks, which were largely concentrated on refugee camps, were a way of deterring the frontline states from giving further assistance to the liberation movements.[35]

Similarly, in this final period of the war, rural Rhodesia was equally convulsed by increasing levels of violence. The nationalist armies concentrated on 'harass[ing] the enemy by attacking the farmers in their isolated homesteads, laying landmines on routes used by enemy troops, assaulting centres of colonial power such as district and police stations, blowing up railway lines and bridges and ambushing enemy convoys.'[36]

Routine wartime activities for Rhodesian troops, in addition to the 'firefights' with guerrillas, included forcible removals of rural people from their villages,[37]

---

[33] Ibid.

[34] Chung, *Re-living the Second Chimurenga*, p. 144.

[35] Ibid., p. 277.

[36] N. Bhebe, *ZAPU and ZANU Guerrilla Warfare and the Evangelical Lutheran Church in Zimbabwe* (Gweru: Mambo Press, 1999) p. 65.

[37] See H. I. Schmidt, 'The Social and Economic Impact of Political Violence in Zimbabwe, 1890-1990: A Case Study of the Honde Valley' (D.Phil. thesis, Oxford University, 1996), for the violent removal of villagers into the so-called protected villages in the Honde Valley.

burning of homesteads, beatings, wanton arrests and torture. Selous Scouts con-ducted an invidious campaign of covert poisoning of guerrilla food and water supplies, and civilian clothing, and the anthrax poisoning of livestock, all in the name of counter-insurgency.[38] Rural villagers also experienced violence meted out by Rhodesian civilian volunteers, often less subject to military discipline and norms and sometimes therefore even more given to wild, random displays of violence. For example, when asked about District Security Assistants (DSAs) in Matabeleland, interviewees recalled:

> they didn't just burn homes but 'If you tried to get your property out, they'd take those things from you and put them in the fire'; they didn't just kill suspects, 'They killed everything, all the donkeys, the goats, even the chickens.' Beating – to extract information on the whereabouts of guerrillas, or simply on suspicion that a home had hosted guerrillas – was common and, again, even extreme. 'The DSAs were the worst. They beat people to death in public places. Wherever they found a suspect – at stores, schools, boreholes – they'd call people to come and watch'.[39]

These brutalities were a last-gasp measure by the Rhodesian forces to intimidate the rural population to stop assisting the guerrillas, a case of depriving 'the fish of the water'.

Untangling the struggle(s)

Cooper has cautioned against the danger of oversimplifying the politics of the late colonial period:

> It is tempting to read the history of the period from 1945 to 1960 [in the case of Rhodesia, 1965 to 1980] as the inevitable triumph of nationalism and to see each social movement taking place within a colony – be it by peasants, women, by workers, or by religious groups – as another piece to be integrated into the coming together of a nation. What is lost in such a reading are the ways in which different groups within colonies mobilized for concrete ends and used as well as opposed the institutions and the niches opened up in the clash of new and old structures. Whether such efforts

---

[38] J. Alexander, J. McGregor and T. Ranger, *Violence and Memory: One Hundred Years in the 'Dark Forests' of Matabeleland* (Harare: Weaver Press; Oxford: James Currey, 2000), pp. 144-5; L. White, 'Poisoned uniforms, poisoned food and anthrax: Or, How guerrillas die in war', *Osiris*, 19, 2004.

[39] Alexander *et al.*, pp. 152-3.

fed into the attempts of nationalist parties to build anti-colonial coalitions needs to be investigated not assumed.[40]

Thus, over and above the armed struggle, there was a complex entanglement of struggles related to, *inter alia*, gender, class, ethnicity and race, which were playing themselves out in Rhodesia;[41] many of these have continued to influence developments in the post-colonial period.

In the contest for citizenship by Africans, some claims negated others. According to Masipula Sithole, '[e]thnicity, class and so forth as factors in the social milieu, are resources which political gladiators utilise in struggles for power.'[42] This power struggle was the source of numerous contradictions that characterised the liberation 'movement'. In their struggle for power, rival groups often sought to overplay ethnic differences in order to garner support for themselves.

The ZAPU-ZANU division in 1963, still a point of debate among scholars, is an example of this conflict. Some have tended to foreground 'ideological differences' and resentment of Nkomo's indecisive approach to the nationalist struggle in explaining the split.[43] Other accounts point to ethnic struggles in ZAPU as having led to the formation of ZANU.[44] Thus, the ZANU leaders dismissed FROLIZI, which they described as 'a nepotistic grouping of cousins and relatives ... determined to undermine the liberation struggle'.[45] Neither was ZANU itself immune to ethnic politics. Such tensions heightened following the assassination of Herbert Chitepo in Zambia in 1975 as the Manyika accused the

[40] F. Cooper, "The dialectics of decolonization: Nationalism and labor movements in post-war French Africa', in F. Cooper and A. Stoler (eds.), *Tensions of Empire: Colonial Cultures in a Bourgeois World* (Berkeley: University of California Press, 1997), p. 406.

[41] This theme has been treated by a number of scholars, for example: M. Sithole, *Struggles within the Struggle* (Harare: Rujeko Publishers, 1999); W. Z. Sadomba, 'Movements within the Movement: Complexities of Zimbabwe's Land Occupations', paper presented to the Economic History Department, Seminar Series, November 2007; N. Kriger, 'The Zimbabwean war of liberation: Struggles within the struggle', *Journal of Southern African Studies*, 14(2), 1988.

[42] M. Sithole, 'Class and factionalism in the Zimbabwean nationalist movement', *African Studies Review*, 27(1), 1984, p. 122. While it may be overly simplistic to reduce everything to a power struggle, Sithole's argument does go a long way in explaining some of the conflicts during the period.

[43] See Martin and Johnson, *The Struggle for Zimbabwe*, pp. 139-42; Bhebe, *Simon Vengayi Muzenda*, pp. 131-6; Sithole, *Struggles within the Struggle*, pp 35-43; N. Shamuyarira, *Crisis in Rhodesia* (New York: Transatlantic Arts, 1966), pp. 173-92.

[44] See Sibanda, *The Zimbabwe African People's Union*, p. 90, and Nkomo, *The Story of My Life*, pp. 117-120, both of whom argue that the grievances over Nkomo's leadership were a red herring to the power interests of the breakaways that rested on ethnic interests of the majority Shona to control the liberation movement.

[45] Cited in Sithole, *Struggles within the Struggle*, p. 120.

Karanga of killing him in order to control the party's external wing.[46] Similar ethnic tensions revisited and plagued ZAPU. The 1971 crisis in ZAPU has been attributed to attempts by two Zezurus, George Nyandoro and James Chikerema, to control the party.[47] The ethnic factor also contributed to the failure of the Zimbabwe Liberation Council. These differences often led to violent fighting between various forces even in the military bases in Zambia. An example is the fighting at Mboroma, Zambia, where ZANU, ZAPU and FROLIZI cadres turned against each other.[48]

There were substantial personality, ideological and ethnic conflicts in the liberation armies. Class tensions also emerged amongst the nationalists and exacerbated existing differences. Class conflict was one of the reasons behind the Nhari Rebellion, a confrontation between members of the ZANU High Command in Zambia and a group of younger freedom fighters. The latter maintained that the leaders enjoyed comfortable lives while 'the fighters faced problems of shortage of food, ammunition and clothing at the battle front'.[49] Sadomba notes the division between the recruits of the Chitepo and ZIPA periods.[50] On the whole, the former were 'poorly educated or even illiterate'[51] while the latter were urbanites or students, many of whom joined the war owing to the attraction of the ideas of the struggle.[52] The ZIPA period recruits, in turn, were referred to as 'those who joined the war by train' or 'those recruited by radio'.[53]

It is interesting to observe the typically repressive way in which both ZANU

---

[46] Sithole, *Struggles within the Struggle*; see also L. White, *The Assassination of Hebert Chitepo: Texts and Politics in Zimbabwe* (Bloomington: Indiana University Press, 2003), p. 46.

[47] See Sithole, *Struggles within the Struggle*, pp. 43-57.

[48] Bhebe, *Simon Vengayi Muzenda*, p. 163. Sadomba also refers to the actions of Tsuro, a member of the ZANU security and intelligence wing, who achieved notoriety by persecuting other guerrillas on ethnic grounds: Sadomba, 'War Veterans in Zimbabwe's Land Occupations', p. 49.

[49] Sadomba, 'War Veterans in Zimbabwe's Land Occupations', pp. 37-8. Sadomba observes that there were divisions among the war veterans in post-colonial Zimbabwe that were linked to the period in which they were recruited. Citing the formation of a splinter group of the Zimbabwe Liberators Platform, whose membership, he alleges, is largely made up of former ZIPA members, he states that the differences between the liberation fighters 'to some extent still play[s] a role in current politics, and explains some of the intricacies of the land movement and the government fast track land reform'.

[50] Sadomba defines the period 1963-1975 as the Chitepo period owing to 'the central leadership role' of Chitepo in 'the initial phase of Zimbabwe's liberation struggle', and April 1975 to January 1977 when ZIPA was functional as the ZIPA period; see Sadomba, 'War Veterans in Zimbabwe's Land Occupations', pp. 34 and 41.

[51] Ibid., p. 38.

[52] Ibid., p. 49.

[53] Ibid. Interestingly, the divisions noted here manifested themselves within the war veterans' movement during the land occupations after 1997.

and ZAPU put down opposition to the party elites. Repression was often accompanied by arrests and lashings in 'underground cells' and, in some cases, even executions. The discipline meted out 'with extreme brutality' on the young proponents of the 1971 crisis in ZAPU is instructive.[54] The quelling of the Nhari Rebellion of 1974 is arguably one of the most outstanding examples of ruthless reprisals to opposition demonstrated by the ZANU leadership during the war. ZANU executed Thomas Nhari and Dakarai Badza and the members who had supported the rebellion, and sentenced many others to death in absentia.[55] Similarly, in the mid-1970s, a group of cadres – which called itself Vashandi (Workers) and espoused Marxist-Leninist ideas and accused the leadership of bourgeois tendencies – was incarcerated in dungeons, only to be released at independence.[56]

The discord among the nationalists must be understood in the light of the fact that not only was the group heterogeneous in nature but the motivations that drove individuals to join the struggle differed as well. Some joined in order to free themselves from the yoke of exploitation, motivated by the issue of land appropriation.[57] As one ex-combatant interviewed in the 1980s explained:

> I had seen my family moved from one of the most fertile lands, in Headlands, to some rocky areas. I had always had this feeling (although I was very young at the time) like, how could we be moved from such an area? So when this exodus started from Zimbabwe, with many of the youth going into Mozambique, I thought that, 'Well, if this is what it means, that when we join the war, when we come back and fight the regime and start all over again, I think it would give us a chance to go back to our fertile lands where we were getting better yields.' So I just left my office and took my keys and started walking into the road.[58]

---

[54] Moore, 'The Contradictory Construction of Hegemony in Zimbabwe', p. 203.

[55] White, *The Assassination of Chitepo*, p. 40. It is believed that more than 250 people were executed.

[56] Bhebe, *Simon Vengayi Muzenda*, pp. 212-14; see also Chung, *Re-living the Second Chimurenga*. On the repressive and authoritarian manner in which the rebels were suppressed, see Sithole, *Struggles within the Struggle*.

[57] J. Nhongo-Simbanegavi, *For Better or Worse? Women and ZANLA in Zimbabwe's Liberation Struggle* (Harare: Weaver Press, 2000), pp. 17-18, states that the issue of appropriated land became the rallying point for the nationalist campaign against white rule.

[58] Interview between 'F.N.' and Teresa Barnes, quoted in Teresa Barnes, 'The heroes' struggle: Life after the liberation war for four ex-combatants', in N. Bhebe and T. O. Ranger (eds.), *Soldiers in Zimbabwe's Liberation War* (Harare: University of Zimbabwe Publications, 1995), pp. 120-1.

Other reasons included poor health provision, unemployment, and the shortage of accommodation in urban areas.[59]

The above notwithstanding, the motives for going to the war were not all as uniformly 'heroic' as nationalist historiography would have us believe. Many who went to the war did so as a result of various 'push and pull' factors. Nhongo-Simbanegavi has shown that joining the war was often seen by women as a chance to put their lives together after some personal misfortune – for example, divorce – and by boys and girls as an escape from responsibilities of parenthood in the case of unplanned pregnancies.[60] Other would-be recruits crossed the borders to join the war as a way of avoiding financial debts. While some were running away from personal problems, others were coerced. Tungamirai, himself a ZANLA commander, acknowledges that recruitment in the earlier period of the war was often far from voluntary. Press-ganging, particularly in schools, was a common practice.[61] Pursuit of adventure and curiosity also informed some decisions to join the war. The motivations for 'going' to war were not static. Those who 'ran away' from domestic problems could also develop a commitment to the nationalist struggle. At the same time, those that went out of indignation at the colonial oppression could also become prone to disillusionment.

The question of guerrilla relations with the peasants during the war remains an area of contentious debate. Nationalist histories have tended to take a 'celebratory' approach to the war. They emphasise the co-operation of young boys and girls who acted as the eyes, ears and porters for the guerrillas (*mujibhas* and *chimbwidos* in the ZANLA areas), and how communities were pleased to provide food, shelter and other support for the guerrillas, risking their lives in the process.[62] Other studies, however, have shown that the violent coercion of peasants in order to gain material support and sexual services was far from uncommon. Kriger, for example, argues that the failure by the guerrillas to establish 'liberated zones' meant that the use of force was inevitable in recruitment and

---

[59] J. Tungamirai, 'Recruitment to ZANLA: Building up a war machine', in Bhebe and Ranger (eds.), *Soldiers in Zimbabwe's Liberation War*, pp. 37-40.

[60] Nhongo-Simbanegavi, *For Better or Worse?* pp. 32-3.

[61] Tungamirai, 'Recruitment to ZANLA', pp. 40-1.

[62] Studies falling in this category include T. O. Ranger, *Peasant Consciousness and Guerrilla War in Zimbabwe: A Comparative Study* (London: James Currey, 1985), which concludes that guerrilla ideology was effective in mobilising the peasants. K. D. Manungo, 'The Role the Peasants Played in the Zimbabwe War of Liberation, with Special Emphasis on Chiweshe District' (D.Phil. thesis, Ohio University, 1991), emphasises the voluntary participation of peasants in aiding the guerrillas at the expense of an examination of the more coercive elements of guerrilla mobilisation. For a review of the literature of the nationalist struggle, see B. Raftopoulos, 'Problematising nationalism in Zimbabwe: A historiographical review', *Zambezia*, 26(2), 1999, pp. 115-34.

mobilisation.[63] T. M. Mashingaidze's study of the Buhera District also indicates the use of violence against the peasants by the guerrillas.[64] Alexander *et al.* point to the existence of abuse and rape of women by some guerrillas in Shangani, although they posit that such practices were infrequent owing to the severe punishment of perpetrators.[65] Tanya Lyons makes the interesting observation that, although the atrocities committed by guerrillas against the civilian population 'have been avoided in the discourse about the war', they have been exposed by frequent reference to them in works of fiction.[66] Indeed, several studies show how the war in general and guerrillas in particular became more brutal in the final stages of the conflict.[67] H. I. Schmidt, for example, records the massacre of 27 civilians by the guerrillas in the Honde Valley on 19 December 1976.[68]

What is clear is that, whether or not coercion was used, the 'co-operation' between guerrillas and peasants was important in ensuring the success of the armed struggle. It is important to avoid a narrow definition of 'fighting' the struggle, which can privilege particular groups to the exclusion of the majority – many ordinary people did not 'cross the border' or 'take up arms' but made significant sacrifices for the liberation of the country. A broader definition is consistent with the philosophy of the nationalist armies that recognised the importance of the 'masses' in the struggle, aptly captured in the Maoist analogy of combatant fish swimming in the water of the people.

Clearly, it would be misleading to portray a rosy picture of a united front of civil co-operation with the freedom fighters against the Rhodesian forces. The reality is that the 'water' was not always of the same colour and density, nor did it always flow in a uniform tide. Out of personal interest, greed, jealousy,

[63] Kriger, 'The Zimbabwean war of liberation', p. 306.

[64] T. M. Mashingaidze, 'The Dynamics of Zimbabwe's Struggle for Liberation: The Case of Buhera District from 1950 to 1990' (MA Dissertation, University of Zimbabwe, 2001).

[65] Alexander *et al.*, *Violence and Memory*, pp. 162-4.

[66] T. Lyons, *Guns and Guerilla Girls: Women in the Zimbabwe Liberation Struggle* (Trenton, NJ: Africa World Press, 2004), p. 146.

[67] See, for example, T. Ranger, 'Bandits and guerrillas: The case of Zimbabwe', in D. Crummey (ed.), *Banditry, Rebellion and Social Protest in Africa* (London: James Currey, 1986), pp. 386-90, and J. Frederikse, *None but Ourselves: Masses vs Media in the Making of Zimbabwe* (Harare: Zimbabwe Publishing House, 1982), pp. 299-318.

[68] Schmidt, 'The Social and Economic Impact of Political Violence in Zimbabwe, pp. 243-4. See also Caute, *Under the Skin*. The 27 victims at Aberfoyle were allegedly killed because they continued working for the estate despite the warnings from the guerrillas. During the liberation struggle, guerrillas generally held that the estates generated capital that was invested in the Rhodesian government's war effort and thus had to be sabotaged. However, this incident, like many of its nature, was characterised by accusations and counter-accusations by the guerrillas and the Rhodesian Forces over responsibility for the massacre of civilians.

Fig. 5.3: An alleged sell-out shows his guerrilla-inflicted injuries, Honde Valley, 1976.
[*Source:* National Archives of Zimbabwe]

family rivalries and animosities, and even as a survival tactic, peasants would often 'sell each other out' to either of the two sides. Alexander *et al.* cite one Jeli Mhlotshwa of Lupane, who states that

> Both sides would beat you if you didn't speak something palatable. Among us, we'll sell each other out – locals could report to the DSAs [District Security Assistants],[69] the child of so and so is among the boys. So then it was an offence.[70]

The larger and wealthier families in the rural areas were usually more vulnerable.[71] One ZAPU leader stated, '[I]f you hated your uncle, that was reason for accusation, as a sellout or as a witch, just to get rid of you.'[72] This was as true in Matabeleland as anywhere else during the war. There were, of course, genuine

---

[69] These were African paramilitaries, recruited from among children of civil servants in rural areas, sometimes by force, who were tasked with assisting in the administration and security of rural areas alongside the District Commissioners and the regular forces. They were regarded to be far more ruthless than the regular forces.

[70] Alexander *et al.*, *Violence and Memory*, p. 152.

[71] Ibid., p. 153. N. Kriger, *Zimbabwe's Guerrilla War: Peasant Voices* (Harare: Baobab Books, 1995), pp. 208-9.

[72] Quoted in Alexander *et al.*, *Violence and Memory*, p. 173.

sell-outs and those perceived as witches; these were punished, often by death, by guerrillas as a necessary war-time act in the case of the former, and in the latter, as a legitimising act to identify guerrillas as 'struggle[rs] against evil'.[73]

Tensions also emerged in the rural areas around the political role of chiefs. Both the nationalist forces and the RF state sought to lure traditional leaders to their side. Where the 'carrot' of increased salaries did not entice them, the 'stick' was used, and a good number of chiefs found themselves in detention for their alleged support of the guerrillas. The use of force was not limited to the RF government. Chiefs perceived to be in support of the government were killed by the guerrillas.[74] To some extent, the balance of power within the rural areas showed a shift from the traditional chiefs, who were linked with the RF government, to the guerrillas, who received the blessing of spirit mediums.[75]

The war also had a contested spiritual element. According to Tungamirai, traditional religion was highly influential in forging a close relationship between the rural population and the guerrillas.[76] A similar view is also expressed by Chung, who reveals how the spirit mediums 'held a special position in the psyche of the freedom fighters'.[77] However, there were significant variations over time and space. During the mid-1970s when ZIPA, which espoused Marxism-Leninism, was in the forefront, religion was generally shunned.[78] The short life of ZIPA, however, meant that traditional religion continued to play a significant role in two key aspects of the struggle: recruitment and mobilisation.

The relationship between the guerrillas and the Christian missions in the country also showed variations. McLaughlin's account of co-operation between the guerrillas and Avila Mission contrasts with the findings of Bourdillon and

[73] D. Lan, *Guns and Rain: Guerrillas and Spirit Mediums in Zimbabwe* (Harare: Zimbabwe Publishing House, 1985), p. 36. Alexander *et al.*, however, argue that, while the issue of witches was frequently raised in ZIPRA-controlled areas, action against people who were so labelled was discouraged as it was not part of ZIPRA strategy and risked losing support for the organisation.

[74] T. Ranger, 'Tradition and travesty: Chiefs and the administration in Makoni district, Zimbabwe, 1960-1980', *Africa*, 52(3), 1982, pp. 20-41.

[75] Lan, *Guns and Rain*, has written about the role the spirit mediums in the Dande area played through their mystical powers, bringing a bonding between the guerrillas and the land, but he errs in generalising the trend of loss of legitimacy among chiefs; see T. Ranger and G. Ncube, 'Religion in the guerrilla war', in N. Bhebe and T. Ranger (eds.), *Society in Zimbabwe's Liberation War* (Harare: University of Zimbabwe Publications; London: James Currey, 1996), p. 45.

[76] Tungamirai, 'Recruitment to ZANLA', p. 41.

[77] Chung, *Re-living the Second Chimurenga*, p. 197.

[78] J. McLaughlin, 'Avila Mission: A turning point in church relations with the state and with the liberation forces', in Bhebe and Ranger (eds.), *Society in Zimbabwe's Liberation War*, p. 92.

Gundani from their study of the south-western part of the country.[79] They conclude that the guerrillas espoused an 'anti-religious secularism' that resulted in the closure of nearly all mission stations in the region, and assert that by 1979 the missionary presence had almost completely vanished.[80] But the attitudes of guerrillas to the Christian churches differed, as some of them were mission-educated. D. J. Maxwell shows how *pungwe*[81] songs were often adapted from church songs, and some *pungwes* opened with prayers.[82] However, despite efforts at forging cordial relations, many missionaries were brutally murdered by guerrillas during the war.[83] Missionaries in isolated rural schools and missions often found themselves in the worst possible position, caught between soldiers and guerrillas. Perhaps the most horrifying example was the ZANLA attack on Elim Mission, a Protestant outpost in the eastern Vumba area, in 1978:

> a band of 20-30 guerrillas visited the school ... They broke open the school stores and distributed food and new uniforms to many of the school children ... They then went to round up the missionaries. The following morning their bodies were found on the sports fields ... [Eight adults], all dead, the bodies of their four children lying beside them; one a three-week old baby girl. Three of the women had been raped. Some yards away lay [another woman missionary], critically ill from her wounds. She never regained consciousness. The nature and degree of violence meted out to the victims defied all imagination. They had been stabbed, bludgeoned and hacked to death; their bodies severely mutilated.[84]

As late as February 1980, a Catholic priest at Berejena Mission, Fr Kilian Heusser, was killed and the church buildings were destroyed by soldiers purportedly pretending to be ZANLA guerrillas.[85] However, the church's attitude to the guerrilla war generally transformed from open hostility in the early period

---

[79] J. McLaughlin, *On the Frontline: Catholic Missions in Zimbabwe's Liberation War* (Harare: Baobab Books, 1996), pp. 108-44. M. Bourdillon and P. Gundani, 'Rural Christians and the Zimbabwe liberation war', in C. Hallencreutz and A. Moyo (eds.), *Church and State in Zimbabwe* (Gweru: Mambo Press, 1988).

[80] Bourdillon and Gundani, 'Rural Christians', p. 52.

[81] *Pungwes* were 'night-time political rallies'; see Tungamirai, 'Recruitment to ZANLA', p. 42.

[82] D. J. Maxwell, 'Christianity and the war of liberation in eastern Zimbabwe: The case of Elim Mission', in Bhebe and Ranger (eds.), *Society in Zimbabwe's Liberation War*, pp. 74-5.

[83] Debate still continues regarding the identity of the murderers, some blaming the Selous Scouts, others the guerrillas; see Ian Linden, 'The Catholic Church and the struggle for Zimbabwe', in Bhebe and Ranger (eds.), *Society in Zimbabwe's Liberation War*; Martin and Johnson, *The Struggle for Zimbabwe*.

[84] Maxwell, 'Christianity and the war in eastern Zimbabwe', p. 69.

[85] Frederikse, *None but Ourselves*, p. 299-318.

to overt support in the 1970s. Several missionaries, as well as Bishop Donal Lamont, were deported for their support of the nationalist cause.[86]

An important aspect of the nationalist armies was the attraction that they held for thousands of black women. The participation of women in the struggle is a topic that has seen heated debate in both historiography and popular culture.[87] It is generally agreed, however, that African women wanted to make a contribution to liberation and thereby be afforded a new kind of respect by their male peers. As one female guerrilla put it,

> [I] wanted to liberate the country because the British colonised us, and there were some jobs only whites could get. I was eighteen years old when I joined. I had not heard about UDI ... as I was too young. We wanted to liberate Zimbabwe. If you are a boy you can come to liberate Zimbabwe. If you are a girl you can come to liberate Zimbabwe.[88]

Ten per cent of ZIPRA's 20,000 guerrillas were women, organised in one brigade 'with its own engineers, communications, other support services and female commanders'.[89] Estimates of trained and fighting women in the ZANLA forces range from 1,000 to 2,000. Refugee camps held many other women, and thousands of female supporters of the guerrilla armies lived inside the country.[90]

Officially, the nationalists advocated gender equality; a report in the ZANU mouthpiece, the *Zimbabwe People's Voice*, stated that

> The emancipation of women is a must and not an act of charity. Women are an indivisible part of society. Their struggle is part of society's struggle for progress. Women should enjoy equal rights with their menfolk. No progress can be reached without the effective participation of women. Women must now totally dedicate themselves to the revolution. Only through conscious participation will Zimbabwean women gain the confidence of their men.[91]

However, the fight against colonial and racial oppression often co-existed with male oppression of females. Kriger notes that some women took advantage

[86] For details of how Bishop Lamont was persecuted by the RF state, see McLaughlin, 'Avila Mission', p. 98.

[87] See T. Barnes, '*Flame* and the historiography of armed struggle in Zimbabwe', in Richard Mendelsohn and Vivian Bickford-Smith (eds.), *Black and White in Colour: African History on Screen* (London: James Currey, 2007).

[88] Lyons, *Guns and Guerilla Girls*, p. 108.

[89] J. Brickhill, 'Daring to storm the heavens: The military strategy of ZAPU, 1976-79', in Bhebe and Ranger (eds.), *Soldiers in Zimbabwe's Liberation War*, pp. 65-6.

[90] Lyons, *Guns and Guerilla Girls*, pp. 159-60.

[91] Cited in ibid., pp. 45-6.

of the presence of the guerrillas to seek intervention in domestic conflicts. With time, however, the guerrillas stopped entertaining such complaints,[92] apparently having realised the folly of alienating the men in the community. Nhongo-Simbanegavi debunks the 'myth' propagated by nationalist parties and some feminist scholars regarding the 'emancipatory' role of the war among women.[93] Women's participation, she points out, was generally limited to the rear, where they served as cooks, nurses, porters and carriers. Luise White also records the complaint by some female cadres in the training camps that 'our [male] comrades were reluctant to show us how to handle a gun'.[94] The response to such complaints was that 'a gun is not an object for you to use as an instrument of showing off, neither is it a certificate that you are equal to men comrades'.[95]

A gender struggle also played itself out in the camps. There is increasing evidence that female guerrillas and ordinary women were sexually exploited during the struggle.[96] Chung points out that the Nhari Rebellion, for example, attracted large numbers of women wanting an end to abuse by military commanders.[97]

The increased visibility of gender roles was not limited to Africans. White women were also involved in the war but, in Lyons's view, did not seek a new status; rather, their function was to support the troops. This, she argues, served to reinforce existing gendered identities and inequalities. A magazine described the experiences of white women in the following terms:

> Typical of frontier folk throughout the world, Rhodesian women have shown great pluck and endurance in the face of terrorism and the economic problems posed by sanctions. They can face drought, fear, armed attacks on their homes, the ever-present risk of being blown up by a terrorist landmine – and emerge as practical and charming as ever.[98]

However, Lyons observes that the war did bring about a degree of emancipation to white women who were often confined to domestic roles. As more men were called-up, women were trained in self-defence methods such as how to handle a gun. This, she points out, was a challenge to the general perception of women as 'domesticated mothers' good for 'nurturing' as opposed to being capable fighters on a par with men.[99]

---

[92] Kriger, *Zimbabwe's Guerrilla War*, pp. 179-95.

[93] Nhongo-Simbanegavi, *For Better or Worse?*, pp. 1-11.

[94] White, *The Assassination of Herbert Chitepo*, p. 21.

[95] Ibid.

[96] Ibid., p. 63; see also Chung, *Re-living the Second Chimurenga*, p. 126.

[97] Chung, *Re-living the Second Chimurenga*, p. 127.

[98] *Focus on Rhodesia*, 1977, quoted in Lyons, *Guns and Guerilla Girls*, p. 131.

[99] Lyons, *Guns and Guerilla Girls*, p. 35.

Fig. 5.4: People dumped in Protected Villages, Honde Valley, 1977.
[*Source:* National Archives of Zimbabwe]

The war also influenced generational tensions in the rural areas. For instance, the young male and female messengers' (*mujibhas* and *chimbwidos*) direct dealings with the guerrillas saw them exercising an unprecedented measure of power over their elders, who risked being reported to the guerrillas as sell-outs or even to the Rhodesian security forces if they dared antagonise them. [100] In the protected villages, for instance, people were subjected to body searches by the young armed guards each time they left or entered.[101] However, when they searched the women, the guards 'made sure they touched every part ... touching the breasts' while their men watched helplessly.[102] This behaviour was not restricted to those executing the day-to-day running of the protected villages. In Nkayi and Lupane, elderly men found the guerrillas 'a source of great concern' because they occasionally entered into involuntary relationships with women. As one ZAPU chairman later recalled, 'it was difficult to control the young guerrillas. They tried to propose girls, but we argued with them, saying "that's not what you're here for".' [103]

---

[100] M. Kesby, 'Arenas for control, terrains of gender contestation: Guerrilla struggle and counter-insurgency warfare in Zimbabwe, 1972-1980', *Journal of Southern African Studies*, 22(4), 1996, p. 570.

[101] M. Nyakudya, 'War, Protected Villages, Environmental Degradation and Social History in Chiweshe, 1972-2005', paper presented at the New Dimensions in History, Seminar Series, History Department, University of Zimbabwe, March 2007.

[102] Kesby, 'Arenas for control', p. 527.

[103] Alexander *et al.*, *Violence and Memory*, p. 164.

A climate for negotiation?

By the late 1970s, the cost of the war had escalated both financially – costs had ballooned to £500,000 a day – and in terms of human resources.[104] Higher taxes were levied on whites to pay for the forty-five per cent increase in the defence budget. Travel and emigration allowances were cut. These increasing difficulties, in turn, led to a rise in emigration rates. In 1976,

> [A]fter a series of monthly losses of around forty, the net departure figure suddenly jumped to 817 in April, the worst result for a single month since 1964. ... But the net average monthly loss of 771 between May and September pinpointed the worsening security situation...[105]

This affected the state's recruitment base, and led Smith to conscript, first, all able-bodied white men under the age of 38, before widening the net to include African males between 18 and 35, with university students being the main target group.[106] Despite the insistence by the RF government that the situation was not yet out of hand, civil administration had broken down and hundreds of schools, clinics and hospitals had closed in the rural areas.

The military gains by the nationalists came, however, at a great cost. The guerrillas began to face debilitating logistical problems. Medicine, clothes, and even food were scarce for both ZANLA and ZIPRA forces as thousands of high school and university students joined the exodus into recruitment camps in Zambia, Botswana, Tanzania and Mozambique. Partly as a result of this, but also due to meagre training, guerrilla casualties began to increase in the late 1970s.

The fact that the Patriotic Front was making significant progress towards winning the war made political repositioning necessary. As international pressure mounted, Smith made attempts to form a government that was acceptable to the international community. This culminated in the 1978 Internal Settlement, which saw the creation of a coalition government comprising Smith, Muzorewa, Sithole and Chief Chirau. Muzorewa and Sithole had at least one thing in common with Smith, their resentment towards the Patriotic Front, and particularly the open support it received from the OAU.[107] The two ostracised leaders fulfilled Smith's criteria for preferred African candidates to assume leadership: neither had an army to talk about, thus they were no security threat, and they were also desperate to pull the political rug from under the feet of the Patriotic Front. Chirau, an African chief with loyalties to Smith, was roped in to give the new

---

[104] Meredith, *The Past Is Another Country*, p. 305.
[105] Godwin and Hancock, *'Rhodesians Never Die'*, p. 163.
[106] Meredith, *The Past Is Another Country*, p. 239.
[107] Nkomo, *The Story of My Life*, p. 193.

white survival package a semblance of support by the traditional authorities. The new state was named Zimbabwe-Rhodesia to give the impression that the arrangement ushered in a new era of racial partnership.

This settlement was an example of the constant repositioning of the belligerents that characterised the period. Smith had neither capitulated nor abandoned his belief in white superiority, and the details of the political arrangements during the period clearly communicated this fact. The property rights of whites were to remain sacred, while the control of the judiciary, the public service, the army and the police was to remain in white hands. Whites were also to be accorded the right to dual citizenship. The constitutional provisions ensured continued white privilege in parliament by allowing 20 seats for whites to be elected on a separate roll, plus another 8 on a common roll, while the 72 remaining seats would be filled by blacks, initially from the three African leaders' party lists.[108]

To authenticate these arrangements, an election was held which pitted the three African signatories against one another. Muzorewa won the elections with a convincing margin, winning 64 seats; Sithole and Chirau won 14 and 6, respectively. Chung and Meredith both argue that the large voter turn-out – an estimated 1.8 million people, despite the boycott campaign by the Patriotic Front – indicated that ordinary people were tired of the war and wanted a return to normal life.[109] On the other hand, De Roche suggests that intimidation by security forces, as well as by Muzorewa and Sithole's militias, formed with the encouragement of Smith, also played a part in influencing the turn-out.[110] The settlement was, however, weakened by a number of factors. To begin with, the war continued because the arrangement had not involved the Patriotic Front. Secondly, it did not receive wide international recognition.[111] Thirdly, popular support for it waned as Smith's dominance became clear.[112] However, Smith's own grip on power was fast becoming precarious as the government was faced by the resignation of high-ranking officials, among them the Internal Affairs Co-Minister, Rollo Hayman, and General John Hickman, clear indications that the end of the regime was near.[113]

---

[108] Chung, *Re-living the Second Chimurenga*, p. 231.

[109] Ibid., p. 233; Meredith, *The Past Is Another Country*, p. 364.

[110] De Roche, *Black, White and Chrome*, p. 274.

[111] Meredith, *The Past Is Another Country*, pp. 365-7.

[112] Ibid., pp. 336-8. Muzorewa's inability to push for the Africans' interests was exposed following his luke-warm reaction to the expulsion of Byron Hove, the Co-Minister of Justice, after alleged subversive comments concerning the continued racial domination of the whites under the new Muzorewa–Smith rule.

[113] See Godwin and Hancock, *'Rhodesians Never Die'*, p. 238, and Chung, *Re-Living the Second Chimurenga*, p.240.

The period after 1978 was arguably the most atrocious of the liberation war. With the government pressing for a ceasefire and the guerrillas continuing with what they believed was a legitimate fight against a 'sell-out' arrangement, the peasants suffered the most. Muzorewa's and Sithole's militias also fought against the Patriotic Front on the government side, although it was also not uncommon for the two militias to fight against each other. The new government was dogged by continuing war and a crumbling economy, and Muzorewa failed to deliver most of the promises he had made in his election campaign. The cumulative impact of one and a half decades of sanctions became even more apparent: basic commodities and fuel were critically scarce; as a result of the shortage of spare parts, the manufacturing and mining industries were operating at low capacity; and the 1978/79 season saw a failure of crops.[114]

The war raged on with greater intensity as guerrilla forces used increasingly sophisticated weapons, such as the Soviet surface-to-air missiles with which ZIPRA guerrillas shot down a civilian Air Rhodesia flight bound for Kariba in September 1978. Eighteen of the fifty-four people aboard survived the crash, but fourteen of them were then shot by the guerrillas.[115] Another plane was shot down in 1979, killing 54 passengers and five crew members.[116] In December 1978, ZANLA sabotage units blew up the oil storage tanks housing Rhodesia's strategic reserves in Salisbury's Southerton industrial area; the resulting fire burned for a week, and was visible from 120 kilometres away.

These events, which proved that white civilian spaces which had always been considered inviolate were actually well within reach of the guerrilla forces, marked the beginning of the end of 'white Rhodesia'. As Ellert has written of the war, by 1979,

> [U]nits of both ZIPRA and ZANLA, in their respective operational sectors, were by now openly parading and showing military authority in rural areas which had long since fallen under their effective control. By the eve of the Lancaster House Constitutional Conference in 1979 the security forces were confined in mine-protected vehicles moving by day in heavily armed convoys. Rural base camps were often subjected to attack by night with mortar rockets and small-arms fire.[117]

This coincided with the August 1979 Commonwealth Heads of Government

---

[114] Godwin and Hancock, 'Rhodesians Never Die', p. 224.

[115] Caute, Under the Skin, p. 274.

[116] Ibid., p. 310.

[117] H. Ellert, The Rhodesian Front War: Counter-insurgency and Guerrilla Warfare, 1962-1980 (Gweru: Mambo Press, 1989), p. 7.

Meeting in Lusaka, where African states reiterated that it was Britain's responsibility to resolve the crisis in Rhodesia. Britain was put under diplomatic pressure by Nigeria, her biggest trading partner in Africa, which threatened to block British investments in Nigeria until the Rhodesian crisis was resolved.[118]

All these pressures culminated in the 1979 Lancaster House conference, chaired by Lord Carrington, the newly appointed British Foreign Secretary. The conference was attended by the Patriotic Front, led by Mugabe and Nkomo, and Muzorewa's delegation, which included Sithole and Smith. The conference was, to a large extent, the result of several forces grown weary of fighting. Zambia and Mozambique, for instance, were desperate to end a war which had led to the serious loss of lives and economic dislocation in their countries. The nationalist leaders were also tired of the war. Guerrillas' logistics had become even more strained. Inside Rhodesia, both the economy and socio-political life were under severe stress.

The major highlights of the Lancaster House Conference settlement were that the minority white population was allowed to retain 20 of the 100 seats in Parliament for at least seven years.[119] The new state was to inherit a debt of $200 million, and agreed to pay pensions to all Rhodesian civil servants, even those who had emigrated. The liberation forces were to be integrated into the regular army. The belligerents also agreed to a ceasefire and to hold fresh elections within three months in order to choose the new leader of independent Zimbabwe.[120] The main point of disagreement was on the issue of land. The Patriotic Front wanted the majority government to be allowed to expropriate unused white commercial land in order to resettle the many land-hungry Africans. However, the Lancaster House Constitution stated that land could not be confiscated, but would have to be bought on a willing-seller–willing-buyer basis.[121] Such an arrangement was, however, beyond the financial ability of the new state.[122] The unresolved land issue was only temporarily rested following British and American promises to buy and develop the white-owned lands, without, however, disclosing how much money they would put up for the compensation exercise.

Under pressure from Presidents Kaunda and Machel,[123] the Patriotic Front

---

[118] Bhebe, *Simon Vengayi Muzenda*, p. 228.

[119] Chung, *Re-living the Second Chimurenga*, p. 246.

[120] Sibanda, *The Zimbabwe African People's Union*, p. 218.

[121] S. Moyo, 'The Land Question', in I. Mandaza (ed.), *Zimbabwe: The Political Economy of Transition, 1980-86* (Dakar: Codesria, 1987), p. 172.

[122] Nkomo, *The Story of My Life*, p. 202. For a more detailed discussion of the land issue at the Lancaster House Conference, see S. Moyo, *The Land Question in Zimbabwe* (Harare: SAPES Books, 1995).

[123] Sibanda, *The Zimbabwe African People's Union*, p. 218.

was forced to accede to this incomplete arrangement, which Joshua Nkomo described as 'a result of muddle and compromise, reached in haste in order to stop the bloodshed'.[124] One commentator likened the agreement to the Africans having been offered 'the driver's seat [while] whites would continue to map the route the car must take and control the fuel which made it run'.[125] These hastily 'settled' issues were to provide material for contest in the post-colonial era.

With the new constitution ready and a ceasefire arranged, the first elections were held to choose the leader of independent Zimbabwe. The fractious alliance that had stood since the Patriotic Front was formed disintegrated; ZAPU and ZANU stood as separate parties: PF-ZAPU and ZANU(PF). In the elections, Mugabe's ZANU(PF) won the majority with 57 seats, while Nkomo's PF-ZAPU won 20 seats and Muzorewa's UANC was a distant third with 3 seats. All but one of PF-ZAPU's seats were won in Matabeleland, while ZANU(PF) won all its seats in Mashonaland – boding ill for the post-independence period.[126] These events culminated in the independence celebrations on 18 April 1980, with Robert Mugabe being installed as the first Prime Minister of independent Zimbabwe.

[124] Nkomo, *The Story of My Life,* p. 204.
[125] Quoted in C. Sylvester, *Zimbabwe: A Terrain of Contradictory Development* (Boulder, CO: Westview Press, 1991), p. 55.
[126] Sibanda, *The Zimbabwe African People's Union,* p. 222.

6

From Buoyancy to Crisis, 1980-1997

James Muzondidya

Introduction

Zimbabwe's post-colonial history has become the subject of many interpretations. This chapter examines the changes in the history of the country from the years of economic buoyancy and politics of reconciliation in the early 1980s, through the crisis of unity in the Gukurahundi period up to the crisis of the state in the late 1990s. The main themes addressed are contestations over the restructuring and reconfiguration of the state after 1980; processes of rule and state-making; questions of justice and equity with regard to land and resource ownership and redistribution; and issues of nationhood and citizenship in the post-colonial state. The chapter begins by focusing on the political economy of Zimbabwe in the first decade of independence, and then reviews the changing nature of the state, politics and society within the context of the economic hardships of the 1990s.

Political and economic restructuring of the state and the nation

The major challenge confronting the post-independence government of ZANU(PF) in 1980 was nation-building in a society deeply divided along the lines of race, class, ethnicity, gender and geography. The other main challenges included post-war reconstruction, restructuring the inherited colonial political economy – especially redressing its racialised imbalances – and democratising the inherited authoritarian colonial state and its institutions.

The government embarked on a programme of post-war reconstruction which aimed to recapitalise and reintegrate the economy into the world economy. To redress some of the inequalities inherited from the old colonial order, it tried to broaden the economy and make it more inclusive by integrating blacks through black economic empowerment, the Africanisation of public service and the active development of a black middle class.[1] In response to black popular aspirations and expectations, and in pursuit of its own developmentalist objectives, the government tried to solve both rural poverty and racial inequality in land ownership

---

[1] I. Kaplan, 'Zimbabwe: Ethnicity and race', *Chapter 2B: Countries of the World*, 1991. <http://www.fb10.uni-bremen.de/anglistik/kerkhoff/AfricanLit/MiniLectures/ZimbaGeneral. htm>; B. Raftopoulos, *Zimbabwe: Race and Nationalism in a Post-colonial State* (Harare: SAPES Books, 1996).

between blacks and whites by introducing a gradual land resettlement pro-gramme targeting peasants in congested communal areas. It also tried to empower rural peasant farmers through positive pricing, and better access to marketing services, credit and inputs. Within a few years of independence, rural agricultural output improved and communal farmers had become the largest producers of maize and cotton.[2]

With the help of local communities and foreign donors, especially from the Scandinavian countries, the government expanded the provision of health and educational facilities to areas previously ignored by the colonial state. It specifically built roads, schools, clinics, boreholes and established sanitation facilities in communal rural lands, which lagged behind urban areas in terms of infrastructural development. By the end of the first decade of independence, as Alois Mlambo has noted, substantial progress had been made in expanding the provision of health care and education.[3] In the educational sector, for instance, enrolment in primary schools rose from 82,000 in 1979 to 2,216,878 in 1985, and in secondary schools from 66,000 to 482,000 during the same period. Between 1980 and 1990, the number of primary and secondary schools had risen by a remarkable 80 per cent from 3,358 to 6,042.[4]

The government made notable progress in the provision of water and sanitation to rural households, and won praise from the World Health Organisation and UNICEF for its ability to provide safe drinking water to 84 per cent of the national population by 1988.[5] There were also improvements in workers' wages and working conditions. A minimum wage was introduced, workers' bargaining strength was improved through the introduction of collective bargaining and companies were compelled to improve living and working conditions for employees and their families.[6]

---

[2] See C. Mumbengegwi, 'Macroeconomic policies and agricultural performance', in C. Mumbe-ngegwi (ed.), *Macroeconomic and Structural Adjustment Policies in Zimbabwe* (London: Macmillan, 2002), p. 240; A. S. Mlambo, *The Economic Structural Adjustment Programme: The Case of Zimbabwe, 1990-1995* (Harare: University of Zimbabwe Publications, 1997), p. 4; S. Moyo, *Land Reform under Structural Adjustment in Zimbabwe: Land Use Change in Mashonaland East Province* (Uppsala: Nordic Africa Institute, 2000), p. 24.

[3] Mlambo, *The Economic Structural Adjustment Programme*, pp. viii, 55-82.

[4] Ibid., p. 59.

[5] M. Musemwa, 'The Politics of Water in Postcolonial Zimbabwe, 1980-2007', Seminar Paper presented at the African Studies Centre, Leiden University, 19 June 2008, p. 6.

[6] S. Dansereau, 'Liberation and opposition in Zimbabwe', in H. Melber (ed.), *Limits to Libera-tion in Southern Africa: The Unfinished Business of Democratic Consolidation* (Cape Town: HSRC Press, 2003), p. 30; G. Kanyenze, 'The Performance of the Zimbabwean economy, 1980-2000', in S. Darnolf and L. Laakso (eds.), *Twenty Years of Independence in Zimbabwe: From Liberation to Authoritarianism* (Basingstoke and New York: Palgrave Macmillan, 2003).

In general terms, the government partially succeeded in addressing the inherited problems and the country achieved some notable economic and social gains. The rapid economic growth in the first two years of independence, averaging 12 per cent a year, and external financing which rose from Z$157 million (then US$157 million) to Z$533 million in 1982 helped the government to introduce qualitative changes in infrastructural development, job creation, and education and health delivery.[7]

However, the gains made in the first decade of independence were limited, unsustainable and ephemerally welfarist in nature. Zimbabwe continued to experience serious social and economic problems as well as redistributive challenges in the 1980s, especially in the spheres of land and the economy, and a number of books have discussed these challenges.[8] The economic boom of the immediate post-independence period did not last long. Zimbabwe's economy experienced mixed fortunes throughout the 1980s, as it went through the negative effects of droughts, weakening terms of trade and high interest rates and oil prices. All this impacted negatively on the state's capacity to finance its programmes. Moreover, mounting pressure from the International Monetary Fund (IMF) and World Bank compelled the government to abandon some of its social policies in 1983 and 1984.

Employment creation was slow during the 1980s, and unemployment grew substantially right from independence. Some critics have attributed the problems to the race between growth of the economy and population growth. From 1982 to 1990, GDP growth rates averaged 1.3 per cent per annum, while the population grew at an average of 3.3 per cent.[9] Only 10,000 new jobs a year were created in the first decade of independence, which did not keep pace with either the population increase or with the large numbers of school leavers (approximately 100,000 by the mid-1980s).[10]

At the same time, the gains of the first decade were unevenly distributed. Elite groups in both rural and urban societies, which included rich peasants

---

[7] See M. Burdette and R. J. Davies, 'The Zimbabwe economy: Prognostications and realities after six years', *Zambezia*, 14(1), 1987, p. 79; Mlambo, *The Economic Structural Adjustment Programme*, pp. 40-1.

[8] S. Moyo, 'The political economy of land acquisition and redistribution in Zimbabwe, 1990-1999', *Journal of Southern African Studies*, 26(1), 2000; I. Mandaza (ed.), *Zimbabwe: The Political Economy of Transition, 1980-1986* (Dakar: Codesria, 1986); C. Stoneman (ed.), *Zimbabwe's Prospects: Issues of Race, Class, State and Capital in Southern Africa* (London: Macmillan, 1988).

[9] See C. Stoneman, 'The economy: Recognising the reality', in Stoneman (ed.), *Zimbabwe's Prospects*, pp. 47-8; Dansereau, 'Liberation and opposition in Zimbabwe', p. 27.

[10] F. Chung, 'Education: Revolution or reform', in Stoneman (ed.), *Zimbabwe's Prospects*, pp. 129-30.

and farmers, business people and educated professionals, benefited most from policies which opened up the state and capital accumulation to blacks.[11] As a result, there was no significant narrowing of income and wealth differentials: it was estimated that 3 per cent of the population, mainly white farmers and a small black bourgeoisie, continued to own the bulk of resources and to control two-thirds of gross national income in the 1980s.[12]

Government policy on rural development, especially the improved support to peasant farmers, did not effectively transform rural economies or lift millions of rural dwellers out of their condition of deprivation. A significant proportion of rural households continued to have inadequate access to productive land in the communal areas. Lack of adequate agricultural land, problems of drought in 1982/83 and 1984/85, and reduced government incentive schemes, led more and more peasants to revert to subsistence farming.[13]

In the urban sphere, generally marginalised in the government's development planning,[14] urban workers were beginning to experience intensified transport problems and shortages in housing by the mid-1980s. Some of the sub-standard houses and hostels built for African workers in townships during the colonial period began to yield to the pressure of increased overcrowding, an unaddressed problem going back to the late 1970s when many rural Africans migrated into towns owing to the intensification of the war.[15]

Besides experiencing growing problems in housing and transport, urban workers were struggling to survive on declining wages. These improved in the first two years of independence, but declined in real terms thereafter by an average of 18 per cent a year.[16] The black middle class also had problems. Those in the business sector continued to suffer from constraints which limited their participation in the productive sectors of the economy. These ranged from difficulties in securing loans from white and foreign-owned financiers and banks

[11] Mandaza (ed.), *The Political Economy of Transition*; Stoneman (ed.), *Zimbabwe's Prospects*.

[12] See Stoneman, 'The economy', pp. 51-2.

[13] L. Cliffe, 'The prospects of agricultural transformation in Zimbabwe', in Stoneman (ed.), *Zimbabwe's Prospects*, pp. 309-25.

[14] The ZANU(PF) government's bias towards rural development was informed by both historical and political considerations – the conscious desire to even the colonially engineered historical imbalance in development between the rural and urban areas and the need to appease a rural-based political constituency which had played a fundamental role in supporting the war in the 1970s and the electoral victory of 1980. See Musemwa, 'The politics of water', p. 5.

[15] J. C. Mafico, *Urban Low-income Housing in Zimbabwe* (Aldershot: Avebury, 1991); L. M. Zinyama, D. Tevera and S. Cumming (eds.), *Harare: The Growth and Problems of the City* (Harare: University of Zimbabwe Publications, 1993).

[16] J. Cobbing, 'Review article: Imperialising of Zimbabwe', *Transformation*, 9, 1999, p. 85.

to hostility from white capital reluctant to lose its historical monopoly.[17] The productive sector, especially manufacturing, continued to be closed to potential black entrepreneurs.[18] A 1989 report on black advancement in the private sector showed the following racial distribution at management level: senior management: 62.5% white, 37.5% black; middle management: 35.5% white, 64.5% black; junior management: 22% white, 78% black.[19] By 1993, the level of business participation by blacks in all sectors of the economy stood at only 2 per cent.[20]

As in the colonial period, when the ambitions of the aspiring black petty bourgeoisie were proscribed by the structures of the colonial state, their aspirations in the post-colonial period were frustrated by the legacy of these structures. The rapid Africanisation of certain sectors of the economy in the early years of independence took place only in the public sector, where the government had direct control. It was not reproduced in the private sector, which remained in the hands of white and international capital. The government tried to redress racial imbalances in the private sector through exhortation and non-preferential legislation, such as the Labour Relations Act (No. 16 of 1985) which outlawed labour market discrimination. The Ministry of Labour, however, had only investigative powers and was not sufficiently resourced to monitor firms effectively.[21]

Throughout the 1980s, then, there was little radical reform or structural change in the Zimbabwean economy. It remained in foreign hands, especially British and South African-based multinational corporations who overwhelmingly owned Zimbabwe's industry.[22] It was estimated in 1985 that 48 per cent of manufacturing was owned by foreign enterprises or individuals. Foreign dominance was more extensive in mining, where an estimated 90 per cent was owned by foreign multinationals.[23] The predominance of foreign-owned companies in the productive sectors of the economy meant that locals continued to be excluded. Joint ventures and partial takeovers, which presented those in power – and those connected to them – with opportunities for personal accumulation,

[17] F. Maphosa, 'Towards the sociology of Zimbabwean indigenous entrepreneurship', *Zambezia*, 25(2), 1998, pp. 176-8.

[18] P. Bond, *Uneven Zimbabwe: A Study of Finance, Development and Underdevelopment* (Trenton, NJ: Africa World Press, 1998).

[19] Raftopoulos, *Race and Nationalism*, p. 6.

[20] *Financial Gazette*, 28 Jan. 1998.

[21] P. Bennell and B. Strachan, 'The Zimbabwean experience: Black occupational advancement', in P. Hugo (ed.), *Redistribution and Affirmative Action: Working on South Africa's Political Economy* (Johannesburg: Southern Books, 1992), p. 30.

[22] Stoneman, 'The economy', pp. 54-5.

[23] Economist Intelligence Unit, *Zimbabwe's First Five Years: Economic Prospects Following Independence* (London: The Unit, Special Report 11, 1981), p. 87; Burdette and Davies, 'The Zimbabwe economy', p. 78.

continued to mask foreign-capital dominance. Many former civil servants and ZANU(PF)'s political clients, for instance, were recruited as middlemen for white-owned corporations.[24]

More critically, the pace of reform in the crucial area of land reform remained very slow. By 1990, the government had acquired only 3.5 m hectares of land, and resettled only 52,000 households of the targeted 162,000 families to be settled on 9 m hectares. Worse, only 19 per cent of the land acquired was prime land. The rest was either in marginal rainfall areas or was unsuitable for agriculture.[25]

A number of factors led to this failure. These included the government's lack of funds to purchase land, and British reluctance to continue bankrolling the programme because of differences with the Zimbabwe government, especially over allegations of land being acquired by government officials and ZANU(PF) politicians.[26] But the key blockage to political and economic reform was the Lancaster House constitution.

The Lancaster House constitution and the legacy of race

The Lancaster House constitution, crafted as part of the deal to end the liberation war in 1979, embodied a series of compromises over minority rights, in particular on the future of land ownership in the country, and guaranteed white representation in parliament. It protected the existing authoritarian bureaucracy and protected private property, thus limiting the scope of redistribution. In effect, it 'gave settler capital a decade-long period of consolidation, during which issues around the radical restructuring of the legacy of economic inequality were effectively put on hold'.[27]

The willing-buyer and willing-seller principle enshrined in the constitution was the main obstacle to successful land reform; it protected the interests of white, large-scale commercial farmers and prevented the government from buying enough land to meet the increasing needs of a growing population.[28] Conscious of the racial protection guaranteed by the constitution, white farmers were generally reluctant to relinquish their colonially inherited privilege. In this respect, the 1979 constitution 'pervaded the process and structures through

---

[24] B. Raftopoulos and D. Compagnon, 'Indigenization, the state bourgeoisie and neo-authoritarian politics', in Darnolf and Laakso (eds.), *Twenty Years of Independence in Zimbabwe.*

[25] Moyo, 'The political economy of land acquisition'.

[26] Ibid., p. 13.

[27] B. Raftopoulos, 'Unreconciled differences: The limits of reconciliation politics in Zimbabwe', in B. Raftopoulos and T. Savage (eds.), *Zimbabwe: Injustice and Political Reconciliation* (Cape Town: Institute for Justice and Reconciliation, 2004), p. 2.

[28] L. Tshuma, *A Matter of (In)justice: Law, State and the Agrarian Question in Zimbabwe* (Harare: SAPES Books, 1997).

which the new state ... sought both to consolidate national independence and provide a basis for genuine economic and social development'.[29]

Apart from safeguarding the economic interests of minority whites by ensuring that 'Zimbabwe inherited the key elements of the white settler colonial apparatus', the constitution hampered the progress towards justice and political reconciliation by entrenching a special parliamentary position for whites.[30] Until the removal of the twenty reserved seats in 1987, politically active whites continued to see themselves as existing outside the new nation state and overwhelmingly supported the conservative Rhodesian Front.[31] After the demise of the Rhodesian Front and the enactment of the constitutional amendment which abolished the separate voters' roll, most whites withdrew from national electoral politics. They only resurfaced in 2000, when their economic livelihoods were threatened by the government confiscation of white commercial farms.[32]

The behaviour of many whites continued to be influenced by what both Ranger and Mandaza have described as the legacy of 'settler culture'.[33] Settler culture is 'the great power exerted by settlers, their virtual monopoly over political and legal institutions, their coercive control over the labour and livelihoods of Africans, their manipulative methods for advancing the economic interests of themselves'.[34] It was also profoundly conservative because it could not allow itself to adapt to the African environment.[35] The legacy of this 'culture', in the sense of 'standardised modes of behaviour and thought', was 'pre-eminently the expression of the white community's tenuously held position of predominance'.[36]

Racial inequalities in land and the economy were also not seriously addressed

[29] I. Mandaza, 'The state in the post-white settler colonial situation', in Mandaza (ed.), *The Political Economy of Transition*, p. 2.

[30] Ibid., p. 42; T. O. Ranger, 'Race and ethnicity in Zimbabwe: A historical overview', in Mass Public Opinion Institute, *The Salience of Race and Ethnicity in Zimbabwe*, forthcoming.

[31] C. Sylvester, 'Zimbabwe's 1985 elections: A search for national mythology', *Journal of Modern African Studies*, 24(2), 1986, p. 252. A more detailed, journalistic account of political conservatism among whites in post-independence can be found in P. Godwin, 'Whose kith and kin now?', *Sunday Times Magazine* [London], 25 Mar. 1984. <http://www.maryellenmark. com/text/magazines/london_sunday_times/904G-000-005.html>, retrieved 28 May 2009.

[32] L. Huyse, 'Zimbabwe: Why reconciliation failed', in D. Bloomfield, T. Barnes and L. Huyse (eds.), *Reconciliation after Violent Conflict: A Handbook* (Stockholm: International Institute for Democracy and Electoral Assistance, 2003), pp. 34-9. <http://www.idea.int/publications/ reconciliation/upload/reconciliation_chapo2cs-zimbabwe.pdf> retrieved 28 May 2009.

[33] Mandaza, 'The state in the post-white settler colonial situation'; Ranger, 'Race and ethnicity in Zimbabwe'.

[34] D. Kennedy, *Islands of White: Settler Society and Culture in Kenya and Southern Rhodesia, 1890-1939* (Durham. NC: Duke University Press, 1987).

[35] Ranger, 'Race and ethnicity in Zimbabwe'.

[36] Ibid.

in the first years of independence because there was little popular pressure on the government at a time when the economy was performing well and social obligations were being met. In the absence of such pressure, the government's indigenisation policies were not coherently defined and were implemented half-heartedly. Its reaction to demands from the black bourgeoisie for greater inclusion in the control and ownership of the economy also lacked urgency and commitment.

In the absence of concerted pressure for justice and economic reform from both the government and the impoverished masses, privileged whites were lulled into a false sense of political and economic security, in which many felt secure in their privileged economic positions over blacks because of their huge capital investments.[37] They did not make much effort to contribute towards addressing the inherited racial imbalances in wealth between blacks and whites or nation-building. Writing in 1982, Kaplan observed that 'whites, acknowledging their loss of political primacy, have focused on maintaining their economic status but have made few attempts to accommodate themselves to a changing social order'.[38] 'The maintenance of their pre-independence privileges was seen as absolutely normal,' Huyse has added, while 'prejudices and the destructive social relations they generated were kept alive.'[39] These unresolved problems became major issues in the 1990s, when the economy began to contract seriously and the social problems of the poor began to mount.

Political reforms, reconciliation and democratisation in rural and urban areas in the 1980s

At independence, the ZANU(PF) government committed itself to establishing an order based on democracy, social justice and equality. Soon afterwards, it enacted laws such as the Legal Age of Majority Act (No. 15 of 1982), giving guardianship powers to anyone over 18 years of age, and the Sex Disqualification Removal Act, giving women rights to be appointed to any post in the civil service and giving them more rights to make individual decisions.[40] The government moved to dismantle colonial institutions and laws promoting oppression, ethnic polarisation and racial disharmony by erasing the legal status of racial distinctions and their institutional supports.[41]

---

[37] C. Banana, *The Politics of Repression and Resistance* (Gweru: Mambo Press, 1996), p. 22.
[38] Kaplan, 'Zimbabwe: Ethnicity and race'.
[39] Huyse, 'Zimbabwe: Why reconciliation failed'.
[40] J. Kazembe, 'The women issue', in Mandaza (ed.), *The Political Economy of Transition*, pp. 386-94.
[41] Kaplan, 'Zimbabwe: Ethnicity and race'.

The government also tried to transform and democratise the structure of governance in urban and rural areas through decentralisation of powers, resources and responsibilities to local authorities and other locally administered bodies.[42] In its attempt to build a more cohesive nation-state, the government adopted a reconciliation policy prioritising reconciliation between blacks and whites.[43]

The national reconciliation policy adopted in 1980 also sought to promote unity among blacks through the promotion of political co-operation between previously antagonistic nationalist parties. In pursuit of this objective, the first government to be formed included not only members from the defeated Rhodesian Front but also individuals from PF-ZAPU, which had come second in the polls. The new army was an integrated unit, consisting of combatants from ZANLA, ZIPRA and former Rhodesian units.[44]

To promote national integration among workers, employment policies emphasised the deployment of public servants to places away from their districts of origin. The language policy emphasised the teaching of both Shona and Ndebele (the languages of the two major ethnic groups in Zimbabwe) to develop a spirit of nationhood among the young. Ndebele and Shona, alongside English, were adopted as official national languages. Other minority languages, such as Kalanga, Shangani, Chewa (Nyanja), Venda, Tonga and Nambya, were also officially recognised for use in education and on radio.[45]

However, the introduction of all these measures in the 1980s did not produce the desired results. The post-colonial project of building a just, equitable and non-racial society was not achieved in the 1980s and the foundation for a truly democratic order was not laid. Nor was reconciliation achieved.

Continuities and discontinuities from the past

A number of scholars who have written about post-independence Zimbabwe politics have pointed to the continuity of authoritarian governance from the Rhodesian Front to ZANU(PF). They have traced the increasingly repressive nature of ZANU(PF) after independence, whether it was dealing with the official

---

[42] R. Weitzer, *Transforming Settler States: Communal Conflict and Internal Security in Northern Ireland and Zimbabwe* (Berkeley: University of California Press, 1990), p. 134.

[43] J. Muzondidya, '"Zimbabwe for Zimbabweans": Invisible subject minorities and the quest for justice and reconciliation in Zimbabwe', in Raftopoulos and Savage (eds.), *Zimbabwe: Injustice and Political Reconciliation*, pp. 213-35

[44] M. Rupiya, 'Demobilisation and integration: "Operation Merger" and the Zimbabwe national defence forces, 1980–1987', *Africa Security Review*, 4(3), 1995, pp. 52-64.

[45] S. Makoni, S. Dube and P. Mashiri, 'Zimbabwe colonial and post-colonial language policy and planning practices', *Multilingual Matters*, 7(4), 2006, pp. 377-414.

opposition, striking workers and students, or civil society.[46] As Welshman Ncube observed, behind the façade of constitutional democracy lay an authoritarian political system characterised by the proscription of democratic space, and serious violation of basic human rights and the rule of law. There was a strong continuity with the Rhodesian state, perpetuated through the application of its repressive laws, such as the Emergency Powers Act (*Chapter 11:04*) and the 1960 Law and Order (Maintenance) Act, which were used to detain political rivals and silence critics.[47]

The government also relied heavily on the coercive tactics developed during the liberation struggle to elicit civilian compliance.[48] As Masipula Sithole has argued:

> The liberation struggle also left a significant mark on Zimbabwe's political culture. The commandist nature of mobilisation and politicisation under clandestine circumstances gave rise to the politics of intimidation and fear. Opponents were viewed in warlike terms, as enemies, and therefore illegitimate. The culture from the liberation struggle was intolerant and violent.[49]

This 'culture of intolerance' badly affected ZANU(PF)'s practice of the democratic ideals it espoused. Although multiparty elections were held regularly

---

[46] See B. Raftopoulos, 'The state in crisis: Authoritarianism, selective citizenship and distortions of democracy in Zimbabwe', in A. Hammar, B. Raftopoulos and S. Jensen (eds.), *Zimbabwe's Unfinished Business: Rethinking Land, State and Nation in the Context of Crisis* (Harare: Weaver Press, 2003); Horace Campbell, *Reclaiming Zimbabwe: The Exhaustion of the Patriarchal Model of Liberation* (Cape Town: David Philip, 2003); J. N. Moyo, *Voting for Democracy: Electoral Politics in Zimbabwe* (Harare: University of Zimbabwe Publications, 1992); W. Ncube, 'Constitutionalism, democracy and political practice in Zimbabwe', in I. Mandaza and L. Sachikonye (eds.), *The One-Party State and Democracy: The Zimbabwe Debate* (Harare: SAPES Trust, 1991); J. Makumbe, 'The 1990 Elections: Implications for democracy', in Mandaza and Sachikonye (eds.), *The One-Party State and Democracy*; Darnolf and Laakso (eds.), *Twenty Years of Independence in Zimbabwe.*

[47] See Ncube, 'Constitutionalism, democracy and political practice in Zimbabwe', pp. 156-77.

[48] For detailed discussion of violence and coercion in nationalist politics during the liberation struggle, see Norma Kriger, *Zimbabwe's Guerrilla War: Peasant Voices* (Cambridge: Cambridge University Press, 1992); F. Chung, *Re-living the Second Chimurenga: Memories from Zimbabwe's Liberation Struggle* (Harare: Weaver Press, 2005), pp. 175-8; D. Moore, 'Democracy, violence and identity in the Zimbabwean war of national liberation: Reflections from the realms of dissent', *Canadian Journal of African Studies*, 3, 1991, pp. 472-95; S. J. Ndlovu-Gatsheni, 'Nationalist-military alliance and the fate of democracy in Zimbabwe', *African Journal of Conflict Resolution*, 6(1), 2006, pp. 49-80.

[49] M. Sithole, 'Zimbabwe: In search of stable democracy', in L. Diamond. J. Linz and S. Lipset (eds.), *Democracy in Developing Countries: Vol. 2, Africa* (Boulder, CO: Lynne Rienner, 1988), p. 245. See also S. J. Ndlovu-Gatsheni, 'Putting people first: From regime security to human security: A quest for social peace in Zimbabwe', in A. G. Nhema (ed.), *The Quest for Peace in Africa* (Addis Ababa: OSSREA, 2004).

throughout the 1980s and 1990s, their organisation betrayed the government's lack of tolerance of political diversity and commitment to democratic politics. ZANU(PF) approached elections as 'battles' and viewed its political opponents as enemies to be annihilated rather than as political competitors. Its electoral dominance was partly achieved through its Gukurahundi strategy, which entailed 'an undisguised, intolerant, commandist and deliberately violent policy towards the opposition'.[50]

However, ZANU(PF) did not win elections through intimidation alone, as its critics and political opponents have often argued. In 1980, for instance, the party's victory was helped by its ability to establish a greater political presence in the areas where ZANLA had operated, which covered about two-thirds of the country.[51] Although ZANU(PF)'s centralist tendencies and politics of violence and tribalism made it unpopular in some constituencies – especially among the urban elites and intellectuals, and in those places, such as Matabeleland and parts of Manicaland, which had been on the receiving end of violence – ZANU(PF) was popular for much of the 1980s and remained the party of choice for many black Zimbabweans. It skilfully articulated populist policies on land, indigenisation of the economy, employment and workers' rights, and initially delivered on some of its social and economic promises.

All the same, violence and coercion remained integral to Zimbabwe's electoral politics throughout the first decade of independence. ZANU(PF) was widely accused of political intimidation in 1980, especially in the areas where its guerrillas had operated during the war,[52] and its supporters also perpetrated widespread violence against the opposition in the 1985 and 1990 elections. Even though the government never proscribed multiparty elections, it never created conditions for them to be free and fair and gave opposition parties very little space to campaign. Besides deploying its violent youth and women's wings to commandeer support during elections, the party marshalled state resources and institutions, such as the army, police, intelligence service, and public radio and television, to ensure its electoral hegemony.[53]

---

[50] M. Sithole and J. Makumbe, 'Elections in Zimbabwe: The ZANU(PF) hegemony and its incipient decline', *African Journal of Political Science*, 2(1), 1997, p. 133.

[51] For a more nuanced analysis of the 1980 election, see M. Sithole, 'The general elections, 1979-1985', in Mandaza (ed.), *The Political Economy of Transition*, pp. 81-5; T. Rich, 'Legacies of the past? The results of the 1980 election in Midlands province, Zimbabwe', *Africa: Journal of the International African Institute*, 52(3), 1982, pp. 42-55.

[52] See Sithole, 'The general elections', pp. 84-5.

[53] See Sithole and Makumbe, 'Elections in Zimbabwe', pp. 122-39; Moyo, *Voting for Democracy*; A. Reynolds, *Electoral Systems and Democratization in Southern Africa* (Oxford: Oxford University Press, 1999), pp. 140-81.

The ruling party's dominance of state institutions and processes was similarly exercised in the governance sphere. The local government decentralisation process started in 1980 was not allowed to take root because of the party's overbearing presence over the sector. The Village Development Committees (VIDCOs) and Ward Development Committees (WADCOs), which were supposed to spearhead development and democracy in rural communities, were not allowed to evolve into inclusive structures of governance. They remained, as Amanda Hammar has noted, local ZANU(PF) party committees and cells carried over from the liberation war but whose partisan and authoritarian practices pervaded both popular participation and democratic developmentalism.[54] Nor were Rural District Councils treated as autonomous units serving the interests of local communities. They remained an appendage of central government, severely marginalised, under-resourced and dependent on central government for both their funding and staffing. The District Administrators, who replaced District Commissioners, were not accountable to local communities but to central government.[55]

In the urban sphere, the ZANU(PF) government sought to control forces challenging its authority, especially workers, youth groups and other civic bodies. For the greater part of its life in the post-colonial period, the labour movement, for instance, was not only weak and divided but also subordinated to the state. Its autonomy, as constituted in the Zimbabwe Congress of Trade Unions (ZCTU), was extremely limited, its capacity to set out and implement its own independent programmes was greatly reduced, and this remained the case for much of the 1980s.[56]

ZANU(PF) relentlessly tried to impose its supremacy after 1980. This was especially so with the establishment at the party's 1984 congress of the Politburo and five new standing committees of the Central Committee, mandated to supervise ministries and secure the authority of party over the government.[57] As the new ruling party set out to stamp its authority on the Zimbabwean polity,

it became clear early on in the post-independence period that its

---

[54] A. Hammar, 'Disrupting Democracy? Altering Landscapes of Local Government in post-2000 Zimbabwe' (London: London School of Economics, Crisis States Development Research Centre, Discussion Paper No. 9, June 2005), p. 19.

[55] E. Masunungure and N. Musekiwa, 'Local Government Policy Review' (Policy Document Prepared for the Zimbabwe Institute, 2005); J. McGregor, 'The politics of disruption: War veterans and the local state in Zimbabwe', *African Affairs*, 101, 2002, pp. 17-23; W. Munro, *The Moral Economy of the State: Conservation, Community Development and State-Making in Zimbabwe* (Athens: Ohio University Press, 1998); E. M. Chiwome, *Masango Mavi* (Gweru: Mambo Press, 1998).

[56] See B. Raftopoulos and L. Sachikonye, (eds.), *Striking Back: The Labour Movement and the Post-Colonial State in Zimbabwe, 1980-2000* (Harare: Weaver Press, 2001).

[57] Weitzer, *Transforming Settler States*, p. 140.

reconciliation policy would be based on the subordination and control both of other political parties and of civil society. The mid-1980s crisis in Matabeleland and the violent state response to it displayed a number of traits that would mark the authoritarian statism of the post-2000 period.[58]

The main characteristics of the post-independence state were lack of tolerance for political diversity and dissent, heavy reliance on force for mobilisation, and a narrow, monolithic interpretation of citizenship, nationalism and national unity.[59] To give one example, the violent and brutal methods used by the state to suppress the activities of a few armed political rebels during the Matabeleland crisis were not only unwarranted but disproportionate to the security threat posed. As detailed in the report *Breaking the Silence*, government forces killed more than 20,000 civilians in Matabeleland and Midlands between 1982 and 1987. The Fifth Brigade's military operation became a bizarre combination of random killing, abduction and torture of PF-ZAPU supporters and Ndebele-speaking civilians, raping of women and girls, cultural imperialism conducted by attempts to force Ndebele-speakers to speak Shona, and indoctrination aimed at forcing people to support ZANU(PF).[60]

The Matabeleland crisis presented the government with the opportunity to crush its only viable opponent, PF-ZAPU. The deployment of both the army and a special militia unit, the Fifth Brigade, in an operation known as Gukurahundi (the rain that sweeps away the chaff), to solve a political problem that could have been resolved through political means, was meant to achieve that. The violence and killings of this period ended only in 1987 after the signing of the Unity Accord between ZANU(PF) and PF-ZAPU and the merging of the two parties into ZANU(PF). While it ended the atrocities in Matabeleland, this political merger effectively emasculated the opposition.[61]

The threat of violence and the hegemonic discourse of unity were not only used to subordinate PF-ZAPU and other opposition parties, but also to control

[58] Raftopoulos, 'Unreconciled differences', p. 4.

[59] Ibid.

[60] Catholic Commission for Justice and Peace in Zimbabwe and Legal Resources Foundation, *Breaking the Silence, Building True Peace: Report on the Disturbances in Matabeleland and the Midlands, 1980-1989* (Harare: CCJPZ and LRF, 1997). See also S. J. Ndlovu-Gatsheni, 'The post-colonial state and Matabeleland: Regional perceptions of civil-military relations, 1980-2002, in R. Williams *et al.* (eds.), *Ourselves to Know: Civil-Military Relations and Defence Transformation in Southern Africa* (Pretoria: ISS, 2003); J. Alexander, 'Dissident perspectives of Zimbabwe's post-independence war', *Africa*, 68(2), 1998, pp. 151-82; J. Alexander, J. McGregor and T. Ranger, *Violence and Memory: One Hundred Years in the 'Dark Forests' of Matabeleland* (Oxford: James Currey, 2000).

[61] Raftopoulos, 'Unreconciled differences', p. 4.

Fig. 6.1: Signing the Unity Accord.   [*Source:* Private collection]

women's groups, labour, students and other civic forces whenever they expressed dissent or organised protests.[62] However, ZANU(PF)'s power continued to be challenged at every level by the country's diverse social and political groups.

Hegemony and resistance

The impression created by most recent accounts of post-independence politics in Zimbabwe, especially those about state authoritarianism, is that ZANU(PF) was able to establish its political hegemony over the country in the 1980s. These analyses have tried to understand Zimbabwe's politics mainly in terms of the history of organised political parties and civic bodies.[63] In the process, they

[62] See ibid., pp. 4-5; L. Sachikonye, 'Sate, Capital, and Trade Unions', in Mandaza (ed.), *The Political Economy of Transition*, pp. 243-73.

[63] This kind of analysis is found mainly in journalistic accounts of post-independence Zimbabwe, such as Martin Meredith, *Our Votes, Our Guns: Robert Mugabe and the Tragedy of Zimbabwe* (Oxford: Public Affairs, 2003); S. Chan, *Robert Mugabe: A Life of Power and Violence* (Michigan: University of Michigan Press, 2003); J. R. Arnold and R. Wienar, *Robert Mugabe's Zimbabwe* (Brookfield, CT: Twenty-First Century Books, 2007).

have not only ignored the democratic tendencies which coexisted uneasily with government authoritarianism in the 1980s but also downplayed the important role played by a wide range of individual voices and other subaltern forces.

Despite its sustained attempts, ZANU(PF) never managed to establish a political hegemony. There continued to be strong voices of dissent throughout the 1980s and 1990s. The judiciary, for instance, resisted executive directives; the government failed in several critical trials, and on several occasions the executive's frustration with the judiciary expressed itself in public attacks on the judges and the courts.[64] President Mugabe himself admitted at the 1988 ZANU(PF) congress that the party's supremacy over the government 'has not been achieved'.[65] Even within the party itself, dissent and disagreements remained very much part of the proceedings, with party leaders and MPs such as Edgar Tekere, Byron Hove, Sydney Malunga, Welshman Mabhena and Lazarus Nzarayebani leading the dissenters.[66] Opinion on a number of national issues, including the two controversial issues of socialism and the one-party state, remained very much divided, and President Mugabe even publicly admitted that the idea of one-party state was facing internal opposition.[67] The dispute culminated in the expulsion of the Secretary-General of the party, Tekere, a vocal critic of the idea, in October 1988. Mobilising his supporters and other dissenters within ZANU(PF), as well as critics of the party around the country, Tekere formed the Zimbabwe Unity Movement which contested the 1990 presidential and parliamentary elections and helped to block the legislated one-party state agenda through its widespread national campaigning and electoral performance.[68]

In the countryside, the leadership of ZANU(PF) tried to impose itself on the rank and file but often met resistance, especially in the selection of election candidates. Although the top hierarchy of the party usually managed to implement their decisions through political chicanery, party supporters did not always endorse or abide by them. As a result, there were always cases of disciplinary

[64] See Weitzer, *Transforming Settler States*, pp. 153-4; O. Saki and T. Chiware, *The Law in Zimbabwe* (Harare: Zimbabwe Lawyers for Human Rights, 2007).

[65] C. Stoneman and L. Cliffe, *Zimbabwe: Politics, Economics and Society* (London: Pinter, 1988), p. 80, cited in Weitzer, *Transforming Settler States*, p. 140.

[66] T. C. Nkiwane, 'Opposition politics in Zimbabwe: The struggle within the struggle', in A. O. Olukoshi (ed.), *The Politics of Opposition in Contemporary Africa* (Uppsala: Nordic Africa Institute, 1997), pp. 97-8.

[67] 'Zanu PF divided over one-party state', *Financial Gazette*, cited in J. Moyo, 'The dialectics of national unity and diversity in Zimbabwe', in Mandaza and Sachikonye (eds.), *The One-Party State and Democracy*, p. 99.

[68] Although ZUM won only 2 of the 120 contested seats, it received 18 per cent of the popular vote. See Makumbe and Sithole, 'Elections in Zimbabwe', p. 128; Moyo, *Voting for Democracy*.

hearings and suspensions of party members and leaders who refused to abide by what they viewed as unfair decisions, policies and practices throughout the 1980s.[69]

Even in rural areas, where the government had a greater hold over people, there were some, including ZANU(PF) supporters, who acted outside the framework of government policy. As Sam Moyo has shown, most of the early land invasions of the 1980s were initiated and carried out by peasants who were frustrated with the government's slow pace of land reform.[70] On a number of occasions, the government used force to evict peasants who had taken over commercial or government land for their own grazing or farming. Moyo has further argued that during the 1980s peasants were more radical than the state, which had to work within the conservative restrictions of the Lancaster House constitution.[71] Government's top-down approach to issues of development was often resisted by peasants who sometimes failed to co-operate with civil servants deployed to their areas without local consultation.[72]

Throughout the 1980s, opposition to unpopular government policies remained very much alive both inside and outside ZANU(PF). Much of this opposition was organised around questions of corruption, the abandonment of the leadership code, workers' and women's rights and democracy. Student demonstrations against the government in October 1989 led to the first closure of the university in post-independence Zimbabwe.[73]

Fig. 6.2: Saying 'No' to corruption.
[Source: The Standard]

[69] Moyo, 'The dialectics of national unity', pp. 99ff.

[70] S. Moyo, 'The Land and Agrarian Question in Zimbabwe' (Conference on the Agrarian Constraint and Poverty Reduction, Addis Ababa, 17-18 December 2004). See also J. Alexander, '"Squatters", veterans and the state in Zimbabwe', in Hammar et al., (eds.), Zimbabwe's Unfinished Business, pp. 83–117; N. Marongwe, 'Farm occupations and occupiers in the new politics of land in Zimbabwe', in Hammar et al. (eds.), Zimbabwe's Unfinished Business, pp. 155-90; A. Chiundura-Moyo, Kuridza Ngoma Nedemo (Harare: Zimbabwe Publishing House, 1985).

[71] Moyo, 'The Land and Agrarian Question in Zimbabwe'.

[72] See Chiwome's brilliant political novel, Masango Mavi.

[73] A. Mutambara, 'The one-party state, socialism and democratic struggles in Zimbabwe: A student perspective', in Mandaza and Sachikonye (eds.), The One-Party State and Democracy, pp. 139-42.

Intellectuals also questioned the state's political and economic agendas. Government indeed tried to restrict this debate, but many – including novelists Dambudzo Marechera, Gonzo Msengezi, Charles Samupindi, Stanley Nyamfukudza and Shimmer Chinodya,[74] law professors Kempton Makamure, Shepherd Nzombe and Welshman Ncube, political scientists Masipula Sithole and Jonathan Moyo – continued to voice their criticism through public seminars, books and articles, novels, poetry and theatre performances, as well as opinion pieces in the media. Their criticisms included government's rhetorical commitment to socialism, its failure to curb corruption in both government and society, the prevailing culture of injustice, the violation of democratic rights, and continued inequalities in ownership of land and the economy. In spite of government attempts to muzzle independent debate, the University of Zimbabwe also remained for much of the 1980s an autonomous space for critical thought and robust criticism.[75]

From the mid-1980s, there also emerged a new type of women's activism, centred on ending continued discrimination against women.[76] It criticised the state for its limited commitment to ending women's subordination and exploitation. Some progressive regulations were indeed introduced in the 1980s, and the government ratified several international conventions aimed at creating an enabling environment for the attainment of gender equity, but there continued to be significant disparities. Women remained marginalised in terms of the control and ownership of economic resources and positions in decision-making processes. The few women who benefited from ZANU(PF) reforms and patronage were usually politically connected,[77] and even they remained sidelined from

[74] Some of the works critical of the post-colonial state produced by these novelists and poets are: D. Marechera, *Mindblast* (Harare: College Press, 1984); D. Marechera, *Cemetery of the Mind: Collected Poems of Dambudzo Marechera* (Harare: Baobab Books, 1992); S. Nyamfukudza, *The Non-Believer's Journey* (London: Heinemann; Salisbury: Zimbabwe Publishing House, 1980); G. H. Msengezi, *The Honourable MP* (Gweru; Mambo Press, 1984); S. Chinodya, *Harvest of Thorns* (Harare: Baobab Books, 1989); Charles Samupindi, *Pawns* (Harare: Baobab Books, 1992); F. Nyamubaya, *On the Road Again: Poems during and after the National Liberation of Zimbabwe* (Harare: Zimbabwe Publishing House, 1986); Chenjerai Hove, *Bones* (Harare: Baobab Books, 1988); Chirikure Chirikure, *Rukuvhute: Muunganidzwa weNhetembo* (Harare: College Press, 1989).

[75] See M. Sithole, 'Should Zimbabwe go where others are coming from?', in Mandaza and Sachikonye (eds.), *The One-Party State and Democracy*, pp. 71-2, 80. See also Mandaza and Sachikonye, 'The Zimbabwe debate on the one-party state and democracy', in Mandaza and Sachikonye (eds.), *The One-Party State and Democracy*, p. 11.

[76] B. Raftopoulos and K. Alexander (eds.), *Reflections on Democratic Politics in Zimbabwe* (Cape Town: IJR, 2006), p. 40.

[77] C. Sylvester 'Vacillations around women: The overlapping meanings of "women" in the Zimbabwean context', in Darnolf and Laakso (eds.), *From Liberation to Authoritarianism*; C. Sylvester, *Producing Women and Progress in Zimbabwe: Narratives of Identity and Work from the 1980s* (London: Heinemann, 2000).

important political and economic spaces, in almost the same way that female activists were marginalised during the anti-colonial struggle.[78]

The government struggled to impose itself and its political ideals on the nation throughout the 1980s. Its coercive nation-building and state-building projects of the early 1980s, which paid little attention to the ethnic, racial, gendered and class configurations of the inherited state, failed to develop a more cohesive nation-state. Important divisions thus continued to surface.[79]

Ethnic and regional divisions within the nation-state

No episode better highlights the broad failure of the government's coercive tactics than the PF-ZAPU–ZANU(PF) conflict that culminated in the Matabeleland crisis. Though originating as a political conflict between two nationalist parties with contrasting visions, it soon assumed ethnic and regional dimensions as a result of a number of events and processes.[80] First, there was the issue of PF-ZAPU's disgruntlement over ZANU(PF)'s use of party slogans, songs and political speeches that portrayed ZANU(PF) as the authentic liberator while disparaging PF-ZAPU and its supporters as villains.[81] PF-ZAPU's leaders and supporters were also aggrieved by the government's narrative of liberation history, which downplayed and denigrated the role of PF-ZAPU and other nationalist parties. Such triumphalism featured the use of Shona pre-colonial heroes and historical monuments while marginalising those of the Ndebele.[82]

Helping to develop a sense of marginalisation among former ZIPRA combatants was the preferential treatment given to ZANLA fighters in the Zimbabwe National Army. Tensions were exacerbated by the 1982 discovery of arms caches in PF-ZAPU-owned properties around Bulawayo and Gweru, the subsequent

---

[78] The most detailed discussion about the marginalisation of women in the nationalist liberation movement is J. Nhongo-Simbanegavi, *For Better or Worse? Women and ZANLA in Zimbabwe's Liberation Struggle* (Harare: Weaver Press, 2000). See also T. Barnes, 'The heroes' struggle: Life after the liberation war for four ex-combatants in Zimbabwe', in Bhebe and Ranger (eds.), *Soldiers in Zimbabwe's Liberation War*, pp. 118-39; T. Lyons, *Guns and Guerilla Girls: Women in the Zimbabwean National Liberation Struggle* (Trenton, NJ: African World Press, 2004).

[79] See J. Muzondidya and S. Ndlovu-Gatsheni, 'Echoing silences: Ethnicity in post-colonial Zimbabwe, 1980-2007', *African Journal of Conflict Resolution*, 27(2), 2007, pp. 275-97; Mandaza (ed.), *The Political Economy of Transition*; Edgar '2-Boy' Zivanai Tekere, *A Lifetime of Struggle* (Harare: SAPES Books, 2006).

[80] From the time of independence in 1980, ZANU(PF) envisaged Zimbabwe as a one-party state while PF-ZAPU regarded itself as an official opposition party in a multiparty democracy.

[81] Alexander, 'Dissident perspectives', pp. 151-82; D. Dabengwa, 'ZIPRA in the Zimbabwe war of national liberation', in N. Bhebe and T. O. Ranger (eds.), *Soldiers in Zimbabwe's Liberation War* (Harare: University of Zimbabwe Publications, 1995).

[82] N. Kriger, *Guerrilla Veterans in Post-War Zimbabwe: Symbolic and Violent Politics, 1980-1987* (Cambridge: Cambridge University Press, 2003), pp. 74-5.

arrest of a number of PF-ZAPU leaders and ZIPRA commanders, and the sacking of PF-ZAPU leaders – including Joshua Nkomo – in the coalition government.[83]

The brutality of the state in suppressing the few rebels operating in the regions of Matabeleland and Midlands between 1982 and 1987 not only left deep scars among the victims but also intensified Matabeleland regionalism. Bjorn Lindgren has argued that this was one of the more serious consequences of the Gukurahundi atrocities.[84] He noted that 'people in Matabeleland accused Mugabe, the government and the Shona in general of killing the Ndebele'.[85] In the eyes of the Ndebele public, what was portrayed as a mission to stamp out dissidents became an anti-Ndebele campaign that deliberately identified Joshua Nkomo, PF-ZAPU, ex-ZIPRA combatants and every Ndebele-speaking person with the political rebels. The Fifth Brigade unit was almost entirely Shona, and justified its violence in political and ethnic terms. For many, this represented a Shona political crusade against the Ndebele.[86]

Feelings of marginalisation also fuelled resistance and opposition in the eastern and south-eastern districts of Chipinge, Chiredzi and Chikombedzi, which lagged behind in infrastructural and economic development for much of the 1980s, especially during the days of the Mozambican civil war when RENAMO rebels attacked Zimbabwean border districts to retaliate against Zimbabwe's deployment of troops to fight alongside FRELIMO government troops. These attacks were not only brutal but also retarded economic development by destroying roads, property, schools, clinics, livestock and lives.[87] Frustrated by both this lack of development and the Zimbabwe government's handling of the war, some villagers offered support to RENAMO, while others expressed their frustration by fanning regionalism and political tribalism against the central state.[88] ZANU(Ndonga) leaders, for instance, successfully mobilised both Ndau ethnicity and local feelings of marginalisation in Chipinge to build a regional

---

[83] Alexander *et al.*, *Violence and Memory*, pp. 180-96; Alexander, 'Dissident perspectives on Zimbabwe's post-independence war'.

[84] B. Lindgren, 'The politics of identity and the remembrance of violence: Ethnicity and gender at the installation of a female chief in Zimbabwe', in V. Broch-Due (ed.), *Violence and Belonging: The Quest for Identity in Post-Colonial Africa* (London: Routledge, 2005), pp. 156-8.

[85] Ibid., p. 158.

[86] Ndlovu-Gatsheni, 'The post-colonial state and Matabeleland'; Alexander *et al.*, *Violence and Memory*, pp. 204-31.

[87] See B. Tauyanago, 'The Renamo War and its Impact in South East Zimbabwe, 1982-1992' (MA thesis, University of Zimbabwe, 2002), pp. 70-95.

[88] See A. Alao, *Brothers at War: Dissidence and Rebellion in Southern Africa* (London: Zed Books, 1994), pp. 122-3.

power base against ZANU(PF). Throughout the 1980s, ZANU(Ndonga) thus received its strongest support in the predominantly Ndau-speaking districts of Chipinge.[89]

Post-colonial expressions of regionalism and political tribalism also remained strong in Masvingo, where senior ZANU(PF) leader and government minister Edison Zvobgo tried to mobilise Karanga identity to dilute what he and his supporters, such as ZANU(PF) provincial chairman Dzikamai Mavhaire and former airforce commander Josiah Tungamirai, viewed as a Zezuru monopoly over power and resources. From independence, Karanga political elites and their supporters constituted themselves as another centre of power that could not be ignored in the politics of ethnic balancing.[90] The roots of this go back to the days of the liberation struggle, when contests for power were mainly between the Karanga and the Manyika.[91] After independence their ethnicity was derived mainly from perceptions about marginalisation from both ZANU(PF) and state politics.

At the same time, minority groups, such as Coloureds and descendents of immigrants from Malawi, Zambia and Mozambique, also continued to feel alienated, suffering discrimination by a post-colonial state which envisioned the new nation in black and white racial binaries and essentialised categories of indigeneity. Studies by Lloyd Sachikonye, Blair Rutherford and Dede Amanor-Wilks, for instance, have all shown how Malawian, Zambian and Mozambican immigrants and their descendants continued to be marginalised both in redistributive programmes and in the dominant politics of belonging and citizenship that unfolded in post-independence Zimbabwe.[92] For years after independence, many of those living and working on the farms and mines did

---

[89] Ndau tribalism in post-independence Zimbabwe also evolved around the controversial ousting of the Chipinge-born and Ndau-speaking Ndabaningi Sithole from the leadership of ZANU in 1975. See M. Sithole, 'Is Zimbabwe poised on a liberal path? The state and prospects of the parties', *Issue: A Journal of Opinion*, 21(1/2), 1993, pp. 37-8.

[90] Muzondidya and Ndlovu-Gatsheni, 'Ethnicity in post-colonial Zimbabwe', pp. 291-2; Tekere, *A Lifetime of Struggle*.

[91] M. Sithole, 'Ethnicity and factionalism in Zimbabwean nationalist politics, 1957-79', *Ethnic and Racial Studies*, 3(1), 1980; M. Sithole, *Zimbabwe: Struggles Within the Struggle* (Harare: Rujeko Publishers, 2nd edn., 1999).

[92] L. M. Sachikonye, *The Situation of Farm Workers after Land Reform in Zimbabwe: A Report Prepared for the Farm Community Trust of Zimbabwe*, May 2003, available at <http://www.oxfam.org.uk/what_we_do/issues/livelihoods/landrights/downloads/zimfwsit.rtf>, retrieved 31 May 2009; D. Amanor-Wilks, *Zimbabwe's Farm Workers and the New Constitution*, 2000, available at <http://www.africaaction.org/rtable/ed0002.htm>, retrieved 15 Feb. 2004; B. Rutherford, 'Belonging to the farm(er): Farm workers, farmers and the shifting politics of citizenship', in Hammar *et al.* (eds.), *Zimbabwe's Unfinished Business*, pp. 191-216.

not have the right to reside in communal land or to vote in local government elections.[93]

Generally, all subject minorities continued to be excluded from the power and governance structures available to other Zimbabwean communities. The post-colonial state displayed either continued ambivalence or outright hostility to these groups. The category of African/Zimbabwean in independent Zimbabwe remained restricted to include only 'ancestral Zimbabweans' (groups that were on Zimbabwean soil before the imposition of colonial rule). Subject minorities were thus left in an anomalous position where they were, depending on the context, regarded as either not indigenous at all or not the right kind of indigenous.[94]

Local feelings about marginalisation also remained strong among other minority groups such as the Shangani, Kalanga, Tonga and Venda, who were located in the borderlands where there was little economic development and less physical and social infrastructure. They complained of political and cultural domination by both the Shona and Ndebele, enforced through such state practices as national-language and educational policies which emphasised the use of Ndebele and Shona at the expense of other national languages. In the southern border town of Beitbridge, the issue of language was an important mark, enforcing identity-group boundaries between the local Venda-speaking people and the Shona, who were considered outsiders.[95] The Shangani-speaking communities in the south-east complained bitterly about the employment of 'Karangas' (derogatively termed *vanyai*, or foreigners) ahead of their sons and daughters. At the same time, intensified competition for limited resources periodically provoked ethnically motivated violence between Shangani-speaking and Karanga-speaking groups living side by side.[96]

Paradoxically, while Zimbabwe was experiencing this internal turmoil, it was still able to build a positive reputation for itself externally. The country played a leading role in both the Southern African Development Co-ordination Conference (SADCC) and the Frontline States; it chaired the Organisation of African Unity (OAU) and the Non-Aligned Movement (NAM); and its President received prestigious awards, including the Africa Prize for Leadership for the Sustainable End of Hunger (1988) and the Jawaharlal Nehru Peace Award

[93] Amanor-Wilks, *Zimbabwe's Farm Workers*; S. Moyo, B. Rutherford and D. Amanor-Wilks, 'Land reform and changing social relations for farm workers in Zimbabwe', *Review of African Political Economy*, 84, 2000, p. 189; Sachikonye, *The Situation of Farm Workers*, p. 18.

[94] J. Muzondidya, '*Jambanja*: Ideological ambiguities in the politics of land and resource ownership in Zimbabwe', *Journal of Southern African History*, 33(2), 2007, pp. 330-3.

[95] R. Mathe, *Making Ends Meet at the Margins: Grappling with Economic Crisis and Belonging in Beitbridge, Zimbabwe* (Dakar: Codesria, 2005), pp. 8-20.

[96] Muzondidya and Ndlovu-Gatsheni, 'Ethnicity in post-colonial Zimbabwe', p. 290.

(1989). In November 1982, Zimbabwe was chosen by the OAU to hold one of the non-permanent seats in the United Nations Security Council for two years, and in 1986 chaired the NAM summit meeting held in Harare. As a member of the UN, Zimbabwe was requested to contribute troops to the 1991 peacekeeping mission in Angola.[97]

As chair of the Frontline States, Zimbabwe campaigned vigorously against apartheid and South Africa's occupation of Namibia. The deployment of around 15,000 soldiers to defend its oil pipeline from Mozambique and to fight alongside FRELIMO against the South Africa-backed RENAMO from 1982 to 1992, though costly to the country in terms of both human and material resources, was seen by many on the continent and in the Third World in general as an example of selfless sacrifice.[98]

However, from the late 1980s onwards, Zimbabwe's positive record abroad could no longer mask the growing social problems and contradictions at home. These problems specifically intensified after 1990, following the country's adoption of an IMF/World Bank economic structural adjustment programme.

The politics and economics of liberalisation, 1990–97

The gains made in the provision of social services were steadily eroded by the economic decline of the 1990s. A series of droughts led to a decline in agricultural productivity and a drastic fall in exports, and the implementation of the IMF/World Bank Economic Structural Adjustment Programme (ESAP) in 1991 saw average economic growth decline from 4 per cent to 0.9 per cent, recovering to only 2.9 per cent in 1998/99.[99] Large numbers of workers were retrenched as industries closed down, and as public spending was cut in line with the structural adjustment policies. By 1994, government statistics revealed that 20,710 workers had lost their jobs since the beginning of the economic liberalisation programme; the Zimbabwe Congress of Trade Unions estimated

[97] J. Muzondidya and N. Samasuwo, *ISS Country Profile: Zimbabwe* (Pretoria: Institute for Security Studies, 2007). Available at <http://www.issafrica.org>.

[98] In the crisis years after 2000, the country has been able to rely on regional support from countries with which it forged political and economic relations during the period of its struggle against colonialism and apartheid – Mozambique, Angola, Namibia and Tanzania – to deflect both local and international criticism over its misrule. The same history has enabled it to mobilise moral and diplomatic support within the OAU and other international organisations such as the African, Caribbean and Pacific (ACP) countries. For a more detailed examination of the way in which Mugabe has exploited African and Third World solidarity in his current political battles, see B. Raftopoulos, 'The Zimbabwean crisis and the challenges for the left', *Journal of Southern African Studies*, 32(2), 2006, pp. 203-19. See also D. Chimanikire, 'Foreign and security policy of Zimbabwe', in Darnoff and Laakso (eds.), *From Liberation to Authoritarianism*.

[99] Kanyenze, 'The performance of the Zimbabwean economy'.

the figure to be over 30,000. Unemployment rose from 32.2 per cent in 1990 to 44 per cent in 1993.[100]

At the same time, the deregulation of prices and the removal of subsidies on basic consumer goods under ESAP resulted in severe hardships for workers, the unemployed and the poor, all of whom battled to afford basic goods as prices skyrocketed and workers' real wages declined. Under structural adjustment, women's and children's suffering intensified, as poor households relied increasingly on these groups' reproductive labour to sustain themselves. Government cutbacks in health and education subsidies made these services inaccessible to the majority of the poor and unemployed, and the introduction of user fees under ESAP further reduced school enrolments. The quality of health services also deteriorated. According to a 1993 UNICEF study, health services had fallen by 30 per cent, twice as many women were dying in childbirth as had before 1990, and fewer people were visiting clinics and hospitals because they could not afford it.[101]

The plight of the rural population also worsened during this period.[102] There was a de-industrialisation of the agro-industrial sector, and rural poverty intensified as a result of ESAP's adverse effects on the agricultural output of the poor. It also exacerbated national and rural income inequalities. The combined result of the reduction in government extension and agricultural input services, the introduction of tight and more expensive credit, and the deterioration in rural roads was a severe decline in both peasant agricultural productivity and peasant earnings. Further, structural adjustment increased pressure on rural land and natural resources as retrenched urban workers either sent their families to their rural homes or went with them.[103] The increased pressure on land and natural resources led to a flare-up of underlying social tensions that had not been resolved in the first decade of independence, such as those concerning racial inequalities and land ownership.

---

[100] Mlambo, *The Economic Structural Adjustment Programme*, p. 91.

[101] See ibid., pp. 83-100, for a more detailed discussion of the effects of the structural adjustment programme.

[102] Studies showed that by 1995 at least a quarter of Zimbabwe's rural population was earning less than the poverty datum figure of Z$4,000 per annum; nor were they growing sufficient crops or keeping enough livestock to feed their families. See CSO, *Demographic and Health Survey*, 1995.

[103] S. Moyo, 'The Land and Agrarian Question in Zimbabwe', p. 9; Moyo, *Land Reform under Structural Adjustment in Zimbabwe*, pp. 58, 90; Chiwome, *Masango Mavi*.

Land, economy and racial politics in the 1990s

By the beginning of the 1990s, it was clear that the country faced a crisis of land use and land allocation. By 1987, the population in the Communal Lands had risen to 5.1m and the national average population density was 36 people per square km, up from 3.9m and 27 in 1982.[104] The failure of the government to deliver land in the wake of continued land hunger posed a challenge to national stability as peasants became more militant in their demands. During the 1990s, land occupations expanded in form and content, as peasants, sometimes led by chiefs and local war veterans, sporadically invaded not only private land but also state land. At the same time, the urban poor were increasingly cultivating both state and municipal lands in a bid to supplement their food resources.[105]

While in the 1980s the government and land owners had managed to control these occupations, often by violent eviction, the intensity of the occupations in the 1990s called for a different approach.[106] To speed up the process of acquisition, the government introduced the Land Acquisition Act (No. 3 of 1992), two years after the expiry of the Lancaster House constitution. The Act sought to do away with the 'willing-seller, willing-buyer' principle and empower the government to compulsorily acquire land for resettlement. However, very little progress was made, and the government's revised targets of resettling some 110,000 families on 5 million hectares never materialised.[107] A number of factors accounted for this failure, including government's failure to commit sufficient resources to the programme, and commercial farmers' resistance.[108]

For this and other reasons, Zimbabwean society continued to be seriously divided along the lines of race. Black opposition to the inequality took an increasingly racial form. Frustrated black business people, for instance, formed pressure groups to push both government and white capital to create more opportunities for their members, while student demonstrations for increases in government support grants were often accompanied by attacks on white motorists or their properties in the affluent northern suburbs.[109] Though black

[104] See Zimbabwe, *Population Census*, 1987.

[105] Moyo, 'The Land and Agrarian Question in Zimbabwe', p. 8; Moyo, *Land Reform under Structural Adjustment in Zimbabwe*.

[106] J. Herbst, *State Politics in Zimbabwe* (Harare: University of Zimbabwe Publications, 1990); Moyo, 'The Land and Agrarian Question in Zimbabwe', p. 8.

[107] Moyo, 'The Political Economy of Land Acquisition'.

[108] When the government designated 1,471 farms for compulsory acquisition in December 1997, a total of 1,393 objections were received, of which 510 were upheld. See Zimbabwe, *Report of the Presidential Land Review Committee Under the Chairmanship of Dr Charles M. B. Utete* (Harare: Government Printers, 2 vols., August 2003), p. 20.

[109] Author's own experiences as a student and later employee at the University of Zimbabwe, between 1988 and 1995.

motorists driving expensive cars were not spared, indicating the class dynamics at play, the attacks were directed mainly against whites. This to some extent reflected a general spirit of resentment against continued white privilege. Even the pro-capital *Financial Gazette* had to caution:

> It is false security and foolhardy for the wealthy few from one section of the population to consider the rest of the population to be content with their [poverty] ... particularly when it is clear that they are from the same race.[110]

In 1990, the Indigenous Business Development Centre (IBDC) was established to push for greater black participation and control of the economy. A conglomeration of various black lobby groups, including the Zimbabwe National Farmers' Union, Women in Business, the Zimbabwe Transport Organisation and the Zimbabwe National Chamber of Commerce, the IBDC agenda was a change in the ownership structure of the economy. Alongside other black affirmative-action lobbies, it also emphasised the de-racialisation of the ownership base of commercial farmland.[111]

Disappointed by the limited success of the IBDC, young black businessmen, led by Philip Chiyangwa and Peter Pamire, formed the Affirmative Action Group (AAG) in 1994 to spearhead a more aggressive campaign for the localisation of ownership in foreign-owned companies. The group soon overshadowed the IBDC, and applied pressure on both government and established business to obtain funding, political support and other policy concessions for black business development.[112]

Initially, the anger and frustration of the aspiring black bourgeoisie was directed against the government, which it saw as having failed them. In July 1996, for instance, the IBDC-affiliated Indigenous Business Women's Organisation (IBWO) accused the government of

> go[ing] out of its way to protect multinationals and ex-settler businesses against competition from outside, so that they can consolidate their hold on this economy ... but has not cushioned aspiring black businesses from evil competition applied by the monopolies and oligopolies in this country.[113]

The black elite's main criticism was reserved for white capital, and it

---

[110] *Financial Gazette*, 25 Feb. 1992.

[111] Maphosa, 'Towards the sociology of Zimbabwean indigenous entrepreneurship', p. 185; Moyo, 'The Land and Agrarian Question in Zimbabwe', p. 13.

[112] Maphosa, 'Towards the sociology of Zimbabwean indigenous entrepreneurship'; R. Sanders, 'Zimbabwe: ESAP's fables', *Southern African Report*, 11(2), 1996, pp. 8-11.

[113] Sanders, 'Zimbabwe: ESAP's fables'.

blamed white businessmen and farmers for blocking their chances of economic success through the practice of institutional racism. Soon after its formation, the AAG, using race as an agency for its own members' private accumulation, unsuccessfully called for a consumer boycott of all firms which had not entered into joint ventures with black entrepreneurs.[114] In July 1994, a coalition of black pressure groups, which included members of the IBDC, AAG, IBWO and the University of Zimbabwe-based youth organisation Sangano Munhumutapa, organised protest marches in Harare to denounce institutional racism in banks and other financial institutions.[115]

Exploiting the power of popular nationalism, the government managed to harness and redirect this anger towards whites by appealing to notions of exclusive black nationalism. It began to give peripheral support to some of the groups which were deploying race as an agency for individual accumulation. At public forums, state and party officials increasingly blamed whites for the problems in the country.[116] The government gradually abandoned both its conciliatory approach and the inclusive nationalism of the early period, and began to adopt a radical, exclusive nationalist stance. It redeployed race in the political and social arena, and tried to reconstitute the whole discourse of rights, justice and citizenship in Zimbabwe. This profound shift in both the official and public discourses denoted, as Jocelyn Alexander has observed, the 'critical shifts in the stakes, terms and alliances marking Zimbabwe's unfolding politics of land' and resource distribution and ownership.[117]

What helped to make race both a divisive issue and a powerful tool for mobilisation was the lack of meaningful social integration since independence and the prevalent racism among some whites. Two decades after independence, there had been little integration in schools, sports, residences and other spaces of social contact. While some whites, especially the younger generation, were socially proactive and integrated, many maintained their isolation and 'largely abdicated from actively engaging in the process of nation building'.[118] As Selby has written in respect of white commercial farmers:

---

[114] Maphosa, 'Towards the sociology of Zimbabwean indigenous entrepreneurship', p. 186.

[115] Maphosa, 'Towards the sociology of Zimbabwean indigenous entrepreneurship'.

[116] See A. Selby, 'Commercial Farmers and the State: Interest Group Politics and Land Reform in Zimbabwe' (D.Phil. thesis, Oxford University, 2006).

[117] Alexander, '"Squatters", veterans and the state in Zimbabwe'; J. Alexander, *The Unsettled Land: State-making and the Politics of Land in Zimbabwe, 1893-2003* (Harare: Weaver Press; Oxford: James Currey, 2006).

[118] K. Alexander, 'Orphans of the empire: An analysis of elements of white identity and ideology construction in Zimbabwe', in Raftopoulos and Savage (eds.), p. 194.

The white community's visible affluence and continued social isolation, which amplified during structural adjustment, provided a target
and a catalyst for anti-white sentiment. An independent consultant
identified the racial exclusiveness of the CFU [Commercial Farmers
Union] as their biggest weakness and greatest threat. Racism
among some whites was still prevalent and mounting scepticism
among farmers towards government was often explained through
condescending cultural perspectives. Some farmers maintained
conservative attitudes with racial undertones.[119]

Notwithstanding the significant role played by many whites who remained
in Zimbabwe after independence, many others had withdrawn into their 'racial
enclaves'.[120] In the urban areas, for instance, some responded to black suburban
encroachment by creating alternative spaces where they continued to keep to
themselves, 'retreat[ing] from public life into the laager of sports club, home
entertaining and the video'.[121] In Harare, affluent whites reacted to the post-
independence movement of blacks into previously white-only areas such as
Mabelreign and Avondale by withdrawing to more exclusive suburbs like Mount
Pleasant and Borrowdale; their counterparts in Bulawayo acted similarly.[122]
Notions of racial boundaries and separation were also maintained through the
setting up of gated communities.[123]

In clubs, diners and restaurants, separation was enforced through practices
such as membership-based admission.[124] In the educational sector, some white
parents responded to the government's de-racialisation of education and the
admission of blacks into formerly white-only (Group A) schools by building
new, independent schools whose fee structures were designed to exclude the

[119] Selby, 'Commercial Farmers and the State', p. 242.

[120] A significant number of Zimbabwean whites responded to the introduction of black
majority rule in 1980 by emigrating to countries such as Canada, Australia and South Africa. By
1984, the white population was estimated to be 100,000, down 63 per cent from its late-1960s
peak of 270,000. See Godwin, 'Whose kith and kin now?'.

[121] Ibid.

[122] C. Pickard-Cambridge, *Sharing the Cities: Residential Desegregation in Harare, Windhoek and Mafikeng* (Johannesburg: Institute of Race Relations, 1988), pp. 1-13; *Financial
Gazette*, 30 Dec. 1999.

[123] For discussions of the process of racialisation of space in post-apartheid South Africa,
see J. Dixon and S. Reicher, 'Intergroup contact and desegregation in the New South Africa',
British Journal of Social Psychology, 36, 1997, pp 361-83; D. Foster, 'Space, place and "race"',
Journal of Community and Health Sciences, 4(1), 1997, pp. 1-10.

[124] The issue of segregation in clubs and restaurants came to the fore in 1996 when the University of Zimbabwe pressure group, Sangano Munhumutapa, carried out a targeted campaign
against 'racist clubs' in Harare. The campaign involved students picketing clubs accused of
practising institutional racism against blacks.

majority of children from middle- and low-income black families.[125] Lack of social integration was similarly experienced in sport, especially in the formerly white codes of rugby and cricket.

While the increasingly unpopular ZANU(PF) state was able to consolidate its power by making alliances with groups such as the frustrated black middle class and rural chiefs, its power in the urban areas was being increasingly weakened by restless urban social groups such as unemployed youths and workers.

Unrest in urban areas and the politics of co-option and confrontation

Pushed to the brink by the social and economic problems associated with ESAP, urban groups were moving increasingly towards militant agitation to air their grievances. During the early 1990s, workers and the unemployed moved towards mass action and responded to the impoverishing effects of ESAP with strike action.[126] The ZCTU gradually distanced itself from the state, became more confrontational, and in this way was able to assert its autonomy. It organised a march against the government's economic reform programme in June 1992, but the event was poorly attended and brutally quashed by the police; the future of ZCTU as a body able to mobilise workers against government and employers came under threat.[127]

However, workers became more and more agitated as their real wages continued to decline. The public-sector strike of June 1996 was the largest strike organised by civil servants in post-independence Zimbabwe; the eight-week wildcat strike by teachers, doctors, nurses and other government workers was supported by student groups, human rights organisations and churches. Although the state initially responded by declaring it illegal, detaining union leaders and refusing to negotiate, the strike almost paralysed the country and delivered a hard blow to the government's cultivated image of unchallenged authority.[128]

Building on this success, the unions organised a series of strikes against both private-sector employers and government, culminating in the general strike of December 1997, which forced the government to abandon its plans to introduce a new levy on workers. The ZCTU's capacity to mobilise workers during this period was strengthened by growing frustration with the slump in the economy, and by

[125] R. J. Zvobgo, 'Education and the challenge of independence', in Mandaza (ed.), *Zimbabwe: The Political Economy of Transition*, p. 337.

[126] R. Saunders, 'Striking ahead: Industrial action and labour movement development in Zimbabwe', in Raftopoulos and Sachikonye (eds.), *Striking Back*, pp. 133-73.

[127] B. Raftopoulos, 'The labour movement and the emergence of opposition politics', in Raftopoulos and Sachikonye (eds.), *Striking Back*, p. 11.

[128] See Raftopoulos, 'The labour movement', pp. 10-11.

Fig. 6.3: Police during the General Strike, 1997.
[*Source:* Private collection]

the government's unbudgeted gratuity payments to war veterans in November 1997. Notably, the general strikes and stay-aways of this period were joined not by workers alone but by other urban social groups, including the unemployed and students, and by civil society organisations working for human rights and democratisation. In this way, a broad alliance between labour and others in the fight for workers' rights and social justice was born and cemented.[129]

During this period, civil society groups, which had hitherto confined themselves to complementing the state's developmental project of the 1980s, gradually became more assertive. They questioned the state's commitment to uprooting poverty and criticised its growing intolerance of dissent.[130] Even the church, which had historically shied away from active involvement beyond 'issues of faith', gradually involved itself in the broader political, social and economic affairs of society. Churches had always played an ambiguous role in terms of social justice, either being co-opted by the state or abdicating responsibility by claiming to remain neutral. Most confined themselves to preaching the gospel, and contributed to national development only through schools, hospitals, humanitarian programmes, and the care of orphans, widows and

---

[129] Raftopoulos, 'The labour movement'; Dansereau, 'Liberation and opposition in Zimbabwe'.
[130] S. Dorman, 'NGOs and the constitutional debate in Zimbabwe: From inclusion to exclusion', *Journal of Southern African Studies*, 29(4), 2003; Raftopoulos and Alexander, *Reflections on Democratic Politics in Zimbabwe*, p. 35.

the disadvantaged.[131] Confronted with the political intolerance of ZANU(PF), which tried to establish its hegemony over autonomous civil institutions after independence, churches avoided criticising government openly and, as both David Maxwell and Sarah Rich Dorman have argued, tried to accommodate themselves to the state.[132]

However, against the backdrop of mounting social and economic pressures, not only did more people turn to the churches for both material and spiritual support but the churches themselves became more critical of the state. In 1994 a small group of church-based NGOs came together under the aegis of the Ecumenical Support Services, formed in the early 1990s, to review the impact of ESAP on their members. The Catholic Commission for Justice and Peace in Zimbabwe (CCJPZ) – with its history of condemning Rhodesian Front atrocities as well as the Gukurahundi killings – the Catholic Church's Silveira House and the Methodist Synod all made efforts to widen the debate about ESAP.[133] Though not necessarily adopting a confrontational stance with the state, some of the more established churches, such as the CCJPZ and the Zimbabwe Council of Churches, took up activities such as policy advocacy, civic education, voter education and election monitoring.[134]

Women's groups, including the Zimbabwe Women's Resource Centre and Network and the Musasa Project, also became more active. With so many men retrenched, the burden of feeding families had fallen increasingly on women – an enormous task, given that most of them had remained on the margins of the economy after independence.[135] Another major issue of concern for these groups was the growing incidence of domestic violence.[136]

As protest increased, government repression intensified. In 1992 the Labour Relations Act was amended in a way that seriously curtailed workers' right to strike, and the controversial Presidential Powers Act (No. 1 of 1986) was occasion-

[131] See D. Maxwell, *Christians and Chiefs in Zimbabwe* (Edinburgh: Edinburgh University Press, 1999); M. Lapsley, *Neutrality or Co-option? Anglican Church and State from 1964 until the Independence of Zimbabwe* (Gweru: Mambo Press, 1986); F. J. Verstraelen, *Zimbabwean Realities and Christian Responses* (Gweru: Mambo Press, 1998).

[132] D. Maxwell, 'The church and democratization in Africa: The case of Zimbabwe', in P. Gifford (ed.), *The Christian Churches and the Democratization of Africa* (Leiden: Brill, 1995); S. R. Dorman, '"Rocking the boat?" Church NGOs and democratization in Zimbabwe', *African Affairs*, 101, 2002, p. 79.

[133] Dorman, 'Rocking the Boat', pp. 82-3.

[134] Ibid., p.81.

[135] N. Kanji and N. Jazdowska, 'Structural adjustment and the implications for low-income urban women in Zimbabwe', *Review of African Political Economy*, 56, 1993, pp. 11-26; Moyo, *Land Reform under Structural Adjustment in Zimbabwe*.

[136] Raftopoulos and Alexander, *Reflections on Democratic Politics in Zimbabwe*, p. 40.

ally deployed to halt or suspend strikes directed against the state.[137] Where it failed to halt strikes and demonstrations, the state increasingly deployed the police and the army to use brutal force.

To consolidate its rule and hold over the population, the government intensified its control over the law, the media and the security services. President Mugabe turned increasingly to the security services, especially the army, for protection against indications of discontent. Through his patronage system, he managed to keep the army leadership close to him.[138]

From the mid-1990s, the Mugabe-led government also turned to the war veterans to deal with growing opposition from inside and outside the party. Since the 1970s war of liberation, the party–military nexus had always been strong in both PF-ZAPU and ZANU(PF), and the military had always had a significant say in party politics.[139] Norma Kriger has argued that war veterans and ZANU(PF) not only relied heavily on violence and appeals to a liberation-war discourse to establish their power and legitimacy but also colluded with and manipulated each other to build power and privilege in the army, the police, the bureaucracy and among other workers.[140]

However, as Kriger herself acknowledges, the relationship had been ambivalent, with strains having been inherited from the liberation war, following such incidents as the 1974 Badza/Nhari rebellion and the Vashandi crisis in 1977.[141] After 1980, veterans' interests often conflicted with those of the politicians, and Fay Chung has argued that many in government feared the power of a united and organised veterans group.[142] Government thus only grudgingly allowed them to form a representative organisation, the Zimbabwe National Liberation War Veterans Association (ZNLWVA), in April 1989. This was 'a reactive initiative taken by ex-combatants when it had became clear that government had

---

[137] L. Madhuku, 'Trade unions and the law', in Raftopoulos and Sachikonye (eds.), *Striking Back*, pp. 105-32.

[138] See UN, 'Final Report of the Panel of Experts on the Illegal Exploitation of Natural Resources and Other Forms of Wealth of the Democratic Republic of the Congo', 16 October 2002. Available at <http://www.afrol.com/Countries/DRC/documents/un_resources_2002_govt_zim.htm>.

[139] See Ndlovu-Gatsheni, 'Nationalist-military alliance'; Sithole, *Struggles within a Struggle*.

[140] N. Kriger, *Guerrilla Veterans in Post-War Zimbabwe*, p. 103; N. Kriger, 'War veterans: Continuities between the past and the present', *African Studies Quarterly*, 7(2&3), [online], <http://web.africa.ufl.edu/asq/v7/v7i2a7.htm>.

[141] D. Moore, 'The Zimbabwean "organic intellectuals" in transition', *Journal of Southern African Studies*, 15, 1988, pp. 96-105; Sithole, *Struggles within the Struggle*; Chung, *Re-living the Second Chimurenga*.

[142] Chung, *Re-living the Second Chimurenga*, p. 302.

failed to assist them'.[143] Even so, the government tried to keep the veterans in line by imposing a politically loyal leadership over them until the emergence of Chenjerai Hunzvi in 1997.

Throughout the 1980s and early 1990s, there was therefore tension between a radical war veterans' agenda, which sought redistribution of land and other resources to the poor, and the ZANU(PF) politicians' agenda, which sought to act within the confines of the constitution and viewed indigenisation in terms of self-aggrandisement and personal accumulation. Although many veterans remained disgruntled over land, unemployment, neglect, and corruption in government throughout the 1980s and 1990s,[144] the government was not too concerned about them, as long as its authority was not seriously challenged from other quarters. It was only from the mid-1990s, when the state was under increasing pressure, that it decided to turn to the war veterans to help consolidate its power.

After initially ignoring the ZNLWVA, the government negotiated with it regarding the War Veterans Administration Bill (1991), the War Veterans Act (No. 4 of 1992) and the War Victims Compensation Act (1993), the latter entitling all ex-combatants injured in the liberation war to financial compensation on a scale proportional to the severity of their injuries.[145] The 'new partnership' was sealed in 1997 when the government agreed to pay unbudgeted gratuities of Z$50,000 (then about US$4,500) and monthly pensions of Z$2,000 after disgruntled war veterans, led by the volatile war veteran leader Chenjerai Hunzvi, had besieged President Mugabe in his party offices.

In the countryside, ZANU(PF) sought to consolidate its power in the 1990s through increasing centralisation of power and authority. As both state and ruling party legitimacy began to slip, the government moved to rekindle its

[143] M. Musemwa, 'The ambiguities of democracy: The demobilisation of the Zimbabwean ex-combatants and the ordeal of rehabilitation, 1980-1993', *Transformation*, 26, 1995, p. 40.

[144] Only 20,000 of around 65,000 ZANLA and ZIPRA guerrillas were integrated into the Zimbabwe National Army in 1980. The others were demobilised and awarded a monthly pension of Z$185 until 1983, but without skills training many slipped into destitution thereafter. For more detailed discussion about war veterans' grievances in post-independence Zimbabwe, see Kriger, *Guerrilla Veterans in Post-War Zimbabwe*; Barnes, 'The heroes' struggle'; Zimbabwe Women Writers (ed.), *Women of Resilience: The Voices of Women Ex-combatants* (Harare: ZWW, 2000); Musemwa, 'The ambiguities of democracy', pp. 31-46.

[145] The implementation of the compensation scheme became chaotic between 1993 and 1996, as party leaders looted money set aside for the fund through the falsification of claims and excluded ordinary war veterans from the scheme. See T. K. Chitiyo, 'Land violence and compensation: Reconceptualising Zimbabwe's land and war veterans' debate', *Track Two*, 9(1), May 2000, Available at <http://ccrweb.ccr.uct.ac.za/archive/two/9_1/zimbabwe.html>.

alliance with chiefs and reassert chiefly authority over rural populations.[146] In 1998, it enacted the Traditional Leaders Act (No. 25 of 1998), which empowered traditional leaders to deal with problems of land and natural resources and to preside over crimes, such as livestock theft, and family disputes. This effectively sidelined the popularly elected VIDCOs and WADCOs and reversed what little progress had been made in democratising rural governance in the early 1980s.[147] The traditional leaders, not accountable to the government, were now supposed to play an important role in consolidating what Mahmood Mamdani has described as 'decentralized despotism'.[148]

Conclusion

Zimbabwe undoubtedly made some limited economic and social progress in the early years of the first decade of independence, especially in infrastructural development, education and health delivery, and agricultural output. Some of these advances helped the country to become more competitive internationally and had a lasting legacy, but most were short-term and welfarist in nature. Many programmes were unsustainable, and did not adequately address the serious challenges of land and economic-resource ownership, justice and equity, the reconfiguration of the nation-state, political inclusiveness and openness, or issues of nationhood and citizenship. As a result, the post-colonial project of building a just, equitable and non-racial society was not achieved in the first decades of independence, and the foundation of a truly democratic order was not laid.

Centrally, there was little radical reform of the colonial economy or of the legacy of economic inequality. Many of the inherited tensions and divisions based on race, ethnicity, regionalism, class and gender were therefore not resolved. These unresolved tensions and divisions widened towards the late 1980s and beginning of the 1990s, when the economy began to contract seriously and the government increasingly struggled to meet its delivery targets as social problems for the poor began to mount. On the political front, state-building projects lacked tolerance of political diversity and dissent, and relied heavily on coercion rather

[146] See Hammar, 'Disrupting Democracy?', pp. 13-21; A. Hammar, 'The making and unma(s) king of local government in Zimbabwe', in Hammar et al. (eds.), Zimbabwe's Unfinished Business, pp. 119-54; J. Alexander, 'State, peasantry and resettlement', Review of African Political Economy, 61, 1994, 325-45; McGregor, 'The politics of disruption', pp. 9-37.

[147] E. Masunungure and N. Musekiwa, 'Local Government Policy Review' (Policy Document Prepared for the Zimbabwe Institute, 2005), pp. 10-11, 13-14, 26-7.

[148] For a more detailed discussion of the concept of 'decentralized despotism', see M. Mamdani, Citizen and Subject: Contemporary Africa and the Legacy of Late Colonialism (Princeton, Princeton University Press, 1996).

than persuasion. The state's hegemonic discourse of citizenship and nationhood also remained narrow and monolithic.

Despite all its efforts, ZANU(PF)'s attempts to proscribe democratic space and to establish its supremacy and dominance over the population were never fully achieved. Throughout the 1980s and early 1990s, the government struggled to impose itself and its political ideals on the nation. Its power continued to be challenged by a number of groups and individuals who felt excluded from both the national project of development and the structures of political and economic power. Such challenges ensured that there were always spaces in which the state's unpopular policies could be questioned, and that democratic tendencies were able to coexist, however uneasily.

7

The Crisis in Zimbabwe, 1998-2008

Brian Raftopoulos

Introduction

From the late 1990s Zimbabwe entered a period that has come to be known generally as the 'Crisis in Zimbabwe'.[1] This upheaval consisted of a combination of political and economic decline that, while it had its origins in the long-term structural economic and political legacies of colonial rule as well as the political legacies of African nationalist politics, exploded onto the scene in the

---

[1] The literature on the Zimbabwe crisis is immense, and what follows is just a select sample of it: A. Hammar, B. Raftopoulos and S. Jensen (eds.), *Zimbabwe's Unfinished Business: Rethinking Land, State and Nation in the Context of Crisis* (Harare, Weaver Press, 2003); Patrick Bond and Masimba Manyanya, *Zimbabwe's Plunge: Exhausted Nationalism, Neoliberalism, and the Search for Social Justice* (Harare: Weaver Press; London: Merlin, 2nd edn., 2003); Jocelyn Alexander, *The Unsettled Land: State-making and the Politics of Land in Zimbabwe, 1893-2003* (Harare: Weaver Press; Oxford: James Currey, 2006); S. Moyo and P. Yeros, 'Land occupations and land reform in Zimbabwe: Towards the national democratic revolution', in S. Moyo and P. Yeros (eds.), *Reclaiming the Land: The Resurgence of Rural Movements in Africa, Asia and Latin America* (Cape Town: David Philip; London: Zed Press, 2005), pp. 165-205; S. Moyo and P. Yeros, 'The radicalised state: Zimbabwe's interrupted revolution', *Review of African Political Economy*, 111, 2007, pp. 103-21; D. Moore, 'Is the land the economy and the economy the land? Primitive accumulation in Zimbabwe', *Journal of Contemporary African Studies*, 19(2), 2001, pp. 253-66; D. Moore, 'Zimbabwe's triple crisis: Primitive accumulation, nation-state formation and democratization in the age of neo-liberal globalization', *African Studies Quarterly*, 7(2&3), 2003, [online], <http://www.africa.ufl.edu/asq/v7/v7i2a2.htm>; B. Raftopoulos and I. Phimister, 'Zimbabwe now: The political economy of crisis and coercion', *Historical Materialism*, 12(4), 2004, pp. 355-82. B. Raftopoulos and L. Sachikonye (eds.), *Striking Back: The Labour Movement and the Post-colonial State in Zimbabwe, 1980-2000* (Harare: Weaver Press, 2001); T. Ranger, 'Nationalist historiography, patriotic history and the history of the nation: The struggle over the past in Zimbabwe', *Journal of Southern African Studies*, 30(2), 2004, pp. 215-34; T. Ranger (ed.), *The Historical Dimensions of Democracy and Human Rights in Zimbabwe: Volume Two: Nationalism, Democracy and Human Rights* (Harare, University of Zimbabwe Publications, 2003); B. Raftopoulos and T. Savage (eds.), *Zimbabwe: Injustice and Political Reconciliation*, (Harare: Weaver Press; Cape Town: Institute for Justice and Reconciliation, 2005); B. Raftopoulos and I. Phimister, 'Mugabe, Mbeki and the politics of anti-imperialism', *Review of African Political Economy*, 101, 2004, pp. 127-43; R. Primorac and S. Chan (eds.), *Zimbabwe in Crisis: The International Response and the Space of Silence* (London: Routledge, 2007); R. Muponde and R. Primorac (eds.), *Versions of Zimbabwe: New Approaches to Literature and Culture* (Harare: Weaver Press, 2005); Martin Meredith, *Our Votes, Our Guns: Robert Mugabe and the Tragedy of Zimbabwe* (New York: Public Affairs, 2002); Heidi Holland, *Dinner with Mugabe: The Untold Story of a Freedom Fighter Who Became a Tyrant* (South Africa: Penguin, 2008).

face of a major threat to the political future of the ruling party, ZANU(PF). The crisis became manifest in multiple ways: confrontations over the land and property rights; contestations over the history and meanings of nationalism and citizenship; the emergence of critical civil society groupings campaigning around trade union, human rights and constitutional questions; the restructuring of the state in more authoritarian forms; the broader pan-African and anti-imperialist meanings of the struggles in Zimbabwe; the cultural representations of the crisis in Zimbabwean literature; and the central role of Robert Mugabe.

As the crisis unfolded, various social forces called on repertoires from both the past and present to construct their version of events. The ruling party drew on a combination of revived nationalism that privileged its role in the liberation of the country, prioritised the centrality of the fight for land, and demonised all those outside the selective 'patriotic history' it espoused. It also represented its stance as part of a longer history of pan-Africanist and anti-imperialist struggles on the African continent and globally. For their part the emergent trade union, civic and political opposition forces called on the anti-colonial struggles for labour, human rights, local government and gender struggles, and the post-1989 global discourses on democratisation, driven by the fall of socialist regimes in Eastern Europe.

A key aspect of the crisis was the rapid decline of the economy, character-ised by, amongst other things: steep declines in industrial and agricultural productivity; historic levels of hyperinflation; the informalisation of labour; the dollarisation of economic transactions; displacements; and a critical erosion of livelihoods. This economic implosion affected the broad balance of social forces in the country and presented enormous challenges of reconstruction. It is these varied aspects of the Zimbabwean crisis that this chapter attempts to address.

The late 1990s and the challenges to the ruling party

The year 1998 opened with an intensification of the pressure on the state by workers and civil bodies. By the end of 1997 several key economic indicators pointed to the challenges facing the state: as a percentage of Gross Domestic Income, the share of wages dropped from 54% in 1987 to 39% in 1997, while the ratio of profit increased from 47% to 61% during the same period; real wages fell from an index of 100.6 between 1985 and 1990 to 86.0 between 1996 and 1999; employment growth declined from an index of 2.4 to 1.5 and inflation increased from 11.6% to 32.6% during this same period; poverty levels increased from 40.4% in 1990/91 to 63% in 1996.[2] Moreover, the involvement of the Zimbabwe

---

[2] G. Kanyenze and B. Chiripanhura, 'The State of Union Organisation in Zimbabwe' (Harare: unpublished paper, 2001).

government in the Democratic Republic of the Congo in 1998, while initially part of a Southern African Development Community (SADC) attempt to stabilise the security situation, found increasing motivation in the economic opportunities offered by the engagement. In particular, the state encouraged entrepreneurs to penetrate the DRC market, citing the 'attractiveness of low-cost, commercially useful, networks' established by the Zimbabwe Defence Forces.[3] The cost of involvement in the DRC added to the failures of the structural adjustment programme by the end of the 1990s. The increasing imbalance between growth and equity, domestic development and export promotion, and the declining possibility of developing a social contract between the state, capital and labour under such conditions led to an impasse over future development strategy. The result was, as Dansereau observes, that ZANU(PF) 'retreated into repression, isolation and a strategy aimed at the support of an economic elite close to the ruling party, using the state to eliminate barriers to its expansion.'[4]

As the economic crisis deepened at the end of the 1980s workers and their unions increasingly demonstrated their opposition to state policies. By the end of 1997 some one hundred job actions had taken place,[5] and in January 1998 food riots, in response to the steep rise in the cost of mealie meal, erupted in the capital city and smaller towns such as Beitbridge, Chegutu, and Chinhoyi. The response of the state was brutal: ten people were killed and hundreds arrested and assaulted by the security forces. This was accompanied by more collective union actions, and the emergence of a coalition of workers, students, intellectuals, human rights organisations, and women's groups to form one of the most effective social movements in the country's history, the National Constitutional Assembly (NCA).

Until the mid-1990s, NGOs had concentrated on income-generating activities, human rights issues, the environment, AIDS, gender struggles, and poverty challenges; subsequent years witnessed the emergence of strong social movements in the fields of labour, constitutionalism and democratisation.[6] More-

[3] M. Nest, 'Ambitions, profits and loss: Zimbabwean economic involvement in the Democratic Republic of the Congo', *African Affairs*, 100, 2001, pp. 469-90.

[4] Suzanne Dansereau, 'Between a rock and a hard place: Zimbabwe's development impasse', in H. Melber (ed.), *Zimbabwe: The Political Economy of Decline* (Uppsala: Nordic Africa Institute, 2005), p. 25.

[5] Suzanne Dansereau, 'Labour and Democratisation: Potential of Labour's Political Challenge in Zimbabwe' (Cape Town: unpublished paper, 2002); R. Saunders, 'Striking ahead: Industrial action and labour movement development in Zimbabwe', in Raftopoulos and Sachikonye (eds.), *Striking Back,* pp. 133-74.

[6] S. Moyo, J. Makumbe and B. Raftopoulos, *NGOs, the State and Politics in Zimbabwe* (Harare: SAPES Books, 2000); B. Raftopoulos, 'Civic Organisations, Governance and Human Development in Zimbabwe' (Harare, unpublished paper, 2000).

over, this process led, in
1999, to the emergence
of the most successful
opposition party in post-
colonial Zimbabwe, the
Movement for Demo-
cratic Change (MDC).
While such movements
developed a critical and
confrontational relation-
ship with the state, the
war veterans' move-
ment, which had begun
in the 1980s but became
more strongly assertive

Fig. 7.1: Morgan Tsvangirai addresses an MDC rally.
[*Photo*: Edwina Spicer/Solidarity Peace Trust]

in the late 1990s, had a relationship with the state that was characterised by a
combination of 'collaboration, conflict and accommodation'.[7]

Labour struggles, constitutional reform and the battle for state power

Following the January 1998 food riots the Zimbabwe Congress of Trade Unions
(ZCTU), continued to press the state over the removal of sales tax, development
levy and price increases that had been imposed in late 1997, as well as over
the need for a properly constituted consultative body on economic policy,
first suggested by the ZCTU in its 1996 document, *Beyond ESAP*.[8] The labour
movement was becoming more aware of its leading role in the struggle for
democracy in Zimbabwe. In the words of its General Council,

> People from all walks of life are crying out for salvation from the
> labour movement. Labour should therefore seriously consider and
> understand the concern of the man in the street. There is need
> to seriously consider going beyond the worker and integrate the
> ordinary people. It was said to be vital for ZCTU to go out there
> and be involved in all levels of change at the same time working
> towards being strongly organised. Workers issues have become
> community issues; as much as linkages and networking with other

[7] N. Kriger, 'Zimbabwe's war veterans and the ruling party: Continuities in political dynamics',
Politique Africaine, 81, 2001, p. 81.

[8] Zimbabwe Congress of Trade Unions [ZCTU]. *Beyond ESAP: Framework for a Long-term
Development Strategy in Zimbabwe beyond the Economic Structural Adjustment Programme*
(Harare: ZCTU, 1996).

civic groups is important, we should be able to control and direct social action to maintain direction. We should be able to put things on course in case of deviation so as to maintain legitimacy.[9]

Throughout 1998 the ZCTU battled with the tension of building its own structures while developing broader alliances with other civic groups, and in April 1998 the Secretary-General, Morgan Tsvangirai, called for a debate on whether 'emphasis should be put on collective bargaining or national issues ... and how best this could be done without losing focus on either issue.'[10] Thus, even as the ZCTU attempted to engage the state through the latter's National Economic Consultative Forum, it maintained an emphasis on mass actions, notably with the organisation of three effective stay-aways in 1998, one in March and two in November. Frustrated by the lack of progress in its attempts to negotiate with the state, the ZCTU declared:

> When workers cannot earn a living wage and decent working con-
> ditions through industrial action at the workplace, they will go
> beyond the shopfloor and bring their issues in the national stage,
> thus politicising the issues. When in addition the Trades Unions
> have been marginalised and cannot successfully address these
> issues through National Reforms in a government that has aband-
> oned the desire to engage in national consensus, the only recourse
> is action at a National level.[11]

In the face of such intensifying labour militancy the state imposed the Presidential Powers (Temporary Measures) Labour Regulations of 1998 (Statutory Instrument 368A of 1998) in November 1998, and imposed heavy penalties on trade unions and employers that incited or facilitated strikes, stay-aways, and other forms of unlawful collective action.

As the labour movement attempted to navigate the course between shop floor and broader political concerns, it had to contend with serious organisational challenges which were apparent by the mid-1990s. Progress in enhancing shop-floor participation in union organisation and skills training was slow, and communication between national and local structures was weak. The ZCTU noted the need to develop district committees since in some areas, such as Masvingo, 'most districts were operating on skeletal [sic] structures and in some instances

[9] ZCTU, 'Minutes of the Special General Council Meeting held at Adelaide Acres on 30 January 1998'.

[10] ZCTU, 'Minutes of the Special General Council Meeting held on 22 April, 1998 at Adelaide Acres'.

[11] ZCTU, 'Special General Council Meeting, 30th January 2008'.

members whose unions are not affiliates are holding key posts in the ZCTU'.[12] In addition, the labour centre faced problems of financial viability owing to the non-payment of subscriptions by its affiliates, and was 'forced therefore to borrow funds from projects to sustain its business'.[13]

Against this background the ZCTU extended its broader political vision through the key role it played in the establishment of the NCA in 1997. Drawing on a history of tensions between labour and nationalist politics dating back to the 1950s and 1960s, the labour movement brought to the emergence of civic and opposition politics not only a long tradition of debate and discussion over the meanings of nationalism and citizenship[14] but also the post-1980 experience of working with other civil society organisations on issues such as ESAP, poverty, human rights and urban residential rights, which proved vital in mobilising around economic and political questions.[15] Thus the ability of the labour movement to combine a national capacity for organisation with extended civic alliances, proved decisive in the emergence of an alternative democratic voice in the late 1990s.

Formed as an initiative from Zimbabwe Council of Churches and with a membership comprised of 'religious organisations, trade unions, professional associations, grassroots structures, media bodies, academic institutions and business, women's, students' and human rights organisations', the NCA contributed to a seismic shift in the development of opposition politics after 1997.[16] On the basis of seed funding provided by the Friedrich Ebert Stiftung,[17] the NCA set out its primary objectives in a meeting in August 1997 prior to its official launch in 1998. These included: To initiate and engage in a process of enlightening the general public on the current constitution in Zimbabwe; to identify shortcomings of the current constitution and to organise debate on possible constitutional reform; to organise the constitutional debate in a way which allows a broad-based participation; to subject the constitution-making process

---

[12] ZCTU, 'Minutes of the Special General Council Meeting held at Adelaide Acres on 29th August 1998'; R. Saunders, 'Trade Union Struggles for Autonomy and Democracy in Zimbabwe' (Harare: unpublished paper, 1996).

[13] ZCTU, 'Minutes of the General Council Meeting held on the 28th July 2000'.

[14] See the discussion and references in chapter three of this book.

[15] A. LeBas, 'Polarization and Party Development: Capturing Constituencies in Democratizing Africa' (Ph.D. thesis, Columbia University, 2006).

[16] E. McCandless, 'Zimbabwean Forms of Resistance: Social Movements, Strategic Dilemmas and Transformative Change' (Ph.D. thesis, American University, 2005), p. 209. For another good discussion of the history of the NCA, see Sara Rich Dorman, 'Inclusion and Exclusion: NGOs and Politics in Zimbabwe' (D.Phil. thesis, University of Oxford, 2001).

[17] National Constitutional Assembly [NCA], 'General Meeting of the 30th January 1998: Task Force Report: 1st Interim Report for 1998'.

to popular scrutiny with a view to entrenching the principles that constitutions are made by, and for, the people; generally to encourage a culture of popular participation in decision making.[18] At its inception many members argued for political pluralism in its membership, but the polarisation of politics in the period leading up to the constitutional referendum in 2000 made this an increasingly difficult proposition. An example of this plea for pluralism was made by Mike Auret of the Catholic Commission for Justice and Peace in Zimbabwe, in July 1997. Auret argued:

> I am thus asking that as this process is very much an ideological one, all task force members declare their political influences and their ideology. The task force must then seek to include members of other ideological persuasions that are unrepresented. As a primary example I believe that both the Liberal Democratic model and the Democratic Socialist model should have representation. I also believe that there is a divide between those that absolutely believe in the ideal of non-racism and the role of affirmative action and black consciousness in the realisation of that goal. There are others that believe in 'indigenisation' as an end in itself and are not particularly interested in the goal of non-racism. These different ideologies and any others must have protection on the task force.[19]

After its official launch at the University of Zimbabwe on 31 January 1998, popularising the work of the NCA proved an immensely challenging task, especially after the state launched its own alternative Constitutional Commission in March 1999. ZANU(PF) Legal Secretary, Edison Zvobgo, dismissed the NCA in the following terms: 'How can a few people sit under a tree and claim to be a National Constitutional Assembly. They are neither constitutional nor an assembly.'[20] Largely deprived of access to the public media and confronted by the impressive outreach of the government's well-funded Commission, the NCA developed its own community-outreach programmes. Even as positions hardened between supporters of the two, there was in the period 1998 to early 2000 sufficient political space for a vibrant political debate to open on the issue of constitutional reform.

---

[18] NCA, 'Second Interim Report of the Taskforce to the Assembly 1997'.

[19] Letter from M. Auret to the NCA Task Force, 21 July 1997. In one of the many ironies of Zimbabwean history, Auret also proposed in this letter that, instead of being called the NCA, the movement should be known as the Movement for a Democratic Constitution.

[20] Quoted in McCandless, 'Zimbabwean Forms of Resistance', p. 210.

In late 1997 the NCA public profile was limited to isolated meetings and seminars. In an early evaluation of its strategy, the NCA observed that

> The experience of seminars so far held points to the sad fact that, collectively, our follow-up strategy has been poor. It has rather been like the Task Force zooms into an area from Mars, pontificates around the constitution even to the excitement of the audiences – and then zooms back to Harare to leave behind life continuing as usual ... it is important that we find ways of strengthening the local ownership of the programme, so that the interest that the Task Force or Assembly generates in the initial contact is not lost.[21]

It was the extensive involvement of NCA organisational members in the programmes of the movement that proved decisive in 'strengthening the local ownership' of the NCA's objectives. In addition to the work of the churches, the ZCTU's key role in utilising its structures was extremely important for the work of the NCA. At its General Council meeting in January 1998 the ZCTU reaffirmed its role in the NCA process, noting that the 'fundamental issue confronting Zimbabwe is how the rules of democratic governance are set'.[22] Although questions were sometimes raised by members of the General Council about the 'status of the ZCTU in the NCA',[23] the labour movement remained committed to the process. Its role in the urban areas was complemented by the growing network of residents' associations in the cities in the late 1990s. Additionally, women's organisations were a key factor in extending the constitutional debate to the rural areas, as were commercial farmers. As Shireen Essof has written, between 1995 and 1998 Zimbabwean women's organisations redefined their strategies for engaging both the state and civil society. This was a strategy that saw the organisational base, rural networks and key individuals 'coming together in various issue-driven configurations and strategic coalitions, forming and disbanding and reforming again as needed'.[24] Within this context the Women's Coalition on the Constitution was launched in June 1999, and played a key mobilisation role.

Between 1999 and the March 2000 referendum the central debate in Zimbabwe revolved around the constitution. The government's Constitutional Commission had been established in 1999 in an attempt to control the process and outcome

---

[21] NCA, 'Second Interim Report 1997'.
[22] ZCTU, 'Special General Council Meeting, 30th January, 1998'.
[23] ZCTU, 'Minutes of the General Council Meeting on the 26th June 1999'.
[24] S. Essof, 'Women in Movement', in K. Alexander (ed.), *The Future of Democratic Politics in Zimbabwe* (Cape Town: Institute for Justice and Reconciliation, 2006), p. 47.

of constitutional reform. It set up a widespread and intensive consultation process that helped to open up political debate in the country. It should be noted that pressure emerged from within ZANU(PF) itself, with its parliamentarians pressing, after 1995, for parliamentary reform, constitutional reform and in some cases a change of leadership. With the limited spaces open for leadership changes in the party, some factions hoped that the constitutional reform process would provide a more acceptable modality for raising such issues.[25]

For many in the civil society movement gathered in the NCA, the heart of this national discussion centred around issues of citizenship, government account-ability and the broadening of democratic spaces. The process of carrying out the reform process, though strongly debated in the NCA, was a major part of the demand of the civic movement, and it was around issues of both process and, later, the proposed composition of the government Commission and its draft constitution – in particular the persistence of concentrated power in the office of the President – that the NCA declined to participate. The NCA objected to the government's failure to put in place 'an agreed upon legal framework to guide the constitution-making process', fearing that the state would use the Commissions of Inquiry Act of 1941 [*Chapter 10:07*] as an executive instrument 'to manipulate the process and results'. The NCA favoured an 'all stakeholder conference and an agreed process based on consensus building and people-centered process'.[26]

The stakes around the constitutional reform process were raised with the formation of the Movement for Democratic Change in September 1999. The MDC emerged out of a range of civic struggles, in particular the labour and constitutional movements, and a formal decision by the civic groups to form the party was taken at a National Working People's Convention in February 1999. On the question of the constitution, the Convention noted that

> the inability to implement any meaningful steps to redress basic economic and social problems emanates from a crisis of govern-ance within the nation. The crisis expresses itself in a failure of government to observe the separation of powers between the executive, legislature, and judiciary; to obey the basic rules of accountability and transparency; to respect human rights and to decentralise power in ways that enable meaningful participation of people in public institutions.[27]

[25] B. Raftopoulos, 'The State, NGOs and Democratisation', in S. Moyo, J. Makumbe and B. Raftopoulos, *NGOs the State and Politics in Zimbabwe*, pp. 21-46.

[26] NCA, 'Task Force Report Presented to the General Assembly 28th October 2000'.

[27] 'Declaration of the National Working People's Convention', Harare, February 1999.

Thereafter, the NCA mobilisation around constitutional reform was linked, in the thinking of both the ruling party and key players in the civic constitutional reform movement, to a change of government. The MDC, with Morgan Tsvangirai as its President, drew much of its leadership from the ZCTU, the NCA and other civil society groups. As the campaign for a rejection of the government's draft constitution intensified, the structures of the MDC, labour movement, the NCA, women's and students' groups and other civic bodies overlapped and cross-fertilised, each drawing from a common pool of support.[28] Moreover, both the NCA and the MDC received support from white farmers, who, in the face of growing threats on their land and the breakdown of their previous consultative arrangements with ZANU(PF) (discussed below), decided in 1999 to engage with the new opposition political developments. Thus, while the NCA worked most effectively in the urban areas, white commercial farmers 'began to mobilise through local exercises, by urging farmworkers to reject the constitution, and by printing T-shirts and leaflets calling for a NO vote'.[29] White farmers were also

an important source of support for the MDC in the 2000 general election.

As a result of the broad coalition of interests that had coalesced around the NCA and MDC the government lost the referendum on its proposed constitution held on 12/13 February; 54 per cent of the 1.3 million citizens who voted cast a 'No' vote.[30]

Fig. 7.2: NCA protest against the government's draft constitution.

[*Photo*: Edwina Spicer/Solidarity Peace Trust]

---

[28] LeBas, 'Polarization and Party Development', p. 157.

[29] A. Selby, 'Commercial Farmers and the State: Interest Group Politics and Land Reform in Zimbabwe' (D.Phil. thesis, Oxford University, 2006), p. 277,

[30] McCandless, 'Zimbabwean Forms of Resistance', p. 483.

Land and politics

The rejection of the government's constitution marked the first major political defeat of the ruling party, against a political and civic opposition that made a national impression in a very short period of time. As a multi-class, cross-racial alliance, the MDC and its allies confronted the state with a language of democratisation, a discourse that resonated in large sections of the population and turned the constitutional referendum into a plebiscite on ZANU(PF)'s rule since 1980. The politics of possibility and change that dominated the MDC was encapsulated in the leading slogan of the party – *chinja maitiro/guqula izenzo*, 'change your ways' – and the open palm which, in opposition to the clenched fist of ZANU(PF), became the symbol of the new party.[31] It also gave notice to the ruling party that it faced a real threat of electoral defeat and loss of state power in the forthcoming general and presidential elections in 2000 and 2002, respectively.

In response to the referendum defeat, a series of land occupations ensued a few weeks later that radically transformed the political and economic landscape of the country. A clause in the rejected constitution provided for the British government to be responsible for the payment of compensation for land confiscated by the Zimbabwean state. Feeling aggrieved at the voting response of the population and drawing on a long post-colonial relationship of collaboration and conflict between the state and the war veterans,[32] the latter embarked on a violent process of land occupations. This move represented a decisive shift of power relations within ZANU(PF) as Mugabe, faced with a growing political opposition from without and the explosive pressures from war veterans within his own party, moved decisively towards a stronger alliance with the veterans.

The land occupations of 2000 and beyond were not the first such protests since independence. In the 1980s there were a number of occupations of land which, abandoned by its owners, was acquired by the government and transferred to the occupiers. In the 1990s there were further occupations owing to a combination of a slow-down in the state's land-reform programme, intensified pressure on land in the communal areas, and economic liberalisation.[33] A prominent instance

---

[31] Both the slogan and the open palm were drawn from the mobilisation activities of the ZCTU; see B. Raftopoulos, 'The labour movement and the emergence of opposition politics in Zimbabwe', in Raftopoulos and Sachikonye (eds.), *Striking Back*, p. 19.

[32] N. Kriger, 'War veterans: Continuities between the past and the present', *African Studies Quarterly*, 7(2&3), [online], <http://web.africa.ufl.edu/asq/v7/v7i2a7.htm>.

[33] S. Moyo, 'The land occupation movement and democratisation in Zimbabwe: Contradictions of neoliberalism', *Millennium: Journal of International Studies*, 30(2), 2001, p. 321; S. Moyo, 'The political economy of land acquisition and redistribution in Zimbabwe, 1990-1999', *Journal of Southern African Studies*, 26(1), 2000, pp. 5-28.

of these occupations was the peasant occupation of commercial farms in the Svosve area near Marondera in Mashonaland East province, which gave impetus to the International Donor Conference on Land, organised by the government in 1998. Mugabe hoped to raise Z$1.5 billion for a five-year programme to resettle 150,000 families on 5 million hectares of land. The governments of the UK and the US refused to fund the programme on the grounds that it would not alleviate poverty and failed to respect property rights.[34]

The new wave of occupations, which would come to be known as the Fast Track land reform and resettlement programme, took place through the modality of what Sam Moyo calls 'centralist models of redistribution'.[35] However, while Moyo has argued that there is continuity in the form of occupations before and after 2000,[36] others have argued that there were 'striking differences in the terms of the leadership and organisation of the occupations, the role and consequences for the state, and their use in attacking a political opposition'.[37] While there were certainly continuities in terms of long-standing grievances on the land question, and while the leadership role of the war veterans was prominent, the organisational, logistical and coercive support provided by the state were crucial distinguishing features of the post-2000 occupations. Most of those who joined the land-occupation movement were drawn from ZANU(PF) youths, and from communal and urban areas,[38] driven by a combination of grassroots initiatives and centralised coercion and violence.

As some analysts have noted, these occupations occurred within the context of 'both longstanding and more recent complexities of the land question', such as struggles within areas of peasant farming, the effects of rural–urban migration, the livelihood crisis of urban households, and the displacement and eviction effects of agricultural export production and eco-tourism during the structural adjustment period.[39] However, the need to contain, coerce and demobilise the structures and support of the opposition played a central role in the politics of land after 2000, and a key characteristic of this process was the restructuring of the state itself, which took several forms.

---

[34] E. McCandless, 'The Case of Land in Zimbabwe: Cause of Conflict, Foundation for Sustained Peace' (Harare: unpublished paper, 2001).

[35] Moyo, 'The land occupation movement', p. 313.

[36] Ibid.

[37] Alexander, The Unsettled Land, p. 185.

[38] Ibid. For an interesting insider account of the war veterans and the land occupations, see Wilbert Sadomba, 'War Veterans in Zimbabwe's Land Occupations: Complexities of a Liberation Movement in an African Post-Colonial Settler Society' (Ph.D. thesis, Wageningen University, 2008).

[39] H. Bernstein, '"Changing before our very eyes": Agrarian questions and the politics of land in capitalism today', Journal of Agrarian Change, 4(1&2), 2004, p. 218.

Firstly the ruling party's nationalist ideology was recast in more authoritarian, selective and racialised notions of citizenship and belonging, constituted around the centrality of the land question and the contribution of ZANU(PF) to the liberation struggle. Mugabe expressed the land issue in the following terms:

> We knew and still know that land was the prime goal for King Lobengula as he fought the British encroachment in 1893; we knew and still know that land was the principal grievance for our heroes of the First Chimurenga, led by Nehanda and Kaguvi. We knew and still know it to be the fundamental premise of the Second Chimurenga and thus a principal definer of the succeeding new Nation and State of Zimbabwe. Indeed we know it to be the core issue and imperative of the Third Chimurenga which you and me are fighting, and for which we continue to make such enormous sacrifices.[40]

This authoritarian nationalism also constructed a series of 'outsiders' and 'enemies of the nation', namely whites, the MDC and the civic movement, urbanites and farmworkers. Mugabe narrated the land struggle as part of a longer and broader history of anti-imperialist and pan-Africanist struggles, casting the opposition and civil society groups as Western surrogates in them. [41]

Secondly, the ruling party embarked on a dramatic reorganisation of state structures. The judiciary was re-formed to ensure that its decisions complied with the dictates of ZANU(PF). In this process the integrity of the legal system was compromised through a combination of pressure on independent judges in the High Court and Supreme Court to resign, repeated refusals by the state to comply with court judgments on the land and other issues, and the issuing of amnesties to people who had carried out acts of violence on behalf of the ruling party.[42] In the civil service, particularly in rural districts, teachers, health workers and local government officials considered to be opposition supporters were dismissed by local war veteran committees, with such actions being given the appearance of a broader appeal as a result of longstanding grievances related to lack of financial capacity, maladministration and corruption on the

---

[40] R. Mugabe, *Inside the Third Chimurenga* (Harare: Government of Zimbabwe, 2001), pp. 92-3.

[41] B. Raftopoulos, 'Nation, race and history in Zimbabwean politics', in Raftopoulos and Savage (eds.), *Zimbabwe: Injustice and Political Reconciliation*, pp. 160-75.

[42] G. Feltoe, 'The Role of Civil Society in Helping Overcome the Crisis in Zimbabwe: The Constitution, the Legal System and Political Violence' (Harare: paper prepared for the Crisis in Zimbabwe Coalition, 2003); K. Saller, *The Judicial Institution in Zimbabwe* (Cape Town: University of Cape Town, 2004).

Fig. 7.3: Calling for land at a ZANU(PF) rally.
[*Photo:* Annie Mpalume]

part of of local government officials. Thus the war veteran leadership took over
the implementation of the Fast Track resettlement programme, sidelining local
development structures.[43]

Thirdly, repressive legislation such as the Public Order and Security Act
(POSA) [*Chapter 11:17*] and the Access to Information and Protection of Privacy
Act (AIPPA) [*Chapter 10:27*] was passed in 2002 to restrict the activities of the
opposition and civic forces in the public sphere and to control the independent
press. In a study of the use of POSA by the state after 2000, several key findings
emerged: POSA was the most commonly cited Act in the arrest of citizens trying
to hold public meetings; it was used in a politically partisan way effectively to
prohibit normal democratic activities; torture, assault and psychological harassment were systematically used by the police and other law enforcement agents
while arresting civilians, and when they were held in custody; the state showed
little inclination to pursue cases against most of those accused and detained,

---

[43] J. McGregor, 'The politics of disruption: War veterans and the local state in Zimbabwe',
African Affairs, 101, 2002, pp. 9-37; A. Hammar, 'The making and unma(s)king of local government in Zimbabwe', in Hammar *et al.* (eds.), *Zimbabwe's Unfinished Business*, pp. 119-54.

indicating that the primary motive was to intimidate and prevent protest actions.[44]

Fourthly, the state turned to an increasing reliance on violence during elections, within the context of a growing militarisation of state structures, as attested to by scores of human rights reports produced during this period. During the 2000 general and 2002 presidential election campaigns the MDC and its supporters were subjected to widespread violence – murder, attempted murder, torture, rape, disappearances and death threats – much of it carried out by the ruling party's youth militia group.

Notwithstanding this onslaught the MDC received 47 per cent of the vote in 2000 compared to ZANU(PF)'s 49 per cent; in the presidential election Mugabe received 56 per cent to Morgan Tsvangirai's 42 per cent. Both elections were conducted under the cloud of enormous electoral discrepancies, and the electoral issues contested by the opposition in these elections were still being contested in the 2005 general election won by ZANU(PF).[45] Moreover, the violence and irregularities of the elections were implemented by a state whose key positions – ranging from the election directorate and Attorney-General's Office to the heads of the Grain Marketing Board, Zimbabwe Electricity Supply Authority, and National Railways of Zimbabwe – Mugabe had filled with military personnel.[46] It is important to note, however, that this widespread violence resulted not only from the ruling party's intention to intimidate and control the opposition but also because of the intense rivalries and weakening of organisational structures in ZANU(PF) itself; thus it also served to bring party structures under the tighter control of the national leadership.[47]

Regarding the outcomes of the land occupations there have been mixed

[44] Solidarity Peace Trust, *Disturbing the Peace: An Overview of Civilian Arrests in Zimbabwe: February 2003 – January 2004'* (2004) Available at <http://www.solidaritypeacetrust.org/reports/disturbing_the_peace.pdf>. For a discussion on the repression of the media, see W. Chuma, 'Liberating or limiting the public sphere? Media policy and the Zimbabwe transition, 1980-2004', in Raftopoulos and Savage (eds.), *Zimbabwe: Injustice and Political Reconciliation*, pp. 119-39.

[45] K. Alexander and B. Raftopoulos (eds.), *The Struggle for Legitimacy: A Long-term Analysis of the 2005 Parliamentary Election and its Implications for Democratic Processes in Zimbabwe* (Cape Town: Institute for Justice and Reconciliation, 2005). D. Moore, 'Marxism and Marxist intellectuals in schizophrenic Zimbabwe: How many rights for Zimbabwe's left?', *Historical Materialism*, 12(4), 2004, pp. 405-26; T. Scarnecchia, 'The "Fascist Cycle" in Zimbabwe, 2000-2005', *Journal of Southern African Studies*, 32(2), 2006, pp. 221-37.

[46] M. Rupiya, 'Evaluating the Security Sector as the Repressive Instrument for the State in Zimbabwe' (Cape Town: paper prepared for the Institute for Justice and Reconciliation, 2006).

[47] A. LeBas, 'Polarization as craft: Party formation and state violence in Zimbabwe', *Comparative Politics*, 38(4), 2006, pp. 419-38.

assessments, and in an important historical sense much more research needs to be undertaken in this area. However, some interim observations can be made. The occupations decisively broke the back of white land ownership in the country, and thereby transformed the legacy of the colonial land dispensation. While in 2000 there were some 4,500 white commercial farmers occupying 11 million hectares of land and producing over 70 per cent of agricultural output, by 2008 this number had been reduced to approximately 500.[48] By 2005 the 'remnants of the white farming community were fragmented and powerless' and the 'production, economic contributions, financial clout and institutional effectiveness' of the white farmers had been eliminated.[49] This enormous transformation in the fortunes of white farmers and their families did not just have significant political and economic implications: it also spurred a new genre of post-colonial 'white writing' that inscribed a new sense of victimhood on white identities. As Ashleigh Harris observes, Mugabe's revocation of the politics of reconciliation through the politics of land occupations, 'has allowed for a white re-imagining of the past that ... exculpates white Zimbabwean involvement in racial tensions through de-historicising that white identity'.[50]

Other major losers in the land reallocation were opposition supporters and farmworkers. A 2002 study of farmworkers noted several indictors relating to the impact of the land reform programme on this group: the occupations led to a huge drop in employment levels, estimated at 70 per cent in the Midlands and 65 per cent in the two Matabeleland provinces; by mid-2000 an estimated 900,000 people had been affected by the evictions; less than 5 per cent of farmworkers were granted land; the loss of incomes and access to housing and safe water affected the capacity of households to care for the sick, in particular those with HIV/AIDS.[51] Their exclusion as beneficiaries of the land occupations was the result of ZANU(PF) branding them either as 'belonging to the farmer' and under the 'domestic government' of commercial farmers, or as foreigners in the politics

[48] P. Matondi, 'Shaping and Stewarding Replacement amidst Uncertainty of Fast Track Land Reform in Zimbabwe' (Harare: unpublished paper, 2008).

[49] A. Selby, 'Commercial Farmers and the State', p. 331.

[50] A. Harris, 'Writing home: Inscriptions of whiteness/descriptions of belonging in white Zimbabwean memoir-autobiography', in Muponde and Primorac (eds.), *Versions of Zimbabwe*, p. 107. Examples of such writing include: A. Fuller, *Don't Let's Go to the Dogs Tonight* (Johannesburg: Picador, 2004); P. Godwin, *Mukiwa: A White Boy in Africa* (London: Picador, 1996); P. Godwin, *When a Crocodile Eats the Sun* (Johannesburg: Picador, 2006); I. Holding, *Unfeeling* (London: Scribner, 2005).

[51] L. M. Sachikonye, *The Situation of Farm Workers after Land Reform in Zimbabwe: A Report Prepared for the Farm Community Trust of Zimbabwe*, May 2003, available at <http://www.oxfam.org.uk/what_we_do/issues/livelihoods/landrights/downloads/zimfwsit.rtf>, retrieved 31 May 2009.

of 'the nation'. Categorised as 'enemies of the state' along with white farmers and the MDC, these workers were subjected to some of the worst election violence of the period 2000-2002. Moreover, through a new citizenship law passed after 2000, their right to vote was severely undermined as, along with white farmers, they were considered foreigners who had to renounce their perceived dual citizenship before being able to vote. For many, the long bureaucratic route to such renunciation effectively resulted in disenfranchisement.[52]

The Fast Track programme also had adverse effects on the agricultural sector; these were apparent in several ways: concerns about the capacity and ability of the beneficiaries; large amounts of vacant and underutilised land; vandalised and deteriorating infrastructure; decline of specialised production systems; drastic decline in seed maize production – exacerbated by drought – that resulted in the need for food assistance to about five million people by the end of 2008; the loss of skilled farmers; the breakdown in production linkages between the agricultural and other sectors; and lack of security of tenure with its associated implications for financial investment on the land.[53] As Matondi writes,

> the overall legal framework for land ownership as an institution itself has remained misty and highly uncertain, witnessed by movements, threats and non-investment in meaningful farm capital. The movements in and out of farms, for whatever reasons, eight years after the commencement of a programme that was declared completed after the second year can be an indicator of the uncertainty that surrounds the overall legal framework for ownership.[54]

On the positive side of this assessment, scholars such as Moyo and Yeros have stressed the significant shift in access to land that took place in the Fast Track programme, noting that 'new petty-commodity-producing establishments' accounted for 93.7 per cent of the new farming establishments, with the large majority of these having their origins in the congested communal areas.[55] Others have documented the continued vibrancy of the livestock sector in

[52] B. Rutherford, 'Belonging to the farm(er): Farm workers, farmers and the shifting politics of citizenship' in Hammar et al. (eds.), Zimbabwe's Unfinished Business, pp. 191-216; B. Rutherford, 'Commercial farm workers and the politics of (dis)placement in Zimbabwe: Colonialism, liberation and democracy', Journal of Agrarian Change, 1(4), 2001, pp. 626-51.

[53] N. Marongwe, 'A Think Piece on Land Reform and the Current Food Crisis: Causes and Consequences', paper prepared for Joint Review of Food Aid in Zimbabwe (EC/ECHO, USAID, DFID, 2006); Matondi, 'Shaping and Stewarding Replacement'.

[54] Matondi, 'Shaping and Stewarding Replacement', p. 13.

[55] Moyo and Yeros, 'Land occupations and land reform in Zimbabwe: Towards the national democratic revolution', p. 195.

southern Zimbabwe through the recasting of racialised production systems and commodity chains and the reconfiguration of the 'relationship between the state and these informal market systems'.[56] Yet, as Cousins observed, the form of 'agrarian populism' formulated by Moyo and Yeros 'ignored the short term need to restore earnings from estates and other specialised, capital- and knowledge-intensive production regimes', as well the importance of feeding urban populations.[57] Moreover, the class differentiation of the land beneficiaries also affected the efficacy of the programme, with a significant number of the best farms going to elites affiliated to the ruling party in the political, military, civil-service and business sectors.

The response of Western governments to the human rights abuses accompanying the land occupations was to impose a series of what were called 'targeted sanctions' against selected individuals in the Mugabe regime. In 2001 the US government passed the Zimbabwe Democracy and Economic Recovery Act, while between 2002 and 2008 the EU and Australia imposed travel and asset sanctions on a growing number of key individuals either involved in the human rights abuses or profiteering under the Mugabe regime. The US, the EU and Canada also imposed arms embargos on the government, and in 2002 Zimbabwe was suspended from the Commonwealth, from which it formally withdrew in 2003.[58]

Meanwhile, the MDC, labour movement and other civil society groups working on democratisation and human rights received both political and financial support from Western governments and donor agencies. Indeed, this support was repeatedly held up by Mugabe as 'proof' of the 'foreign control' of the MDC and the civics in Zimbabwe, an assertion that always avoided the strong national roots of opposition politics in the country.[59] However, the major economic restrictions imposed by the IMF was a result of the Mugabe regime's failure to make repayments to the Bretton Woods institutions in 1999.[60] The political and economic disruptions caused by the Fast Track programme, and the international

[56] B. Z. Mavedzenge, J. Mahenehene, F. Murimbarimba, I. Schoones and W. Wolmer, 'The dynamics of real markets: Cattle in southern Zimbabwe following land reform', *Development and Change*, 39(4), 2008, p. 619.

[57] B. Cousins, 'Reply to Mamdani article in *London Review of Books*, 4 December 2008' (Cape Town: unpublished paper, 2008).

[58] Reuters. 'Factbox – Sanctions on Zimbabwe', 26 Jan. 2009, cited on the *Zimbabwe Situation* <http://www.zimbabwesituation.com/jan27_2009.html>.

[59] McCandless, 'Zimbabwe Forms of Resistance'; Dorman, 'Inclusion and Exclusion'; LeBas, 'Polarization and Party Development'; P. Yeros, 'The Political Economy of Civilisation: Peasant Workers in Zimbabwe and the Neo-colonial World' (Ph.D. thesis, London School of Economics and Political Science, University of London, 2002).

[60] P. Bond, 'Reply to Mamdani' (Durban: unpublished paper, 2008).

implications of this process, impacted disastrously on the rest of the economy, affecting the capacity of social forces in the country to respond to the deepening crisis.

Economic decline and deepening political impasse

The reasons for the cataclysmic decline of the Zimbabwean economy from the late 1990s have both long-term and more contemporary causes. The long-term legacies of colonial resource inequalities, narrow forms of capital accumulation that failed to build a broader productive base, a labour reproduction system based on low wages and migrant labour, and problematic development strategies in both the 'welfarist' 1980s and the neoliberal 1990s provide a schematic historical backdrop to the crisis that unfolded between 1998 and 2008.[61] The more immediate causes lay in a combination of the increased 'threat' around the land reform, the large payouts made to war veterans and the involvement in the conflict in the Democratic Republic of the Congo. The confluence of these issues became manifest on 14 November 1997, when the Zimbabwe dollar lost 74 per cent of its value within a four-hour period.[62]

After 2000, the Zimbabwean economy spiralled rapidly into a world record decline. By 2006 GDP per capita was 47 per cent lower than it was in 1980 and 53 per cent below its 1991 peak.[63] Formal-sector income levels also experienced a drastic decline. At the end of December 2006, the average minimum wage for agriculture and domestic workers of Z$2,800, was only 3 per cent of the Food Datum Line, while the average minimum wage of Z$57,000 in the same period was 16.6 per cent of the Poverty Datum Line, prompting the chief economist of the ZCTU to label these 'starvation wages'. As wages declined, their share in the Gross Domestic Income decreased from an average of 49 per cent between 1985 and 1990, to 41 per cent between 1991 and 1996, and dropping dramatically to 29 per cent between 1997 and 2003. This decline took place in the context of formal-sector employment shrinking from 1.4 million in 1998 to 998,000 in 2004.[64]

[61] For useful discussions on this debate see: P. Bond, 'Competing explanations of Zimbabwe's long economic crisis', *Safundi: The Journal of South African and American Studies*, 8(2), 2007, pp. 149-81; R. Davies, 'Memories of underdevelopment: A personal interpretation of Zimbabwe's economic decline', in Raftopoulos and Savage (eds.), *Zimbabwe: Injustice and Political Reconciliation*, pp. 19-42; Moore, 'Is the land the economy and the economy the land?'.

[62] Bond, 'Competing explanations', p. 170.

[63] P. Robinson, 'Macro-Economic Paper produced for the Zimbabwe Institute' (Cape Town, 2007), p. 4.

[64] G. Kanyenze, 'The Labour Market, Sustainable Growth and Transformation in Zimbabwe' (Harare: unpublished paper, 2007), pp. 31-5.

Hyperinflation reached an official level of 230 million per cent by the end of 2008, devaluing both earnings and savings. Peter Robinson explained the effects of this process on the various classes in the economy:

> Hyperinflation is ... notorious for concentrating incomes in the hands of the rich while impoverishing the poor, often making already highly unequal societies even more divided. In Zimbabwe's case, this undesirable process has been magnified through being accompanied by high levels of patronage. Key resources in a highly distorted environment (such as cheap credit and foreign currency at the official rate) have been allocated to selected individuals and groups, enabling them to amass enormous levels of wealth in a very short space of time. Those with political clout have borrowed heavily from the banks and then declined to pay, waiting for inflation to remove the burden of the original debt and claiming the 'in duplum' rule to evade paying interest. The small depositors bear the cost, in effect subsidizing the rich.[65]

This process contributed to the share of profit in Gross Domestic Income rising from an average of 50 per cent between 1985 and 1990 to 73 per cent between 1997 and 2003, while the estimate of Zimbabweans living below the Poverty Datum Line was 85 per cent in 2006.[66] The combination of the agrarian crisis, formal-sector employment decline and the growing informalisation of the economy created huge challenges for workers. The loss of formal-labour remittances to rural households severely impacted on the capacity of rural-urban linkages to be maintained, and thus affected the food security of both rural and urban families.

The colonial political economy of indirect consumer subsidies of food, and low wages, was replaced in this period by hyperinflation and rapidly decreasing real wages.[67] This vulnerability of labour was greatly exacerbated by the government's Operation Murambatsvina (translated as 'clear out the filth') in May 2005, a massive onslaught on the informal sector carried out as a militarised urban 'clean-up'. A UN report estimated that 650,000-700,000 people were directly affected by the operation, and a further 1.7 million indirectly by its economic effects.[68]

---

[65] Robinson, 'Macro-Economic Paper', p. 15.

[66] Kanyenze, 'The Labour Market', p. 32.

[67] L. Cliffe and B. Raftopoulos, 'An Assessment and Review of the Joint Donor Review of Food Aid in Zimbabwe (Leeds and Cape Town: EC/ECHO, USAID, DFID, 2007).

[68] United Nations, 'Report of the Fact-Finding Mission to Zimbabwe to Assess the Scope and Impact of Operation Murambatsvina by the UN Special Envoy on Human Settlements Issues in Zimbabwe Mrs. Anna Kajumulo Tibaijuka' (UN, 2005); L. M. Sachikonye, 'The Impact of Operation Murambatsvina/Clean Up on the Working People in Zimbabwe' (Harare: Report prepared for the Labour and Economic Development Research Institute of Zimbabwe, 2006).

Several reasons were suggested for the operation: punishment of the urban areas for their consistent support of the MDC after 2000; an adherence to urban planning that was technocratic, bureaucratic and modernist; and a desire to decrease the presence of the poor in the cities

Fig. 7.4: A woman is forced to destroy her own home in Operation Murambatsvina.

[*Photo:* Edwina Spicer/Solidarity Peace Trust]

because of an incapacity to provide sufficient food and fuel for them.[69] Operation Murambatsvina was based on an assumption that those pushed out of the urban areas could 'return' to homes in the rural areas, but by 2001 half of them were urban-born and did not have a rural home to return to.[70]

The other side of this impoverishment was the adoption of what Rob Davies called a 'pure *rentier* economy', in which the ruling party created incentives for trading goods in short supply 'not only as a way to become rich but also as virtually the only way to survive'. The rewards for long-term investment in production were minuscule compared to the rapid profits of buying cheap and selling dear.[71] Additionally, the informalisation of production structures that intensified in this period also provided new opportunities for entrepreneurs with links to the party and the state to accumulate wealth in the gold- and diamond-mining sectors. In such sectors reliance on the state's monopoly of coercion

[69] D. Potts, '"Restoring order"? Operation Murambatsvina and the urban crisis in Zimbabwe', *Journal of Southern African Studies*, 32(2), 2006, pp. 273-91; A. Kamete, 'Cold-hearted, negligent and spineless? Planning, planners and the (r)ejection of "filth" in urban Zimbabwe', *International Planning Studies*, 12(2), 2007, pp. 153-71.

[70] D. Potts, '"You must go home": Manipulating narratives of rural linkages for Operation Murambatsvina', Paper presented at the Conference on 'Political Economies of Displacement in Post-2000 Zimbabwe', University of the Witwatersrand, 9-11 June 2008.

[71] R. Davies, 'Economic Recovery in Zimbabwe' (Harare: unpublished paper, 2008).

and selective law enforcement was a central factor in this race for riches.[72] As one report on the 'diamond rush' in the Marange area of Manicaland province noted,

> A prison official in Mutare said top figures in the ruling ZANU-PF party and security officials are running the illegal diamond trade here.
>
> 'The people in the police, prisons service, army and CIO [Central Intelligence Organization] have got groups of people who are working for those lieutenants, known as syndicates,' says the official. 'Usually these high-ranked officers in the armed forces are working for the ministers, governors and other ZANU-PF bigwigs.'[73]

However, even as the elite scrambled for these informal mining deposits under the guise of 'indigenisation', the large-scale mining operations remained under foreign control and domination.[74]

Another major effect of the economic meltdown in the country, in particular of the dizzying speed of hyperinflation, was the rapid loss of value of the Zimbabwean currency and the resulting 'dollarisation' of economic transactions. As the Zimbabwe dollar lost its value, those with the capacity to do so transferred a significant share of their assets into foreign currency; and as goods and services were increasingly available only for foreign currency, more people left the country. Zimbabwe has a long history of migration: to the South African mines and cities during the colonial period; from the mid-1980s as a result of the Gukurahundi killings in Matabeleland and the Midlands; and from drought-prone areas such as Masvingo, Midlands and Matabeleland South. However, it was only after 2000 that large numbers left as a result of political violence, forced removals and the general economic meltdown. Estimates of the numbers involved range from one to three million, and the main destinations were South Africa, Botswana, the UK and the USA.

---

[72] S. Mawowa, 'Crisis, State and Accumulation in Zimbabwe' (MA Thesis, University of Kwa-Zulu Natal, 2007).

[73] Robyn Dixon, 'Zimbabwe's deadly diamond fever', *Los Angeles Times*, 4 Dec. 2008.

[74] R. Saunders, 'Painful paradoxes: Mining, crisis and regional capital in Zimbabwe', *At Issue EZINE*, 8(4), 2008, pp. 17-49, available at <http://www.africafiles.org/atissueezine. asp?issue=issue8#art3>; Solidarity Peace Trust, *A Difficult Dialogue: Zimbabwe-South Africa Economic Relations since 2000* (Johannesburg, 2007).

As these migrant workers – *majoni-joni/amadouble-up*[75] – found ways to survive and make their livelihoods in other countries, they drew on the historical networks that first emerged during the colonial period. Burial societies, church organisations, social football clubs, and shebeens were all key focuses of social support and solidarity during colonial rule.[76] After 2000, Zimbabwean migrants set up burial societies such as the Masasane, Maranda and Mberengwa in Johannesburg and Pretoria, while the Zionist churches provided important support structures, especially for women. In more informal settings 'boozers' soccer' clubs and shebeens provided space for social interaction and an exchange of information about home.[77] Of vital importance were the remittances that such workers sent back to their families, which became an essential part of the survival strategies of such families. In 2005/6 it was estimated that half of the families in the two major cities in Zimbabwe were in receipt of remittances from workers in the diaspora,[78] while a study of Zimbabweans in Leeds, UK, reported that over 80 per cent of respondents were sending 'everyday necessities' back to their families.[79]

Migrants to South Africa developed a variety of responses to issues of citizenship and identity, ranging from calls for regional citizenship and pan-Africanism to attempts at assimilation into South Africa by those with strong cultural and linguistic ties to the country. Others vied for more particularistic ethnic claims

[75] This section draws heavily on the work of James Muzondidya, 'Majoni-Joni: Survival Strategies among Zimbabwean Migrants in South Africa', Paper presented at the International Conference on the Political Economies of Displacement in Zimbabwe', University of the Witwatersrand, 9-11 June 2008. As Muzondidya explains, the term *majoni-joni* is derived from 'the popular belief that all migrants heading for South Africa work in Johannesburg (*Joni*). The term has historical resonance going back to the days of colonial migration, and it is widely used by both migrants and locals based in Zimbabwe. In the Ndebele-speaking parts of the country, unskilled Zimbabweans in South Africa are called *"amadouble-up"*, a term referring to their use of informal routes and channels to get to their destination', p. 17. See also Solidarity Peace Trust, *No War in Zimbabwe: An Account of the Exodus of a Nation's People* (Johannesburg, November 2004). For Zimbabwean migrants in the UK, see, J. McGregor, '"Joining the BBC (British Bottom Cleaners)": Zimbabwean migrants and the UK care industry', *Journal of Ethnic and Migration Studies*, 33(5), 2007, pp. 801-24.

[76] T. Yoshikuni, *African Urban Experiences in Colonial Zimbabwe: A Social History of Harare before 1925,* (Harare: Weaver Press, 2006); T. Yoshikuni, *African Urban Experiences in Colonial Zimbabwe: A Social History of Harare before the Mid-20th Century* (Tokyo: Impact Shuppankai, 2005).

[77] J. Muzondidya, 'Majoni-Joni'.

[78] S. Bracking and L. Sachikonye, *Remittances, Poverty Reduction and Informalisation in Zimbabwe 2005-6: A Political Economy of Dispossession?* Brooks World Poverty Institute Working Paper No. 28, 9 Sept. 2008. Available at SSRN: <http://ssrn.com/abstract=1265516>.

[79] F. Magunha, A. Bailey and L. Cliffe, 'Remittance Strategies of Zimbabweans in Northern England' (University of Leeds, 2009).

or a revived 'patriotic nationalism' in which national symbols were fervently embraced in response to continued xenophobia and racism. The widespread xenophobic violence that broke out in South Africa in the first half of 2008 only enhanced such patriotic sentiments.[80] Zimbabweans working on farms in the border zone faced competing claims of authority and sovereignty over their status from South African farmers and the state, even as they attempted to find ways to fight for their rights in conditions of such vulnerability.[81] All these indicators of economic decline evoked no constructive response from the Zimbabwean state, and not even its 'Look East' policy, in particular the reliance on Chinese investment, could reverse the trend.

Under these conditions of rapid economic deterioration both the MDC and the civil society movement faced severe challenges in confronting the Mugabe regime. For the MDC – increasingly frustrated by electoral violence and irregularities, harassment, torture and murder of party officials and parliamentarians, the arrest of its leadership, and constant vilification in the media as 'foreign agents', 'unpatriotic' and outsiders in 'legitimate national politics' – the task of winning state power through electoral means looked remote. In the urban areas, where MDC support was dominant and where it consistently won parliamentary and local government elections between 2000 and 2008, the ruling party carried out a concerted campaign to undermine the democratic vote.

Through the abuse of such laws as the Urban Councils Act [*Chapter 29:15*], the Public Order and Security Act, the Constitution of Zimbabwe, the Electoral Act [*Chapter 2:01*] and the Provincial Councils and Administration Act [*Chapter 29:11*], the ruling party either removed or intimidated MDC councils and mayors, and used its vast powers to 'interfere in local affairs in order to modify, cripple or destroy local councils'.[82] Civic organisations such as the Combined Harare Residents' Association (CHRA) fought long legal and civic struggles with the central state to enforce the democratic rights of urban citizens who were characterised by the ruling party as 'totemless strangers' and were a persistent

---

[80] J. Muzondidya, 'Makwerekwere: Migration, Citizenship and Identity among Zimbabweans in South Africa', in J. McGregor and R. Primorac (eds.), *Displacement and Survival: Zimbabwe's Diasporic Identities and Connections* (Oxford: Berghahn, forthcoming).

[81] B. Rutherford, 'Zimbabweans living in the South African border-zone: Negotiating, suffering and surviving', *Association of Concerned African Scholars*, 80, 2008, pp. 36-42. Available at <http://concernedafricascholars.org/docs/acasbulletin80-6.pdf>.

[82] A. Kamete, 'The return of the jettisoned: ZANU-PF's crack at "re-urbanising" in Harare', *Journal of Southern African Studies*, 32(2), 2006, p. 270; A. Kamete, 'In defence of national sovereignty? Urban governance and democracy in Zimbabwe', *Journal of Contemporary African Studies*, 21(2), 2003, pp. 193-213.

threat to ZANU(PF) rule.[83] While during the colonial period the central state was confronted with stubborn local councils determined to protect only the rights of white residents, CHRA and the MDC faced an authoritarian state determined to enforce its rule against the democratic mandate. Thus the battle for control and representation between central and local governments was part of a longer history of such struggles in Zimbabwe.[84]

The strategic dilemma of confronting a violent, authoritarian regime through peaceful means also resulted in a build-up of major tensions within the opposition: issues of accountability, capacity, strategy, intra-party violence and ethnicity became zones of contestation, leading to a split in the party in 2005. The immediate cause given for the split was the decision to participate in a Senate election called by ZANU(PF) for 2006. However, the broader problems mentioned above were major factors, and they continued to challenge the viability of the party after the division. In 2006, two MDC formations came into existence, the larger led by Morgan Tsvangirai and the other by former student leader Arthur Mutambara, with most of the civic movement and popular sentiment going behind the Tsvangirai party.[85]

While the MDC faced these obstacles, its civil society allies were being worn down by both the repression of the state and the corrosive effects of economic deterioration. The ZCTU lost much of its impetus after 2000 owing to state harassment, employment shrinkage and declining union membership (down from 16 per cent of the labour force in 1990 to 12 per cent in 2000).[86] The Zimbabwe Federation of Trade Unions, established by the ruling party in 2000, also weakened the ZCTU by creating splinter unions in nine sectors of the economy: furniture and timber, engineering, catering, leather, clothing, commerce, agriculture, sugar plantations and construction.[87] The general informalisation of the economy made it extremely difficult for the labour movement to organise, as informal sector workers turned to various methods of survival in the 'kukiya-kiya economy', which Jones describes as 'the space of suspension, where

[83] Mike Davies [Chair of CHRA], 'Citizens or Subjects? Housing Rights in Zimbabwe'. Paper presented at the World Social Forum, Nairobi, January 2007.

[84] T. Ranger, 'City versus state in Zimbabwe: Colonial antecedents of current crisis', *Journal of East African Studies*, 1(2), 2007, pp. 161-92.

[85] B. Raftopoulos, 'Reflections on opposition politics in Zimbabwe: The politics of the Movement for Democratic Change (MDC)', in B. Raftopoulos and K. Alexander (eds.), *Reflections on Democratic Politics in Zimbabwe* (Cape Town: IJR, 2006), pp. 6-29.

[86] Kanyenze and Chiripanhura, 'The State of Union Organisation'.

[87] ZCTU, 'Annual Report of the Organising Department for the year ended 2004'.

normal rules and/or procedures do not necessarily apply'.[88] In this context of growing reliance on individualised strategies of survival, the public strikes and stay-aways deployed so effectively in the 1990s became much more difficult to organise after 2000. This diminished capacity to organise and mobilise workers and other citizens affected other civic bodies like the NCA, Women of Zimbabwe Arise (WOZA) and the Crisis in Zimbabwe Coalition, whose persistent attempts to demonstrate against the state were characterised more by the bravery of their leaders and membership than by their capacity to mobilise people in large numbers. The growing debilitation of the social base of the opposition was exacerbated by the humanitarian crisis that emerged around the cholera epidemic in the last quarter of 2008. As a result of the state's incapacity to supply clean water and the breakdown of the public health system, the humanitarian crisis effectively signalled the loss of the state's capacity to provide basic services for its citizens. A report by the Physicians for Human Rights wrote of the crisis as follows:

> The health and healthcare crisis in Zimbabwe is a direct outcome of the malfeasance of the Mugabe regime and the systematic violation of a wide range of human rights, including the right to participate in government and in free elections and egregious failure to respect, protect and fulfill the right to health.[89]

This continuing deterioration resulted in a palpable loss of hope that was vividly captured in Valerie Tagwira's novel, *The Uncertainty of Hope*. Exhausted from talking about the fallout from Operation Murambatsvina, Katy says in exasperation: 'Isn't there something else we can talk about? What can we say or do to change anything, anyway?'[90] The seemingly hopeless condition of the unfortunate heroine of the story is rescued by the philanthropic intervention of a businessman against the background of the apparent defeat of forces for change in the country. Tagwira's plot provides a good example of what Eagleton calls 'a kind of providential redemption of the bunglings and injustices of everyday life.'[91]

In the politics of this period such 'redemption' emerged out of the continued political struggles in the country. During the years covered in this chapter, the

---

[88] J. Jones, '"Nothing is Straight in Zimbabwe": The Rise of Kukiya-kiya Economy 2000-2008'. Paper presented at the International Conference on the Political Economies of Displacement in post-2000 Zimbabwe, 2008), p. 15.

[89] Physicians for Human Rights, *Health in Ruins: A Man-Made Disaster in Zimbabwe* (Cambridge MA: Physicians for Human Rights, 2008/09), p. viii.

[90] V. Tagwira, *The Uncertainty of Hope* (Harare: Weaver Press, 2006).

[91] T. Eagleton, *The English Novel: An Introduction* (Oxford: Blackwell, 2005), p. 60.

church was largely divided over the politics of the state; some key players in the major churches were drawn to Mugabe's nationalism, others towards the critical civic movement, while growing congregations like the Pentecostals drew on their doctrines to 'make the best of rapid social change'.[92] In March 2007 the police brutally disrupted a prayer meeting organised by the Christian Alliance in the high-density Harare suburb of Highfield; leaders of the MDC and the civic movement as well as fifty others attending the meeting were arrested and beaten up. The incident received worldwide publicity, indicating once again the repressive nature of the Mugabe regime as well as the sense of impunity demonstrated by the state. While ZANU(PF) had since 2004 been embroiled in its own succession battles, exemplified by the attempt to remove Mugabe through the Mnangagwa-inspired 'Tsholotsho plot' in that year, the ruling party was united in its repression against the opposition; notwithstanding its Byzantine power struggles, the ruling party's brutal response to opposition politics remained undiminished.[93]

Mediation, electoral crisis and political agreement

The global coverage of this event, and the resultant renewed international pressure on the Mugabe government, pushed SADC into a new effort to deal with the Zimbabwe crisis. From the beginning of his presidency South African President Thabo Mbeki adopted what became known as 'quiet diplomacy'. In political terms this meant attempting to walk the tightrope of 'keeping South Africa's continental ambitions alive [by not coming out in opposition to Mugabe] without totally sacrificing Western support'.[94] In 2002, in conjunction with the Nigerian government, Mbeki initiated a dialogue between ZANU(PF) and the MDC, which did not make much headway. Under the changed conditions after the March 2007 events in Harare, Mbeki received a mandate from an Extraordinary Summit of SADC held in Tanzania on 29 March, to facilitate dialogue in Zimbabwe between the major political parties. The central objective of the facilitation was to create the conditions for broadly acceptable elections in the country that would, in Mbeki's words,

---

[92] D. Maxwell, '"Delivered from the spirit of poverty?" Pentecostalism, prosperity and modernity in Zimbabwe', *Journal of Religious Affairs*, 28(3), 1998, p. 351. For the divided role of the church, see W. Anderson, 'The Role of the Church in Zimbabwe: A Willing Servant' (Unpublished paper, 2008).

[93] E. Masunungure, 'The Dynamics of ZANU(PF) in the Post-Tsholotsho Phase' (Zimbabwe Institute, Cape Town, 2006).

[94] L. Freeman, 'South Africa's Zimbabwe policy: Unravelling the contradictions', *Journal of Contemporary African Studies*, 23(2), 2005, p. 156.

Fig. 7.5: MDC and civic leaders are released from custody
after severe beatings by the security services on 11 March 2007.
Left to right (foreground): Arthur Mutambara, Morgan Tsvangirai,
Lovemore Madhuku and Tendai Biti.

[*Photo:* Edwina Spicer]

begin the process leading to the normalisation of the situation
in Zimbabwe and the resumption of its development and
reconstruction process intended to achieve a better life for all
Zimbabweans on a sustained and sustainable basis.[95]

After a long-drawn-out process that involved distrust, recriminations between
the parties, growing tension between Mbeki and Tsvangirai, disagreements
within the ANC alliance in South Africa, and continued diplomatic pressure
from the West on SADC, some progress was made by the end of 2007 towards
creating conditions for a reasonable election to be held in 2008. Though serious
disagreements remained over the conditions for free and fair elections, one key
reform agreed on in the mediation was the requirement that voting results be
posted outside polling booths to ensure greater transparency. This was to prove

[95] Letter from President Thabo Mbeki to Morgan Tsvangirai and Arthur Mutambara, copied
to Robert Mugabe, 4 April 2007.

vital for the MDC in the March 2008 parliamentary, local government and presidential elections.[96]

The elections took place in the context of the SADC mediation and with relatively little violence. After a month's delay in the release of the results, it became clear that for the first time in its 28 years in government ZANU(PF) had lost its parliamentary majority. The combined MDC won 109 seats against ZANU(PF)'s 97, while the presidential vote failed to deliver a decisive winner with a '50 per cent plus one' majority, thus requiring a run-off election. Tsvangirai polled 47.9 per cent of the vote to Mugabe's 43.2 per cent. ZANU(PF)'s loss was a result both of divisions in the party and its growing loss of legitimacy amongst the electorate. The defection of former stalwart Simba Makoni to stand as an independent presidential candidate showed the fissures in the ruling party and opened the political space for the election, even though it did not translate into a political victory for Makoni himself. Despite the fact that the combined MDC won the parliamentary elections, its divided participation probably prevented an even larger victory.

It was, however, the violence that preceded the presidential run-off at the end of June, that plunged the country into further political uncertainty. The violence inflicted by the ruling party on the electorate, as punishment for its loss in the March election and as a warning against the repeat of such a vote, was the worst seen in the country since the Gukurahundi massacres in the mid-1980s. Directed by the Joint Operations Command of the armed forces, most of the violence took place in the three Mashonaland provinces, former strongholds of ZANU(PF).[97] Faced with this widespread violence, MDC candidate Tsvangirai withdrew from the run-off, signalling a universal lack of recognition for Mugabe's resulting solo 'victory'.

The period between July and December was marked by further SADC attempts to bring finality to the mediation efforts, with strong criticism from the West, as well as from church and civic bodies in Zimbabwe and the southern Africa region, about the perceived complicity of SADC in not bringing stronger pressure to bear in ending Mugabe's rule. Both ZANU(PF) and the MDCs faced limited options outside of the mediation process. While the former retained the monopoly of coercive force in the country, it had little prospect of dealing with

[96] For a discussion of the SADC mediation and the processes leading up to the harmonised elections in March 2008, see Solidarity Peace Trust, *Punishing Dissent, Silencing Citizens: The Zimbabwe Elections 2008*, (Johannesburg, May 2008).

[97] Solidarity Peace Trust, *Desperately Seeking Sanity: What Prospects for a New Beginning in Zimbabwe?*, (Johannesburg, July 2008); J. Alexander and B-M. Tendi, 'A tale of two elections: Zimbabwe at the polls in 2008', *Association for Concerned African Scholars Bulletin*, 80, 2008, pp. 5-17. Available at <http://concernedafricascholars.org/docs/acasbulletin80-2.pdf>

Fig. 7.6: Mugabe Must Go!   *[Photo:* Annie Mpalume]

the unfolding economic and humanitarian disasters. The MDC, while strongly supported by the West and civic bodies in the region, continued to face suspicion in SADC, where regional governments refused to go beyond Mbeki's 'quiet diplomacy' strategy. The political settlement that was signed by the two MDC formations and ZANU(PF) under the SADC mediation on 11 September 2008 thus represented the outcome of this balance of forces and the threat of a deepening political quagmire that was the likely alternative to such an agreement.[98]

The terms of the agreement left Mugabe very much in control of the security apparatus of the state, but also gave the MDC a share of political power in an envisaged inclusive government. It took another four month for the parties to agree on the final sharing of power, amidst more SADC summits and pressure from the West and the UN. In January 2009 the political parties finally agreed to form an inclusive government. The agreement presented severe threats and opportunities, seemingly unresolvable contradictions, and a small opening for moving beyond the political impasse. It continued to have its critics and opponents both in ZANU(PF) and the MDC, with most in the civic movement unconvinced by the settlement. Thus it was not surprising that, on publicly

[98] B. Raftopoulos, 'Elections, mediation and deadlock in Zimbabwe?', *Real Instituto Elcano*, 119, 2008, pp. 1-7. Available at <http://www.realinstitutoelcano.org/wps/portal/rielcano_eng/ Content?WCM_GLOBAL_CONTEXT=/Elcano_in/Zonas_in/ARI119-2008>.

declaring his decision to join the inclusive government, Morgan Tsvangirai's statement was marked by the nervous optimism of his decision and the weight of historic expectations and doubts that he carried:

> Let us make no mistake, by joining an inclusive government, we are not saying that this is a solution to the Zimbabwe crisis, instead our participation signifies that we have chosen to continue the struggle for a democratic Zimbabwe in a new arena. This agreement is a significant milestone on our journey to democracy but it does not signify that we have arrived at our destination – we are committed to establishing a democratic Zimbabwe regardless of how long that struggle takes us.[99]

Conclusion

This final chapter tracked the explosion of ideas of sovereignty, nationalism, citizenship and belonging that marked this period, with the politics of land occupations, 'patriotic nationalism', civil and constitutional rights, contesting and reshaping the meanings of these terms in the context of crisis. From the first decade and a half of independence in which the language and politics of modernisation, development and bureaucratic regularity dominated the discourse of the nation, the politics of the crisis period brought to the fore the fact that throughout Zimbabwe's history there has been, as Hammar and other scholars have shown, an 'intimate and sustained' relationship between displacements of various forms, violent assertions of sovereignty and the making of the state.[100]

The failure of ESAP in the 1990s brought with it a descent into authoritarian politics, and as the informal economy became the dominant form of production, the ruling party created a state based less on formal bureaucratic procedures than on the politics of coercion and the politics of patronage. In such conditions of a failing market economy, popular organisations like the labour movement that had built their structures in the conditions and regulation of the formal economy had to contend with a declining membership that was forced to eke out a livelihood in the more desperate conditions of the informal sector. As the state singled out particular groups for demonisation in the name of sovereignty, opposing ideas of citizenship and nation emerged from the political opposition and civic movement. While the state fought its political struggles through a repressive

[99] D. Muleya and H. Radebe, 'MDC to join government', *The Weekender*, 31 Jan. 2009.

[100] A. Hammar, 'Reflections on displacement in Zimbabwe', *Association of Concerned African Scholars Bulletin*, 80, 2008, pp. 28-35, available at <http://concernedafricascholars.org/docs/acasbulletin80-5.pdf>, and 'In the name of sovereignty: Displacement and state making in post-independence Zimbabwe', *Journal of Contemporary African Studies*, 26(4), 2008, pp. 417-34.

nationalism and an appeal to a broader pan-Africanist tradition, opposition groups relied on the liberal notions of rights and democratic accountability. In a region only recently emerging from settler colonial domination it took some time for the realities of repression underlying the Mugabe regime to become part of a critical debate. The displacement of the Zimbabwe crisis into other southern African countries, and the spread of Zimbabwe's humanitarian disaster in the region, added urgency to the region's attempts to find a 'settlement' to the Zimbabwe question.

While a formal political agreement was established at the beginning of 2009, the political and economic challenges that confronted the country were formidable. Amongst the most urgent was the task of building new, more tolerant forms of citizenship and nation, as the millions who had been subjected to the brutishness of ZANU(PF)'s politics of sovereignty yearned to add democratic credentials to that notion.

Bibliography

Agamben, G. *Homo Sacer: Sovereign Power and Bare Life* (Palo Alto, CA: Stanford University Press, 1998).

Alao, A. *Brothers at War: Dissidence and Rebellion in Southern Africa* (London: Zed Books, 1994).

Alexander, J. 'Dissident perspectives of Zimbabwe's post-independence war', *Africa: Journal of International African Institute*, 68(2), 1998.

Alexander, J. *The Unsettled Land: State-making and the Politics of Land in Zimbabwe, 1893-2003* (Harare: Weaver Press; Oxford: James Currey, 2006).

Alexander, J., J. McGregor and T. O. Ranger *Violence and Memory: One Hundred Years in the 'Dark Forests' of Matabeleland* (Harare: Weaver Press; Oxford: James Currey, 2000).

Amanor-Wilks, D. *Zimbabwe's Farm Workers and the New Constitution*, 2000, available at <http://www.africaaction.org/rtable/ed0002.htm>.

Arnold, J. R. and R. Wienar *Robert Mugabe's Zimbabwe* (Brookfield, CT: Twenty-First Century Books, 2007).

Astrow, A. *Zimbabwe: A Revolution that Lost Its Way?* (London: Zed Books, 1983).

Banana, C. *The Politics of Repression and Resistance* (Gweru: Mambo Press, 1996).

Banana, C. (ed.) *Turmoil and Tenacity* (Harare: College Press, 1989).

Bannerman, J. H. 'Hlengweni: The history of the Hlengweni of the lower Save and Lundi rivers from the late 18th century to the mid-20th century', *Zimbabwean History*, 12, 1981.

Barnes, T. '"So that a labourer could live with his family": Overlooked factors in social and economic strife in urban colonial Zimbabwe, 1945-52', *Journal of Southern African Studies*, 21(1), 1995.

Barnes, T. *'We Women Worked So Hard': Gender, Urbanization, and Social Reproduction in Colonial Harare, Zimbabwe, 1930-1956* (Portsmouth, NH: Heinemann; Oxford: James Currey, 1999).

Barnes, T. and E. Win, *To Live a Better Life: An Oral History of Women in Harare, 1930-70* (Harare: Baobab Books, 1992).

Beach, D. N. '"Chimurenga": The Shona Rising of 1896-97', *Journal of African History*, 20(3), 1979.

Beach, D. N. *Mapondera: Heroism and History in Northern Zimbabwe, 1840-1904* (Gweru: Mambo Press, 1989).

Beach, D. N. 'Second thoughts on the Shona economy: Suggestions for further research', *Rhodesian History*, 7, 1976.

Beach, D. N. *The Shona and Zimbabwe, 900-1850* (Gwelo: Mambo Press, 1980).

Beach, D. N. *The Shona and their Neighbours* (Oxford: Blackwell, 1994).

Beach, D. N. *War and Politics in Zimbabwe, 1840-1900* (Gweru: Mambo Press, 1986).

Beach, D. N. *Zimbabwe before 1900* (Gweru: Mambo Press, 1984).

Beach, D. N. *A Zimbabwean Past* (Gweru: Mambo Press, 1994).

Beinart W. and J. McGregor (eds.) *Social History and African Environments* (Oxford: James Currey, 2003).

Berman, B., D. Eyoh and W. Kymlicka (eds.), *Ethnicity and Democracy in Africa* (Oxford: James Currey, 2004).

Bhabha, H. K. *The Location of Culture* (London: Routledge, 2nd. edn., 2004).

Bhebe, N. *Benjamin Burombo: African Politics in Colonial Zimbabwe, 1945-1958* (Harare: College Press, 1989).

Bhebe, N. M. *Christianity and Traditional Religion in Western Zimbabwe* (London: Longman, 1979).

Bhebe, N. 'Ndebele trade in the nineteenth century', *Journal of African Studies*, 1(2), 1974.

Bhebe, N. *Simon Vengayi Muzenda and the Struggle for and Liberation of Zimbabwe* (Gweru: Mambo Press, 2004).

Bhebe, N. M. B. 'Some aspects of Ndebele relations with the Shona in the 19th century', *Rhodesian History*, 4, 1973.

Bhebe, N. *ZAPU and ZANU Guerrilla Warfare and the Evangelical Lutheran Church in Zimbabwe* (Gweru: Mambo Press, 1999).

Bhebe N. and T. O. Ranger (eds.) *The Historical Dimensions of Democracy and Human Rights in Zimbabwe, Volume One: Pre-Colonial and Colonial Legacies* (Harare: University of Zimbabwe Publications, 2001).

Bhebe, N. and T. Ranger (eds.) *Society in Zimbabwe's Liberation War* (Harare: University of Zimbabwe Publications; London: James Currey, 1996).

Bhebe, N. and T. Ranger (eds.) *Soldiers in Zimbabwe's Liberation War* (Harare: University of Zimbabwe Publications; London: James Currey, 1995).

Bhila, H. H. K. *Trade and Politics in a Shona Kingdom: The Manyika and Their Portuguese and African Neighbours, 1575-1902* (Harlow: Longman, 1982).

Blake, R. *A History of Rhodesia* (London: Eyre Methuen, 1977).

Blennerhassett, Rose and Lucy Sleeman *Adventures in Mashonaland* (Bulawayo: Books of Rhodesia, 1969 [1893]).

Bloomfield, D., T. Barnes and L. Huyse (eds.) *Reconciliation after Violent Conflict: A Handbook* (Stockholm: International Institute for Democracy and Electoral Assistance, 2003).

Boahen, A. A. *African Perspectives of Colonialism* (London: James Currey, 1989).

Bond, P. *Uneven Zimbabwe: A Study of Finance, Development and Underdevelopment* (Trenton, NJ: Africa World Press, 1998).

Bond, Patrick and Masimba Manyanya *Zimbabwe's Plunge: Exhausted Nationalism, Neoliberalism, and the Search for Social Justice* (Harare: Weaver Press; London: Merlin, 2nd edn., 2003).

Bowman, L. W. *Politics in Rhodesia: White Power in an African State* (Cambridge, MA: Harvard University Press, 1973).

Bratton, M. 'Settler state, guerrilla war and rural underdevelopment in Rhodesia', *Issue: A Journal of Opinion*, 9(1/2), 1979.

Broch-Due, V. (ed.) *Violence and Belonging: The Quest for Identity in Post-Colonial Africa* (London: Routledge, 2005).

Bullock, C. *The Mashona* (Cape Town: Juta, 1928).

Burden, G. N. *Nyasaland Native Labour in Southern Rhodesia* (Salisbury: [n.p.], 1938).

Burdette, M. and R. J. Davies 'The Zimbabwe economy: Prognostications and realities after six years', *Zambezia*, 14(1), 1987.

Burke, T. *Lifebouy Men, Lux Women* (Durham, NC: Duke University Press, 1996).

Campbell, H. *Reclaiming Zimbabwe: The Exhaustion of the Patriarchal Model of Liberation* (Cape Town: David Philip, 2003).

Catholic Commission for Justice and Peace in Zimbabwe and Legal Resources Foundation *Breaking the Silence, Building True Peace: Report on the Disturbances in Matabeleland and the Midlands, 1980-1989* (Harare: CCJPZ and LRF, 1997).

Caute, D. *Under the Skin: The Death of White Rhodesia* (Evanston, IL: Northwestern University Press; London: Allen Lane, 1983).

Chan, S. *Robert Mugabe: A Life of Power and Violence* (Michigan: University of Michigan Press, 2003).

Chanaiwa, D. 'Politics and long distance trade in the Mwene Mutapa empire during the sixteenth century', *The International Journal of African Historical Studies*, 5(3), 1972.

Chaza, G. A. *Bhurakuwacha: Black Policeman in Rhodesia* (Harare: College Press, 1998).

Chinodya, S. *Harvest of Thorns* (Harare: Baobab Books, 1989).

Chirikure, C. *Rukuvhute: Muunganidzwa weNhetembo* (Harare: College Press, 1989).

Chitiyo, T. K. 'Zimbabwe's military historiography', *Southern African Diaspora Review*, 1(Summer), 2006.

Chiundura-Moyo, A. *Kuridza Ngoma Nedemo* (Harare: Zimbabwe Publishing House, 1985).

Chiwome, E. M. *Masango Mavi* (Gweru: Mambo Press, 1998).

Chung, F. *Re-living the Second Chimurenga: Memories from Zimbabwe's Liberation Struggle* (Harare: Weaver Press, 2005).

Clarke, D. G. *Contract Workers and Underdevelopment in Rhodesia* (Gwelo: Mambo Press, 1974).

Clarke, D. G. 'Settler ideology and the African underdevelopment in post-war Rhodesia', *Rhodesia Journal of Economics*, 8(1), 1974.

Clements, Frank *Rhodesia: The Course to Collision* (London: Pall Mall Press, 1969).

Cobbing, J. 'The absent priesthood: Another look at the Rhodesian rising of 1896-1897', *Journal of African History*, 18(1), 1977.

Cobbing, J. R. D. 'The Ndebele under the Khumalos' (Ph.D. thesis, University of Lancaster, 1976).

Cobbing, J. 'Review article: Imperialising of Zimbabwe', *Transformation*, Vol. 9, 1999.

Coillard, F. *On the Threshold of Central Africa* (London: Frank Cass, 1897).

Comaroff, Jean *Body of Power, Spirit of Resistance: The Culture and History of a South African People* (Chicago: University of Chicago Press, 1985).

Comaroff, John L. and Jean Comaroff *Of Revelation and Revolution: The Dialectics of Modernity on a South African Frontier: Volume Two* (Chicago: University of Chicago Press, 1997).

Cooper, F. *Colonialism in Question: Theory, Knowledge, History* (Berkeley and Los Angeles: University of California Press, 2005).

Cooper, Frederick *Decolonization and African Society: The Labour Question in French and British Africa* (Cambridge: Cambridge University Press, 1996).

Cooper, F. and A. Stoler (eds.) *Tensions of Empire: Colonial Cultures in a Bourgeois World* (Berkeley: University of California Press, 1997).

Cosmin, B. A. 'The Pioneer Community of Salisbury in November 1897', *Rhodesian History*, 2, 1971.

Creighton, T. R. M. *The Anatomy of Partnership: Southern Rhodesia and the Central African Federation* (London: Faber, 1960).

Crummey, D. (ed.) *Banditry, Rebellion and Social Protest in Africa* (London: James Currey, 1986).

Daneel, M. *The God of the Matopo Hills* (The Hague: Mouton, 1970).

Dangarembga, T. *The Book of Not* (Banbury: Ayebia Clarke Publishing, 2006).

Darnolf, S. and L. Laakso (eds.) *Twenty Years of Independence in Zimbabwe: From Liberation to Authoritarianism* (Basingstoke: Palgrave Macmillan, 2003).

Day, John *International Nationalism* (London: Routledge, 1967).

De Roche, A. *Black, White and Chrome: The United States and Zimbabwe, 1953-1998* (Trenton, NJ: Africa World Press, 2001).

Diamond, L., J. Linz and S. Lipset (eds.) *Democracy in Developing Countries: Vol. 2, Africa* (Boulder, CO: Lynne Rienner, 1988).

Dixon, J. and S. Reicher 'Intergroup contact and desegregation in the New South Africa', *British Journal of Social Psychology*, 36, 1997.

Dorey, Anne *The Victoria Incident and the Anglo-Matabele War of 1893* (Salisbury: Central African Historical Association, Local Series No. 16, 1966).

Dorman, S. R. 'NGOs and the constitutional debate in Zimbabwe: From inclusion to exclusion', *Journal of Southern African Studies*, 29(4), 2003.

Dorman, S. R. '"Rocking the boat?" Church NGOs and democratization in Zimbabwe', *African Affairs*, 101, 2002.

Dorman, S., D. Hammett and P. Nugent (eds.) *Making Nations, Creating Strangers* (Leiden and Boston: Brill, 2007).

Drinkwater, M. 'Technical development and peasant impoverishment: Land use policy in Zimbabwe's Midlands province', *Journal of Southern African Studies*, 15(2), 1989.

Dumbutshena, E. *Zimbabwe Tragedy* (Nairobi: East African Publishing House, 1975).

Economist Intelligence Unit, *Zimbabwe's First Five Years: Economic Prospects Following Independence* (London: The Unit, Special Report 11, 1981).

Elkins, C. and S. Pedersen (eds.) *Settler Colonialism in the Twentieth Century: Projects, Practices, Legacies* (New York: Routledge, 2005).

Ellert, H. *The Rhodesian Front War: Counter-insurgency and Guerrilla Warfare, 1962-1980* (Gweru: Mambo Press, 1989).

Ellert, H. *Rivers of Gold* (Gweru: Mambo Press, 1993).

Eppel, S. and B. Raftopoulos *Prospects for Transitional Justice in Zimbabwe* (Pretoria: IDASA, 2008).

Etherington, N. *The Great Treks: The Transformation of Southern Africa, 1815-1854* (London: Pearson Education, 2001).

Fitzpatrick, P. *Through Mashonaland with Pick and Pen* (Johannesburg: Argus, 1892 [Harper, 1973 reprint]).

Foster, D. 'Space, place and "race"', *Journal of Community and Health Sciences*, 4(1), 1997.

Frederikse, J. *None but Ourselves: Masses vs Media in the Making of Zimbabwe* (Harare: Zimbabwe Publishing House, 1982).

Fullard, M. and N. Rousseau 'Uncertain borders: The TRC and the (un)making of public myths', *Kronos*, 34(November), 2009.

Gale, W. *The Years Between, 1923-1973: Half a Century of Responsible Government in Rhodesia* (Salisbury: H. C. P. Andersen, 1973).

Gifford, P. (ed.) *The Christian Churches and the Democratization of Africa* (Leiden: Brill, 1995).

Godwin, P. and I. Hancock *'Rhodesians Never Die': The Impact of War and Political Change on White Rhodesia, c.1970-1980* (Oxford: Oxford University Press, 1993; Harare: Baobab Books, 1995).

Hallencreutz, C. and A. Moyo (eds.) *Church and State in Zimbabwe* (Gweru: Mambo Press, 1988).

Halsey, P., G. Morlan and M. Smith (eds.) *If You Want to Know Me* (New York: Friendship Press, 1976).

Hammar, A., B. Raftopoulos and S. Jensen (eds.) *Zimbabwe's Unfinished Business: Rethinking Land, State and Nation in the Context of Crisis* (Harare: Weaver Press, 2003).

Hanlon, J. *Beggar Your Neighbours: Apartheid Power in Southern Africa* (London: Catholic Institute for International Relations, 1986).

Hansen, T. Blom and F. Stepputat (eds.) *States of Imagination: Ethnographic Explorations of the Post-Colonial State* (Durham, NC: Duke University Press, 2001).

Harris, Peter 'Industrial workers in Rhodesia, 1946-1972: Working class elites or lumpenproletariat?', *Journal of Southern African Studies*, 1(2), 1975.

Herbst, J. *State Politics in Zimbabwe* (Harare: University of Zimbabwe Publications, 1990).

Hobsbawn, E. and T. Ranger (eds.) *The Invention of Tradition* (Cambridge: Cambridge University Press, 1983).

Hobson, J. A. *Imperialism: A Study* (London: Allen and Unwin, 1948).

Holderness, Hardwicke *Lost Chance: Southern Rhodesia 1945-58* (Harare: Zimbabwe Publishing House, 1985).

Holland, R. (ed.) *Emergencies and Disorder in the European Empires after 1945* (London: Frank Cass, 1994).

Hove, C. *Bones* (Harare: Baobab Books, 1988).

Hove, M. M. 'Notes on the vaNgowa tribe', *NADA*, 20, 1943.

Hughes, D. M. *From Enslavement to Environmentalism: Politics on a Southern African Frontier* (Seattle: University of Washington Press, 2006).

Hugo, P. (ed.) *Redistribution and Affirmative Action: Working on South Africa's Political Economy* (Johannesburg: Southern Books, 1992).

Huffman, T. N. *Handbook to the Iron Age: The Archaeology of Pre-colonial Farming Societies in Southern Africa* (Scottsville: University of KwaZulu-Natal Press, 2007).

Huffman, T. N. *The Leopard's Kopje Tradition* (Salisbury: Trustees of the National Museums and Monuments of Rhodesia, 1974).

Huffman, T. N. *Snakes and Crocodiles: Power and Symbolism in Ancient Zimbabwe* (Johannesburg: Witwatersrand University Press, 1996).

Hyam, R. 'The geopolitical origins of the Central African Federation: Britain, Rhodesia and South Africa, 1948-1953', *Historical Journal*, 30(1), 1987.

Isaac, Julius *British Post-War Migration* (Cambridge: Cambridge University Press, 1954).

Isaacman, A. F. and B. S. *Slavery and Beyond: The Making of Men and Chikunda Ethnic Identities in the Unstable World of South-Central Africa, 1750-1920* (Portsmouth, NH: Heinemann, 2004).

Itote, Waruhui *'Mau Mau' General* (Nairobi: East African Publishing House, 1967).

Jacobs, S. and J. Mundy (eds.) 'Reflections on Mahmood Mamdani's "Lessons of Zimbabwe"', *Concerned African Scholars Bulletin*, 82(Spring).

Jardim, J. *Sanctions Double Cross: Oil to Rhodesia* (Bulawayo: Books of Rhodesia, 1979).

Jeater, D. *Law, Language and Science: The Invention of the 'Native Mind' in Southern Rhodesia, 1890-1930* (Portsmouth, NH: Heinemann, 2007).

Junod, H. A. 'The Balemba of the Zoutpansberg (Transvaal)', *Folklore*, 19(3), 1908.

Kanji, N. and N. Jazdowska 'Structural adjustment and the implications for low-income urban women in Zimbabwe', *Review of African Political Economy*, 20(56), 1993.

Kapungu, L. *The United Nations and Economic Sanctions Against Rhodesia* (Lexington: Lexington Press, 1973).

Kennedy, D. *Islands of White: Settler Society and Culture in Kenya and Southern Rhodesia, 1890-1939* (Durham, NC: Duke University Press, 1987).

Keppel-Jones, A. *Rhodes and Rhodesia: The White Conquest of Zimbabwe, 1884-1902* (Pietermaritzburg: University of Natal Press, 1983).

Kesby, M. 'Arenas for control, terrains of gender contestation: Guerrilla struggle and counter-insurgency warfare in Zimbabwe, 1972-1980', *Journal of Southern African Studies*, 22(4), 1996.

Kolapo, F. J. and K. O. Akurang-Parry (eds.) *African Agency and European Colonialism: Latitudes of Negotiations and Containment* (Lanham, MD: University Press of America, 2007).

Kriger, N. *Guerrilla Veterans in Post-War Zimbabwe: Symbolic and Violent Politics, 1980-1987* (Cambridge: Cambridge University Press, 2003).

Kriger, N. 'War veterans: Continuities between the past and the present', *African Studies Quarterly*, 7(2&3), [online], <http://web.africa.ufl.edu/asq/v7/v7i2a7.htm>.

Kriger, N. *Zimbabwe's Guerrilla War: Peasant Voices* (Cambridge: Cambridge University Press, 1992; Harare: Baobab Books, 1995).

Kriger, N. 'Zimbabwe's war veterans and the ruling party: Continuities in political dynamics', *Politique Africaine*, 81, 2001.

Kriger, N. 'The Zimbabwean war of liberation: Struggles within the struggle', *Journal of Southern African Studies*, 14(2), 1988.

Kurebwa, J. 'The Politics of Multilateral Economic Sanctions on Rhodesia during the Unilateral Declaration of Independence period, 1965-1979' (D.Phil. thesis, University of Zimbabwe, 2000).

Lan, D. *Guns and Rain: Guerrillas and Spirit Mediums in Zimbabwe* (Harare: Zimbabwe Publishing House, 1985).

Lancaster, C. S. 'Ethnic identity, "history", and tribe in the middle Zambezi valley', *American Ethnologist*, 1(4), 1974.

Lancaster, C. and K. P. Vickery (eds.) *The Tonga-Speaking Peoples of Zambia and Zimbabwe: Essays in Honor of Elizabeth Colson* (Lanham, MD: University Press of America, 2007).

Lapsley, M. *Neutrality or Co-option? Anglican Church and State from 1964 until the Independence of Zimbabwe* (Gweru: Mambo Press, 1986).

Leisegang, G. J. 'Aspects of Gaza Nguni history', *Rhodesian History*, 6, 1975.

Leonard, A. *How We Made Rhodesia* (Bulawayo: Books of Rhodesia, 1896).

Le Sueur, J. D. (ed.) *The Decolonization Reader* (New York: Routledge, 2003).

Lindgren, B. 'Power, education and identity in post-colonial Zimbabwe: Representations of the fate of King Lobengula of Matabeleland', *African Sociological Review*, 1(5), 2002.

Loney, Martin *Rhodesia: White Racism and Imperial Response* (Harmondsworth: Penguin, 1975).

Loubser, J. 'Oral traditions, archaeology and the history of Venda *mitupo*', *African Studies*, 49(2), 1990.

Louis, R. W. M. *Decolonization and African Independence: The Transfers of Power, 1960-1980* (New Haven: Yale University Press, 1988).

Lyons, T. *Guns and Guerilla Girls: Women in the Zimbabwean National Liberation Struggle* (Trenton, NJ: Africa World Press, 2004).

McGregor, J. 'The politics of disruption: War veterans and the local state in Zimbabwe', *African Affairs*, 101, 2002.

Machingaidze, V. E. M. 'Agrarian change from above: The Southern Rhodesia Native Land Husbandry Act and African responses', *International Journal of African Historical Studies*, 24(3), 1991.

McKenzie, J. A. 'Commercial Farmers in the Governmental System of Colonial Zimbabwe' (D.Phil. thesis, University of Zimbabwe, 1989).

Mackenzie, J. M. 'Colonial labour in the chartered company period', *Rhodesian History*, 1, 1970.

McLaughlin, J. *On the Frontline: Catholic Missions in Zimbabwe's Liberation War* (Harare: Baobab Books, 1996).

Mafico, J. C., *Urban Low-Income Housing in Zimbabwe* (Aldershot: Avebury, 1991).

Majonga, M. 'The Struggle Continues: African Trade Unions and Workers' Responses in Rhodesia, 1965-1980' (MA dissertation, University of Zimbabwe, 1998).

Makaye, P. 'The Underdevelopment of Matsai Communal Area before and after the Second Chimurenga' (MA dissertation, University of Zimbabwe, 2000).

Makoni, S., S. Dube and P. Mashiri 'Zimbabwe colonial and post-colonial language policy and planning practices', *Multilingual Matters*, 7(4), 2006.

Mamdani, M. *Citizen and Subject: Contemporary Africa and the Legacy of Late Colonialism* (Princeton: Princeton University Press, 1996).

Mamdani, M. 'Reconciliation without justice', *Southern African Review of Books*, Nov./Dec. 1996.

Mandaza, I. (ed.) *Zimbabwe: The Political Economy of Transition, 1980-1986* (Dakar: Codesria, 1986).

Mandaza, I. *Race, Colour and Class in Southern Africa: A Study of the Coloured Question in the Context of an Analysis of the Colonial and White Settler Racial Ideology and African Nationalism in Twentieth Century Zimbabwe, Zambia and Malawi* (Harare: SAPES Books, 1997).

Mandaza, I. (ed.) *Zimbabwe: The Political Economy of Transition, 1980-1986* (Dakar: Codesria, 1986).

Mandaza, I. and L. Sachikonye (eds.) *The One-Party State and Democracy: The Zimbabwe Debate* (Harare: SAPES Trust, 1991).

Mandivenga, E. 'The history and "re-conversion" of the vaRemba of Zimbabwe', *Journal of Religion in Africa*, 9(2), 1989.

Manungo, K. D. 'The Role the Peasants Played in the Zimbabwe War of Liberation, with Special Emphasis on Chiweshe District' (D.Phil. thesis, Ohio University, 1991).

Manyanga, M. *Resilient Landscapes: Socio-environmental Dynamics in the Shashi-Limpopo Basin, Southern Zimbabwe c.AD 800 to the Present* (Uppsala: Studies in Global Archaeology, 2007).

Maphosa, F. 'Towards the sociology of Zimbabwean indigenous entrepreneurship', *Zambezia*, 25(2), 1998.

Marechera, D. *Cemetery of the Mind: Collected Poems of Dambudzo Marechera* (Harare: Baobab Books, 1992).

Marechera, D. *Mindblast* (Harare: College Press, 1984).

Martin, D. and P. Johnson *The Struggle for Zimbabwe* (Harare: Zimbabwe Publishing House, 1981).

Mashingaidze, T. M. 'The Dynamics of Zimbabwe's Struggle for Liberation: The Case of Buhera District from 1950 to 1990' (MA Dissertation, University of Zimbabwe, 2001).

Masunungure, E. and N. Musekiwa 'Local Government Policy Review' (Policy Document Prepared for the Zimbabwe Institute, 2005).

Mathe, R. *Making Ends Meet at the Margins: Grappling with Economic Crisis and Belonging in Beitbridge, Zimbabwe* (Dakar: Codesria, 2005).

Maxwell, D. *Christians and Chiefs in Zimbabwe* (Edinburgh: Edinburgh University Press, 1999).

Mavedzenge, B. Z., J. Mahenehene, F. Murimbarimba, I. Schoones and W. Wolmer 'The dynamics of real markets: Cattle in southern Zimbabwe following land reform', *Development and Change*, 39(4), 2008.

Mazarire, G. C. 'Defence consciousness as way of life: "The refuge period" and Karanga defence strategies in the 19th century', *Zimbabwean Prehistory* 25, 2005.

Mazarire, G. C. 'Women, politics and the environment in pre-colonial Chivi, c.1830-1900', *Zambezia*, 30(1), 2003.

Mbembe, A. *On the Postcolony* (Berkeley and Los Angeles: University of California Press, 2001).

Megahey, A. *Humphrey Gibbs: Beleaguered Governor* (London: Macmillan, 1998).

Melber, H. (ed.) *Limits to Liberation in Southern Africa: The Unfinished Business of Democratic Consolidation* (Cape Town: HSRC Press, 2003).

Mendelsohn, Richard and Vivian Bickford-Smith (eds.) *Black and White in Colour: African History on Screen* (London: James Currey, 2007).

Meredith, M. *Our Votes, Our Guns: Robert Mugabe and the Tragedy of Zimbabwe* (Oxford: Public Affairs, 2003).

Meredith, M. *The Past Is Another Country: Rhodesia UDI to Zimbabwe* (London: Pan, 1980).

Minter, W. and E. Schmidt 'When sanctions worked: The case of Rhodesia re-examined', *African Affairs*, 87(347).

Mlambo, A. S. 'Building a white man's country: Aspects of white immigration into Rhodesia up to World War Two', *Zambezia*, 25(2), 1998.

Mlambo, A. S. *The Economic Structural Adjustment Programme: The Case of Zimbabwe, 1990-1995* (Harare: University of Zimbabwe Publications, 1997).

Mlambo, A. S. '"Some are more white than others": Racial chauvinism as a factor in Rhodesian immigration policy, 1890-1963', *Zambezia*, 27(2), 1998.

Mlambo, A. S. *White Immigration into Rhodesia: From Occupation to Federation* (Harare: University of Zimbabwe Publications, 2002).

Mlambo, A. S., E. S. Pangeti and I. Phimister *Zimbabwe: A History of Manufacturing, 1890-1995* (Harare: University of Zimbabwe Publications, 2000).

Mlambo, Alois and Ian Phimister, 'Partly protected: The origin and growth of colonial Zimbabwe's textile industry', *Historia*, 51(2), 2006.

Mlambo, Eshmael *Rhodesia: The Struggle for a Birthright* (London: C. Hurst, 1972).

Moore, D. B. 'The Contradictory Construction of Hegemony in Zimbabwe: Politics, Ideology and Class in the Formation of a New African State' (D.Phil. thesis, York University, 1990).

Moore, D. 'Democracy, Violence and Identity in the Zimbabwean War of National Liberation: Reflections from the Realms of Dissent', *Canadian Journal of African Studies*, 3, 1991.

Moore, D. 'The Zimbabwean "organic intellectuals" in transition', *Journal of Southern African Studies*, 15, 1988.

Moore, D. S. *Suffering for Territory: Race, Place, and Power in Zimbabwe* (Harare: Weaver Press, 2005).

Moore-King, Bruce *White Man, Black War* (Harare: Baobab Books, 1988).

Morley, D. and K-H. Chen *Stuart Hall: Critical Dialogues in Cultural Studies* (London: Routledge, 1996).

Mothibe, T. H. 'Zimbabwe: African working class nationalism, 1957-1963', *Zambezia*, 23(2), 1996.

Moyana, V. *The Political Economy of Land in Zimbabwe* (Gweru: Mambo Press, 2nd. edn., 2002).

Moyo, J. N. *Voting for Democracy: Electoral Politics in Zimbabwe* (Harare: University of Zimbabwe Publications, 1992).

Moyo, S. 'The land occupation movement and democratisation in Zimbabwe: Contradictions of neoliberalism', *Millennium: Journal of International Studies*, 30(2), 2001.

Moyo, S. *The Land Question in Zimbabwe* (Harare: SAPES Books, 1995).

Moyo, S. *Land Reform under Structural Adjustment in Zimbabwe: Land Use Change in Mashonaland East Province* (Uppsala: Nordic Africa Institute, 2000).

Moyo, S. 'The political economy of land acquisition and redistribution in Zimbabwe, 1990-1999', *Journal of Southern African Studies*, 26(1), 2000.

Moyo, S., J. Makumbe and B. Raftopoulos *NGOs, the State and Politics in Zimbabwe* (Harare: SAPES Books, 2000).

Moyo, S. and P. Yeros *Reclaiming the Land: The Resurgence of Rural Movements in Africa, Asia and Latin America* (Cape Town: David Philip; London: Zed Books, 2005).

Moyo, S., B. Rutherford, and D. Amanor-Wilks 'Land reform and changing social relations for farm workers in Zimbabwe', *Review of African Political Economy*, 84, 2000.

Mseba, A. 'Money and Finance in a Closed Economy: Rhodesia's Monetary Experience, 1965-1980' (MA dissertation, University of Zimbabwe, 2007).

Msengezi, G. H. *The Honourable MP* (Gweru: Mambo Press, 1984).

Msindo, E. 'Ethnicity and nationalism in urban colonial Zimbabwe: Bulawayo, 1950-1963', *Journal of African History*, 48, 2007.

Mudenge, S. I. G. *A Political History of Munhumutapa c.1400-1902* (Harare: Zimbabwe Publishing House, 1988).

Mumbengegwi, C. (ed.) *Macroeconomic and Structural Adjustment Policies in Zimbabwe* (London: Macmillan, 2002).

Munro, W. *The Moral Economy of the State: Conservation, Community Development and State-Making in Zimbabwe* (Athens: Ohio University Press, 1998).

Musemwa, M. 'The ambiguities of democracy: The demobilisation of the Zimbabwean ex-combatants and the ordeal of rehabilitation, 1980-1993', *Transformation*, 26, 1995.

Mushunje, S. S. 'The Development of Agricultural Credit Systems in Zimbabwe, with Special Reference to the Agricultural Finance Corporation, 1971 to 1986' (MA dissertation, University of Zimbabwe, 1988).

Mutasa, N. M. *Misodzi, Dikita neRopa* (Gweru: Mambo Press, 1991).

Mutema, L. 'Salt making, myth and conflict in Chireya', *Zimbabwea*, 4, 1996.

Muzondidya, J. '*Jambanja*: Ideological ambiguities in the politics of land and resource ownership in Zimbabwe', *Journal of Southern African History*, 33(2), 2007.

Muzondidya, J. *Walking a Tightrope: Towards a Social History of the Coloured People of Zimbabwe* (Asmara: Africa World Press, 2004).

Muzondidya, J. and S. Ndlovu-Gatsheni 'Echoing silences: Ethnicity in post-colonial Zimbabwe, 1980-2007', *African Journal of Conflict Resolution*, 27(2), 2007.

Muzondidya, J. and N. Samasuwo *ISS Country Profile: Zimbabwe* (Pretoria: Institute for Security Studies, 2007).

Muzorewa, A. T. *Rise Up and Walk: An Autobiography* (London: Evans, 1979).

Ncube, G. T. *A History of Northwest Zimbabwe* (Kadoma: Mond Books, 2004).

Ndlovu-Gatsheni, S. J. 'African Criminality in Southern Rhodesia, 1900-1923' (MA thesis, University of Zimbabwe, 1995).

Ndlovu-Gatsheni, S. J. 'The Dynamics of Democracy and Human Rights among the Ndebele of Zimbabwe, 1818-1934' (Ph.D. thesis, University of Zimbabwe, 2004).

Ndlovu-Gatsheni, S. J. 'Nationalist-military alliance and the fate of democracy in Zimbabwe', *African Journal of Conflict Resolution*, 6(1), 2006.

Ndlovu-Gatsheni, S. J. 'Quarrying African indigenous political thought on govern-
    ance: A case study of the Ndebele state in the 19th century', *Indilinga: African
    Journal of Indigenous Knowledge Systems*, 4(2), 2005.
Ndlovu-Gatsheni, S. J. 'Re-thinking the colonial encounter in Zimbabwe in the early
    twentieth century', *Journal of Southern African Studies*, 33(1), 2007.
Ndlovu-Gatsheni, S. J. and F. J. Ndhlovu 'Twilight of patriarchy in a southern African
    kingdom: A case study of captives and women in the Ndebele state of Zimbabwe',
    UNISWA Research Journal, 19, 2005.
Nelson, Harold D. *et al. Area Handbook for Southern Rhodesia* (Washington, DC:
    American University, Foreign Area Studies, 1975).
Newitt, M. *A History of Mozambique* (London: Hurst, 1995).
Ngwenya, B. 'The Rise and Fall of Copper Mining at Mhangura, *c.*1957-2000' (MA
    dissertation, University of Zimbabwe, 2007).
Nhema, A. G. (ed.) *The Quest for Peace in Africa* (Addis Ababa: OSSREA, 2004).
Nhongo-Simbanegavi, J. *For Better or Worse? Women and ZANLA in Zimbabwe's
    Liberation Struggle* (Harare: Weaver Press, 2000).
Nkomo, J. *The Story of My Life* (London: Methuen, 1984; Harare: SAPES Books,
    2001).
Nugent, P. and A. J. Asiwaju (eds.) *African Boundaries: Barriers, Conduits and
    Opportunities* (London: Pinter, 1996).
Nyagumbo, M. *With the People* (Salisbury: Graham Publishing, 1980).
Nyambara, P. S. 'Immigrants, "traditional" leaders and the Rhodesian state: The
    power of "communal" land tenure and the politics of land acquisition in Gokwe,
    Zimbabwe, 1963-1979', *Journal of Southern African Studies*, 27(4), 2001.
Nyambara, P. S. 'Madheruka and Shangwe: Ethnic identities and the culture of
    modernity in Gokwe, northwestern Zimbabwe, 1963', *Journal of African History*,
    42, 2002.
Nyambara, P. S. 'The politics of land acquisition and struggles over land in the
    "communal" areas of Zimbabwe: The Gokwe region in the 1980s and 1990s', *Africa*,
    71(2), 2001.
Nyamfukudza, S. *The Non-Believer's Journey* (Harare: Zimbabwe Publishing House,
    1980).
Nyamubaya, F. *On the Road Again: Poems During and after the National Liberation
    of Zimbabwe* (Harare: Zimbabwe Publishing House, 1986).
Nyathi, P. *Mthwakazi: Imbali YamaNdebele 1820-1894* (Gweru: Mambo Press, 1995).
Olukoshi, O. A. (ed.) *The Politics of Opposition in Contemporary Africa* (Uppsala:
    Nordic Africa Institute, 1997).
Omer-Cooper, J. D. *The Zulu Aftermath: Revolution in Bantu Africa* (London:
    Longman, 1966).
Palley, C. *The Constitutional History and Law of Southern Rhodesia, 1898-1965*
    (Oxford: Oxford University Press, 1966).

Palmer, R. H. *Aspects of Rhodesian Land Policy, 1890-1936* (Salisbury: Central Africa Historical Association, Local Series No. 22, 1968).

Palmer, Robin *Land and Racial Domination in Rhodesia* (London: Heinemann, 1977).

Palmer, Robin and I. Birch, *Zimbabwe: A Land Divided* (Oxford: Oxfam, 1992).

Palmer, R. and N. Parsons (eds.) *The Roots of Rural Poverty in Central and Southern Africa* (London: Heinemann, 1977).

Pangeti, E. S. 'The State and the Manufacturing Industry: A Study of the State as Regulator and Entrepreneur in Zimbabwe, 1930-1990' (D.Phil. thesis, University of Zimbabwe, 1995).

Phimister, I. 'Ancient mining near Great Zimbabwe', *Journal of the South African Institute of Mining and Metallurgy*, 74(6), 1974.

Phimister, I. *An Economic and Social History of Zimbabwe, 1890-1948: Capital Accumulation and Class Struggle* (London: Longman, 1988).

Phimister, I. 'Peasant production and underdevelopment in Southern Rhodesia, 1890-1914', *African Affairs*, 73(291), 1974.

Phimister, I. 'Rethinking the reserves: Southern Rhodesia's Land Husbandry Act reviewed', *Journal of Southern African Studies*, 19(2), 1993.

Phimister, I. and B. Raftopoulos '"Kana sora ratswa ngaritswe": African nationalists and black workers: The 1948 general strike in colonial Zimbabwe', *Journal of Historical Sociology*, 13(3), 2000.

Pickard-Cambridge, C. *Sharing the Cities: Residential Desegregation in Harare, Windhoek and Mafikeng* (Johannesburg: Institute of Race Relations, 1988).

Pikirayi, I. 'David Beach, Shona history and the archaeology of Zimbabwe', *Zambezia*, 26(2), 1999.

Pikirayi, I. *The Zimbabwe Culture: Origins and Decline of Southern Zambezian States* (Walnut Creek: Altamira Press, 2001).

Pollak, O. 'The impact of the Second World War on African labour organisation in Rhodesia', *Rhodesian Journal of Economics*, 7(3), 1973.

Posselt, F. W. T. *Fact and Fiction* (Bulawayo: Books of Rhodesia, 1935).

Pwiti, G. *Continuity and Change: An Archaeological Study of Farming Communities in Northern Zimbabwe* (Uppsala: Studies in African Archaeology 13, 1996).

Pwiti, G. 'Trade and economies in southern Africa: The archaeological evidence', *Zambezia*, 18, 1991.

Raftopoulos, B. 'Gender, nationalist politics and the fight for the city: Harare 1940-1950s', *Safere: Southern African Feminist Review*, 1(2), 1995.

Raftopoulos, B. 'Problematising nationalism in Zimbabwe: A historiographical review', *Zambezia*, 26(2), 1999.

Raftopoulos, B., 'The Zimbabwean crisis and the challenges for the left', *Journal of Southern African Studies*, 32(2), 2006.

Raftopoulos, B. *Zimbabwe: Race and Nationalism in a Post-colonial State* (Harare: SAPES Books, 1996).

Raftopoulos, B. and K. Alexander (eds.) *Reflections on Democratic Politics in Zimbabwe* (Cape Town: Institute for Justice and Reconciliation, 2006).

Raftopolous, B. and I. Phimister (eds.) *Keep on Knocking: A History of the Labour Movement in Zimbabwe, 1900-1997* (Harare: Baobab Books, 1997).

Raftopoulos, B. and L. Sachikonye (eds.) *Striking Back: The Labour Movement and the Post-Colonial State in Zimbabwe 1980-2000* (Harare: Weaver Press, 2001).

Raftopoulos, B. and T. Savage (eds.) *Zimbabwe: Injustice and Political Reconciliation* (Cape Town: Institute for Justice and Reconciliation, 2004).

Raftopoulos, B. and T. Yoshikuni *Sites of Struggle* (Harare: Weaver Press, 1999).

Ralushai, N. M. N. and J. R. Gray 'Ruins and traditions of the Ngona and Mbedzi among the Venda of the Northern Transvaal', *Rhodesian History*, 8, 1977.

Ranchod-Nilsson, S. 'Gender politics and the pendulum of political and social transformation in Zimbabwe', *Journal of Southern African Studies*, 32(1), 2006.

Ranger, T. *The African Voice in Southern Rhodesia, 1898-1930* (London: Heinemann, 1970).

Ranger, T. *Are We Not Also Men? The Samkange Family and African Politics in Zimbabwe* (Harare: Baobab Books, 1995).

Ranger, T. 'City versus State in Zimbabwe: Colonial antecedents of the current crisis', *Journal of East African Studies*, 1(2), 2007.

Ranger, T. 'Connexions between "primary resistance" movements and modern mass nationalism in east and central Africa', *Journal of African History*, 9(3/4), 1968.

Ranger, T. (ed.) *The Historical Dimensions of Democracy and Human Rights in Zimbabwe, Volume Two: Nationalism, Democracy and Human Rights* (Harare: University of Zimbabwe Publications, 2001).

Ranger, T. 'Historiography, patriotic history and the history of the nation: The struggle over the past in Zimbabwe', *Journal of Southern African Studies*, 30(2), 2004.

Ranger, T. *The Invention of Tribalism in Zimbabwe* (Gweru: Mambo Press, 1985).

Ranger, T. 'Nationalist historiography, patriotic history and the history of the nation: The struggle over the past in Zimbabwe', *Journal of South African History*, 30(2), 2004.

Ranger, T. *Peasant Consciousness and Guerrilla War in Zimbabwe: A Comparative Study* (London: James Currey, 1985).

Ranger T. *Revolt in Southern Rhodesia, 1896-7: A Study in African Resistance* (London: Heinemann, 1967).

Ranger, T. 'Tradition and travesty: Chiefs and the administration in Makoni District, Zimbabwe, 1960-1980', *Africa*, 52(3), 1982.

Ranger, T. *Voices from the Rocks: Nature, Culture and History in the Matopos Hills of Zimbabwe* (Harare: Baobab Books; Oxford: James Currey, 1999).

Ranger, T. and O. Vaughan (eds.), *Legitimacy and the State in Twentieth-century Africa* (London: Macmillan, 1993).

Ransford, O. *The Rulers of Rhodesia* (Bulawayo, Books of Rhodesia, 1968).

Rasmussen, R. Kent *Migrant Kingdom: Mzilikazi's Ndebele in South Africa* (Cape Town: Rex Collings, 1978).

Reynolds, A. *Electoral Systems and Democratization in Southern Africa* (Oxford: Oxford University Press, 1999).

Rich, T. 'Legacies of the past? The results of the 1980 election in Midlands province, Zimbabwe', *Africa: Journal of the International African Institute*, 52(3), 1982.

Rupiya, M. 'Demobilisation and integration: "Operation Merger" and the Zimbabwe national defence forces, 1980-1987', *Africa Security Review*, 4(3), 1995.

Russell, L. (ed.) *Colonial Frontiers: Indigenous-European Encounters in Settler Societies* (Manchester: Manchester University Press, 2001).

Sachikonye, L. M. *The Situation of Farm Workers after Land Reform in Zimbabwe: A Report Prepared for the Farm Community Trust of Zimbabwe*, May 2003, available at <http://www.oxfam.org.uk/what_we_do/issues/livelihoods/landrights/downloads/zimfwsit.rtf>.

Sadomba, W. Z. 'War Veterans in Zimbabwe's Land Occupations: Complexities of a Liberation Movement in an African Post-Colonial Settler Society' (D.Phil. thesis, Wageningen University, 2008).

Said, E. *Orientalism* (London: Routledge, 1978).

Saki, O. and T. Chiware *The Law in Zimbabwe* (Harare: Zimbabwe Lawyers for Human Rights, 2007).

Salim, A. I. (ed.) *State Formation in Eastern Africa* (Nairobi: Heinemann, 1984).

Samkange, S. *The Origins of Rhodesia* (Heinemann, London, 1968).

Samkange, S. *What Rhodes Really Said About Africans* (Harare: Zimbabwe Publishing House, 1982).

Samupindi, C. *Pawns* (Harare: Baobab Books, 1992).

Scarnecchia, T. 'Poor women and nationalist politics: Alliances and fissures in the formation of a nationalist political movement in Salisbury, Rhodesia, 1950-56', *Journal of African History*, 37(3), 1996.

Scarnecchia, T. *The Urban Roots of Democracy and Political Violence in Zimbabwe: Harare and Highfield, 1940-1964* (Rochester, NY: University of Rochester Press, 2008).

Schmidt, H. I. 'The Social and Economic Impact of Political Violence in Zimbabwe, 1890-1990: A Case Study of the Honde Valley' (D.Phil. thesis, Oxford University, 1996).

Schoffeleers, J. M. (ed.) *Guardians of the Land* (Gwelo: Mambo Press, 1979).

Schulz, Barry M. 'Homeward bound? A survey study of the limits of white Rhodesian nationalism and permanence', *Ufahamu*, 5(3), 1975.

Selby, A. 'Commercial Farmers and the State: Interest Group Politics and Land Reform in Zimbabwe' (D.Phil. thesis, Oxford University, 2006).

Shamuyarira, Nathan *Crisis in Rhodesia* (London: Deutsch, 1965).

Shillington, Kevin *History of Africa* (New York: Macmillan, 2nd. edn, 2005).

Shutt, A. K. '"The natives are getting out of hand": Legislating manners, insolence and contemptuous behaviour in Southern Rhodesia c.1910-1963', *Journal of Southern African Studies*, 33(3), 2007.

Shutt, Alison K. 'The settlers' cattle complex: The etiquette of culling cattle in colonial Zimbabwe, 1938', *Journal of African History*, 43(2), 2002.

Shutt, A. '"We are the Best Poor Farmers": Purchase Area Farmers and Economic Differentiation in Southern Rhodesia, c.1925-1980' (D.Phil. thesis, University of California, 1995).

Sibanda, E. *The Zimbabwe African People's Union, 1961-87: A Political History of Insurgency in Southern Rhodesia* (Trenton, NJ: Africa World Press, 2005).

Sinclair, P. J. J. *Space, Time and Social Formation: A Territorial Approach to the Archaeology and Anthropology of Zimbabwe and Mozambique c.0-1700AD* (Uppsala: Societas Archaeologica Upsaliensis, 1987).

Sithole, M. 'Class and factionalism in the Zimbabwean nationalist movement', *African Studies Review*, 27(1), 1984.

Sithole, M. 'Ethnicity and factionalism in Zimbabwean nationalist politics, 1957-79', *Ethnic and Racial Studies*, 3(1), 1980.

Sithole, M. 'Is Zimbabwe poised on a liberal path? The state and prospects of the parties', *Issue: A Journal of Opinion*, 21(1/2), 1993.

Sithole, M. *Zimbabwe: Struggles Within the Struggle* (Harare: Rujeko Publishers, 2nd edn., 1999).

Sithole, M. and J. Makumbe 'Elections in Zimbabwe: The ZANU(PF) hegemony and its incipient decline', *African Journal of Political Science*, 2(1), 1997.

Sithole, N. *African Nationalism* (London: Oxford University Press, 1968).

Smith, Ian *The Great Betrayal* (London: Blake, 1997).

Stiff, Peter *Selous Scouts: Top Secret War* (Alberton: Galago, 1982).

Stokes, E. and R. Brown (eds.) *The Zambesian Past: Studies in Central African History* (Manchester: Manchester University Press, 1966).

Stoneman, C. (ed.) *Zimbabwe's Inheritance* (London: Macmillan, 1981).

Stoneman, C. (ed.) *Zimbabwe's Prospects: Issues of Race, Class, State and Capital in Southern Africa* (London: Macmillan, 1988).

Stoneman, C., and L. Cliffe *Zimbabwe: Politics, Economics and Society* (London: Pinter, 1988).

Storry, J. G. 'The settlement and territorial expansion of the Mutasa dynasty', *Rhodesian History*, 7, 1976.

Strack, H. R. *Sanctions: The Case of Rhodesia* (Syracuse, NY: Syracuse University Press, 1978).

Summers, C. *Colonial Lessons* (Portsmouth: NH, Heinemann, 2002).

Sutcliffe, P. 'The political economy of Rhodesian sanctions', *Journal of Commonwealth Political Studies*, 7(July), 1979.

Sylvester, C. *Producing Women and Progress in Zimbabwe: Narratives of Identity and Work from the 1980s* (London: Heinemann, 2000).

Sylvester, C. *Zimbabwe: A Terrain of Contradictory Development* (Boulder, CO: Westview Press, 1991).

Sylvester, C. 'Zimbabwe's 1985 elections: A search for national mythology', *Journal of Modern African Studies*, 24(2), 1986.

Tapson, R. R. 'Some notes on the Mrozwi occupation of Sebungwe district', *NADA*, 21, 1944.

Tauyanago, B. 'The Renamo War and its Impact in South East Zimbabwe, 1982-1992' (MA thesis, University of Zimbabwe, 2002).

Tekere, Edgar '2-Boy' Zivanai *A Lifetime of Struggle* (Harare: SAPES Books, 2006).

Theal, G. M. *History of South Africa before 1795* (London: Swan Sonnenschein, 1910).

Thomas, T. M. *Eleven Years in Central South Africa* (London: Routledge, 1971 [1873]).

Todd, J. *The Right to Say No* (London: Sidgwick and Jackson, 1972).

Tshuma, L. *A Matter of (In)justice: Law, State and the Agrarian Question in Zimbabwe* (Harare: SAPES Books, 1997).

Tsomondo, M. 'Shona reaction and resistance to the European colonisation of Zimbabwe', *Journal of Southern African Affairs*, 2, 1977.

Turino, T. *Nationalists, Cosmopolitans and Popular Music in Zimbabwe* (Chicago: University of Chicago Press, 2000).

Unesco. *Sociological Theories: Race and Colonialism* (Paris: Unesco, 1980).

United Nations. *Final report of the Panel of Experts on the Illegal Exploitation of Natural Resources and Other Forms of Wealth of the Democratic Republic of the Congo,* 16 October 2002.

United Nations. 'Report of the Fact-Finding Mission to Zimbabwe to Assess the Scope and Impact of Operation Murambatsvina by the UN Special Envoy on Human Settlements Issues in Zimbabwe Mrs. Anna Kajumulo Tibaijuka' (UN, 2005).

Vambe, Lawrence *An Ill-Fated People* (London: Heinemann, 1972).

Vambe, Lawrence *From Rhodesia to Zimbabwe* (London: Heinemann, 1976).

Van Onselen, C. *Chibaro: African Mine Labour in Southern Rhodesia, 1900-1933* (London: Pluto Press, 1976).

Van Warmelo, N. J. (ed.) *The Copper Mines of Musina and the Early History of the Zoutpansberg* (Pretoria: Department of Native Affairs, 1940).

Vera, Y. *Nehanda* (Harare: Baobab Books, 1993).

Verstraelen, F. J. *Zimbabwean Realities and Christian Responses* (Gweru: Mambo Press, 1998).

Von Sicard, H. 'The Dumbuseya', *NADA*, 5, 1968.

Von Sicard, H. 'Lemba Clans', *NADA*, 34, 1962.

Von Sicard, H. 'The origin of some tribes in the Belingwe Reserve', *NADA*, 27, 1950.

Wallis, J. P. R. (ed.) *The Matabele Journals of Robert Moffat, 1829-1860* (London: Chatto and Windus, 2 vols., 1945).

Weinrich, A. K. H. *Chiefs and Councils in Rhodesia: The Transition from Patriarchal to Bureaucratic Power* (London: Heinemann, 1971).

Weitzer, R. *Transforming Settler States: Communal Conflict and Internal Security in Northern Ireland and Zimbabwe* (Berkeley and Los Angeles: University of California Press, 1990).

Welensky, R. *Welensky's 4000 Days: The Life and Death of the Federation of Rhodesia and Nyasaland* (London: Collins, 1964).

Wentzel, P. J. *Nau dzabaKalanga: A History of the Kalanga* (Pretoria: Unisa Press, 1983).

Wentzel, P. J. *The Relationship Between Venda and Western Shona* (Pretoria: Unisa Press, 1983).

Werbner, R. and T. Ranger (eds.), *Postcolonial Identities in Africa* (London: Zed Books, 1996).

West, M. O. *The Rise of an African Middle Class: Colonial Zimbabwe 1898-1965* (Bloomington: Indiana University Press, 2002).

Wetherell, Iden 'Settler expansionism in central Africa: The imperial response of 1931 and subsequent implications', *African Affairs*, 78, 1979.

White, L. *The Assassination of Hebert Chitepo: Texts and Politics in Zimbabwe* (Bloomington: Indiana University Press, 2003).

Williams, P. and L. Chrisman (eds.) *Colonial Discourses and Post-Colonial Theory: A Reader* (New York: Columbia University Press, 1994)

Williams, R. *et al.* (eds.) *Ourselves to Know: Civil-Military Relations and Defence Transformation in Southern Africa* (Pretoria: ISS, 2003).

Wills, A. J. *An Introduction to the History of Central Africa* (Oxford: Oxford University Press, 3rd. edn., 1973).

Wood, J. R. T. *So Far and No Further!: Rhodesia's Bid for Independence during the Retreat from Empire, 1959-1965* (Victoria, BC: Trafford, c.2005).

Yoshikuni, Tsuneo *African Urban Experiences in Colonial Zimbabwe: A Social History of Harare before 1925* (Harare: Weaver Press, 2007).

Zimbabwe. *Report of the Presidential Land Review Committee under the Chairmanship of Dr Charles M. B. Utete* (Harare: Government Printers, 2 vols., August 2003).

Zimbabwe Women Writers (eds.) *Women of Resilience: The Voices of Women Ex-combatants* (Harare: Zimbabwe Women Writers, 2000).

Zinyama, L. M., D. Tevera and S. Cumming (eds.) *Harare: The Growth and Problems of the City* (Harare: University of Zimbabwe Publications, 1993).

Zvarevashe, I. M. *Dzinza ravaGovera vaChirumhanzu naMutasa* (Gweru: Mambo Press, 1998).

Notes on Contributors

Teresa Barnes is Associate Professor at the University of Illinois, Urbana-Champaign, with a joint appointment in History and Gender/Women's Studies. She received a BA from Brown University, and MA and Ph.D. degrees from the University of Zimbabwe. Her major work on Zimbabwean history is 'We Women Worked So Hard': Gender, Urbanization, and Social Repro-duction in Colonial Harare, Zimbabwe, 1930-1956 (1999). From 1997 to 2007 she worked in the History Department at the University of the Western Cape, South Africa, where her interests moved to questions of gender and institutional culture in higher education. Her publications are in the areas of gender and Zimbabwean history, and African higher education.

Gerald Chikozho Mazarire is a lecturer in History at the University of Zimbabwe, with special interest in Karanga oral traditions within the general pre-colonial history of Zimbabwe. His doctoral research focuses on the 'The Political and Social History of Chishanga: South-Central Zimbabwe c.1750-2000'. He has been a Visiting Research Fellow at the Centre of African Studies, University of Edinburgh, and has published articles in the *Journal of Southern African Studies*, *Historia*, *Zambezia* and *African Historical Review*, as well as chapters on Zimbabwean early colonial history in edited collections.

Professor Alois S. Mlambo works in the Department of Historical and Heritage Studies, University of Pretoria, and has written extensively on Zimbabwe's social and economic history. His publications include: *White Immigration into Rhodesia: From Occupation to Federation* (2002); *The Economic Structural Adjustment Programme: The Case of Zimbabwe 1990-1995* (1997); [with E. S. Pangeti and I. Phimister] *Zimbabwe: A History of Manufacturing 1890-1995* (2000); and [with E. S. Pangeti] *The Political Economy of the Sugar Industry in Zimbabwe 1920-90* (1996). He has recently edited *African Scholarly Publishing: Essays* (2007), and is currently working on the history of South Africa's hegemony in Southern Africa since the 1960s.

Dr Joseph Mtisi received his Ph.D. from the University of Ibadan and is currently a lecturer in the Department of Economic History at the University of Zimbabwe. He has taught at the universities of Ibadan and Swaziland, and his research interests are the agrarian and labour history of Africa. Presently he is working on the history of the tea industry, and tea and forest plantation labour in Zimbabwe.

Dr James Muzondidya is a senior researcher at the Human Sciences Research Council in Pretoria. He lectured in the History Department of the University of Zimbabwe, where he received his BA and MA degrees before proceeding to the University of Cape Town for his Ph.D. His research interests are in post-colonial citizenship and identity politics, and he has published a number of chapters and journal articles on historical and contemporary Zimbabwe.

Dr Sabelo J. Ndlovu-Gatsheni is Lecturer in African Studies at the Ferguson Centre for African and Asian Studies at the Open University in England. He is also affiliated to the Department of History at the Open University. He was formerly a Senior Lecturer and Head of the Department of International Studies at Monash University's South Africa Campus in Johannesburg. He has published widely on the history and politics of Zimbabwe and South Africa, including *The Ndebele Nation: Reflections on Hegemony, Memory and Historiography*.

Munyaradzi Nyakudya has an MA in African History from the University of Zimbabwe, where he lectures in African history. He has researched widely on the 'protected villages', a counter-insurgency measure adopted by the Rhodesian Front government to curb the intensifying guerrilla onslaught in Zimbabwe's rural areas. For his doctoral thesis he is researching the socio-political and economic dynamics of cattle in shaping the colonial state's relations with the peasantry in Zimbabwe's Mazowe District.

Brian Raftopoulos was Associate Professor of Development Studies at the University of Zimbabwe, and is now Director of Research and Advocacy at the Solidarity Peace Trust, a human rights organization based in South Africa but working on Zimbabwe. He has published widely on Zimbabwean history, politics and economics. He was a founder member of the National Constitutional Assembly and the first Chair of the Crisis Coalition. He is also a Research Fellow at the Centre for Humanities Research, University of the Western Cape, and a Research Associate in the Department of Historical Studies, University of Cape Town.

Index

LaVergne, TN USA
19 October 2009
161314LV00003B/8/P